ENCYCLOPEDIA
OF MARY

ENCYCLOPEDIA
OF MARY

Monica & Bill Dodds

Our Sunday Visitor Publishing Division
Our Sunday Visitor, Inc.
Huntington, Indiana 46750

Nihil Obstat: Rev. Michael Heintz, Censor Librorum
Imprimatur: ✠ John M. D'Arcy
Bishop of Fort Wayne-South Bend
August 9, 2007

Copyright © 2007 by Our Sunday Visitor Publishing Division,
Our Sunday Visitor, Inc. Published 2007

11 10 09 08 07   1 2 3 4 5 6 7 8 9

Our Sunday Visitor Publishing Division
Our Sunday Visitor, Inc.
200 Noll Plaza
Huntington, IN 46750

ISBN: 978-1-59276-150-0 (Inventory No. T201)
LCCN: 2007929037
Cover design: Lindsey Luken
Cover image: *The Virgin of the Annunciation* by Pompeo Batoni; courtesy Art Resource
Interior design: Sherri L. Hoffman

PRINTED IN THE UNITED STATES OF AMERICA

In loving memory of
Steve Green
1952–2005
A true friend of Mary

and for his precious family:
Mary Ann, Jolene, and Emily

INTRODUCTION

Our Loving Mother

It's been an honor and a privilege to write this book.

It's also been a challenge because there's so much material worldwide about the Blessed Mother. Choosing what to put in and what to leave out wasn't always easy.

We apologize if we failed to mention your favorite image, devotion, or prayer. Or if, in writing about one, we focused on a certain pious tradition but you're more familiar with a different explanation of its origin. The same holds true if the translation or version of a Marian prayer isn't your favorite wording.

We've discovered that, when it comes to Our Lady, many individuals *do* have favorites. That there's a particular image, devotion, or prayer, that touches the heart, eases the mind, and soothes the soul in a particular way. That Mary, universally a mother to us all, is — in a unique way — a mother to each individual who loves her.

If anything, this book demonstrates that Mary has been beloved continuously since New Testament times — that, truly, all generations have called and still call her blessed.

A Word of Thanks

We want to thank Fr. Thomas A. Thompson, S.M., for reading through our manuscript and offering corrections and suggestions. (Any errors that made it into print are the authors'.) Fr. Thompson is the Director of the Marian Library at the University of Dayton in Dayton, Ohio; a professor at the International Marian Research Institute; treasurer of the Mariological Society of America; and editor in chief of MSA's scholarly journal, *Marian Studies*.

Our thanks also to Fr. Thompson and to Dr. Geraldine M. Rohling, archivist at the Basilica of the National Shrine of the Immaculate Conception in Washington, DC, for their help in supplying artwork for this book.

— MONICA AND BILL DODDS

AD CAELI REGINAM

Encyclical *Proclaiming the Queenship of Mary,* promulgated by Pope Pius XII on October 11, 1954, near the close of a Marian Year observed in connection with the 100th anniversary celebration of the proclamation of the dogma of the Immaculate Conception, and four years after the proclamation of the dogma of the Assumption.

The encyclical begins by pointing out:

From the earliest ages of the Catholic Church a Christian people, whether in time of triumph or more especially in time of crisis, has addressed prayers of petition and hymns of praise and veneration to the Queen of Heaven. And never has that hope wavered which they placed in the Mother of the Divine King, Jesus Christ; nor has that faith ever failed by which we are taught that Mary, the Virgin Mother of God, reigns with a mother's solicitude over the entire world, just as she is crowned in heavenly blessedness with the glory of a Queen.

Explaining that he was also instituting the liturgical feast of the Queenship of Mary (now celebrated on August 22) as a fitting conclusion to the Marian Year, and "in response to petitions which have come to us from all over the world," Pope Pius said, "We do not wish to propose a new truth to be believed by Christians, since the title and the arguments on which Mary's queenly dignity is based have already been clearly set forth, and are to be found in ancient documents of the Church and in the books of the sacred liturgy."

The encyclical goes on to mention references to Christ's royalty in scripture (such as he "will reign in the house of Jacob forever" [Lk. 1:32]; "the Prince of Peace" [Is. 9:6]; the "King of Kings and Lord of Lords" [Rev. 19:16]) and says "when Christians reflected upon the intimate connection that obtains between a mother and a son, they readily acknowledged the supreme royal dignity of the Mother of God. Hence it is not surprising that the early writers of the Church called Mary 'the Mother of the King' and 'the Mother of the Lord,' basing their stand on the words of St. Gabriel the archangel, who foretold that the Son of Mary would reign forever (Lk. 1:32, 33) and on the words of Elizabeth who greeted her with reverence and called her '"the Mother of my Lord' (Lk.1:43). Thereby they clearly signified that she derived a certain eminence and exalted station from the royal dignity of her Son."

Quoting from several Fathers of the Church (including Sts. John Damascene, Gregory Nazianzen, and Jerome), the pontiff noted that title was used in both the Eastern and Western Churches:

The theologians of the Church, deriving their teaching from these and almost innumerable other testimonies handed down long ago, have called the most Blessed Virgin the Queen of all creatures, the Queen of the world, and the Ruler of all.

Ad Caeli Reginam goes on to cite pontifical writing dating as far back as the seventh century, when St. Martin I called Mary "our glorious Lady, ever Virgin," and the eighth, when Gregory II referred to Our Lady as "the Queen of all, the true Mother of God," and "the Queen of all Christians."

Pope Pius XII also noted that "for all these reasons St. Alphonsus Liguori, in collecting the testimony of past ages, writes these words with evident devotion: 'Because the virgin Mary was raised to such a lofty dignity as to be the mother of the King of kings, it is deservedly and by every right that the Church has honored her with the title of 'Queen'.'"

The encyclical goes on to say:

> Furthermore, the sacred liturgy, which acts as a faithful reflection of traditional doctrine believed by the Christian people through the course of all the ages both in the East and in the West, has sung the praises of the heavenly Queen and continues to sing them.

And:

> Finally, art which is based upon Christian principles and is animated by their spirit as something faithfully interpreting the sincere and freely expressed devotion of the faithful, has since the Council of Ephesus portrayed Mary as Queen and Empress seated upon a royal throne adorned with royal insignia, crowned with the royal diadem and surrounded by the host of angels and saints in heaven, and ruling not only over

nature and its powers but also over the machinations of Satan. Iconography, in representing the royal dignity of the Blessed Virgin Mary, has ever been enriched with works of highest artistic value and greatest beauty; it has even taken the form of representing colorfully the divine Redeemer crowning His mother with a resplendent diadem.

See also Queenship of Mary.

AD DIEM ILLUM LEATISSIMUM

Encyclical *On the Immaculate Conception*, promulgated by Pope Pius X on February 2, 1904, to mark the 50th anniversary of the proclamation of dogma of the Immaculate Conception.

In it, the pope explained:

Pope St. Pius X

But the first and chief reason, Venerable Brethren, why the fiftieth anniversary of the proclamation of the dogma of the Immaculate Conception should excite a singular fervor in the souls of Christians lies for us in that restoration of all things in Christ which we have already set forth in our first encyclical letter [*E supremi*, "On the restoration of all things to Christ," 1903]. For can anyone fail to see that there is no surer or more direct road than by Mary for uniting all mankind in Christ and obtaining through Him the perfect adoption of sons, that we may be holy and immaculate in the sight of God? For if to Mary it was truly said: "Blessed art thou who hast believed because in thee shall be fulfilled the things that have been told thee by the Lord" (Luke 1:45); or in other words, that she would conceive and bring forth the Son of God and if she did receive in her breast Him who is by nature Truth itself in order that "He, generated in a new order and with a new nativity, though invisible in Himself, might become visible in our flesh" (St. Leo the Great, Ser. 2, *De Nativ. Dom.*): the Son of God made man, being the "author and consummator of our faith"; it surely follows that His Mother most holy should be recognized as participating in the divine mysteries and as being in a manner the guardian of them, and that upon her as upon a foundation, the noblest after Christ, rises the edifice of the faith of all centuries.

See also Immaculate Conception.

AD JESUM PER MARIAM

See Consecration to Jesus through Mary.

ADMIRABLE HEART OF MARY, THE

Treatise written by St. John Eudes in 1681 to promote devotion to the Immaculate Heart of Mary.

> Mary is truly admirable in all her perfections and in all her virtues,

the saint wrote in the large book, which resembles a summary. He goes on:

St. John Eudes

But what is most admirable in her is her virginal Heart. The Heart of the Mother of God is a world of marvels, an abyss of wonders, the source and principle of all the virtues which we admire in our glorious Queen: 'All the glory of the king's daughter is within.' It was through the humility, purity and love of her most holy Heart that she merited to become the Mother of God and to receive the graces and privileges with which God enriched her on earth. These same sublime virtues of her immaculate Heart have rendered her worthy of the glory and happiness that surround her in heaven, and of the great marvels that God has wrought in and through her.

The book also said:

The Admirable Heart of Mary is the perfect image of the most Divine Heart of Jesus. It is the pattern and model for our own hearts, and all our happiness, perfection and glory consists in striving to transform them into so many living images of the sacred Heart of Mary, just as her holy Heart is a consummate likeness of the adorable Heart of Jesus. The sovereign devotion is to imitate what we honor, says St. Augustine, so who can fail to perceive that in encouraging the faithful in devotion to the most amiable Heart of the Mother of God, we are also exhorting them to imitate the most eminent virtues that adorn it.

St. John founded the Society of the Admirable Heart of Mary to foster devotion to the Immaculate Heart. He also established a feast celebrated in honor of the Heart of Mary, first at Autun in 1648, and afterwards in a number of French dioceses. Although he was unable to get approval from Rome for an office and feast, devotion to the Admirable Heart of Mary continued to grow.

See also Immaculate Heart of Mary.

ADMIRABLE SECRET OF THE MOST HOLY ROSARY — *See* Secret of the Rosary, The.

ADORATION

Worship directed to God alone.

In *Lumen Gentium* (*The Dogmatic Constitution on the Church*), the bishops at the Second Vatican Council wrote:

Placed by the grace of God, as God's Mother, next to her Son, and exalted above all angels and men, Mary intervened in the mysteries of Christ and is justly honored by a special cult in the Church. Clearly from earliest times the Blessed Virgin is honored under the title of Mother of God, under whose protection the faithful took refuge in all their dangers and necessities. . . . This cult, as it always existed, although it is altogether singular, differs essentially from the cult of adoration which is offered to the Incarnate Word, as well to the Father and the Holy Spirit, and it is most favorable to it. The various forms of piety toward the Mother of God, which the Church within the limits of sound and orthodox doctrine, according to the conditions of time and place, and the nature and ingenuity of the faithful has approved, bring it about that while the Mother is honored, the Son, through whom all things have their being and in whom it has pleased the Father that all fullness should dwell, is rightly known, loved and glorified and that all His commands are observed (66).

See also Cult; Veneration of Mary.

ADVOCATE OF GRACE

Title used in the Litany of Mary, Queen, referring to Mary's unique role in salvation history.

In his 1987 encyclical *Redemptoris Mater* (*Mother of the Redeemer*), Pope John Paul II explained:

> At the [Second Vatican] Council Paul VI solemnly proclaimed that Mary is the Mother of the Church, "that is, Mother of the entire Christian people, both faithful and pastors." Later, in 1968, in the Profession of Faith known as the "Credo of the People of God," he restated this truth in an even more forceful way in these words: "We believe that the Most Holy Mother of God, the new Eve, the Mother of the Church, carries on in heaven her maternal role with regard to the members of Christ, cooperating in the birth and development of divine life in the souls of the redeemed."

> The Council's teaching emphasized that the truth concerning the Blessed Virgin, Mother of Christ, is an effective aid in exploring more deeply the truth concerning the Church. When speaking of the Constitution Lumen Gentium, which had just been approved by the Council, Paul VI said: "Knowledge of the true Catholic doctrine regarding the Blessed Virgin Mary will always be a key to the exact understanding of the mystery of Christ and of the Church. Mary is present in the Church as the Mother of Christ, and at the same time as that Mother whom Christ, in the mystery of the Redemption, gave to humanity in the person of the Apostle John. Thus, in her new motherhood in the Spirit, Mary embraces each and every one in the Church, and embraces each and every one through the Church. In this sense Mary, Mother of the Church, is also the Church's model. Indeed, as Paul VI hopes and asks, the Church must draw from the Virgin Mother of God the most authentic form of perfect imitation of Christ."

> Thanks to this special bond linking the Mother of Christ with the Church, there is further clarified the mystery of that "woman" who, from the first chapters of the Book of Genesis until the Book of Revelation, accompanies the revelation of God's salvific plan for humanity. For Mary, present in the Church as the Mother of the Redeemer, takes part, as a mother, in that "monumental struggle against the powers of darkness" which continues throughout human history. And by her ecclesial identification as the "woman clothed with the sun" (Rev. 12:1) it can be said that "in the Most Holy Virgin the Church has already reached that perfection whereby she exists without spot or wrinkle." Hence, as Christians raise their eyes with faith to Mary in the course of their earthly pilgrimage, they "strive to increase in holiness." Mary, the exalted Daughter of Sion, helps all her children, wherever they may be and whatever their condition, to find in Christ the path to the Father's house.

> Thus, throughout her life, the Church maintains with the Mother of God a link which embraces, in the saving mystery, the past, the present and the future, and venerates her as the spiritual mother of humanity and the advocate of grace. (No. 47)

On December 8, 2004, the 150th anniversary of the proclamation of the dogma of the Immaculate Conception, Pope John Paul II concluded his homily with a prayer addressing Mary as the advocate of grace:

To you, Immaculate Virgin, predestined by God above every other creature as advocate of grace and model of holiness for his People, I renew this day in a special way the entrustment of the whole Church.

May you guide your children on the pilgrimage of faith, rendering them ever more obedient and faithful to the Word of God.

May you accompany every Christian on the path of conversion and holiness, in the struggle against sin and in the search for true beauty, which is always the sign and reflection of divine Beauty.

May you, again, obtain peace and salvation for all peoples. May the eternal Father, who willed you to be the Immaculate Mother of the Redeemer, renew also in our time, through you, the wonders of his merciful love. Amen!

AFRICA, OUR LADY OF

A bronze, dark-colored statue of the Immaculate Conception with European features brought from Lyon, France, to Algiers, Algeria, in 1840.

After the French conquered Algiers in the early 19th century, the first bishop — with no church, residence, or funds — was not welcomed by the local Muslims. On returning to Lyon, France, he told the sisters at the Convent of the Religious of the Sacred Heart about his situation, and the Sodality of Our Lady offered him the statue as a gift. The donors suggested the image should be considered the patroness of Muslims and blacks.

On returning to his own diocese, the bishop gave custody of the statue to the Trappist Fathers. It was his successor who oversaw the building of a church (now the Basilica of Our Lady of Africa) and asked the Trappists for the return of the statue, which was to be placed in it. The Trappists — who had displayed the statue at the entrance to their monastery — reluctantly agreed.

Soon, the image became known as Our Lady of Africa, Consolation of the Afflicted, and was visited by soldiers, sailors, the disabled, and others asking for Mary's help. Donations attested to cures attributed to her miraculous intercession. To show her gratitude, one woman sewed a white gown for the image. Another made a blue silk mantle. Later Pope Pius IX donated a golden crown with precious stones.

Algiers' Cardinal Charles Lavigerie — founder of the White Fathers (Missionaries of Our Lady of Africa) and White Sisters (Missionary Sisters of Our Lady of Africa) — placed the orders under the protection of Our Lady of Africa. These sisters are privileged to replace the gown and the mantle of the statue.

Our Lady of Africa is venerated by Muslims as well as Christians. The followers of Islam ask *Lala Meriem,* as they call the Blessed Virgin, for her special favors.

See also Islam, Mary in.

AGREDA, VENERABLE MARY OF

Spanish mystic and author of *The Mystical City of God,* book detailing private revelations from the Blessed Mother.

Mary was born in 1602 in Spain, one of the four children of Francis and Catherine Coronel, a wealthy and pious couple. Eventually, her father and brothers became Franciscan brothers, and she, her sister, and her mother became Franciscan sisters. The family castle became a convent and the family's money was given to the poor. Mary was chosen abbess in 1627 and remained in that position until her death in 1665.

A mystic and visionary, she was given to ecstasies and reputed to have the gift of bilocation. It is said she visited the areas of what are now New Mexico and Texas and taught the native people about Christ. There she was known as the "Lady in Blue."

Her four-volume work on the life of the Virgin Mary, *The Mystical City of God*, is based on private revelations. Written at the request of the Blessed Mother, it tells the story of Our Lady from her Immaculate Conception to her coronation in heaven.

Abridged translations of the work are still in print as is an edited version, titled *The Divine Life of the Most Holy Virgin*.

An excerpt from *The Mystical City of God*, describing the visit of the Magi to Mary and the Christ Child, reads:

The heavenly Mother awaited the pious and devout kings, standing with the Child in her arms. Amid the humble and poor surroundings of the cave, in incomparable modesty and beauty, She exhibited at the same time a majesty more than human, the light of heaven shining in her countenance. Still more visible was this light in the Child, shedding through the cavern effulgent splendor, which made it like a heaven. The three kings of the East entered and at the first sight of the Son and Mother they were for a considerable space of time overwhelmed with wonder.

They prostrated themselves upon the earth, and in this position they worshiped and adored the Infant, acknowledging Him as the true God and man, and as the Savior of the human race.

Adoration of the Magi

See also Most Blessed Sacrament, Our Lady of the; Revelation, Divine and Private.

AIN-KARIN

Town four miles from Jerusalem, home of Elizabeth and Zechariah, parents of John the Baptist. The second Joyful Mystery of the Rosary, the visitation, is Mary's traveling from Nazareth to Ain-Karin to spend time with her kinswoman, Elizabeth.

See also Magnificat; Scripture, Mary in.

AKATHISTOS

Byzantine hymn to Mary. By the fifth century, it was called *Akathistos,* although this is not its original name but a rubric. *A-kathistos* in Greek means "not seated." The Church stipulated that it be sung or recited standing, as when the Gospel is read, as a sign of reverence for Mary.

The structure of the hymn is inspired by a description of the heavenly Jerusalem found in Rev. 21. Mary is identified with the Church, the "Bride" with no earthly spouse, the Virgin Bride of the Lamb, in all splendor and perfection.

The *Akathistos* is made up of twenty-four stanzas, the number of letters in the Greek alphabet, and is structured according the alphabet with each stanza beginning with the succeeding letter. Within that are two distinct parts — history and faith — offering a perspective on Christology and ecclesiology. Each of those two is, in turn, divided into two sections of six stanzas. The hymn is both Christological and Marian.

The author is unknown. The Latin translation — which was edited by Bishop Christopher of Venice around the year 800 and greatly influenced the piety of the medieval West — has the name of Germanus of Constantinople (733). Today scholars tend to attribute its composition to one of the Fathers of Chalcedon, which means this hymn has its roots in the most ancient tradition of the undivided Church of the first centuries.

In the Byzantine liturgy from which it is taken, the *Akathistos* was originally celebrated on the fifth Saturday of Lent, called "Saturday of the *Akathistos.*" This was not only because the date is near the feast of the Annunciation (in which a passage from the *Akathistos* still appears) but also because the hymn, rich with Marian theology and spirituality, links the mystery of Christmas to the mystery of Easter: Christ's birth and his death and Resurrection, and the rebirth for all through the sacraments, to the motherhood of Mary at Bethlehem, to her maternal presence at the baptismal font.

Besides celebrating the hymn on the fifth Saturday of Lent and singing a section of it on the four preceding Saturdays, monks, priests, and faithful recite it on many other occasions, even daily. Almost all Byzantine monasteries and churches contain painted scenes from the *Akathistos* on the walls of their sacred buildings, on vestments, on liturgical furnishings, or surrounding the most celebrated icons. Excerpts from the hymn read:

> *O Mother, worthy of all hymn-tributes,*
> *who brought forth the Word, Most Holy*
> *of all the holy, accept the present offering,*
> *deliver all from every evil, and save from*
> *future suffering all who cry to thee.*
> *Alleluia.*

> *Hail, through whom joy shall shine forth!*
> *Hail, through whom evil shall end!*
> *Hail, restorer of fallen Adam!*
> *Hail, redemption of Eve's tears!*

> *Hail, Mother of the Lamb and of the*
> *Shepherd!*
> *Hail, Sheepfold of rational sheep!*

Hail, Mother of the unsetting Star!
Hail, Splendor of the mystic Day!

Hail, Sea that did overwhelm the wise
*   Pharaoh!*
Hail, Rock that gave life to the thirsty!

Hail, Tabernacle of God and the Word!
Hail, unshaken Tower of the Church!
Hail, inexpugnable Wall!
Hail, through whom trophies are lifted up!
Hail, through whom enemies fall down!
Hail, healing of my body!
Hail, safety of my soul!

*See also **Eastern Church, Mary in the.***

AKITA, OUR LADY OF

In June, August, and October of 1973, Sister Agnes Sasagawa of the Order of Handmaids of the Eucharist reported a supernatural event. After seeing a bright light, Sister Agnes heard a voice that seemed to come from a weeping three-foot wooden statue of Our Lady. Others report that since 1973, the statue has continued to cry tears which scientific study identified as human.

Sister Agnes received three messages from Our Lady. The first message was a prayer:

Most Sacred Heart of Jesus, truly present in the Holy Eucharist, I consecrate my body and soul to be entirely one with Your Heart, being sacrificed at every instant on all the altars of the world, and giving praise to the Father, pleading for the coming of His Kingdom.

The second and third messages told of the need for prayer, penance, and sacrifices. If the messages are ignored, Our Lady warned, there would be "a terrible punishment on all humanity."

The apparition was approved for devotion by John Shojiro Ito, Bishop of Niigata, Japan, in April 1984. It received final Church approval in June 1988 by then-Cardinal Joseph Ratzinger of the Congregation for the Doctrine of the Faith.

*See also **Revelation, Divine and Private.***

Our Lady of Akita

ALEXANDER VII

Pope from 1655 to 1667. At that time, the Spanish monarchs were involved in the discussion of Mary's Immaculate Conception, and Philip IV carried on a twenty-two-year correspondence (1643–1665) with a cloistered Franciscan and mystic, Sister Mary de Agreda, who strongly favored the teaching. Philip made it a state matter by regularly sending delegates to Rome to promote the teaching. The Spanish Plaza (*Piazza di Spagna*) in Rome, with its column surmounted with the statue of the Immaculate Conception, decorated each December 8, is a reminder of this period.

In reply to the Spanish intervention, Alexander VII issued in 1661 a decree (*Sollicitudo omnium ecclesiarum*), frequently considered the turning point in the development of the doctrine, which, without condemning the opposing opinion, stated the preference of the Holy See for the pious belief. In 1695, the observance of the Office and Mass of the Conception of Mary was granted to the whole church, and in 1708, it was established as a holy day of obligation.

In his 1853 apostolic constitution *Ineffabilis Deus*, proclaiming the dogma of the Immaculate Conception, Pope Pius IX quoted from the 1661 decree when he wrote:

> Alexander VII . . . authoritatively and decisively declared the mind of the Church: "Concerning the most Blessed Virgin Mary, Mother of God, ancient indeed is that devotion of the faithful based on the belief that her soul, in the first instant of its creation and in the first instant of the soul's infusion into the body, was, by a special grace and privilege of God, in view of the merits of Jesus Christ, her Son and the Redeemer of the human race, preserved free from all stain of original sin. And in this sense have the faithful ever solemnized and celebrated the Feast of the Conception."

See also Agreda, Venerable Mary of; Immaculate Conception.

ALL SOULS' ROSARY

Chaplet that uses a standard Rosary but replaces the Apostles' Creed with Psalm 130, which begins:

> "Out of the depths I cry to thee, O Lord! Lord, hear my voice! Let thy ears be attentive to the voice of my supplications!"

ALMA REDEMPTORIS MATER

Marian antiphon traditionally sung at the end of the Evening Prayer in the Liturgy of the Hours, from the first Sunday in Advent to the feast of the Purification. The title is the first line of the hymn which, in English, is "Loving Mother of the Redeemer."

Probably composed by the tenth-century monk Herman the Cripple (who was severely physically disabled), it is mentioned both by the author of the *Ancrene Riwle* (a religious classic of Middle English literature) and in Chaucer's *The Canterbury Tales*.

The hymn reads:
Loving Mother of the Redeemer,
Gate of Heaven, Star of the Sea,
Assist your people who have fallen
yet strive to rise again.
To the wonder of nature, you bore your Creator,
Yet remained a virgin after as before.
You who received Gabriel's joyful greeting,
have pity on us poor sinners. Amen.

See also Antiphons of Our Lady.

ALMUDENA, OUR LADY OF

Image of a standing, crowned Mary holding the crowned Christ Child in both arms, patroness of Madrid.

The devotion dates back to the eleventh century and the battles between the Christians and the Moors. A Moor citadel was conquered in 1085 by Alfonso VI in his advance towards Toledo. He reconsecrated the mosque — which had been named for Mary — as the Church of the Virgin of Almudena (*almudin*, the garrison's granary).

A pious legend about the vision of an image of the Virgin on the outer wall of the citadel on November 9, 1085, also dates back to this era. This is the image of the Virgin of Almudena, patroness of Madrid. St. Isidore (1082–1172), the patron of Madrid, had a great devotion to Our Lady of Almudena.

Madrid's cathedral is named in her honor. Charles V was the first king to express an interest in constructing a cathedral in Madrid, but it was not until 1883, when Alfonso XII laid the first stone, that work actually begun. Only the crypt was completed by 1911. In 1920, the architect Juan Moya was put in charge of the project and worked on the cathedral until the start of the Spanish Civil War. In 1944, after discussion on the original Gothic design, a competition was held and new architects chose a classical style, more in keeping with the Royal Palace nearby. Although work continued until 1999, Our Lady of Almudena Cathedral was officially declared completed in 1993.

The feast of Our Lady of Almudena is November 9.

See also **Atocha, Our Lady of.**

ALTAGRACIA, OUR LADY OF

One of two Marian titles chosen to be the patroness of the Dominican Republic. (The second is Our Lady of Mercy.)

Documents show that in 1502, Mary was honored as *Virgen de la Altagracia* (The Virgin of High Grace) in Santo Domingo. The name came from a painting brought from Spain by Alfonso and Antonio Trejo, brothers who were among the first European settlers there. When they later moved to the city of Higuey, they took the image with them and offered it to the parish church so that everyone could venerate it. The first shrine was completed in 1572; the present basilica was consecrated in 1971.

The portrait, painted on fine cloth, is about thirteen inches wide and eighteen inches high and is thought to be a primitive work of the Spanish school, dating back to the end of the fifteenth or beginning of the sixteenth century. It depicts Mary, her hands folded in prayer, in front of the Infant Jesus in a manger. Our Lady wears the traditional Marian colors and dress (a red tunic and blue mantle) and has a white scapular with white sleeves. The painting's frame is gold, precious stones, and enamel, the work of an unknown eighteenth-century artisan.

The image has been crowned twice: in 1922, during the pontificate of Pius XI; and in 1979, by Pope John Paul II, during his visit there.

ALTÖTTING, OUR LADY OF

Image and devotion. This small wooden statue of Mary and the Christ Child carved in the early fourteenth century is kept in an octagonal stone chapel dating back to the seventh century in Altötting, Bavaria, Germany.

Tradition holds that in 1489, a child who had drowned came back to life after being placed before the image. Many cures and miracles have since been attributed to the intercession of Our Lady of Altötting, to the point where the region is sometimes called the "Lourdes of Germany." For more than five centuries, that small stone chapel has been a destination for pilgrims, whose many gifts and donations make it one of the richest shrines in Europe. St. Conrad of Parzham (1818–1894) was its doorkeeper for more than thirty years, and Pope John Paul II visited the chapel in 1980.

ANCESTORS OF MARY

While there is no historical evidence of Mary's ancestry, scripture scholars note that biblical prophecies make her a member of the House of David because, by blood, it is through her and not Christ's foster father, Joseph, that Christ, too, is a member that line.

Jesus' lineage is recorded in both Mt. 1:1–16 and Lk. 3:23–38. Matthew uses a descending order from Abraham to Christ. Luke's is ascending, from Christ to Adam. The nature of the genealogies was not to provide archival or family records but preach who Jesus was and what he means for the salvation of all. At the time of the evangelists, paternity — including adoption or "levirate" (marrying a brother's widow), for example — was sufficient by itself to confer all hereditary rights. The rights in these lists are those of the messianic line.

There is a theory (to which many scholars do not subscribe) that Matthew is listing Christ's lineage through Joseph and Luke through Mary.

In the Middle Ages, Mary's lineage from David was sometimes depicted in a series of stained-glass windows. The series is called a "Jesse Tree" because Mary's ancestry begins with Jesse of Bethlehem, the father of David.

See also Apocryphal Writing, Mary in; Scripture, Mary in.

ANGELIC SALUTATION

Words addressed by the archangel Gabriel to Mary at the Annunciation: "Hail, full of grace, the Lord is with you!" (Lk. 1:28). Also, a term used for the prayer called the Hail Mary, which begins with the salutation.

A similar Byzantine prayer from the fourth century reads:

Hail, Virgin Mother of God, full of grace, the Lord is with you. Blessed are you among women and blessed is the fruit of your womb, for you have borne Christ, the Savior and Deliverer of our souls. Amen.

See also Ave Maria.

ANGELS, OUR LADY OF THE

Title since the early Church, sometimes called Queen of the Angels; also, stone image also known as *La Negrita*, "The Little Black One," and "Virgin de los Angeles."

Carved on dark stone, the image of Our Lady of the Angels is about three inches high and depicts the Blessed Mother carrying the Christ Child.

Pious tradition holds that while searching for firewood on August 2, 1635, a poor native woman named Juana Pereira found the image on a path outside Cartago, Costa Rica. She took it home with her, but it soon disappeared and was later found at the same spot on the trail. After that strange occurrence had happened five times, local residents understood it to mean Our Lady wanted a shrine built there. It soon became a pilgrimage destination, especially for the poor. In 1935, Pope Pius XI declared the shrine of the Queen of Angels a basilica.

An ornate cloak covers the entire image except for the faces of Mary and Jesus. Over time, the stone on which the statue had been placed was worn down by pilgrims touching it; a spring of water appeared beneath the stone and its water was collected and taken to the sick Now, the statue is displayed in a large gold monstrance. The image was solemnly crowned in 1926.

Our Lady of the Angels is the patroness of Costa Rica, where her feast day is August 2.

The title is also used for other famous shrines, including the Basilica of Santa Maria degli Angeli in Assisi, Italy, where St. Francis recognized his vocation. In Rome, Santa Maria degli Angeli was designed and built by Michelangelo.

There is also St. Mary of the Angels in Engeber, Switzerland; Notre Dame du Angles near Lurs, France; Our Lady of the Angels in London; and Our Lady of the Angels Cathedral in Los Angeles.

ANGELUS

A prayer traditionally repeated three times daily — morning, noon, and evening — at the sound of a bell.

Some historians note the devotion may trace its roots to at least the early thirteenth century and the custom of saying three Hail Marys at sunset, or when the Compline (evening prayer) bell tolled. It was a general practice throughout Europe by the fourteenth century and recommended by Pope John XXII in 1318 and 1327. The custom of reciting the prayers in the morning came later and, at noon, later still.

The version as it is now recited does not appear before the second decade of the seventeenth century. At about that time, the substitution of the *Regina Caeli* for the *Angelus* at Easter time was recommended and finally became the standard practice.

The title of the prayer comes from its first word in the Latin:

V. Angelus Domini nuntiavit Mariae.
R. Et concepit de Spiritu Sancto.

In English, the prayer reads:

V. The angel of the Lord declared unto Mary;
R. And she conceived by the Holy Spirit.

Hail Mary . . .

V. Behold the handmade of the Lord.
R. Be it done unto me according to your word.

Hail Mary . . .

V. And the Word was made flesh,
R. And dwelt among us.

Hail Mary . . .

V. Pray for us, O holy Mother of God,
R. That we may be made worthy of the
*   promises of Christ.*

Let us pray:
Pour forth, we beseech you, O Lord, your
grace into our hearts, that we, to whom the
incarnation of Christ, your Son, was made
known by the message of an angel, may by his
passion and cross be brought to the glory of
his resurrection, through the same Christ our
Lord. Amen.

See also **Regina Caeli.**

ANGLICAN CHURCH, MARY IN THE

As noted in the 2005 Anglican-Roman Catholic International Commission's statement of agreement, titled *Mary: Grace and Hope in Christ,* devotion to Mary, often seen as a distinctively Roman Catholic or Orthodox practice, has roots in Scripture and the early Christian tradition. This makes it part of Anglicans' heritage as well.

The Anglican liturgical calendar marks major events in the life of Mary, and in their formal prayers, Anglicans refer to her as "ever virgin" and as "Mother of God Incarnate."

But the document also notes that, because Anglicans and other non-Catholics do not recognize the infallibility of the pope, and because Mary's conception and assumption are not mentioned explicitly in Scripture, the two dogmas have been considered major obstacles to Christian unity. Still, "it is impossible to be faithful to Scripture and not to take Mary seriously," the document said, and "Anglicans and Roman Catholics together affirm" that Mary was biologically Jesus' mother, that she was a virgin, and that Jesus was conceived by the power of the Holy Spirit.

However, the document explained, by the sixteenth century, reformers were calling for greater restraint in Marian devotion that had seemed to move far beyond Scripture and tradition. "In popular religion, Mary came widely to be viewed as an intermediary between God and humanity, and even as a worker of miracles with powers that verged on the divine." Reformers reacted "against devotional practices which approached Mary as a mediatrix (mediator) alongside Christ or sometimes even in his place." It was the reformers' emphasis on Jesus as the only mediator between God and humanity that led them to reject the "real and perceived abuses surrounding devotion to Mary. It also led to the loss of some positive aspects of devotion and the diminution of her place in the life of the church."

On the other hand, "to be Roman Catholic came to be identified by an emphasis on devotion to Mary," the statement noted. The growth in devotion contributed to the consensus among Roman Catholics that led to the solemn definitions of Mary's Immaculate Conception and Assumption.

While Anglicans may object to the way the dogmas were proclaimed, commission members said, the teachings make sense when seen in the light of a scriptural pattern through which God prepares those he has called to fulfill a special mission and reward those who cooperate with him.

In the statement's conclusion, the authors reaffirmed:

— that any interpretation of the role of Mary must not obscure the unique mediation of Christ;

— that any consideration of Mary must be linked with the doctrines of Christ and the Church;

— that we recognize the Blessed Virgin Mary as the *Theotókos*, the mother of God incarnate, and so observe her festivals and accord her honor among the saints;

— that Mary was prepared by grace to be the mother of our Redeemer, by whom she herself was redeemed and received into glory;

— that we recognize Mary as a model of holiness, faith, and obedience for all Christians; and

— that Mary can be seen as a prophetic figure of the Church.

ANNA

Prophetess who recognized the infant Jesus as the Messiah (Lk. 2:36ff).

See also Scripture, Mary in.

ANNE — *See Joachim and Anne.*

ANNOCIADE

An old form of the French word for the Annunciation. *Annociade* is still used by some religious orders of women, including the *Annonciades* of Bourges, founded by St. Joan Valois in 1501, and the Blue *Annonciades,* founded by Blessed Victoria Strata in 1605.

ANNUNCIATA, THE

A painting of the Annunciation commissioned in 1252 for the Friar Servants of Mary's house in Florence. Pious tradition says the artist fell asleep at his easel and awoke to see the piece completed. St. Aloysius Gonzaga made his vow of chastity in front of the painting in 1579. The small chapel of the Servites was rebuilt in the fifteenth century and decorated by Andrea del Sarto.

ANNUNCIATION

Announcement of the Archangel Gabriel to the Virgin Mary that she would become the mother of Christ (Lk. 1:26–38); solemnity celebrated on March 25 to commemorate that event.

Celebrated in the Eastern Church as early as the fifth century, this feast was introduced into the West during the sixth and seventh centuries. In some regions of Spain, it was marked on December 18, until the eleventh century; then, they adopted the Roman date but retained their own feast. In the eighteenth century, the December commemoration was replaced with a feast of the "Expectation of Birth of the Blessed Virgin Mary." Until 1918, the feast was a public holiday in many Catholic countries.

In the early Church, March 25 was observed in a special way as the Day of the Incarnation; tradition claimed that it was also the date of the Crucifixion. By medieval times, the anniversaries of several other events in salvation history were placed on this date.

Annunciation

It was an ancient custom of the papal Curia to start the year on March 25 in all their documents, calling it the Year of the Incarnation. The practice was even adopted by civil governments for the legal dating of documents. In fact, the Feast of the Annunciation, called "Lady Day," marked the beginning of the legal year in England until 1752.

In the Greek Church, the feast was called *Evangelismos* (Glad Tidings); Eastern Rite Slavs referred to it as *Blagovescenije Marii* (Glad Tidings of Mary); and, for Arabic Christians, it was it *Id Al-bishara* (Feast of Good News). Central Europeans knew it as the Feast of Swallows, because of the general belief that the first swallows returned from their migration on or about this day.

The feast returned to its Christological orientation by the reform of the calendar in 1969.

See also **Daughter of Zion;** **Fiat** *in the Name of Humanity;* **Scripture, Mary in.**

ANNUNCIATION BREAD

A Russian sacramental: large wafers of wheat flour blessed by the priest and given to the faithful.

In the home, a father would hand a small piece of the wafer to each member of the family and to the servants, who received it with a bow and ate it in silence. Later, they would take the crumbs of the Annunciation bread into the fields and, with pious superstition, bury them in the ground as a protection against blight, hail, frost, and drought.

In a similar tradition in central Europe, farmers put a picture of the Assumption in the seed grain while asking for Our Lady's help with the crop.

ANTIGUA, OUR LADY OF

Image and devotion; patroness of Panama.

The painting *Nuestra Señora de la Antigua* is about six feet high and two-and-a-half feet wide and shows a standing Mary holding the Christ Child in her left arm. Both figures have gold-plated silver imperial crowns superimposed.

Tradition holds that the image was brought to Panama in the seventeenth century and, although most of the city was destroyed when the pirate Henry Morgan attacked and set fire to the city in 1671, the image remained intact. Now, the painting is displayed in the temple of Chirivi in Tunja, a very popular shrine located near the Turine River, and the feast of Our Lady of la Antigua is celebrated on the third Sunday of January.

Other Marian images and devotions in Panama include: the painting of Our Lady of Mercy in Panama City; *La Virgen Hallada* (*The Virgin Found*), a stone sculpture of Our Lady of Mount Carmel that is venerated in Montijo; *Our Lady of Tarivá,* a 1571 painting in the village of that name; and *Our Lady of Sopetrán,* a painting in the village of Hita, dating back to 1615.

ANTIPHONS OF OUR LADY

Hymns, echoing scriptural themes, sung at the conclusion of Night Prayer in the Liturgy of the Hours.

These antiphons are suited to the various seasons of the liturgical year: *Alma Redemptoris Mater* (Advent and Christmas); *Ave Regina Caelorum* (Lent); *Regina Caeli* (Easter); and *Salve Regina* (ordinary time).

The Antiphons of Our Lady are sung daily in some monasteries. Some religious orders customarily sing them, especially the *Salve Regina,* each evening before the statue of Mary. That practice began with the Dominicans under Jordan of Saxony (d. 1237), the second Master of the Order, then spread to other orders and, eventually, to the universal Church.

See also **Alma Redemptoris Mater; Ave Regina Caelorum; Regina Caeli; Salve Regina.**

ANTIPOLO, OUR LADY OF

Wooden statue carved and blessed in Acapulco, Mexico, and then taken by the new Governor General of the Philippines to Manila, the Philippines, in 1626, aboard the El Almirante and placed in the Jesuit church of San Ignacio. It is said that because of the safe voyage across the Pacific, the Marian image was named *Nuestra Señora de la Paz y Buenviaje*: Our Lady of Peace and Good Voyage. After the governor died, the Jesuits became the custodians of the statue, and it was taken to Santa Cruz by the new pastor of that region.

Our Lady of Antipolo

According to pious tradition, the statue disappeared at least twice from the church, and each time was found in the branches of a *tipulo* (breadfruit) tree. A church was built near the site, and the tree was cut down and made into a pedestal for "The Brown Virgin."

The name *tipulo* prefixed by the Tagalog article *ang* ("the") forms the name "Antipolo."

During the World War II occupation of the Japanese, the statue — accompanied by five hundred devotees — was evacuated to the mountains of Angono. After being kept for a time in the Ocampo residence at Quiapo, it was moved to the Quiapo church where it stayed until October 15, 1945, when it was returned to the original site Our Lady had "chosen" centuries before. In 1950, Antipolo was proclaimed the national shrine of Our Lady by the bishops of the country.

Each year the faithful commemorate the statue's return from 8 P.M. on April 30 until dawn on May 1. Thousands visit the shrine during the month of May.

APARECIDA, OUR LADY

Image and devotion: *Nossa Senhora Aparecida,* "Our Lady Who Appeared." Patroness of Brazil.

Pious tradition holds that in October 1717, three fishermen with a devotion to Mary were working their trade near Guarantinqueta, a small city in the Paraiba River valley, when they netted first a headless statue, and then, the remainder of the image. It depicted Our Lady of the Immaculate Conception. Asking for Mary's intercession, they hauled in a large catch, the first miracle attributed to Our Lady Aparecida.

Although it is not known how the small (less than three feet high) statue ended up at the bottom of the river, art historians say it is the work of Agostino de Jesus, a monk from São Paulo who made clay sculptures. They believe the image was made around 1650 and must have stayed submerged in the river for many years because it had lost its original colors.

It is now clothed in a heavily embroidered mantle which allows only the face and hands to be seen. The statue was crowned in 1904, and in 1930, Pope Pius XII proclaimed her principal patroness of Brazil. Her October 12 feast day is a national holiday there.

APOCRYPHAL WRITING, MARY IN

The apocrypha is writing that uses the same style as the books of the Old and New Testaments but is not part of the sacred canon. The word itself comes from the Greek meaning "secret" or "hidden." The apocrypha falsely assert divine inspiration by claiming, for example, to have been written by one of the patriarchs, a great prophet, or an apostle. Apocryphal writings imply that they pass on true revelation that clarifies what is found in canonical Scripture.

Mary is written about at length in several apocryphal books: the *Protoevangelium of James* (first titled *The Nativity of Mary*), the *Gospel of Pseudo-Matthew*, and the *Passing of Mary*. Others texts include the *Sibylline Oracles,* the *Ascension of Isaiah,* the *History of Joseph the Carpenter,* the *Arabic Gospel of the Infancy,* and the *Book of the Resurrection of Christ.*

The *Protoevangelium of James* probably dates back to the second century and seems to be the first Christian writing demonstrating an independent interest in Mary.

Written in a legend style, the book recounts the background and life of Mary, offering elaborate details to the basics presented in the four Gospels. There is her miraculous birth after her parents, Joachim and Anne, are visited by an angel; her presentation in the Temple when she was three; and her engagement to Joseph.

In this book, the archangel Gabriel appears to Mary twice: first, while she is drawing water at the well; then, when she is spinning wool at home. Other scenes include the birth of Christ in a cave outside Bethlehem, the midwife's testimony of Mary's virginity, and Mary's vindication before the High Priest.

Historians note that the *Protoevangelium* is significant because it promoted three Marian feasts: the Conception of Mary, the Nativity of Mary, and the Presentation of Mary in the Temple.

An excerpt from the *Protoevangelium of James* describing Mary's presentation in the Temple and engagement to Joseph reads:

Presentation of Mary

And the child was two years old, and Joachim said: Let us take her up to the temple of the Lord, that we may pay the vow that we have vowed, lest perchance the Lord send to us, and our offering be not received. And Anna said: Let us wait for the third year, in order that the child may not seek for father or mother. And Joachim said: So let us wait. And the child was three years old, and Joachim said: Invite the daughters of the Hebrews that are undefiled, and let them take each a lamp, and let them stand with the lamps burning, that the child may not turn back, and her heart be captivated from the temple of the Lord. And they did so until they went up into the temple of the Lord. And the priest received her, and kissed her, and blessed her, saying: The Lord has magnified thy name in all generations. In thee, on the last of the days, the Lord will manifest His redemption to the sons of Israel. And he set her down upon the third step of the altar, and the Lord God sent grace upon her; and she danced with her feet, and all the house of Israel loved her.

And her parents went down marveling, and praising the Lord God, because the child had not turned back. And Mary was in the temple of the Lord as if she were a dove that dwelt there, and she received food from the hand of an angel. And when she was twelve years old there was held a council of the priests, saying: Behold, Mary has reached the age of twelve years in the temple of the Lord. What then shall we do with her, lest perchance she defile the sanctuary of the Lord? And they said to the high priest: Thou standest by the altar of the Lord; go in, and pray concerning her; and whatever the Lord shall manifest unto thee, that also will we do. And the high priest went in, taking the robe with the twelve bells into the holy of holies; and he prayed concerning her. And behold an angel of the Lord stood by him, saying unto him: Zacharias, Zacharias, go out and assemble the widowers of the people, and let them bring each his rod; and to whomsoever the Lord shall show a sign, his wife shall she be. And the heralds went out through all the circuit of Judea, and the trumpet of the Lord sounded, and all ran.

And Joseph, throwing away his axe, went out to meet them; and when they had assembled, they went away to the high priest, taking with them their rods. And he, taking the rods of all of them, entered into the temple, and prayed; and having ended his prayer, he took the rods and came out, and gave them to them: but there was no sign in them, and Joseph took his rod last; and, behold, a dove came out of the rod, and flew upon Joseph's head. And the priest said to Joseph, Thou hast been chosen by lot to take into thy keeping the virgin of the Lord. But Joseph refused, saying: I have children, and I am an old man, and she is a young girl. I am afraid lest I become a laughing stock to the sons of Israel. And the priest said to Joseph: Fear the Lord thy God, and remember what the Lord did to Dathan, and Abiram, and Korah; how the earth opened, and they were swallowed up on account of their contradiction. And now fear, O Joseph, lest the same things happen in thy house. And Joseph was afraid, and took her into his keeping. And Joseph said to Mary: Behold, I have received thee from the temple of the Lord; and now I leave thee in my house, and go away to build my buildings, and I shall come to thee. The Lord will protect thee.

APOSTLES — *See Scripture, Mary in.*

APOSTOLIC ROSARY

Popular term for Rosary beads that have been blessed by the pope.

The name also refers to the apostolic indulgences attached to objects of devotion. The indulgence may be given by any priest who has been granted the necessary permission and may be obtained by performing the good works prescribed by the pope.

APPARITIONS OF MARY

Visions or appearances of Mary that have taken place after her death.

Since the fourth century, many visions and appearances of Mary have been reported throughout the world. Within the Church, a distinction is made between an apparition during apostolic times and one following the end of public revelation, with the death of the last apostle. A Catholic is not required to believe in an apparition that is a "private revelation," even one the Church judges "worthy of belief" (for example, revelations made to St. Juan Diego at Guadalupe, St. Bernadette at Lourdes, or the children at Fatima).

Phenomena such as apparitions and visions do not constitute an essential element of Christian holiness and are not proof of the holiness of the visionary. Some reported visions (and "locutions," or inner voices) can be the result of hallucination or an unknown natural cause. Because it is not permissible to presume that a cause is supernatural, cases require careful investigation and discernment.

In a vision, a body is not objectively present although, for example, an angel who appears in a vision will "assume" a body. In an apparition, a person is present at a definite location in space and time and is visible (in some instances, to more than one witness).

Throughout the history of the Church following the end of public revelation, there have been many reports of apparitions, but few have been judged "worthy of belief." When called to evaluate a given claim, the Church has considered the facts of the phenomenon itself (the ecstasy, the visionary), the doctrine that emerged, and the spiritual and other fruits. These three central themes have been systematized into sets of positive and negative criteria by the Sacred Congregation for the Doctrine of the Faith:

Positive Criteria

1. Moral certitude or a high probability that the facts are consistent with what has been claimed.
2. The persons involved are psychologically balanced, honest, living a good moral life, sincere, and respectful toward Church authority.
3. That there is immunity from error in theological and spiritual doctrine.
4. That there be sound devotion and spiritual fruits, such as the spirit of prayer, testimony of charity, and true conversion.

Negative Criteria

1. That there be no manifest error regarding the facts of the event.
2. That there be no doctrinal errors attributed to God, Mary, or a saint.
3. That there be no evidence of material or financial motives connected with the event.
4. That there be no gravely immoral acts by the person on the occasion of the revelations or apparitions.
5. That there be no psychopathic tendency in the person which might enter into the alleged supernatural event; no psychosis or collective hysteria of some type.

See also particular name of apparition; Revelation, Divine and Private.

ARANTZAZU, OUR LADY OF

Tiny — less than twelve inches — statue of Mary with the Christ Child found in a hawthorn tree in the Guipúzcoa province of Spain in 1469 by a shepherd named Rodrigo de Balzategui after he had had a vision. The image gets its name from the shepherd's comment to it — *"Arantzan zu!"* — which in Basque means, "You, in the hawthorn!"

The statue is kept in the Shrine of *Nuestra Señora de Arantzazu*, which has been a pilgrimage site for centuries. Among those who visited was St. Ignatius of Loyola; it was before Our Lady of Arantzazu that the founder of the Society of Jesus made a vow of chastity to Mary and entrusted her to take him under her protection and patronage.

On September 9, the feast day of Our Lady of Arantzazu, people from all over the Basque country come to the shrine on a traditional pilgrimage.

ARCACHON, OUR LADY OF

Statue of Mary holding the Christ Child, found by Blessed Thomas Illyricus of Osimo (born in the mid-fifteenth century), a Franciscan who had moved to the forest solitude of Arcachon, France. Tradition says he came upon the statue on the seashore as it was being battered by the waves. Carved from alabaster, the statue is about twenty inches tall and appears to be the work of the thirteenth century.

Blessed Thomas immediately built a wooden chapel for the image. A century later, that building was replaced by a stone sanctuary, but nearby drifting sand dunes made it necessary to build a new church in 1723 on a hill overlooking the Bay of Arcachon. The image was given a crown by Pius IX in 1870.

ARCHAEOLOGY AND MARY

Archaeological work points to the early Church's devotion to Mary and the role in salvation history it attributed to her.

Franciscan archaeologists excavating at the site of Nazareth's Church of the Annunciation have concluded that prior to the building of a Byzantine church there in the first half of the first millennium, Christians had already constructed a place of worship at this site. Excavations revealed also a primitive baptismal font, a mosaic floor, and a flight of seven steps that led down toward a grotto. To the west of the shrine was another cave that had been made into a devotional site.

Architectural elements and decorations indicate the construction of a "public" building, which the archaeologists identify with a church-synagogue. Among these architectural remains the researchers found various graffiti including the Greek characters *XE MAPIA (Ch(air)e Maria)* which can be translated as "Hail Mary," the angel's greeting at the Annunciation. It is the oldest of its kind to have been discovered.

Scientists say it was written before the Council of Ephesus (431), which first addressed the role of Mary and devotion to her. Other graffiti, all now conserved at an adjacent museum, confirm the Marian nature of the shrine. One in Armenian reads "beautiful girl" (referring to Mary) and another one in Greek reads "on the holy site of M(ary) I have written."

Inscriptions from second-century catacombs under St. Peter's Basilica in Rome show Mary as the protector of Christians who have died and their mediatrix with Christ. An inscription from an early Jewish burial site in Egypt affirms the tradition of Mary's virginity.

ARK OF THE COVENANT

Marian title used in the Litany of the Blessed Virgin Mary (also known as the Litany of Loreto) which was originally approved in 1587 by Pope Sixtus V.

Chapters 25 and 40 of the book of Exodus include a description of the Ark of the Covenant, a symbol of God's presence to Israel. Placed in the ark were the Commandments of the Law, God's covenant with the Chosen People. Mary is referred to as the "Ark of the Covenant" in the sense that her womb contained the maker of the Law, God the Son.

See also Litany of the Blessed Virgin Mary.

ART, MARY IN

Since the third century, portrayals of Mary have been a constant theme in Christian art in all Orthodox and Catholic countries.

A mother and child from the catacomb of St. Priscilla (third century), perhaps referring to Isaiah's prophecy (7:14), is thought to be the oldest image. The theme of a seated mother with her child on her lap can also be found in the Cappella dells Velata, in the same catacomb, but from a later date. A full-face image in the Cemeterium Major was painted in the fourth century. An image of Our Lady praying was also portrayed on the bottom of gilt glasses.

Following the Council of Ephesus in 431 and its teaching of Mary as *Theotokos* — God bearer — portrayals became more regal. A mosaic in St. Mary Major in Rome (now lost) showed Mary enthroned with the Christ Child. The clothing was stereotypical. Mary wore an eastern *maphorion* (a veil) and red slippers. In the *Adoration of the Magi* in S. Appolinare Nuovo in Ravenna, Mary is shown full-face with a solemn expression. This style was used in apses (depicting Our Lady surrounded by angels) and on ivory diptychs (hinged, two-paneled works).

Art historians say at this point, many modes developed. In Byzantium, Mary was portrayed on liturgical icons. Pious tradition holds that St. Luke painted *Odigitria* (or *Hodegetria*) — Our Lady, Guide of Wayfarers — which was brought from Jerusalem to the Odigôn monastery in Constantinople. The painting shows a standing Mary, holding the Child in her left arm as he gives his blessing. Her right arm is either touching the Child or raised. Another version, in the diptych of Etschmi-

Madonna of the Streets by Ferruzzi

adzin, shows the Madonna seated. This style often features an angel on either side of her. The *Odigitria,* which is the most common style of this image of Our Lady, is enthroned in the apses and votive panels of churches (as in Hagia Sophia, Constantinople). In the mosaics in Kiti, Cyprus, she is standing.

A different portrayal that shows Mary praying, either alone or with a medallion of the Christ Child on her breast, is called the *Orans.* Among the early images of "the praying Madonna" is the *Virgin Blachernistissa* in Constantinople's Blachernae monastery, which Augusta Pulcheria founded in the fifth century in honor of Mary.

Yet another style depicted an intercessory Mary in three-quarters profile with her hands uplifted. Mary stands to the right, and John the Baptist to the left, with Christ in the center. This portrayal was common in apses and in tombs. *Galaktotropphousa,* or the "nursing Madonna,"* appeared early in Egypt and is an adaptation of the Egyptian goddess Isis nursing her son Horus.

A ninth-century ivory work of either Egyptian or Syrian origin shows the *Eleousa,* or *Virgin of Tenderness.* The *Glykophilousa* shows the Christ Child kissing his mother. Art historians say these are predominantly folkloric and, though sometimes found in churches, are most often seen in minor arts.

All types of Marian styles — alone or with the Child — are included in Byzantine seals. The Virgin with Child is the symbolic theme of the *Zoodocho Pigi (Source of Life)* in the illustration of the *Akathistos.* Marian litrugical art also features her principal feast based on the cycle of her life and death.

To a large extent, Russian art adopted the Byzantine motifs. The *Blachernistissa* becomes the *Snmenie* and the *Virgin of Tenderness* the *Umileniye.* Many other Russian types were derived from Byzantine works, most notably the *Pokrov,* or *Protection of the Mantle of Our Lady,* from the Greek *Episkepsis,* which is similar to the *Blachernistissa.*

The West also relied heavily on Byzantium, but the picture of Mary as a crowned empress (*Maria Regina*) was a Western conception originating in the sixth century. The Queen of Heaven in an attitude of prayer can be found in the mosaic of the Oratory of John VII (from the early eighth century and now in Florence). Regina reappears during the Middle Ages, in the Romanesque and Gothic periods. The Virgin in Majesty, *Majestas Mariae* — derived from the *Odigitria* — is enthroned in the apses of Roman churches, in Romanesque statuary, and on the tympanums of cathedrals.

Eleousa, the "Virgin of Tenderness"

Italians adopted the Byzantine styles and first kept the Eastern manner of treatment before portraying Mary according the Renaissance interpretation of idealized beauty. Gothic art includes many examples of the Madonna standing with the Christ Child. In Western art, Mary still typically is personified as the ideal woman.

As depicted in art, traditional Marian colors and dress are a red tunic and blue mantle. An example is Raphael's *Madonna Connestabile,* painted in 1503–1504.

The West has also created a number of types often linked with a particular place or group such as a sanctuary, shrine, or association. Some motifs are based on the events of her life. For example, the Immaculate Conception, developed particularly in the seventeenth century by Spanish artists; the Virgin of Expectation or Our Lady of Good Hope; Mary before the birth of Christ; and the Sorrowful Virgin, including the *Pietá,* inspired by the Passion of Christ. The term "Black Madonnas" is used for hundreds of images of Mary that portray her as dark-skinned.

***See also* Akathista, *Black Madonnas,* Eleousa *and* Oumilenie, Pietá, *Mother of God.*

ASSOCIATE OF THE REDEEMER

Title referring to Mary's unique role in salvation history as one "who already shares fully in the fruits of the Paschal Mystery" (*Marialis Cultus*, 22).

In his 1974 apostolic exhortation, *Marialis Cultus*, subtitled "for the right ordering and development of Marian devotion," Pope Paul VI also wrote:

> The examination of the revised liturgical books leads us to the comforting observation that the postconciliar renewal has, as was previously desired by the liturgical movement, properly considered the Blessed Virgin in the mystery of Christ, and, in harmony with tradition, has recognized the singular place that belongs to her in Christian worship as the holy Mother of God and the worthy Associate of the Redeemer.

In his general audience on May 4, 1983, Pope John Paul II explained:

> Dearest brothers and sisters, in the month of May we raise our eyes to *Mary, the woman who was associated in a unique way in the work of mankind's reconciliation with God.* According to the Father's plan, Christ was to accomplish this work through his sacrifice. However, *a woman would be associated with him, the Immaculate Virgin who is thus placed before our eyes as the highest model of cooperation in the work of salvation....*
>
> The "Yes" of the Annunciation constituted not only the acceptance of the offered motherhood, but signified above all Mary's commitment to service of the mystery of the Redemption. Redemption was the work of her Son; Mary was associated with it on a subordinate level. Nevertheless, her participation was real and demanding. Giving her consent to the angel's message, Mary agreed to collaborate in the whole work of mankind's reconciliation with God, just as her Son would accomplish it.

See also Co-Redemptrix, Co-Redemptorist.

The Sistine Madonna by Raphael

ASSUMPTION

A dogma of faith Pope Pius XII solemnly defined on November 1, 1950. In his apostolic constitution *Munificentissimus Deus*, Pius wrote:

> We pronounce, declare and define it to be a divinely revealed dogma: that the Immaculate Mother of God, the ever Virgin Mary,

having completed the course of her earthly life, was assumed body and soul into heavenly glory.

Pius' use of the phrase "was assumed" indicates that the Assumption is different from Christ's Ascension. And his "having completed the course of her earthly life" does not say whether or not Mary actually experienced death.

Tradition favors the theological opinion that Mary died and was most likely buried near the Garden of Gethsemane in Jerusalem. And, as with the body of Christ, her body did not undergo decomposition after her death and burial, but was assumed intact. Theologians note that, as in the case of the Resurrection, what the dogma of the Assumption defines is seen as a reality and a truth only by those with the gift of faith, by those who accept and respond to what is contained in Divine Revelation.

There is no explicit biblical evidence for the Assumption but, based on theological reasoning and Tradition, there is the implicit belief that Christ took his mother to himself at the moment of her leaving this life because she is one declared "full of grace" and the "highly favored daughter" of God the Father (Lk. 1:28). In *Munificentissimus Deus*, Pius quotes the apostle Paul:

When the perishable puts on the imperishable, and the mortal puts on immortality, then shall come to pass the saying that is written: "Death is swallowed up in victory" (1 Cor. 15:54). Because of the unique role Mary played in the life of Christ, she also shares in the victory of his Resurrection, his conquering sin and death. They are the new

Assumption

Adam and the new Eve foretold in Gen. 3:15: "I will put enmity between you [the serpent] and the woman, and between your seed and her seed."

Pope Pius also noted the great Scholastic theologians and doctors of the Church of the thirteenth century (Sts. Albert the Great, Thomas Aquinas, and Bonaventure) considered the Assumption "the fulfillment of the most perfect grace granted to the Blessed Virgin and the special blessed that countered the curse of Eve."

Other Doctors of the Church who promoted this teaching were St. Bernadine of Siena (1380–1444), St. Robert Bellarmine (1542–1621), St. Francis de Sales (1567–1622), St. Peter Canisius (1521–1597), and St. Alphonsus Liguori (1696–1787).

Pius' decision to solemnly define the Assumption of Mary as a dogma was also strongly influenced by "outstanding agreement of the Catholic prelates and faithful." Between 1849 and 1950, a remarkable number of petitions for a solemn declaration were sent to Rome from the Church worldwide. This includes 113 cardinals, 18 patriarchs, 2,505 archbishops and bishops, 32,000 priests and men religious, 50,000 women religious, and 8 million laypersons.

Just as Pope Pius IX had done in the nineteenth century in reference to the Immaculate Conception, Pius XII issued an encyclical, *Deiperae Virginis*, addressed to the bishops of the world, asking whether or not Mary's bodily Assumption was definable and whether their priests and people wished it to be defined at this time. The answer was an overwhelming "yes."

Later, at the Second Vatican Council, the bishops wrote in *Lumen Gentium* (*The Dogmatic Constitution on the Church*) that Mary's Assumption offers both a reminder of the bodily resurrection of all people at the end of time (*CCC* 366) and comfort now for those grieving the death of a loved one:

> In the bodily and spiritual glory which she possesses in heaven, the Mother of Jesus continues in this present world as the image and the first flowering of the Church as she [the Church] is to be perfected in the world to come. Likewise, Mary shines forth on earth, until the day of the Lord shall come (cf. 2 Pet. 3:10), as a sign of sure hope and solace for the pilgrim People of God (No. 68).

ASSUMPTION, FEAST OF THE

One of the oldest and most solemn feasts of Mary, now a solemnity and holy day of obligation celebrated on August 15.

A Memorial of Mary, which celebrated all her privileges as the Mother of God, was already being held during the fifth century. In the Eastern Church this was marked on August 15 and, over time, came to be known

St. Francis de Sales

as the "falling asleep" (the dormition) of Mary. (Early Christians believed that a body "fell asleep" at death and rested until it woke in the glory of the next life.) Emperor Mauricius Flavius (582–602) ordered that the liturgical feast of the Dormition of Mary be celebrated throughout the Byzantine Empire on August 15. A basilica was built in Gethsemane where tradition held her tomb was located, and Byzantine preachers began to proclaim her Assumption as well as her death. Today in Eastern liturgies, the feast is commonly called the Assumption or "Journey of the Blessed Mother of God into Heaven."

Rome adopted the feast in the seventh century and, during the pontificate of St. Adrian I (772–795), its title became Assumption. From the very beginning, Mary's being assumed body and soul into heaven was the focus of this feast in the Western Church. In the West, there is testimony to it dating as far back as the writing of St. Gregory of Tours, who died in 593. By the eighth century, the doctrine was entirely accepted in the East.

In the sixteenth century, the Assumption became the greatest of the Marian liturgical celebrations and one of the most prominent feasts of the Church year.

ATHANASIAN CREED

A profession of faith approved and used in the West but not generally recognized in the East although it appears in the Greek liturgical book *Herologian* and in the service books of the Russian Church from the seventeenth century. The creed probably dates back to the fourth or fifth century. First attributed to St. Athanasius, its authorship is now placed by scholars to southern Gaul (France) and was, perhaps, written by St. Ambrose. It is divided into halves, dealing with the doctrines of the Trinity and the Incarnation, with references to assorted dogmas. It begins and ends with the declaration that belief in the truth is essential for salvation.

Passages directly related to Mary read:

It is necessary for eternal salvation that one also faithfully believe that our Lord Jesus Christ became flesh. For this is the true faith that we believe and confess: That our Lord Jesus Christ, God's Son, is both God and man.

He is God, begotten before all worlds from the being of the Father, and he is man, born in the world from the being of his mother — existing fully as God, and fully as man with a rational soul and a human body; equal to the Father in divinity, subordinate to the Father in humanity.

Although he is God and man, he is not divided, but is one Christ. He is united because God has taken humanity into himself; he does not transform deity into humanity. He is completely one in the unity of his person, without confusing his natures. For as the rational soul and body are one person, so the one Christ is God and man.

ATOCHA, OUR LADY OF

A small — less than two feet tall — Enthroned Madonna, holding an apple in her right hand and the blessing Christ Child on her left knee and arm. The image's face is of dark complexion. The wooden sculpture has artistic characteristics indicating it was made in the twelfth or thirteenth century, but the image of Our Lady of Atocha is much older. Ildephonsus of Toledo mentioned its existence in the seventh century and included a reference to the apple in Mary's hand. Because its history is obscure, some devotees have attributed its origin to St. Luke.

By 1162, devotion to Our Lady of Atocha had spread through Spain, and the statue was kept in the Church of St. Leocadio in Toledo. The image of the Child — *Niño de Atocha* — is detachable; devout families would borrow it when a woman was about to give birth. Pious legend says *el Nino* escaped from his mother, and, according to other sources, brought food and drink to Christians incarcerated by the Moors at a place called Atocha.

In 1523, King Charles V paid for a huge church and placed the statue of Our Lady of Atocha under the care of the Dominicans. This Madrid parish is still in existence. Originally a hermitage, it became a simple sanctuary, intentionally kept small by the then-Moorish government. In 1863 Pope Pius IX elevated it to the rank of basilica.

In past centuries, the statue has been clothed in precious robes and jewels, as was the custom especially since Reformation times. Queens and future queens would frequently donate their wedding garments to Our Lady. Among the treasures of Our Lady of Atocha is the *terciopelo* (velour cape) of Isabel II.

Our Lady of Atocha is the secondary patroness of Madrid, together with the *Virgin de la Paloma*. The principal patroness is Our Lady of Almudena.

See also Almudena, Our Lady of.

ATONEMENT, OUR LADY OF

The Rosary League of Our Lady of the Atonement was formed in 1901 "to pray and work for the restoration of Mary's Dowry, England, to our Virgin Queen, the Holy Mother of God." Later, its purpose became more extensive, including not only the conversion of England but the entire world.

Our Lady of Atonement

The league was started by Fr. Paul Wattson and Mother Lurana Mary Francis White, members of the Anglican Communion until they, with fifteen others, were received into the Catholic Church in 1909. The community grew and is now known as the Franciscan friars and sisters of Graymoor. In 1919, Pope

Benedict XV gave his approval and apostolic recognition to the title of Our Lady of Atonement.

The image *Our Lady of Atonement* shows Mary with a red mantle, symbolizing the Precious Blood of which she was the immaculate source, and by which she was made immaculate. She wears a blue inner tunic and holds the infant Jesus in her arms.

AVE MARIA

Latin for "Hail, Mary," the Archangel Gabriel's greeting to Mary at the Annunciation; Latin name for the most popular and universally recited Marian prayer, the Hail Mary.

The opening line ("Hail Mary, full of grace. The Lord is with you") comes from Lk. 1:28. Its second line ("Blessed are you among women, and blessed is the fruit of your womb") is Elizabeth's greeting to Mary, Lk. 1:42.

The two salutations were joined in Eastern Rite formulas by the sixth century and were used in a similar way in the West in the seventh. The insertion of Jesus' name at the closing of the second line was probably made by Pope Urban IV around 1262.

The prayer concludes with a petition based on the Council of Ephesus. The present form was incorporated into the breviary in 1514 and codified by the Council of Trent.

In English, the prayer reads:

Hail Mary, full of grace, the Lord is with you. Blessed are you among women and blessed is the fruit of your womb, Jesus. Holy Mary,

Mother of God, pray for us sinners, now and at the hour of our death. Amen.

And in Latin, it is:

Ave Maria, gratia plena. Dominus tecum, benedicta tu in mulieribus, et benedictus fructus ventris tui, Jesus. Sancta Maria, Mater Dei, ora pro nobis peccatoribus, nunc et in hora mortis nostrae. Amen.

See also Annunciation; Ephesus, Council of; Hymns, Marian; Rosary; Scripture, Mary in.

AVE MARIA SALUTATION

A Marian prayer written by St. John Eudes in the seventeenth century. A copy of the prayer was found in a book belonging to St. Margaret Mary Alacoque after her death. The prayer was strongly promoted by Father Paul of Moll, O.S.B. (1824–1896), of Belgium.

The prayer reads:

Hail Mary! Daughter of God the Father.
Hail Mary! Mother of God the Son.
Hail Mary! Spouse of God the Holy Spirit.
Hail Mary! Temple of the Most Blessed Trinity.
Hail Mary! Pure Lily of the Effulgent Trinity, God.
Hail Mary! Celestial Rose of the ineffable Love of God.
Hail Mary! Virgin pure and humble, of whom the King of Heaven willed to be born and with your milk to be nourished.
Hail Mary! Virgin of Virgins.
Hail Mary! Queen of Martyrs, whose soul a sword transfixed.

Hail Mary! Lady most blessed! Unto whom all power in Heaven and earth is given.

Hail Mary! My Queen and my Mother. My life, my sweetness and my hope.

Hail Mary! Mother most amiable.

Hail Mary! Mother most admirable.

Hail Mary! Mother of Divine Love.

Hail Mary! Immaculate! Conceived without sin.

Hail Mary Full of Grace. The Lord is with you. Blessed are you among women and blessed the fruit of your womb, Jesus.

Blessed by your spouse, St. Joseph.

Blessed by your father, St. Joachim.

Blessed by your mother, St. Anne.

Blessed by your guardian, St. John.

Blessed by your holy angel, St. Gabriel.

Glory be to God the Father, who chose you.

Glory be to God the Son, who loved you.

Glory be to God the Holy Ghost, who espoused you.

O glorious Virgin Mary, may all men love and praise you.

Holy Mary, Mother of God, pray for us and bless us, now, and at death in the name of Jesus, your Divine Son.

AVE MARIS STELLA

Latin for "Hail, Star of the Sea"; title of hymn used at Vespers on Marian feasts. Probably initially intended for use on the feast of the Annunciation, this song is considered one of the greatest of the Marian hymns. It is unique from most of early hymns of the breviary in that it has remained in its original form. Its author is unknown. It has been incorrectly attributed to St. Bernard (1090–1153) but

predates him. It was found in a manuscript from the ninth century.

One translation reads:

Hail thou star of ocean, portal of the sky,

Ever virgin Mother, of the Lord Most High.

Oh, by Gabriel's Ave, uttered long ago

Eva's name reversing, established peace below.

Break the captive's fetters, light on blindness pour,

All our ills expelling, every bliss implore.

Show thyself a Mother, offer Him our sighs,

Who for us incarnate did not thee despise.

Virgin of all virgins, to thy shelter take us,

Gentlest of the gentle, chaste and gentle make us.

Still as on we journey, help our weak endeavor

Till with thee and Jesus, we rejoice forever.

Through the highest heaven, to the almighty three,

Father, Son, and Spirit, One same glory be.

AVE REGINA CAELORUM

Hymn based on scriptural texts that traditionally was sung at the conclusion of Evening Prayer, in the Liturgy of the Hours, from the feast of the Purification until Holy Thursday. It was originally sung for None on the Feast of the Assumption. The author is unknown, but the earliest plainchant manuscript dates back to the twelfth century. There are slightly different versions.

Most authorities break the antiphon into two rhymed stanzas. It was a processional antiphon, and — even though it was used during Lent — it repeatedly greets Mary in words that echo happiness and sureness in her intercession, similar to biblical allusions used in the ancient Eastern hymn, the *Akathistos.*

The title comes from the opening line of the hymn in Latin.

One translation reads:

Welcome, O Queen of Heaven.

Welcome, O Lady of Angels.

Hail! thou root,

Hail! thou gate from whom unto the world,
a light has arisen.

Rejoice, O glorious Virgin,

Lovely beyond all others,

Farewell, most beautiful maiden,

And pray for us to Christ.

V. Allow me to praise you, O sacred Virgin.

R. Against your enemies give me strength.

Grant unto us, O merciful God, a defense
against our weakness, that we who
remember the holy Mother of God, by
the help of her intercession, may rise
from our iniquities, through the same
Christ our Lord. Amen.

See also Akathistos; *Antiphons of Our Lady.*

AVIOTH, OUR LADY OF

Statue of seated Mary dating back to medieval times that, according to pious legend, traveled to Avioth, Verdun, France, from the nearby St. Brice. A Gothic church built on that spot — Notre Dame de Avioth — remains a place of pilgrimage. Now a basilica, it is also known as The Cathedral of the Fields.

BAI DAU, OUR LADY OF

Image and devotion.

A shrine to her in the coastal city of Vung Tau, Vietnam, features a sixty-five-foot-tall statue of Mary holding up the infant Jesus as if presenting him to the world. After the fall of Saigon to the communists in 1975, as tens of thousands of Vietnamese fled their homeland by boat from Vung Tau, the statue *Our Lady of Bai Dau* was the last image many of them had of their homeland. She is honored as the "mother of refugees."

In 2005–2006 the Knights of Columbus sponsored a program for a two-foot-tall traveling pilgrim statue of Our Lady of Bai Dau to be hosted in Vietnamese parishes throughout the United States and Canada.

BANNEUX, OUR LADY OF

Marian title based on apparitions in Banneux, Belgium, seen by eleven-year-old Mariette Beco on eight occasions between January 15 and March 2, 1933.

Mariette reported seeing a young lady in the garden by her house. The smiling woman, surrounded by an oval light, stood bent slightly forward and to the left, and was "more beautiful than any statue." She wore a long white gown with blue sash and a transparent white veil. There was a golden rose on her right foot.

She held a rosary with gold cross and chain on her right arm. Her hands were joined, and her lips moved as she prayed.

Over the course of the sightings, Our Lady beckoned to Mariette and led her to a spring of water, telling her the water was "reserved for all nations, to relieve the sick." Mary referred to herself as the "Virgin of the Poor," said she had come to relieve suffering, and urged Mariette to pray frequently.

As at Lourdes, there have been reports of miraculous healings at this site. In May 1942, the bishop of Liège approved the evidence of a miracle. The apparitions received preliminary Vatican approval in 1947, and final Church approval was granted in 1949.

Today several million people honor Our Lady of Banneux by belonging to the International Union of Prayer, by visiting the shrine near Liège, and by attending prayers at any of the more than one hundred shrines worldwide dedicated to Mary under this title.

See also Apparitions of Mary.

BEADS

Small, ball-shaped pieces of glass, metal, wood or other material pierced for stringing. A rosary or chaplet is a string of beads of a certain number based on the number of prayers being recited. The word "bead" comes from the Middle English *bede*, meaning a prayer or prayer bead. The Middle English is derived from the Old English, *gebed* meaning prayer. To "count (or say or tell) one's beads" is a colloquialism meaning to pray the Rosary. The sacramental itself is sometimes referred to as one's "beads."

See also Chaplet; Rosary; Sacramentals, Marian.

BEAURAING, OUR LADY OF

Title of Mary following an apparition in Beauraing, Belgium, in 1932 and 1933. Five children — Andree and Gilbert Degeimbre, and Albert, Fernande, and Gilberte Voisin — reported seeing a lady dressed in white, walking above the neighborhood bridge. They described her as a young woman, suspended a little above the ground, her feet hidden by a cloud. She was dressed in a glowing white gown, her hands in prayer, with blue eyes that were raised to heaven. When questioned by their families, they explained they knew they were not seeing a statue because her knees moved when she walked, and she smiled at them. Over two months, the children reported thirty-three visits, and Our Lady often appeared while the children prayed the Rosary. She was silent during the first visits but later spoke to the children, referring to herself as "Immaculate Virgin" and "Mother of God, Queen of Heaven." She also used the title "Virgin with a Golden Heart," and during the last several visits, the children saw Our Lady with a gold heart surrounded by rays of glowing light.

This apparition was acknowledged by the bishop of Namur, Belgium, on February 19, 1943. The feast of the Virgin with a Golden Heart is August 21.

In 1949, the Pro Maria Committee was founded to make better known the story of Our Lady's appearances and promote an Association of Prayers called the Marian Union of Beauraing. It also distributes pamphlets, leaflets, a book, and medals.

See also Apparitions of Mary.

BENEDICT XV, POPE

Pontiff (1914–1922) whose statements on Mary's co-redemptive role were later referred to by popes when teaching about Mary's unique role in salvation history.

Speaking of Mary on March 22, 1918, Pope Benedict said: "She suffered so much for us, almost to the point of dying with her suffering and dying Son. Therefore we may rightfully say that she has, with Christ, redeemed the human race."

And in his homily on May 13, 1920, for the canonization of St. Gabriel of the Sorrowful Virgin and St. Margaret Mary Alacoque, he declared:

But the sufferings of Jesus cannot be separated from the sorrows of Mary. Just as the first Adam had a woman for an accomplice in his rebellion against God, so the new Adam wished to have a woman share in his work of re-opening the gates of heaven for men. From the cross, he addressed his own Sorrowful Mother as the "woman," and proclaimed her the new Eve, the Mother of all men, for whom he was dying that they might live.

See also Co-Redemptrix, Co-Redemptorist.

BENEDICT XVI, POPE

Pontiff elected in 2005. He concluded his first encyclical, *Deus Caritas Est* (*God is Love,* 2005), with a section on Mary:

> 41. Outstanding among the saints is Mary, Mother of the Lord and mirror of all holiness. In the *Gospel of Luke* we find her engaged in a service of charity to her cousin Elizabeth, with whom she remained for "about three months" (1:56) so as to assist her in the final phase of her pregnancy. "*Magnificat anima mea Dominum*", she says on the occasion of that visit, "My soul magnifies the Lord" (*Lk* 1:46). In these words she expresses her whole programme of life: not setting herself at the centre, but leaving space for God, who is encountered both in prayer and in service of neighbour — only then does goodness enter the world. Mary's greatness consists in the fact that she wants to magnify God, not herself. She is lowly: her only desire is to be the handmaid of the Lord (cf. *Lk* 1:38, 48). She knows that she will only contribute to the salvation of the world if, rather than carrying out her own projects, she places herself completely at the disposal of God's initiatives. Mary is a woman of hope: only because she believes in God's promises and awaits the salvation of Israel, can the angel visit her and call her to the decisive service of these promises. Mary is a woman of faith: "Blessed are you who believed", Elizabeth says to her (cf. *Lk* 1:45). The *Magnificat* — a portrait, so to speak, of her soul — is entirely woven from

Pope Benedict XVI

threads of Holy Scripture, threads drawn from the Word of God. Here we see how completely at home Mary is with the Word of God, with ease she moves in and out of it. She speaks and thinks with the Word of God; the Word of God becomes her word, and her word issues from the Word of God. Here we see how her thoughts are attuned to the thoughts of God, how her will is one with the will of God. Since Mary is completely imbued with the Word of God, she is able to become the Mother of the Word Incarnate. Finally, Mary is a woman who loves. How could it be otherwise? As a believer who in faith thinks with God's thoughts and wills with God's will, she cannot fail to be a woman who loves. We sense this in her quiet gestures, as recounted by the infancy narratives in the Gospel. We see it in the delicacy with which she recognizes the need of the spouses at Cana and makes it known to Jesus. We see it in the humility with which she recedes into the background during Jesus' public life, knowing that the Son must establish a new family and that the Mother's hour will come only with the Cross, which will be Jesus' true hour (cf. *Jn* 2:4; 13:1). When the disciples flee, Mary will remain beneath the Cross (cf. *Jn* 19:25-27); later, at the hour of Pentecost, it will be they who gather around her as they wait for the Holy Spirit (cf. *Acts* 1:14).

42. The lives of the saints are not limited to their earthly biographies but also include their being and working in God after death. In the saints one thing becomes clear: those who draw near to God do not withdraw from men, but rather become truly close to them. In no one do we see this more clearly than in Mary. The words addressed by the crucified Lord to his disciple — to John and through him to all disciples of Jesus: "Behold, your mother!" (*Jn* 19:27) — are fulfilled anew in every generation. Mary has truly become the Mother of all believers. Men and women of every time and place have recourse to her motherly kindness and her virginal purity and grace, in all their needs and aspirations, their joys and sorrows, their moments of loneliness and their common endeavours. They constantly experience the gift of her goodness and the unfailing love which she pours out from the depths of her heart. The testimonials of gratitude, offered to her from every continent and culture, are a recognition of that pure love which is not self-seeking but simply benevolent. At the same time, the devotion of the faithful shows an infallible intuition of how such love is possible: it becomes so as a result of the most intimate union with God, through which the soul is totally pervaded by him — a condition which enables those who have drunk from the fountain of God's love to become in their turn a fountain from which "flow rivers of living water" (*Jn* 7:38). Mary, Virgin and Mother, shows us what love is and whence it draws its origin and its constantly renewed power. To her we entrust the Church and her mission in the service of love:

Holy Mary, Mother of God, you have given the world its true light, Jesus, your Son — the Son of God. You abandoned yourself completely to God's call and thus became a wellspring of the goodness which flows forth from him. Show us Jesus. Lead us to him. Teach us to know and love him, so that we too can become capable of true love and be fountains of living water in the midst of a thirsting world.

BETHLEHEM — *See Scripture, Mary in.*

BETROTHAL TO JOSEPH — *See Scripture, Mary in.*

BIRTH OF MARY

Feast celebrated in both the East and the West, dating back to the sixth or seventh century, to mark the nativity of Mary. There are no scriptural references to Mary's birth, but it was written about in several apocryphal books, most notably the *Protoevangelium of James* (first titled *The Nativity of Mary*).

Historians trace the origin of the liturgical feast to the consecration of a church in Jerusalem in the sixth century traditionally known as St. Anne's Basilica. The original church was constructed in the fifth century on the spot known as the shepherd's field and thought to have been the home of Mary's parents, Sts. Joachim and Anne. After it was destroyed and rebuilt, the new basilica was named in honor of Mary's mother.

By the seventh century the liturgy was also celebrated in Rome where it had been introduced by monks from the East. From there, it spread throughout the West, and by the thirteenth it had developed to a solemnity with a major octave (eight days of commemoration prior to the liturgy) and a solemn vigil which prescribed a fast day. Pope Sergius I (687–701) established a procession (a *litania*) from the Roman Forum to St. Mary Major for the feast.

September 8 was chosen because it was the eighth day (an octave) after the former Byzantine New Year. Throughout the centuries, Mary birth had been celebrated on various dates but September 8 was, by far, the most common. When a liturgy was later instituted to celebrate Mary's Immaculate Conception, December 8 was chosen to correspond to nine months before the feast marking her birth.

In the East, Mary's birthday is celebrated as one of the twelve great liturgies and its title is "The Birth of Our Exalted Queen, the Birthgiver of God and Ever-Virgin Mary." Around 560, Romanos the Melodist wrote a *kontakion* (a poetic form that was significant in early Byzantine liturgical music) for the celebration. The oldest existing sermon for the liturgy was written by St. Andrew of Crete (d. 740).

The Church usually celebrates the death of a person to mark his or her entry into eternal life. Besides the birth of Christ, the Christian liturgy celebrates only two other birthdays: that of St. John the Baptist and of Mary. Both liturgies celebrate their role in salvation history.

See also Apocryphal Writing, Mary in.

BISTRICA, OUR LADY OF

Statue of Mary and the Christ Child dating back to the early fifteenth century, to which miracles have been attributed.

The statue was first venerated in a chapel on a hill called *Vinski vrh,* about two miles from the parish church in the Bistrica region of Croatia. At that time, the Ottoman army was attacking the area and, concerned that the chapel and statue could be desecrated, the

Our Lady of Bistrica

parish priest — without telling anyone — secretly moved the statue to the parish church and sealed it in a wall below the choir loft. It remained there for more than four decades, and its existence was nearly forgotten.

In 1588, that statue was discovered by the priest then serving the parish but, for unknown reasons, it was sealed inside the wall behind the main altar in 1650. Due to the efforts of Bishop Martin Borkovic, the statue was found again on July 16, 1684, and placed on display for veneration. As devotion increased, it was necessary to enlarge the shrine within the church.

In 1710, the Croatian Parliament issued a ruling that a votive altar be built in the church; later, the church was renovated and enlarged. Since its consecration in 1731, the former parish of Sts. Peter and Paul has been known as the Shrine of Our Lady of Bistrica. During the course of again renovating and enlarging the building in 1880, a fire broke out, destroying everything in the structure except the main altar and the statue. On December 4, 1923, Pope Pius XI elevated the church in Bistrica to the rank of minor basilica.

Marija Bistrica is now officially The Croatian National Shrine of Our Lady of Bistrica. Since 1987, the Feast of Our Lady of Bistrica has been celebrated on July 13.

BLACKBIRDS, OUR LADY OF THE

Original name of the Abbey of St. Sulpice at Rennes, France, founded by Blessed Ralph de la Futaye around 1096.

BLACK MADONNA, THE — *See Czestochowa, Our Lady of.*

BLACK MADONNAS

Designation for hundreds of images of Mary that portray her as dark-skinned. Among the better known pilgrimage sites that have Black Madonnas are Altötting, Germany; Czestochowa, Poland; Einsiedeln, Switzerland; Loreto, Italy; and Montserrat, Spain.

In some cases, the pigmentation is unintentional and due to discoloration through age and grime. In others, the dark hue is simply the color of wood from which the statue was made. There are also Madonnas whose facial characteristics and skin color match a particular dark-skinned indigenous population, such

Our Lady of Einsiedeln

Madonna and Child of Soweto

as Our Lady of Guadalupe, and Larry Scully's *Madonna and Child of Soweto*, painted in 1973, which hangs in the Regina Mundi Church in Soweto.

BLACK SCAPULAR — *See Scapular of St. Camillus; Scapular of the Seven Sorrows.*

BLACK VIRGIN — *See Chartres, Our Lady of.*

BLESSED AMONG ALL WOMEN — *See Scripture, Mary in.*

BLESSED FOR HAVING HEARD THE WORD OF GOD AND KEPT IT — *See Scripture, Mary in.*

BLESSED ROSES

A pious custom celebrated on the feast of the Holy Rosary, October 7, in Dominican and other parishes.

Traditionally, the rose has symbolized the Rosary, with the leaves representing the joyful mysteries; the thorns the sorrowful; and the blossoms the glorious.

In the Roman Ritual, the blessing reads:

O God, Creator and Preserver of mankind, deign to pour out Thy heavenly benediction upon these roses, which we offer to Thee through devotion and reverence for Our Lady of the Rosary. Grant that these roses which are made by Thy Providence to yield an agreeable perfume for the use of men and women, may receive such a blessing by the sign of Thy holy cross that all the sick on whom they be laid and all who shall keep them in their houses may be cured of their ills; and that the devils may fly in terror from these dwellings, not daring to disturb Thy servants.

BLESSED (TITLE OF MARY)

In its broadest use, "blessed" refers to any person's being graced by God. Officially within the Catholic Church, it is the title conferred after an individual has been beatified, the final step before canonization.

While Mary is sometimes referred to as "Saint" (as in the case of St. Mary Major Basilica in Rome), generally the title of blessed is used in a unique way when referring to her, as in the "Blessed Virgin Mary" or the "Blessed Mother." That designation was first used at the time of the Visitation, when Mary visited her kinswoman Elizabeth and was greeted with:

"Blessed are you among women and blessed is the fruit of your womb" (Lk. 1:42).

BLUE, COLOR ASSOCIATED WITH MARY — *See Art, Mary in.*

BLUE ARMY

International association dedicated to spreading the message of Our Lady of Fatima. Founded by Msgr. Harold Colgan in October 1947 in Plainsfield, N.J., it is now known as the Blue Army World Apostolate of Fatima and is in more than 40 nations with millions of members. Its headquarters is in Fatima, Portugal.

The apostolate promotes Eucharistic prayer and the Rosary as well as penance, especially the acceptance of the duties of one's state in life. It offers a variety of spiritual programs, including prayer cells (where individuals meet for weekly prayer in the parish or home setting), First Saturday devotions, all-night vigils, a Sacred Heart Home Enthronement Program, and Family Consecrations to the Sacred Heart of Jesus and the Immaculate Heart of Mary. It also sponsors the National Blue Army Pilgrim Virgin Statue, which makes a statue available to dioceses for three-week tours at parishes, hospitals, schools, and nursing homes. The custodian accompanying the statue distributes information about Mary's message of Fatima.

In 2005, the apostolate was approved by the Holy See as a Public Association of the Faithful for the universal Church. As such, it is the only organization approved by the Catholic Church to be responsible for the propagation of the message of Fatima.

BLUE SCAPULAR — *See Scapular of the Immaculate Conception.*

BLUE VIRGIN OF PARAGUAY — *See* Caacupé, Our Lady of the Miracles of.

BOOK OF COMMON PRAYER, MARY IN THE

The official prayer book of the Church of England and of Anglican churches in other countries. The first complete version appeared in 1549 at the time of the Reformation. The book includes references to Mary in the recitation of creeds and the baptismal ceremony, and in the saying of the Magnificat during evening prayer.

See Anglican Church, Mary in the.

BOULOGNE, OUR LADY OF

Statue that, according to pious legend, was washed up on the French coast around 633 in a boat without oars, sails, or sailors. Sculpted of wood, the statue was about three-and-a-half

Blue Army logo

feet high and depicted Mary holding the Christ Child in her left arm.

A shrine was built to "the Virgin of the Sea" (*Nôtre Dame-de-Boulogne-sur-mer*), which was visited by sailors on both sides of the English Channel and by English and French royalty. Chaucer mentions Boulogne as a pilgrimage site in the prologue to his *Canterbury Tales*.

Nearly a millennium after the statue was found, Henry VIII had it stolen and taken to England, but after extended negotiations between the two countries, it was finally returned to France.

Though the original image — stolen, hidden, and returned many times — was eventually destroyed during the French Revolution, it has been replaced by two others. One, made of marble, is a skiff with the seated Madonna holding the Christ Child. It is known as *Our Lady of the Great Return*. The second is made of wood and depicts Mary standing and holding the Christ Child on her left arm. In her right is a golden scepter. Both Mary and Jesus wear jeweled crowns. The solemn crowning took place in 1885.

BOWED HEAD, OUR LADY OF THE
— *See* **Grace, Our Lady of.**

BRIGETTINE OFFICE

Office modeled on the Divine Office of the Roman Rite of the Middle Ages and used by members of the religious order founded by St. Bridget of Sweden (1303–1373). The Brigettine Office features a series of twenty-one readings covering the life of Mary and Marian doctrine.

While commonly mistaken to be a variant of one of the several versions of the Little Office of the Blessed Virgin, it is not.

In the very late middle ages, a brother of Syon Abbey composed the famous *Mirror of Our Lady*, printed in 1530. Offering a detailed commentary on the Brigettine Office, it became popular among clergy and laity. There is no direct evidence as to authorship, but research suggests it was Thomas Fishbourne (d. 1428), one of Syon Abbey's Brigettine monks and its first confessor-general.

BRIGETTINE ROSARY

Chaplet instituted and promoted by St. Bridget of Sweden (1303–1373). The devotion features six decades of Hail Marys. Each begins with an Our Father and ends with the Apostles' Creed. After the six decades, there is an Our Father and three Hail Marys.

The sixty-three Hail Marys are in remembrance of the sixty-three years of Mary's earthly life according to one traditional account. The seven Our Fathers, said on the large beads between each decade, are in remembrance of Mary's Seven Sorrows and Seven Joys.

Fifteen of the mysteries of this chaplet are the same as the traditional fifteen-decade Rosary. In each of the three five-decade divisions, there is a sixth mystery. The first of the joyful is the Immaculate Conception. The sixth of the sorrowful is the dead Christ in the arms of his mother. And the sixth glorious is the patronage of Mary.

See also Chaplet; Rosary; Seven Joys of Mary; Seven Sorrows of Mary.

BROWN SCAPULAR — *See Scapular of Our Lady of Mount Carmel.*

BROWN VIRGIN

Thirteenth-century icon of Mary, believed to have been brought to Naples before 1268. In 1500, Neapolitans took the image to Rome on a pilgrimage. As Pope John Paul II noted in a letter marking the 500th anniversary of the visit, "This event led to the widespread practice of the 'Wednesdays of Mount Carmel,' an expression of Marian devotion in which, as in other similar displays of popular faith, one can see a reflection of the motherly kindness of Mary Most Holy."

In 1990 in Naples, the pope visited the icon and prayed: "O Mother, protect the city of Naples! Guide her sons and daughters along the path of justice and brotherhood! Strengthen their faith, make them courageous witnesses of the Gospel and ardent builders of peace."

The term "Brown Virgin" is also used for *Our Lady of Antipolo*, because of the dark wood from which the statue is made, and *Our Lady of Guadalupe*, because of Mary's skin color.

See also **Antipolo, Our Lady of; Guadalupe, Our Lady of.**

BYZANTINE CHURCH, MARY IN THE
— *See Eastern Rites, Mary in the.*

C

CAACUPÉ, OUR LADY OF THE MIRACLES OF

Image and devotion dating back to early sixteenth-century Paraguay.

According to pious tradition, a native who had converted to Catholicism was in danger of being killed by members of another tribe opposed to Christianity. The man hid in the forest in a large tree trunk and promised Mary that if his life was spared, he would use the wood to carve an image of her. He kept his vow and made two statues, giving the larger one to the church in Tobati and keeping the smaller one for himself.

Tradition also says, years later, it was the second image that a local priest, Father Luis de Bolaños, used to bless the water when the area was threatened by a potentially devastating flood. The region was spared, and from then on, the statue was called *La Virgen de los Milagros* (*The Virgin of Miracles*).

The twenty-inch image depicts Our Lady with blues eyes and blond hair, standing on a sphere resting on a large half-moon. Her hands are folded in prayer. Mary wears a white tunic and a sky-blue cloak, both embroidered with gold thread. The statue is kept in the National Marian Shrine of Our Lady of Caacupé.

The city of Caacupé remains the religious center of Paraguay, the meeting place of Church and state. Every December 8, the worldwide feast of the Immaculate Conception, the local feast of *Maria de Caacupé* is celebrated. On this national holiday, thousands of pilgrims visit the shrine to show their love and gratitude to the *Virgen Azul de Paraguay* (*The Blue Virgin of Paraguay*).

CALVARY— *See Scripture, Mary in.*

CANA — *See Scripture, Mary in.*

CANDELARIA

An image of Mary in which she holds a candle as a sign of purity. Devotion to the *Candelaria,*

Candelaria

also known as the *Purísima* (the Most Pure), is very popular in many Hispanic countries and regions where the festival of the *Virgen de la Candelaria* is celebrated on February 2, the feast of the Presentation.

Examples of *Candelaria* include *Our Lady of Chapi, Our Lady of Cocharcas,* and *Our Lady of Copacabana.*

See also Candlemas; **Chapi, Our Lady of; Cocharcas, Our Lady of; Copacabana, Our Lady of.**

CANDLEMAS

Former name for the feast of the Purification of the Blessed Virgin Mary celebrated on February 2 and now called the Presentation of the Lord. The term Candlemas was used because candles are blessed on this day. That custom, probably in commemoration of Christ who was the Light to enlighten the Gentiles, became common about the eleventh century.

See also Presentation of Jesus in the Temple, Feast of the.

CANTICLE

A scriptural chant or prayer differing from the psalms. Three canticles prescribed for use in the Liturgy of the Hours are: the *Magnificat,* the Canticle of Mary (Lk. 1:46–55); the *Benedictus,* the Canticle of Zechariah (Lk. 1:68–79); and the *Nunc Dimittis,* the Canticle of Simeon (Lk. 2:29–32).

See also **Magnificat.**

CANTICLE OF MARY — *See* **Magnificat.**

CAP-DE-LA-MADELEINE, SHRINE OF
— *See* **Cape, Our Lady of the.**

CAPE, OUR LADY OF THE

Marian title associated with national Canadian shrine dating back to the mid-seventeenth century; also known as Our Lady of the Holy Rosary and the Shrine of Cap-de-la-Madeleine.

In 1659, Jesuit missionaries built a chapel on a piece of land named "Blessed Mary's field," and in 1694, the Confraternity of the Holy Rosary was established there. Almost three decades later, in 1720, the first stone church was constructed. It later became known as the "Old Shrine" and is the oldest church in Canada.

In 1854, during the year of the proclamation of the dogma of the Immaculate Conception, a parishioner donated a statue of Mary that is still venerated in the shrine.

In March 1879, construction was to begin on a new church, but because of a mild winter, the St. Lawrence River was not frozen solidly enough to allow teams of horses to transport building stones across the ice to the construction site. Parishioners prayed the Rosary, asking for Mary's help, while the pastor vowed not to tear down the small church already there and to dedicate it to Our Lady. The river froze, and for one week, the stones were brought to the site. This became known as the Rosary Bridge.

Nine years later, in 1888, the small church was dedicated to Mary and became the shrine. Fr. Frederic Janssoone, O.F.M., who gave the homily that day, served as pilgrimage director until 1902. On the evening of the dedication, three witnesses reported seeing the statue of Mary with the eyes wide open. In 1904, the statue — now known as Our Lady of the Cape — was crowned by a delegate of Pope Pius X.

From 1947 to 1954, the image became a pilgrim statue and was taken throughout Canada before being crowned once again, this time by a delegate of Pope Pius XII at a National Marian Congress.

From 1955 to 1964, a basilica was constructed, and in 1973, an annex to the small shrine was built with stones which had been transported over the Rosary Bridge. Pope John Paul II visited Notre-Dame-du-Cap Shrine in 1984; during the shrine's centennial year of 1988, he beatified Fr. Janssoone in Rome. For more than a century, the shrine has been staffed by members of the Missionary Oblates of Mary Immaculate and now receives more than 600,000 visitors annually.

CARAVAGGIO, OUR LADY OF

Marian shrine, also know as Our Lady of the Fountain, located in Caravaggio, Italy. Devotion dates back to a vision of Mary seen by Giovanna Vacchi in 1432 and at which time it was reported a blind man was cured by water from a font that had sprung up during the apparition. A church stood on the spot from the sixteenth to eighteenth century, and more recently, the location has been called "the Lourdes of Italy."

During a gathering there with young people from three local dioceses in 1992, Pope John Paul II noted, "It is truly a gift from God to be able to meet you this evening in the shadow of the beautiful shrine of Caravaggio, a place of prayer and meditation, a temple of living faith and Marian devotion."

Other Marian sites and titles in the Lombard regions associated with water and miracles include:

- Camairago: "Shrine of the Virgin of the Fountain." In 1682, a small boy unable to speak from birth was cured after drinking water from the fountain.
- Cerlongo: "Church of the Virgin of Pozzenta." The water from this well is considered a blessing for new mothers.
- Trezzo sull'Adda: "Shrine of the Madonna of Milk." Contains a spring said to have been the source of many miracles.

See also Apparitions of Mary; Miracle.

CAREGIVER, OUR LADY'S

A reference to St. John the Evangelist, to whom Jesus entrusted his mother as He died on the cross (Jn. 19:26–27).

Our Lady's Caregiver

CARMEL OF THE MAIPÙ, OUR LADY OF

Devotion dating back to 1785, when Don Martin de Lecuna ordered a sculptor in Quito, Chile, to carve a statue of Our Lady of Mount Carmel.

Since then, Our Lady of Carmel of the Maipú has been associated with the struggles for Chile's independence. In 1817, General José de San Martin placed his baton in the right hand of the image and named her Patroness of the Army of the Andes. Later, she was named patroness and general of the Chilean armed forces. Fulfilling a vow after asking for Our Lady's protection against Spanish armed forces, Chileans built a shrine to her. The present church housing the image was finished in 1974.

In 1923, at the request of the Chilean bishops, the Vatican proclaimed the Virgin of Carmel principal patroness of all Chileans — not just of the army and navy, as she had been until then.

There is a second Carmel image that Chileans especially venerate. Now located in the Basilica of the Savior in Santiago, it was made in France and solemnly crowned in 1926.

The feast of Our Lady of Carmel of the Maipú is the last Sunday in September.

CARMEL, MOUNT

Promontory just above the port city of Haifa which is associated with early Christians' devotion to Mary.

Mount Carmel divides the central plain of Israel into the Plan of Acco to the north and the Plain of Sharon to the south. Since ancient times, it has played a role in the religious life of the people in the area. During the Old Testament era, it was associated with the activities of Elijah and Elisha (1 Kings 18:19–46; 2 Kings 2:25; 4:25). The Carmelite Order venerates the spot as the site of its foundation.

See also **Carmel, Our Lady of Mount.**

CARMEL, OUR LADY OF MOUNT

Marian image and early devotion associated with the Carmelites, an order that began in the late twelfth century in Carmel.

At that time, pilgrims on their way to Jerusalem reported the presence of the Carmelites at the Fountain of Elijah and said the oratory was dedicated to the Virgin Mary. That devotion has remained a focal point of the order.

As the political and religious situation worsened in the Holy Land, order members started to move from Mount Carmel in 1238 to such places as Cyprus, Sicily, France, and England. By 1291, after a century's existence there, all the Carmelites had left the Fountain of Elijah.

The Marian tradition of the Carmelites is united with the Elijah tradition in an ancient book of the order titled *The Institution of the First Monks.* This work dates back at least to the late fourteenth century, when it was first circulated among the Carmelites.

In it, when Elijah sends his servant to look out to sea during a drought in Israel, the servant tells of seeing a small cloud. To Elijah, God revealed four mysteries about the cloud: l) the future birth of a girl born without sin; 2) the time of her birth; 3) that she would be

Our Lady of Mount Carmel

the first woman to take the vow of virginity (after Elijah, who was the first man to do so); and 4) that the Son of God would be born of this virgin.

The Carmelites then understood that these mysteries were fulfilled in Mary and devoted themselves to her, choosing her as their patroness. From that point, they considered Mary their sister and were known as the "Brothers of the Blessed Virgin of Mount Carmel." As early as 1252, papal documents contain that title in reference to the Carmelites.

Other early members, including the Frenchman Jean de Cheminot in 1337 and the Englishman John Baconthorpe (d. 1348), wrote about the relationship of Mary and Elijah in Carmelite tradition.

The Carmelite habit is the theme of the final section of *The Institution of the First Monks*. The habit is understood as a sign of poverty, humility, separation from the world, dedication to God, and a common fraternity.

The scapular itself is viewed as the yoke of obedience.

It is important, too, to understand that for some 150 years, the scapular was identified not with Mary but with the Christological theme of obedience. The first reference to the scapular is found in the Carmelite Constitutions of 1281:

> The Brothers are to sleep in their tunic and scapular under the pain of severe penalty.

No mention is made of the scapular vision of St. Simon Stock in any of the documents of the thirteenth century.

An account written in the late fourteenth century tells of an appearance by Mary to Simon Stock who, perhaps, was elected prior general of the Carmelite Order in 1254 at the general chapter held in London, England. According to this account, Mary held the scapular in her hand and said that the one who died in it would be saved. However, this event is not written about for decades after it is supposed to have happened.

A more contemporary approach to the scapular devotion understands the scapular as an expression of devotion to Mary, a sign of her protection and care, some type of affiliation to the Carmelites, and a willingness to imitate her prayerful submission to God's plan of salvation.

In a recent publication, the North American Carmelite superiors wrote:

> The Brown Scapular of Our Lady of Mount Carmel is best understood in the context of the Catholic Faith. It offers us a rich spiritual tradition that honors Mary as the first and foremost of her Son's disciples. This

scapular is an outward sign of the protection of the Blessed Virgin Mary, our sister, mother, and queen. It offers an effective symbol of Mary's protection to the Order of Carmel — its members, associates, and affiliates — as they strive to fulfill their vocation as defined by the Carmelite Rule of St. Albert "to live in allegiance to Jesus Christ."

While Christ alone has redeemed us, the Blessed Virgin Mary has always been seen by Catholics as a loving mother and protector. The Blessed Virgin has shown her patronage over the Order of Carmel from its earliest days. This patronage and protection came to be symbolized in the scapular, the essential part of the Carmelite habit.

Stories and legends abound in Carmelite tradition about the many ways in which the Mother of God has interceded for the Order, especially in critical moments of its history. Most enduring and popular of these traditions, blessed by the Church, concerns Mary's promise to an early Carmelite, St. Simon Stock, that anyone who remains faithful to the Carmelite vocation until death will be granted the grace of final perseverance. The Carmelite Order has been anxious to share this patronage and protection with those who are devoted to the Mother of God and so has extended both its habit (the scapular) and affiliation to the larger Church.

[Because private revelation can neither add to nor detract from the deposit of faith in the Catholic Church,] therefore, the Brown Scapular of Our Lady of Mount Carmel simply echoes the promise found in Divine Revelation, i.e., "The one who holds out to the end is the one who will see salvation" (Mt. 24:13).

"Remain faithful until death and I will give you the crown of life" (Rev. 2:10). The Brown Scapular of Our Lady of Mount Carmel must be regarded as a reminder to its wearers of the saving grace which Christ gained for all upon the cross for all people, and that there is no salvation for anyone other than that won by Christ himself. It is the Sacraments which mediate this saving grace to all the faithful. The sacramentals however, including the scapular, do not mediate this saving grace but prepare the faithful to receive grace and dispose them to cooperate with it.

The feast of Our Lady of Mount Carmel is July 16.

See also Novena to Our Lady of Mount Carmel; Sabbatine privilege.

CARMELITES — *See* Carmel, Our Lady of Mount.

CARRYING THE VIRGIN

An Alpine Advent custom. On each of the nine nights leading up to Christmas, an image of Mary is taken from house to house while the occupants join in prayer.

CARTAGO, OUR LADY OF — *See Angels, Our Lady of the.*

CASA SANTA MARIA

Motherhouse of the Pontifical North American College in Rome. Located at the bottom of Quirinale Hill, this is where American clergy working toward graduate degrees pray, study, and live during their time in the school. The building was founded as a Dominican monastery for young noble women in 1601, and in 1616, the cloister was dedicated and blessed under the patronage of Mary. The official title for the church and monastery is *La Chiesa della Santa Maria Asunta al monastero dell'Umiltà*. The monastery continued for some two centuries until it was suppressed under Napoleon. After his defeat, the Church regained control of the property, which was administered by the Congregation for the Propagation of the Faith.

In 1859, Pope Pius IX gave the property to the American bishops, who established the North American College on December 7, 1859, for the purpose of training priests for the growing United States.

Seminarians lived and studied in the house and attended classes at two Roman universities: the Gregorian and the Urbaniana. Residence continued until World War II when the students and faculty were sent home for their own safety. In 1947, the seminary was reestablished under the administration of Bishop Martin J. O'Connor.

Due to an increase in the number of students, the American bishops used property they had purchased in 1926 (near the Vatican on the Gianicolo Hill), and built the new Seminary of the North American College. It was inaugurated on October 14, 1953, by Pope Pius XII. The former seminary became the residence for American clergy studying in Rome.

Throughout the Casa Santa Maria chapel are numerous depictions of Our Lady and other female saints both in fresco and marble. Above the tabernacle is a nineteenth century copy of the famous image known as the *Madonna of Mercy*.

CASIMIR'S HYMN, ST. — *See* Daily, Daily, Sing to Mary.

CATACOMBS, OUR LADY OF THE

Image discovered in the Roman catacomb known as the cemetery of St. Priscilla, beneath the Basilica of St. Sylvester. The picture, which dates from the second half of the second century, shows Mary seated with the Christ Child on her lap.

To her left, according to historians and theologians, is the prophet Isaiah, who wrote: "Therefore, the Lord himself will give you a sign. Behold, a young woman shall conceive and bear a son, and shall call his name Emmanuel" (7:14).

There is a star between Isaiah and Mary, representing the Star of Bethlehem, and to the left of the prophet are branches of a blossoming tree extending over the group. The tree represents another prophecy: "Therefore, shall come forth a shoot from the stump of Jesse, and a branch shall grow out of his roots" (Is. 11:1).

The crypt church in the Basilica of the National Shrine of the Immaculate Conception in Washington, D.C., is dedicated to Our Lady of the Catacombs.

See also Art, Mary in.

CATECHISM OF THE CATHOLIC CHURCH, MARY IN THE

First published in 1992, the *Catechism of the Catholic Church* includes basic teaching on Mary's role in salvation history, in the Church, and in individuals' lives.

At the end of his 1992 apostolic letter, *Fidei Depositum*, (on the publication of the *Catechism of the Catholic Church*), Pope John Paul II included a prayer to Mary:

> At the conclusion of this document presenting the *Catechism of the Catholic Church*, I beseech the Blessed Virgin Mary, Mother of the Incarnate Word and Mother of the Church, to support with her powerful intercession the catechetical work of the entire Church on every level, at this time when she is called to a new effort of evangelization. May the light of the true faith free humanity from the ignorance and slavery of sin in order to lead it to the only freedom worthy of the name (cf. Jn 8:32): that of life in Jesus Christ under the guidance of the Holy Spirit, here below and in the Kingdom of heaven, in the fullness of the blessed vision of God face to face (cf. 1 Cor 13:12; 2 Cor 5:6-8)!"

The English translation of the *Catechism's* Latin text's *Index Analyticus* lists the following under "Mary" (numbers refer to numbered paragraphs in the *Catechism*):

Christ's Mother by the power of the Holy
  Spirit, 437, 456, 484–86, 723–26
    the Church and active example and
    type of the Church, 967
    Church reaches towards perfection in,
    829

place in the mystery of the Church,
    773, 963–72
spiritual motherhood, 501

Mary in the economy of salvation
    Annunciation, 484, 490
    assent, 148, 490, 494
    Assumption, 966
    conception by the Holy Spirit, 437,
    456, 484–86, 495, 723
    the Immaculate Conception,
    490–493
    mediatrix of grace, 969
    predestination of, 488–89, 508
    preserved from sin, 411
    virginity, 496–98, 502–07
    visitation to Elizabeth as God's visitation to his people, 717
    works of the Holy Spirit, 721–26

Mary as exemplar
    of holiness, 2030
    of hope, 64
    of obedience of faith, 144, 148–49,
    494
    of prayer in the "Fiat" and "Magnificat," 2617, 2619
    of union with the Son, 964
    and witness of faith, 165, 273

titles of Mary
    Advocate, Help, Benefactress, Mediatrix, 969
    Assumed into heaven, 966
    Eschatological icon of the Church,
    967, 972
    Ever Virgin, 499–501
    Full of grace, 722, 2676
    Handmaid of the Lord, 510

"Hodigitria" or "She shows the way,"
2674
Immaculate, 491–92
Mother of Christ, 411
Mother of the Church, 963–70
Mother of God, 466, 495, 509
Mother of the living, 494, 511
The New Eve, 411
"Panagia" or All Holy, 493
Seat of Wisdom, 721

veneration of Mary
faith concerning the veneration of
Mary based on faith concerning
Christ, 487
liturgical feasts of, 2043, 2177
in the liturgical year, 1172, 1370
not adoration, 971
prayer to, 2675–79
respect for the name of, 2146

CAUSE OF OUR JOY

Marian title used in the Litany of the Blessed Virgin Mary (also known as the Litany of Loreto) which was originally approved in 1587 by Pope Sixtus V.

Mary is referred to as "the cause of our joy" because she gave birth to the Redeemer and, in so doing, shared in the work of redemption.

See also Liesse, Our Lady of; Litany of the Blessed Virgin Mary.

CENACLE, OUR LADY OF THE

Image and devotion.

The Cenacle — a term from the Latin *cenaculum*, meaning a dining room which was usually on an upper floor — was the room chosen by Jesus for the Last Supper (Lk. 22:7–13). It was also where Mary and the apostles waited for the coming of the Holy Spirit on Pentecost, a period which can be considered the first Christian "retreat" or "novena" (Acts 1:13–14).

Tradition places the Cenacle in the southwest quarter of Jerusalem. Early Christian reverence for the spot prompted the Emperor Hadrian to destroy it and replace it with a pagan temple. Crusaders later used stones from that era to build a chapel there. Today it is a mosque. Islamic authorities allow the Patriarch of Jerusalem to celebrate Mass there once a year, on Holy Thursday. The original Cenacle, the Upper Room, has been called the first Christian church.

Images of Our Lady in the Cenacle typically show Mary with upraised hands, praying for the coming of the Holy Spirit. Devotion to her under this title is promoted by the Religious of the Cenacle, an international congregation founded in 1826 in La Loubesc, France, by St. Thérèse Couderc and Fr. Etienne Terme.

The Marian Movement of Priests promotes devotion to Mary with its Cenacle Prayer Groups. Meetings include the recitation of Rosary, prayers for the pope, and the Act of Consecration to the Immaculate Heart of Mary.

See also Immaculate Heart of Mary, Consecration to the; Marian Movement of Priests.

La Virgen Del Cerro San Cristobal

CERRO SAN CRISTÓBAL, LA VIRGEN DEL

Large statue of Mary, the Immaculate Conception, in Santiago, Chile.

Located in a municipal park at the top of Cerro San Cristóbal (St. Christopher's Hill), *La Virgen del Cerro San Cristóbal* looks out over the city and is a pilgrimage site on December 8, the feast of the Immaculate Conception.

The statue, made in 1904 to commemorate the fiftieth anniversary of the declaration of the dogma of the Immaculate Conception, is fifty feet tall and stands on a twenty-five-foot base. The extended arms are thirty feet wide.

CHAPI, OUR LADY OF

Image and devotion popular in southern Peru.

The Virgen de Chapi Shrine is in the heart of a very narrow, barren valley in the Andean Peruvian region of Arequipa.

Tradition holds that after the image was found by a group of sixteenth-century pilgrims, a fountain of water appeared miraculously, and there were other clear signs of where Mary wanted a shrine built. The sanctuary is frequently called the "Little Lourdes"

because of the great number of miraculous healings.

This two-foot-tall Spanish image of the Virgin Mary is of a type known as a *Candelaria* because she holds a candle in her right arm, as a symbol of purity.

The feast of Our Lady of Chapi is celebrated on May 1.

See also Candelaria.

CHAPLET

From the French for "rosary" (*chapelet*), a chaplet is a string of beads used to count prayers. A five-decade rosary is the most common chaplet. Others vary in size and may use different assigned prayers for each bead.

Chaplets are intended to honor and ask the help of God, Mary, the angels, or saints. New chaplets are written to also spread devotion to a particular saint or to reinforce devotion to a mystery or aspect of the faith. Some chaplets trace their history to reported private revelations, although the origins of many older chaplets are unknown.

Reciting a chaplet could typically include the repetition of basic prayers (the Our Father, Hail Mary, Glory Be), prayers addressed to a particular divine image (Christ the King, for example), Marian image, angel or saint; and a litany.

See also specific name of particular chaplet; Rosary.

Our Lady of Charity of El Cobre

CHARITY OF EL COBRE, OUR LADY OF

Image and devotion; the patroness of Cuba, affectionately called *Cachita*.

The statue *Our Lady of Charity of El Cobre* is about sixteen inches high. The head is made of baked clay, covered with a polished coat of fine white powder. Mary stands on a moon that has silver clouds at either end of it and three golden-winged cherubs beneath it. She holds the Christ Child in her left arm and a gold crucifix in her right. Jesus raises one hand in blessing; in the other hand, he holds a golden globe. The statue's original robes were white, but most often, Our Lady wears a cloak with gold and silver embroidery, including the national shield of Cuba.

Pious tradition holds that around 1608, two brothers, Rodrigo and Juan de Hoyos, and a ten-year-old slave boy named Juan Moreno, left Santiago del Prado (modern El Cobre) to find salt to preserve meat for local copper miners. Halfway across the Bay of Nipe, they went to shore because of a bad storm; the next morning, a small white bundle floated across the water toward them. It was the statue, completely dry, attached to a board that had the inscription "I am the Virgin of Charity." Not long after that, people in the region built a shrine (and later a church) to house the image, and it soon became a pilgrimage destination.

In 1916, at the request of the veterans of Cuba's War of Independence, Pope Benedict XV declared Our Lady of Charity the patroness of that country. The statue was crowned during a Eucharistic Congress at Santiago de Cuba in 1936. In 1977, Pope Paul VI raised the church to the status of a basilica, and in 1998, Pope John Paul II crowned the statue again.

CHARTRES, OUR LADY OF

There are three famous Marian shrines in Our Lady of Chartres Cathedral in Chartres, France.

The building itself is considered a leading example of High Gothic architecture. It is the first Gothic cathedral originally designed to make use of flying buttresses for structural support. Construction of a Romanesque style building began in 1120 on the site of a previous church, but that cathedral was almost completely destroyed by fire in 1194. Work on the current structure began that year and, for the most part, was completed about a quarter-century later. Work on the interior and additions continued for several centuries.

Out of almost two hundred images of Mary in the cathedral, the three most famous are:

— *Notre Dame de Sous-Terre* (*Our Lady Underground*), which is said to be the oldest shrine of Our Lady in the world, because its origins date back to pre-Christian, Druidic times. Chartres had been the center of Druidic worship in Gaul, and in a grotto on the hill where the cathedral now stands, there was an altar to the *Virgo Paritura*, or "the Virgin who should conceive," to whom the local king and his people had dedicated themselves. When Christian missionaries reached Chartres in the third century, they considered it a shrine already built to the Mother of the God.
— *Vierge Noire de Notre-Dame-du-Pilier* (*The Black Virgin*) in the upper church.
— *Voile de la Vierge* (*Veil of the Blessed Virgin*), where a piece of silk about sixteen feet long is kept. Pious tradition holds this relic is Mary's veil.

See also Relics.

CHILD OF MARY

The expression "A devout child of Mary (or "servant of Mary") will never be lost" was used by many founders of Marian movements and congregations during the nineteenth century and the first half of the twentieth. Scholars maintain that it may be said that the expression was coined by Benedictines for Benedictines and stands for the spiritual result of an intense meditation on the Incarnation and Our Lady's divine motherhood. The classical formulation is most often attributed to St. Anselm of Canterbury (1033–1109), and St. Alphonsus Liguori (1696–1787) is considered the greatest promoter of the teaching.

CHILDREN OF MARY

Members of a specific confraternity of Mary. Blessed Peter de Honestis founded the oldest known Children of Mary sodality in Italy in the thirteenth century. The most famous was begun in 1847 by the Vincentian Fathers and the Daughters of Charity to promote the Miraculous Medal.

See also Confraternity, Archconfraternity; Miraculous Medal; Sodalities of Our Lady. For siblings of Jesus, see Virginity of Mary, Perpetual.

CHINA, OUR LADY OF

Marian images and devotion.

There are a number of popular titles for Mary in China, including Our Mother of Mercy; Holy Mother of Tonglu; Queen of Peace; Help of Christians; and Our Lady of Peking (Beijing), Empress of China.

Our Lady of Peking depicts Mary as an empress of the Qing dynasty, with a long string of pearls around her neck. With her left arm, she supports the Christ Child, dressed in the robe of an imperial prince, who stands on her lap.

The image of *Our Lady of China*, depicted in the Basilica of the National Shrine of the Immaculate Conception, was a gift of the Chinese-American Catholics. The mosaic is based

Our Lady of China

on a painting by John Lu Hung Nien, who was born in Beijing in 1914. Trained there in the Academy of Fine Arts at the Catholic University (run by the Divine Word Missionaries until the communists took over), Lu converted to Catholicism and came to be recognized as a master of religious art, particularly for his Madonna.

Thomas Tien Keng-Hsin, S.V.D., (1890–1967) the first Chinese cardinal, used this image for the prayer card for the persecuted in China and promoted the following prayer in the United States and Canada:

Almighty and eternal God, Comforter of the afflicted, and Strength of the Suffering, grant that our brothers of China who share our faith may obtain, through the intercession of the Blessed Virgin Mary and our Holy Martyrs, peace in Thy service, strength in time of trial, and grace to glorify Thee, through Jesus Christ our Lord. Amen.

CHIQUINQUIRA, OUR LADY OF

Image and devotion dating back to the sixteenth century; patroness of Colombia.

Painted on a native cotton blanket, the piece shows a standing Our Lady of the Rosary holding the Christ Child in her left arm. St. Anthony of Padua stands on her right side and St. Andrew on her left.

The chronicles of New Spain say that in 1563, Don Antonio de Santana, the Spanish chief of Sutamarchan, had a particular devotion to Our Lady of the Rosary and a painting of her in his chapel. It was the work of Alonso de Narvaez, given to him by a Dominican brother. Over time, the cloth developed holes, and dirt and time caused the paint to fade. Finally, in 1578, a priest took it down from the chapel; from there, it ended up at a nearby ranch belonging to Don Santana at Chiquinquira. There, resembling little more than an old rag, the painting was used to carry and sort seed.

In 1585, Maria Ramos, a relative of Don Santana, came to work at the ranch as a maid in the home of his widow. She noticed the painting and, after being told it had once been an image of Our Lady, did her best to clean it. Even so, the images were almost too faded to see. But undeterred, she took over a little hut that had been a shed for the ranch's pigs and dog and made it into a little chapel, placing the picture on the wall. Each day, she prayed in front of the ragged picture, begging Our Lady to console her. Homesick for her native land, she asked Mary to make herself a little more visible so that the woman could pray better.

The chronicles go on to report that on the morning of December 26, 1586, a Christian Indian named Isabel was passing the door of the little hut-chapel, carrying her four-year-old son, Miguel, when the child cried out, "Mama, Mama, look at the Mother of God who is on the floor!" Isabel turned and saw the painting surrounded by a bright light that lit up the entire chapel. She shouted to Maria Ramos, "Look, look, Señora, the Mother of God has come down from where she was, and it seems as if she is burning!" Maria Ramos came and realized that things were as the Indian had described, so she knelt in front of the image and began to pray. Hearing the cries of the two women, others came and saw what was happening: the painting had burst into flames and restored itself with beautiful colors.

When news of the event spread, the priest came from Sutamarchan to see what had happened. A commission was established to study the miracle; on January 10, 1587, the archbishop of Bogota pronounced the restoration as a supernatural occurrence. The fame of the picture spread throughout the country, and people of all walks of life began to beg Our Lady for favors, which she granted. Twice, in times of a virulent epidemic that was killing many of the native Colombians, the picture was carried out in procession and the epidemics ceased. Through the years, there have been many miracles attributed to the intercession of Our Lady of Chiquinquira, but the one favor most granted is that of conversions. To this day, the people ask her for a change of heart for their loved ones who have lost their way, and Our Lady is credited with giving faith to thousands.

Until her death, Maria Ramos was the main guardian of the miraculous picture of *Our Lady of the Rosary of Chiquinquira*. Since 1636, it has been in the custody of the Dominican Fathers. In 1829, Pope Pius VII declared her patroness of Colombia, and she was canonically crowned in 1919. Pope John Paul II paid homage to Our Lady of Chiquinquira when he visited Colombia in 1986.

CHOSEN DAUGHTER OF THE FATHER

Marian title referring to Mary's being selected by God to be the mother of Christ. The phrase "chosen daughter of the Father" is part of the Litany of Mary, Queen.

See also Litany of Mary, Queen; **Theotokos.**

CHRISTI MATRI — *See Paul VI.*

CHRISTIAN LIFE COMMUNITY

Worldwide network of small communities of Catholic lay people committed to a way of life

St. Ignatius Loyola

inspired and sustained by Ignatian spirituality. Prior to 1967, they were called Sodalities of Our Lady.

Christian Life Community traces its roots back to St. Ignatius Loyola and his conversion experience while recovering from battle wounds. The former soldier sought to help others by speaking with them in groups about the work of God in their lives. As he guided many toward God by drawing on his own spiritual experiences, over time he designed his Spiritual Exercises to help future leaders do the same. These Spiritual Exercises played a role in the development of the Society of Jesus (the Jesuits).

In Rome in 1563, John Leunis, a young Jesuit, founded the first CLC by gathering a group of young lay students at the Roman College to help them unite their everyday lives with Christian values. Originally called the Sodality of Our Lady, the movement grew and was confirmed by Pope Gregory XIII in 1584. By 1920, there were 80,000 sodalities worldwide. In the 1950s in the United States, more than two million teenagers were members. Following Vatican II, groups such as the Sodality were encouraged to rediscover their original roots — the link with the Spiritual Exercises, which was rediscovered and renewed at that time.

CIRCUMCISION, FEAST OF — *See Solemnity of Mary, Mother of God.*

CLARETIANS

Religious order, formally known as the Congregation of the Missionary Sons of the Immaculate Heart of Mary, founded in Spain in 1849

St. Anthony Claret

by St. Anthony Mary Claret for preaching and catechizing. At their religious professions, members make a solemn vow to promote devotion to the Immaculate Heart of Mary.

COCHARCAS, OUR LADY OF

Image and devotion.

Our Lady of Cocharcas is a sculpture ordered in 1598 by Sebastián Quiminchi from San Pedro de Cocharacas, Peru, in appreciation for miracles he attributed to the intercession of Our Lady of Copacabana in Bolivia. The statue is located in the Church of Our Lady of Cocharcas, which was dedicated in 1623 and is the oldest church in South America named for Mary. The feast of Our Lady of Cocharchas is September 8.

See also **Candelaria; Copacabana, Our Lady of.**

COINS

As early as Byzantine times, coins have been stamped with images of Mary.

The oldest show her alone; later ones have her holding the Christ Child. She is also depicted blessing the emperor and is described as "blessed" and "glorious."

In the West, "Holy Mary" was mentioned on the coins of Charlemagne, but there was no image. In later centuries, she was depicted standing on the sickle of the moon or as a heavenly queen on the throne. Her head is adorned with a veil and, later, a crown. Some show her surrounded by a halo or stars and holding a scepter.

Among the types of coins on which she can be seen are talers, ducats, grochen, and pfennigs. Some countries depicted her as their patroness and showed her showering blessings on a country or town. Many spiritual and civil leaders — including the pontiff — decorated their coins with an image of Mary, sometimes shown amid saints.

Even following the Reformation, states and towns that followed Luther still did not consistently abolish pictures of Mary on coins, because the motif was too popular and symbolic. On the other hand, in the years of the Counter-Reformation, Mary and the Christ Child were shown with special intensity and variety on the coins of Catholic rulers.

COLLECTION OF MASSES OF THE BLESSED VIRGIN MARY

A compilation of more than forty Mass formularies in honor of Mary.

The collection was promulgated in Latin in 1986. A partial translation in English was published in 1988 and the complete work in English in 1990.

In preparing the *Collection*, the Congregation for Divine Worship used Marian propers (parts of the Mass that are variable according to the day or feast being observed) from dioceses and religious orders, often adapting the texts and adding a proper preface for each formulary. The Introduction to each Mass contains doctrinal, liturgical, and spiritual material.

The Masses are designated by Marian titles or mysteries and ordered for the liturgical year. (For example, formularies for Advent include Masses to Our Lady "of the Annunciation" and "of the Visitation.") For Ordinary Time, numerous titles are taken from the Litany of the Blessed Virgin Mary (also known as the Litany of Loreto) or a popular devotion (e.g., Mother of Divine Providence).

While the Masses are intended to be used primarily at Marian shrines, the General Introduction notes that the collection will be helpful "to those ecclesial communities that wish to celebrate the Saturday memorial in honor of Our Lady according to the rubrics."

See also Litany of the Blessed Virgin Mary.

COLUMN, ST. MARY'S

Column in Munich, Germany, built in 1638 by Maximilian I, Duke of Bavaria, to commemorate the survival of the city during the Thirty Years' War. In recent times, the site has been the weekly meeting place for members of the Legion of Mary to pray the Rosary.

COMFORTER OF THE AFFLICTED — *See Consolation, Our Lady of.*

COMMUNION OF SAINTS

The spiritual union among the saints (all souls) in heaven, the souls in purgatory, and the faithful on earth. Mary is a member of the Communion of Saints.

In the words of the Second Vatican Council's *Dogmatic Constitution on the Church* (*Lumen Gentium*), it is "the living communion which exists between us and our brothers who are in the glory of heaven or who are yet being purified after their death" (n. 51).

The document also declares:

Our community with the saints joins us to Christ, from whom as from its fountain and head issues all grace and the life of the People of God itself. It is most fitting, therefore, that we love those friends and co-heirs of Jesus Christ who are also our brothers and outstanding benefactors, and that we give due thanks to God for them, humbly invoking them, and having recourse to their prayers (50).

COMPANY OF MARY

Also known as the Montfort Missionaries, an international religious congregation dedicated to the establishment of the Kingdom of God under the patronage of Mary.

St. Louis Marie de Montfort founded the order in 1713, and it now has some 1,100 priests and brothers who carry out their mission in thirty different countries. The congregation's constitution notes:

The Marian character of the Company is an essential possession of our Congregation. Mary is not present in the life of the missionaries in some accidental fashion: devotion toward her is an integral part of their spiritual life and apostolate. The "total consecration" to Jesus through Mary is the most outstanding mark of the Marian character of our inspiration.

CONFERENCE, MARIAN — *See Congress, Marian.*

CONFIDENCE, OUR LADY OF

Image and devotion.

Madonna della Fiducia (*Our Lady of Confidence*, also known as *Our Lady of Trust* and *Our Lady of Good Hope*) depicts Mary in the traditional red tunic and blue mantle, holding the Christ Child. It is the work of the Italian painter Carlo Maratta (1625–1713), who was knighted by Pope Clement XI in 1704 and made court painter by Louis XIV that same year.

Tradition says Maratta gave the painting to a young noble woman, Clara Isabel Fornari, who later became the abbess of the Convent of Poor Clares of St. Francis in the city of Todi and has since been declared venerable.

The abbess was known to have lived a life of penance and was said to have been blessed with many mystical experiences, including receiving the stigmata. She also had a deep love for Mary, particularly as *Madonna della Fiducia*. She reported that Mary promised to help her and others who sought the intercession of Our Lady of Confidence.

The original image remains in Todi, but there is also a famous duplicate. After a priest who was the abbess' confessor (and a confessor at the Roman Seminary) was healed through the intercession of *Madonna della Fiducia*, he had a copy painted for the school. Only the first of many duplicates, today it can be found in the small chapel of St. Mary's Seminary at the Lateran Basilica in Rome. Our Lady of Confidence is the school's patroness, and in thanksgiving for her protection over centuries, the seminarians have crowned the images of Mary and Jesus.

The feast of Our Lady of Confidence is celebrated on the Sunday before Ash Wednesday. There is also a novena to her as well as the simple prayer, "My Mother, my confidence."

See also Kevelaer, Our Lady of.

CONFRATERNITY, ARCHCONFRATERNITY

Voluntary association of clergy or laity established under Church authority. Though the Code of Canon Law uses the term "associations of the faithful," "confraternity" is still preferred by many groups.

In the early centuries of the Church, Christians established groups to promote devotion, care for the sick, and give Christian burial. During the Middle Ages, both societies and guilds were dedicated to works of charity and to the construction and embellishment of churches, bridges, and other public buildings. In the fifteenth and sixteenth centuries, numerous sodalities and pious associations began in Rome to assist pilgrims from other countries.

Present-day confraternities focusing on a particular Marian image, devotion, or spirituality include:

- Brown Scapular Confraternity of Carmel, tracing its history back to 1251 and Mary's appearing to St. Simon Stock, a Carmelite.

- Confraternity of the Immaculate Conception of the Most Blessed Virgin Mary, dating back to the late seventeenth century, and under the guidance of the Marian Order, to promote the Blue Scapular.

- Confraternity of the Immaculate Conception of Our Lady of Lourdes, formed in 1874 to distribute Lourdes water.

- Confraternity of Mary, Help of Christians, founded by Capuchin Friars in Munich, Germany, in 1627.

- Confraternity of Mary, Queen of All Hearts, established in 1899 and based on the works of St. Louis Marie de Montfort.

- Confraternity of the Most Holy Rosary, an international association established in the fifteenth century under the spiritual guidance of the Dominican Order.

- Confraternity of Our Mother of Perpetual Help, dating back to the Redemptorist church of San Alfonso in Rome in 1871.

- Confraternity of Our Lady of Sorrows, established in 1645, and under the auspices of the Servite Order.

- Confraternity of the Lady of All Nations, begun in 1998 in Cebu, the Philippines.

CONGRESS, MARIAN

A worldwide, national, or local gathering to deepen devotion to, and understanding of, Mary.

The first International Marian Congress was held in Lyon, France, in 1900, and continued biannually through 1912. The meetings were discontinued from the start of World War I to the conclusion of World War II, then resumed in 1950.

At the closing Mass of the twentieth gathering in 2000 — marking both the International Mariological-Marian Congress and the World Jubilee of Marian Shrines — Pope John Paul II noted:

Dear brothers and sisters! Before this mystery of grace one clearly sees how appropriate for the Jubilee Year are the two events which this Eucharistic celebration brings to a close: the International Mariological-Marian Congress and the World Jubilee of Marian Shrines. Are we not celebrating the 2,000th anniversary of Christ's birth? It is therefore natural that the Jubilee of the Son should also be the Jubilee of the Mother!

It is therefore to be hoped that among the fruits of this year of grace, as well as that of a stronger love for Christ, there should also be that of a renewed Marian devotion. Yes, Mary must be deeply loved and honored, but with a devotion which, to be authentic:

— must be firmly grounded in Scripture and Tradition, making the most of the liturgy first of all and drawing from it a sound orientation for the most spontaneous demonstrations of popular piety;

— must be expressed in an effort to imitate the All Holy in a way of personal perfection;

— must be far from every form of superstition and vain credulousness, accepting in the right way, in accordance with ecclesial discernment, the extraordinary manifestations in which the Blessed Virgin often likes to grant herself for the good of the People of God;

— must always be able to go back to the source of Mary's greatness, becoming a ceaseless Magnificat of praise to the Father, to the Son and to the Holy Spirit.

Dear Brothers and Sisters! "Whoever receives one such child in my name receives me," Jesus said to us in the Gospel. He could say to us even more aptly: "whoever receives my Mother, receives me." And Mary, on her part, received with filial love, once again points out the Son to us as she did at the wedding of Cana: "Do whatever he tells you" (Jn 2:5).

Dear friends, may this be the consignment of today's Jubilee celebration, which combines Christ and his most holy Mother in one praise. I hope that each of you will receive abundant spiritual fruits from it, and be encouraged to authentic renewal of life. *Ad Iesum per Mariam!* [To Jesus through Mary.] Amen.

See also Pontifical International Marian Academy.

CONSECRATION TO JESUS THROUGH MARY

Pledge promoted by St Louis Marie de Montfort (1673–1716) who was noted for fostering devotion to Mary and the Rosary.

One form reads:

I, a faithless sinner, renew and ratify today into your hands, O Immaculate Mary, the vows of my baptism. I renounce forever Satan, his pomps and works, and I give myself entirely to Jesus Christ, the Incarnate Wisdom, to carry my cross after him all the days of my life and to be more faithful to him than I have ever been before. In the presence of all the heavenly court, I choose you today for my

Mother and Mistress. I deliver and consecrate to you, as your loving slave, my body and soul, my good, both interior and exterior and even the value of all my good actions, past, present and future, leaving to you the entire and full right of disposing of me and of all that belongs to me, without exception, according to your good pleasure, for the greater glory of God, in time and in eternity. Amen.

In his prayers of consecration of the world to Mary, Pope John Paul II used the word "entrustment" rather than "slavery."

CONSOLATION, CHAPLET OF OUR LADY OF

Also known as the Corona of Our Lady of Consolation and the Augustinian Rosary, this prayer is associated with the Archconfraternity of Sts. Augustine and Monica and composed of thirteen couplets — one Our Father and one Hail Mary — and concludes with the Hail, Holy Queen.

When prayed in a group, the devotion begins by calling to mind the scene in the Cenacle when the Apostles, along with Mary and other women, devoted themselves to constant prayer. Each pair of beads begins with the announcement of each of the twelve articles of the Apostles' Creed, followed by a brief reading from the writings of St. Augustine or other writings of the Augustinian tradition, and then the recitation of the Hail Mary and Our Father.

See also Cenacle; Chaplet; Consolation, Our Lady of.

CONSOLATION, OUR LADY OF

Ancient title and devotion.

In the second century, St. Ignatius of Antioch wrote, "Mary, knowing what it is to suffer, is ever ready to administer consolation." An icon of Mary and the Christ Child is titled "Mother of Consolation." Mary and the Christ Child are shown in royal vestments. Mary's mantle features a large star and her halo has twelve small ones. Her tunic is fastened with a black cincture, typical of the one worn by Augustinian monks. This memorial is celebrated on September 4.

Our Lady of Consolation is the patroness of Luxembourg, and the title "Comforter of the afflicted" is used in the Litany of the Blessed Virgin Mary.

Pious tradition holds that in the fourth century, sick with grief and anxiety for her then-wayward son, St. Augustine, St. Monica confided her troubles to Mary, who appeared to St. Monica in mourning clothes and wearing a shining cincture. Our Lady gave the belt St. Monica as a sign of her support and compassion, directing St. Monica to encourage others to wear it. St. Monica gave it to her son, who later handed it on to his community — which is why, as a token of fidelity to Our Lady of Consolation, members of the Order of St. Augustine wore a cincture.

The Augustinian monks promoted this devotion to Mary beginning in 1436, with the foundation of the confraternity of the Holy Cincture of Our Lady of Consolation in Bologna, Italy.

A second tradition, seemingly separate, dates from the fourteenth century and tells of a Roman nobleman awaiting death in the

Capitoline prison. Reflecting on execution, he dictated in his will that his son was to have a Madonna and Child painted and placed near the gallows for the consolation of all who would die in that place in the future. The son followed his father's wishes; when, in 1470, a youth who had been unjustly convicted was miraculously saved from the hangman's noose as his mother prayed before the picture, the place became a popular shrine. More miracles followed, and a church was built. The painting was given the title Mother of Consolation. Visiting pilgrims returned home and spread the devotion throughout Europe.

In the seventeenth century, when plague ravaged the city of Luxembourg, the people began a special devotion to Mary, Consoler of the Afflicted. A statue of her with the Christ Child was enshrined in a small chapel built on the outskirts of town and many favors were authenticated among visiting pilgrims.

A small portrait of the Luxembourg image was used when a shrine in her honor was established in Kevelaer, Germany, in 1642. In 1652, the pope fostered devotion to Mary under this title by establishing a confraternity.

The devotion eventually spread to the United States, where the first shrine to Our Lady of Consolation was built in Carey, OH. A replica statue was commissioned and arrived from Luxembourg in 1875. Today, the Basilica and National Shrine of Our Lady of Consolation, which features relics from the original image, is administered by the Conventual Franciscan Friars.

A shrine in Turin, Italy, is also associated with Our Lady of Consolation, known there as Our Lady of Consolata. It houses a fifth-century icon of Our Lady of Consolation; a religious order placed under her protection, the Consolata Missionaries, was founded there in 1901.

See also Kevelaer, Our Lady of.

COPACABANA, OUR LADY OF

Image and devotion that originated on Copacabana, a peninsula in Lake Titicaca, Bolivia, near the islands of the Sun and Moon, which were sacred sites of the Incas. Also known as the *Most Blessed Virgin de la Candelaria, Our Lady of Copacabana,* the *Dark Virgin of the Lake,* and *La Coyeta.*

The four-foot statue is made of plaster and fiber from the maguey plant and is completely covered with gold leaf, except for the face and hands. Our Lady holds the Christ Child as if he were about to fall and both faces have features similar to inhabitants of the region. The colors and style of Mary's clothes are those of an Inca princess, although the statue's original shape is hidden by robes and cloaks, and its carved hair has been covered by a wig.

The statue is the work of Francisco Tito Yupanqui, a descendant of the Inca Huayna Capac. It was placed in a simple adobe church on February 21, 1583, making it one of the oldest Marian shrines in the Americas.

The present church dates from 1805, and the image was crowned during Pius XI's pontificate. Over the centuries rich donors were generous with their gifts, but later, the shrine was looted by presidents, dictators, and generals. Today, the Marian image has precious stones around her neck, and on her hands and ears. Her right hand holds a straw basket and a baton, the gift and souvenir of the visit of the viceroy of Peru in 1669.

The original image never leaves the sanctuary, which became a basilica in 1949; a copy is used for processions. A replica was taken to Brazil in the nineteenth century and enshrined in an area near a Brazilian beach which came to be called Copacabana.

Originally, the feast of Our Lady of Copacabana was celebrated on February 2, which was the Purification of Mary. Later it was transferred to August 5, with its own liturgy and large local celebration.

See also **Candelaria.**

CORD

A long rope of linen or hemp, tasseled at the ends, used to confine the alb at the waist. Also known as a cincture or girdle, it is a symbol of purity.

Wearing a cord or cincture in honor of a saint is of ancient origin, and an early mention of this practice is found in the life of St. Monica. During the Middle Ages, cinctures were often worn by the faithful in honor of saints and, later, ecclesiastical authority established special blessings for cinctures in honor of Our Lady, the Most Precious Blood, St. Francis of Paula, St. Francis of Assisi, St. Thomas Aquinas, St. Joseph, and others.

In the East, August 31 — the last day of their liturgical year — was the feast of the Cincture (or Girdle) of Our Lady, commemorating the enshrinement of Mary's cincture in the church of Khalkoprateia, Turkey, in 940. Pious tradition said this relic was brought from Jerusalem in ancient times, as one of the rare remains of Mary's garments.

See also Consolation, Our Lady of; Relics.

CO-REDEMPTRIX, CO-REDEMPTORIST

Title used to describe Mary's relation to Jesus and her unique role in salvation history.

Scholars say the term entered theology in the fourteenth century. Although popes as recent as Benedict XV and Pius XI have used it, Popes Pius XII and Paul VI did not. Pope John Paul II used the title but — despite advocates promoting the move — did not solemnly proclaim Mary "co-redemptrix."

Marian theologians say the bishops at Vatican II did not include the title in those documents because they did not want to encourage invoking her by that name; it is too easily misinterpreted as making her a fellow redeemer with Christ.

While the title can be explained in such a way as to avoid that basic misconception, the prefix "co-" ordinarily means a mutually cooperative effort between or among equals. The theologians continued that using the prefix "con-" — denoting "with" — does not have the same ambiguity; it applies to one who both cooperates with, and is completely dependent on and subordinate to, another or others. It is in this sense in which Mary may be said to cooperate with her Son, the sole redeemer of humanity.

See also Mediatrix.

COROMOTO, OUR LADY OF

Title and image.

According to tradition, Our Lady appeared several times to the leader of the Coromoto tribe in Venezuela in 1652. During the last apparition, concerned that Mary was going to scold him for continuing his sinful ways, the leader jumped up to grab her but instead found himself holding an image of her instead.

The tiny artwork, made of parchment or tissue paper, measures about one inch by three-quarters on an inch. It appears to have been drawn with a fine pen in India ink with dots and dashes. Mary is painted seated with the Christ Child on her lap. Both are crowned. The back of the throne supporting them has two columns joined together by an arch. Mary wears a red cloak, white veil, and light yellow tunic. Jesus wears a white tunic.

The image is kept inside an ornate monstrance in the National Sanctuary of the Virgin of Coromoto, a meeting place of great pilgrimages, which was declared a basilica by Pope Pius XII on May 24, 1949.

At the request of the nation's bishops, on October 7, 1944, Pius XII declared her Patroness of the Republic of Venezuela, and her canonical coronation was celebrated on the third centenary of her apparition, on September 11, 1952. Cardinal Manuel Arteaga Betancourt, Archbishop of Havana, representing Pope Pius XII, crowned the sacred image.

The Venezuelans celebrate their patroness each year on different occasions: February 2 and September 8 and 11.

CORONA OF OUR MOTHER OF CONSOLATION — *See Consolation, Chaplet of Our Lady of.*

CORONATION OF THE BLESSED VIRGIN MARY

The fifth glorious mystery of the Rosary; any of a number of images or paintings of Mary surrounded by saints and angels as she is crowned Queen of Heaven and Earth; the act (practiced in both the East and the West) of crowning a statue or other image of Mary.

In his 1954 encyclical *Ad Caeli Reginam*, Pope Pius XII wrote that a coronation "is one form of reverence frequently shown to images of the Blessed Virgin Mary. . . ."

From the end of the sixteenth century the practice became widespread in the West for the faithful — both religious and laity — to crown images of the Blessed Virgin. The popes not only endorsed this devout custom but "on many occasions, either personally or through bishop-delegates, carried out the coronation of Marian images."

A special rite was written in the seventeenth century for the coronation of religious images of Jesus, Mary, and the saints. In the nineteenth, a rite was written for crowning images of Mary. New rites were approved by the Congregation for the Sacraments and Divine Worship in Rome on March 25, 1981, and the English translation was approved by the Administrative Committee of the United States Conference of Catholic Bishops five years later.

The new *Order of Crowning* includes three types of coronation: within Mass, within evening prayer, and within a celebration of the Word of God.

The *Order* points out that Mary is shown this particular honor because:

> She is the Mother of the Son of God, who is the messianic King. Mary is the Mother of Christ, the Word incarnate. . . . "He will be great and will be called the Son of the Most High; and the Lord God will give him the throne of his father David; and he will reign over the house of Jacob for ever; and of his kingdom there will be no end" (Luke 1:32-33). . . . Elizabeth greeted the Blessed Virgin, pregnant with Jesus, as "the Mother of my Lord" (Luke 1:41-43).

> She is the perfect follower of Christ. The maid of Nazareth consented to God's plan; she journeyed on the pilgrimage of faith; she listened to God's word and kept it in her heart; she remained steadfastly in close union with her Son, all the way to the foot of the cross; she persevered in prayer with the Church. Thus in an eminent way she won the "crown of righteousness," (See 2 Timothy 4:8) the "crown of life," (See James 1:12; Revelation 2:10) the "crown of glory" (See 1 Peter 5:4) that is promised to those who follow Christ.

The *Order of Crowning* is an official, liturgical act carried out by the diocesan bishop or his delegate. It may take place at any time of the year, most appropriately on solemnities and feasts of Mary.

The *Order* adds:

> It should be noted that it is proper to crown only those images to which the faithful come with a confidence in the Mother of the Lord so strong that the images are of great renown and their sites centers of genuine liturgical cultus and of religious vitality. For a sufficient period before the celebration of the rite, the faithful should be instructed on its meaning and purely religious nature. . . . The crown . . . should be fashioned out of material of a kind that will symbolize the singular dignity of the Blessed Virgin.

Even so, the instructions say the crown should be simple and avoid "opulence."

A similar custom — although not an official liturgical act — is a coronation popularly known as a "May crowning" because often it takes place during that month. In parishes and schools, and at Marian shrines and grottos, an individual is chosen to place a wreath of flowers on Mary's image. It often takes place during Benediction, the recitation of the Rosary, or at the end of Mass.

See also May; Queenship of Mary; Rosary.

CROSIER ROSARY

Rosary beads or chaplets blessed by the Crosier Fathers, the Canons Regular of the Order of Holy Cross.

In the sixteenth century, Pope Leo X granted an indulgence of 500 days for each time an Our Father or Hail Mary is said on the blessed beads.

The order was founded in the year 1210 by Blessed Theodore de Celles and his companions. The name Crosier — meaning crossbearer — comes from the French *croisés;* that is, those signed with the cross. In medieval England, Crosiers were known as the

Crutched (crossed) Friars. The primary feast of the Crosiers, the Triumph of the Cross, reflects a spirituality focused on the triumphal cross of Christ and the glorified Lord. One of the distinctive marks of the Crosiers is the red and white crusaders' cross worn on the scapular of their religious habit.

CROWNING OF MARY — *See Coronation of the Blessed Virgin Mary.*

CROWN OF SEVEN DECADES — *See Rosary of the Seven Joys of Our Lady.*

CROWN OF THE BLESSED VIRGIN MARY, LITTLE

Chaplet based on Rev. 12:1: "I saw a woman clothed with the sun, with the moon beneath her feet, and a crown of twelve stars on her head." This was a favorite prayer of Sts. John Berchmans (1599–1621) and Louis Marie de Montfort (1673–1716).

This devotion consists of praying three Our Fathers and twelve Hail Marys in honor of her twelve privileges, from her Immaculate Conception to her power of intercession. St. Louis Marie de Montfort recommended it in his *True Devotion to Our Blessed Virgin.*

One version of the prayer reads:

I. Crown of Excellence

(To honor the divine maternity of the Blessed Virgin, her ineffable virginity, her purity without stain, and her innumerable virtues.)

Our Father, Hail Mary...

Blessed art thou, O Virgin Mary, who didst bear the Lord, the Creator of the world; thou didst give birth to Him Who made thee, and remainest a virgin forever.

Rejoice, O Virgin Mary; rejoice a thousand times!

Hail Mary...

O holy and immaculate Virgin, I know not with what praise to extol thee, since thou didst bear in thy womb the very One Whom the heavens cannot contain.

Rejoice, O Virgin Mary; rejoice a thousand times!

Hail Mary...

Thou art all fair, O Virgin Mary, and there is no stain in thee.

Rejoice, O Virgin Mary; rejoice a thousand times!

Hail Mary...

Thy virtues, O Virgin, surpass the stars in number.

Rejoice, O Virgin Mary; rejoice a thousand times!

Glory be to the Father...

II. Crown of Power

(To honor the royalty of the Blessed Virgin, her magnificence, her universal mediation and the strength of her rule.)

Our Father, Hail Mary...

Glory be to thee, O Empress of the world! Bring us with thee to the joys of Heaven.

Rejoice, O Virgin Mary; rejoice a thousand times!

Hail Mary...

Glory be to thee, O treasure house of the Lord's graces! Grant us a share in thy riches.
Rejoice, O Virgin Mary; rejoice a thousand times!

Hail Mary . . .

Glory be to thee, O Mediatrix between God and man! Through thee may the Almighty be favorable to us.
Rejoice, O Virgin Mary; rejoice a thousand times!

Hail Mary . . .

Glory be to thee who destroyest heresies and crushest demons! Be thou our loving guide.
Rejoice, O Virgin Mary; rejoice a thousand times!

Glory be to the Father . . .

III. Crown of Goodness

(To honor the mercy of the Blessed Virgin toward sinners, the poor, the just and the dying.)

Our Father, Hail Mary . . .

Glory be to thee, O refuge of sinners! Intercede for us with God.
Rejoice, O Virgin Mary; rejoice a thousand times!

Hail Mary . . .

Glory be to thee, O Mother of orphans! Render the Almighty favorable to us.
Rejoice, O Virgin Mary; rejoice a thousand times!

Hail Mary . . .

Glory be to thee, O joy of the just! Lead us with thee to the joys of Heaven.

Rejoice, O Virgin Mary; rejoice a thousand times!

Hail Mary . . .

Glory be to thee who art ever ready to assist us in life and death! Lead us with thee to the kingdom of Heaven!
Rejoice, O Virgin Mary; rejoice a thousand times!

Glory be to the Father . . .

Let us pray.

Hail, Mary, Daughter of God the Father; Hail, Mary, Mother of God the Son; Hail, Mary, Spouse of the Holy Ghost; Hail, Mary, Temple of the most Holy Trinity; Hail, Mary, my Mistress, my treasure, my joy, Queen of my heart; my Mother, my life, my sweetness, my dearest hope — yea, my heart and my soul! I am all thine and all that I have is Thine, O Virgin blessed above all things! Let thy soul be in me to magnify the Lord; let thy spirit be in me to rejoice in God. Set thyself, O faithful Virgin, as a seal upon my heart, that in thee and through thee I may be found faithful to God. Receive me, O gracious Virgin, among those whom thou lovest and teachest, whom thou leadest, nourishest and protectest as thy children. Grant that for love of thee I may despise all earthly consolations and ever cling to those of Heaven until, through thee, His faithful spouse, Jesus Christ thy Son, be formed in me for the glory of the Father. Amen.

See also Privileges of Mary.

CROWN OF TWELVE STARS

Chaplet that dates back to an ancient devotion of the Order of Our Lady of Mercy, based on Rev. 12:1: "And a great sign appeared in heaven; a woman clothed with the sun, and the moon under her feet, and on her head a crown of twelve stars."

The final section of the prayer is said for the Catholic Church, for the propagation of the Faith, for peace among Christian peoples, and the extermination of heresy

The congregation referred to in this prayer is the Order of Our Lady of Ransom — the Mercedarians, now called the Order of Our Lady of Mercy. It was founded by St. Peter Nolasco (c. 1189–1256) and St. Raymond of Peñafort (1185–1275) to ransom Christian slaves from the Moors. In addition to the usual three vows, the Mercedarians took a fourth vow: to give themselves up, if necessary, in exchange for a slave.

The prayer reads:

Let us offer praise and thanksgiving to the Most Holy Trinity, who has shown us the Virgin Mary, clothed with the sun, the moon under her feet, and on her head a mystic crown of twelve stars. Forever and ever. Amen.

Let us give praise and thanks to the Eternal Father, who chose her for his daughter. Amen.

Our Father . . .

Praised be the Eternal Father, who predestined her to be the Mother of his Divine Son. Amen.

Hail Mary . . .

Praised be the Eternal Father, who preserved her from all stain of sin in her conception. Amen.

Hail Mary . . .

Praised be the Eternal Father, who adorned her at her birth with his most excellent gifts. Amen.

Hail Mary . . .

Praised be the Eternal Father, who gave her Saint Joseph to be her companion and most pure spouse. Amen.

Hail Mary . . .

Glory be . . .

Let us give praise and thanks to the Divine Son, who chose her for his Mother. Amen.

Our Father . . .

Praised be the Divine Son, who became incarnate in her womb and there abode for nine months. Amen.

Hail Mary . . .

Praised be the Divine Son, who was born of her and was nourished at her breast. Amen.

Hail Mary . . .

Praised be the Divine Son, who in his childhood willed to be taught by her. Amen.

Hail Mary . . .

Praised be the Divine Son, Who revealed to her the mystery of the redemption of the world. Amen.

Glory be . . .

Let us give praise and thanks to the Holy Spirit, who took her for his spouse. Amen.

Our Father...

Praised be the Holy Spirit, who revealed first to her his name of Holy Spirit. Amen.

Hail Mary...

Praised be the Holy Spirit, by whose operation she was at once Virgin and Mother. Amen.

Hail Mary...

Praised be the Holy Spirit, by whose power she was the living temple of the ever-blessed Trinity. Amen.

Hail Mary...

Praised be the Holy Spirit, by whom she was exalted in heaven above every living creature. Amen.

Let us praise Mary, who has done so much for our good, and let us say to her: God hail thee, Mary, Mother of Clemency, Comfortress of the Afflicted, Redemptress of Captives. Thou art the glory of Jerusalem, thou art the joy of Israel, thou art the honor of our people.

V. Remember thy congregation, O Mary.
R. Which belongs to thee from the beginning.

Let us pray: O God, who by means of the most glorious Mother of thy Divine Son, didst enrich the Church with a new religious family for the redemption of the faithful of Christ from pagan oppression, grant, we beseech Thee, that we may be freed from our sins and from the bondage of the devil by the merits and intercession of her whom we devoutly venerate as the foundress of so great a work. Amen.

See also Ransom, Our Lady of.

CUAPA, NICARAGUA

Site of a series of Marian apparitions in 1980 and 1981 reported by Edward Bernardo Martinez, a parish sacristan.

Martinez said that several weeks before the first vision, a parish statue of Our Lady seemed bathed in a unusual light, and then on May 15, while out fishing and gathering mangos:

Suddenly I saw a lightning flash. I thought and said to myself: "It is going to rain." But I became filled with wonder because I did not see from where the lightning had come. I stopped but I could see nothing; no signs of rain. Afterwards I went over near a place where there are some rocks. I walked about six or seven steps. That was when I saw another lightning flash, but that was to open my vision and she presented herself. I was then wondering whether this could be something bad, whether it was the same statue as in the chapel... But I saw that she blinked... that she was beautiful.... There was a little norisco tree over the rocks and over that tree was the cloud. That is how high the cloud was . . . the cloud was extremely white . . . it radiated in all directions, rays of light with the sun. On the cloud were the feet of a very beautiful lady. Her feet were bare. The dress was long and white. She had a celestial cord around the waist. Long sleeves. Covering her was a veil of a pale cream color with gold embroidery along the edge. Her hands were held together over her breast. It looked like the statue of the Virgin of Fatima.

Martinez said the woman — who, when asked, identified herself with "I come from heaven. I am the Mother of Jesus" — told him to promote praying the Rosary daily as a family ("with biblical citations"), taking part in the first Saturday devotions of Mass and confession, and putting "into practice the Word of God."

The visions continued through 1981. The following year, they received local approval from Bishop Bosco M. Vivas Robelo, the auxiliary bishop and vicar general of Managua.

See also Apparitions of Mary.

CULT

Ecclesiastically speaking, a term that broadly refers to a devotion or honor afforded to a person or persons. This act itself is divided into various categories, differing both in their degree of intensity and in the level of official approval given the cult by Church authority. There is, for example, "the cult of Mary" and "the cult of the saints."

The word itself is not to be confused with the term generally used to describe an aberrant or bizarre organization or pseudo-religion.

See also **Dulia, Hyperdulia, Latria.**

CZESTOCHOWA, CHAPLET OF OUR LADY OF

Chaplet consisting of a string of nine beads with a crucifix on one end and a medal of Our Lady of Czestochowa on the other.

The devotion includes three Our Fathers, three Hail Marys, and three Glory Bes, and begins or ends with this prayer:

O Almighty and merciful God! You gave the Polish Nation a wondrous help and defense in the most holy Virgin Mary and you hon-

ored her sacred image at Jasna Gora with remarkable veneration of the faithful. Grant in your mercy that, under her protection, we may struggle confidently throughout our lives and at the moment of death be victorious over our enemy. We ask this through Christ our Lord. Amen.

Lady of Jasna Gora, our Mother, Queen of the Polish Nation! Trusting in your maternal goodness and powerful intercession with your Son, we place before You our humble prayers and petitions. To you we commend all our needs, in particular _____, and all children of the Polish Nation whether in their native land or elsewhere in the world.

CZESTOCHOWA, OUR LADY OF

Image also known as *Our Lady of Jasna Gora*, after the name of the Polish monastery in which it has been kept for six centuries.

It is also called the *Black Madonna* because of the dark pigment on Our Lady's face and hands. This coloration is believed to be the result both of age and of being hidden for long periods in places where the only light was from candles, which colored the painting with smoke.

Art historians believe *Our Lady of Czestochowa* was initially a Byzantine icon used from the sixth to ninth centuries. During a fifteenth-century restoration in Krakow, it was painted again, because restorers scraped it clean after being unable to apply their tempera colors over the original wax paint.

According to pious legend, the portrait of Mary and the Christ Child dates back to the time after St. John took Mary under his care following the Crucifixion. When Our Lady moved into his home, among her personal possessions was a table built by Jesus in St. Joseph's workshop. When other women asked St. Luke to paint a portrait of Mary, he used the table's top for his canvas. As he painted, he listened to Mary talk about Jesus and her life with him, facts he later included in the Gospel he wrote.

Legend also says the painting remained in the Holy Land until it was discovered by St. Helena in the fourth century. The painting and other relics were taken to Constantinople, where Helena's son, Constantine the Great, built a church to hold them. The painting remained there for some 500 years, and miracles were attributed to Mary's intercession, until it became part of several dowries and ended up under the protection of the Polish prince, Ladislaus, in a region of Russia that later became part of Poland.

When Ladislaus' castle was besieged, an enemy shot an arrow through a chapel window and hit the painting, leaving a scar on Mary's neck. The tear remains there to this day. Wishing to make sure it was not further damaged or taken by the enemy, Ladislaus decided to move it to his hometown, Opala. To get there, he had to travel through Czestochowa, where he decided to spend the night. While there, the image was taken to Jasna Gora (a name meaning "bright hill") and placed in a small wooden church named for the Assumption.

The following morning, the image was put into a wagon to make the rest of the journey to Opala, but the team of horses refused to budge. Seeing this as a sign from heaven, the prince chose to leave the portrait at the church. This was on August 26, 1382, a date still marked as the feast of Our Lady of Czestochowa. The future St. Ladislaus ordered that

the painting be guarded by holy men; so, a church and monastery were built for the Pauline Fathers. The image has been under their care for the last six centuries.

Our Lady of Czestochowa

In 1430, robbers attacked and plundered the monastery and stole the Marian image. But again, according to legend, after traveling only a short distance, the wagon's team of horse refused to move. Aware of what had happened almost five decades earlier, the men threw the icon on the ground, breaking it into three pieces. One man slashed Mary's face with a sword twice, but died before he could do it a third time.

After the painting was returned to Jasna Gora, Mary was credited with interceding to protect the monastery from an attack in 1655.

The following year, King Casimir declared her *Krolowa Polski*, the Queen of Poland.

Our Lady's intercession has also been credited with stopping the Russian army from invading Warsaw in 1920. During the Nazi occupation of Poland in World War II, Hitler ordered all religious pilgrimages stopped, but a half million Poles went to the sanctuary in defiance of his decree. After Poland was liberated in 1945, a million and a half people expressed their gratitude to Our Lady by praying before the image.

When the Soviets took control of the country in 1948, more than 800,000 Poles made a pilgrimage to the sanctuary at Czestochowa on the Feast of the Assumption. According to Lech Walesa — the first democratically elected president of Poland after the defeat of Communism — Our Lady of Czestochowa played a central role in the Solidarity movement in the 1980s, which led to Poland peacefully regaining its freedom and, later, to the fall of the Soviet Union.

Papal recognition of the image was made by Pope Clement XI in 1717. After the image's first official crown was stolen in 1909, it was replaced by Pope Pius X. Pope John Paul II, a native of Poland, visited Jasna Gora six times during his pontificate and, in gratitude for Mary's protection, gave the shrine the sash he wore the day he was shot in 1981. The sash — with the bullet hole, drops of blood, and the pope's coat of arms visible — is encased on display next to the icon of Our Lady of Czestochowa.

See also Black Madonnas.

DAILY, DAILY SING TO MARY

Medieval hymn attributed to the twelfth-century author Bernard of Cluny and to St. Anselm (1033–1109), but which is most often associated with St. Casimir (1460–1483), the patron saint of Poland and Lithuania.

Casimir was the third of thirteen children of King Casimir IV and Elizabeth of Austria, daughter of Albert II of Habsburg. As a youth and young man, he was known for his holiness, including his devotion to Mary. After he died of consumption, he was buried at Vilnius, Lithuania, and his tomb became famous for miracles.

When his casket was opened more than a century after his death, his body was found to be incorrupt. The coffin also held a copy of the hymn written in his own hand; at the top of the paper was written, "Everyday prayer of the most noble Prince Casimir." He was canonized in 1522.

The opening stanza of the hymn in Latin reads:

Omni die dic Mariae
Mea laudes anima:
Ejus festa, ejus gesta
Cole devotissima.
Contemplare et mirare
Ejus celsitudinem:
Dic felicem genitricem,
Dic beatam Virginem.

In English, the hymn — which now has some five dozen stanzas — begins:

Daily, daily sing to Mary,
Sing, my soul, her praises due:
All her feasts, her actions honor
With the heart's devotion true.
Lost in wond'ring contemplation,
Be her majesty confessed:
Call her Mother, call her Virgin,
Happy Mother, Virgin blest.

DARK VIRGIN OF THE LAKE — *See* Copacabana, Our Lady of.

DAUGHTER OF ZION

Title referring to a biblical designation.

In the Old Testament, it can be seen to represent Jerusalem, the suffering virgin Israel awaiting the coming of the Messiah. The idea that Mary is the Daughter of Zion is based on both the words the angel Gabriel speaks to her and Rev. 12. In Vatican II's *Lumen Gentium*, the bishops call Mary the "exalted Daughter of Zion."

In a general audience of May 1, 1996, Pope John Paul II explained how the Old Testament title applies to Mary:

At the time of the Annunciation, Mary, the "exalted daughter of Zion" (*Lumen Gentium*,

n. 55), is greeted by the angel as the representative of humanity, called to give her own consent to the Incarnation of the Son of God. . . .

Our thoughts turn first of all to the Prophet Zephaniah. The text of the Annunciation shows a significant parallelism with his oracle: "Sing aloud, O daughter of Zion, shout, O Israel! Rejoice and exult with all your heart, O daughter of Jerusalem!" (Zeph. 3:14). There is the invitation to joy: "Rejoice and exult with all your heart" (v. 14). Mention is made of the Lord's presence: 'The King of Israel, the Lord, is in your midst' (v. 15). There is the exhortation not to be afraid: "Do not fear, O Zion let not your hands grow weak" (v. 16). Finally, there is the promise of God's saving intervention: "The Lord your God is in your midst, a warrior who gives victory" (v. 17). The comparisons are so numerous and regular that they lead one to recognize Mary as the new "daughter of Zion," who has full reason to rejoice because God has decided to fulfill his plan of salvation.

[. . .]

Also significant is the oracle of Zechariah, cited in connection with Jesus' entry into Jerusalem (Mt. 21:5, Jn. 12:15). In it the reason for joy is seen in the coming of the Messianic king: "Rejoice greatly, O daughter of Zion! Shout aloud, O daughter of Jerusalem! Lo your king comes to you; triumphant and victorious is he, humble . . . and he shall command peace to the nations" (Zech. 9:9–10) . . .

The three reasons for the invitation to joy: God's saving presence among his people, the coming of the messianic king and gratuitous and superabundant fruitfulness, find their fulfillment in Mary. They justify the pregnant meaning attributed by Tradition to the angel's greeting. By inviting her to give her assent to the fulfillment of the messianic promise and announcing to her the most high dignity of being Mother of the Lord, the angel could not but invite her to rejoice. Indeed, as the Council reminds us: "After a long period of waiting the times are fulfilled in her, the exalted daughter of Zion and the new plan of salvation is established, when the Son of God has taken human nature from her, that he might in the mysteries of his flesh free man from sin" (*Lumen Gentium*, n. 55).

The account of the Annunciation allows us to recognize in Mary the new "daughter of Zion," invited by God to deep joy. It expresses her extraordinary role as mother of the Messiah, indeed as mother of the Son of God. The Virgin accepts the message on behalf of the people of David, but we can say that she accepts it on behalf of all humanity, because the Old Testament extended the role of the Davidic Messiah to all nations (cf. Ps. 2:8; 71 [72]:8). In the divine intention, the announcement addressed to her looks to universal salvation.

To confirm this universal perspective of God's plan, we can recall several Old and New Testament texts which compare salvation to a great feast for all peoples on Mount Zion (cf. Is. 25:6f.) and which announce the final banquet of God's kingdom (cf. Mt. 22:1–10).

As "daughter of Zion," Mary is the Virgin of the Covenant which God establishes with all humanity. Mary's representational role in this event is clear. And it is significant that it is a woman who carries out this function.

As the new "daughter of Zion," Mary in fact is particularly suited to entering into the spousal Covenant with God. More and better than any member of the Chosen People, she can offer the Lord the true heart of a Bride.

With Mary, "daughter of Zion" is not merely a collective subject, but a person who represents humanity and, at the moment of the Annunciation, she responds to the proposal of divine love with her own spousal love. Thus she welcomes in a quite special way the joy foretold by the prophecies, a joy which reaches its peak here in the fulfillment of God's plan.

See also Annunciation.

DAUGHTERS OF MARY, HELP OF CHRISTIANS

Religious order of women, also known as the Salesian Sisters, founded by St. John Bosco (1815–1888) and St. Maria Mazzarello (1837–1881).

As with the members of the Society of St. Francis de Sales (the Salesians), the Daughters of Mary, Help of Christian has focused its apostolic work on needy youth.

The institute began in Mornese, Italy, from an association founded in 1855. John Bosco gave it the definitive form of a society in 1872, with the adoption of the habit and the profession of faith. The Vatican approved the institute in 1922. Today, there are some 16,000 Salesian Sisters in more than 1,500 houses around the world.

St. Maria Mazzarello

DAUGHTERS OF MARY IMMACULATE

Congregation of women religious founded by Blessed William Joseph Chaminade (1761–1850) and Adèle de Batz de Trenquelléon (1789–1828).

Following the French Revolution, the pair formed service-oriented lay communities as a way to re-Christianize France. These "pious societies" grew and eventually some women and men formed the nucleus of two religious congregations. The Marianist Sisters — officially called the Daughters of Mary Immaculate — began in 1816. The Society of Mary (Brothers and Priests) was founded in 1817.

Blessed William Joseph Chaminade

The "Marianist Family" also includes the Alliance Mariale and Marianist Lay Communities.

See also Society of Mary.

DAUGHTERS OF OUR LADY OF COMPASSION

Commonly known as the Sisters of Compassion, a congregation of women religious founded in New Zealand in 1892 by Suzanne Aubert (1835–1926).

The order's ministry focus on the needs of the elderly, the sick, and the disadvantaged, and its headquarters is in Wellington, Island Bay.

DAUGHTERS OF OUR LADY OF MERCY

Congregation of women religious founded by St. Mary Josepha Rossello (1811–1881).

Born in Italy, Mary Joseph was one of nine children, and although pious from her youth, she was not allowed to enter religious life because of her frail health and because her family's sparse income meant it could not afford a dowry.

At age sixteen, she became a Franciscan tertiary. Later, her bishop learned of her skill at teaching religion to girls and gave her a house which she and three other young women made into two classrooms. This became the Institute of the Daughters of Mercy in 1837, which Mary Joseph placed under the protection of Our Lady of Mercy and St. Joseph.

Members devoted themselves to teaching children and caring for the sick, and any deserving girl was accepted by the community, even if her family was unable to provide a dowry. Sr. Mary Joseph served as the congregation's superior for more than forty years. In 1875, it opened its first house in the Americas, in Buenos Aires, Argentina. Pope Pius XII canonized St. Mary Joseph in 1949.

DAUGHTERS OF OUR LADY OF THE HOLY ROSARY

Congregation of women religious founded by Bishop Dominic Mary Hồ Ngọc Cẩn (1876–1948) of the Diocese Bùi Chu, Vietnam, where he served as co-adjutor for one year and ordinary from 1939–1948.

When Bishop Hồ came to the diocese, there were already several groups of women religious who had joined together for apostolic work but he saw a need for a diocesan congregation. In 1940, he sent a letter to Rome asking for permission to establish a religious order, but his application was lost during World War II.

He sent a second request and, on June 10, 1946, received a response from the Holy See allowing him to establish a religious order with simple vows for women. On September 8, 1946, the feast of the Birth of Mary, Bishop Hồ officially announced the Holy See's approval of the establishment of the Congregation of the Daughters of Our Lady of The Holy Rosary, and the convent at Trung Linh was chosen to be the motherhouse of the new religious order.

Bishop Dominic Mary HồNgọc Cẩn

DAUGHTERS OF OUR LADY OF THE SACRED HEART

Congregation of women religious founded in France in 1882 by Fr. Jules Chevalier (1824–1907), who wanted members to be dedicated to a particular participation in the saving mission of Jesus. Earlier (in 1854), he had already founded a congregation of priests and brothers known as the Missionaries of the Sacred Heart.

Sisters' ministries in France, Australia, the United States, Belgium, Spain, Italy, Holland, England, and Ireland, include teaching, nursing, social work, and parish work.

DEATH OF MARY — *See Assumption.*

DECADE

Section of the Rosary made up of one Our Father, ten Hail Marys, and one Glory Be. The prayers are said while meditating on a mystery assigned to the decade.

See Rosary.

DEDICATION OF BASILICA OF ST. MARY MAJOR

An optional memorial, celebrated on August 5, commemorating the rebuilding and dedication by Pope Sixtus III (432–440) of a church in honor of Mary: the Basilica of St. Mary Major on the Esquiline Hill in Rome. An earlier building had been erected during the pontificate of Liberius (352–366).

See St. Mary Major, Basilica of.

DEIPARA

Latin translation of the Greek *Theotokos*, meaning "God-bearer," the title given to Mary at the Council of Ephesus in 431 that says she is the Mother of God.

See also Ephesus, Council of; Mother of God.

DE LA ROCHE (DE RUPE), O.P., BLESSED ALAN

French Dominican priest (1428–1475), theologian, and visionary, known for his holiness and for re-establishing devotion to the Rosary. In the two centuries after the death of St. Dominic (1170–1221), Europe was hit by a number of devastating plagues as well as heresies. After they had subsided, Mary told Blessed Alan to revive the Confraternity of the Most Holy Rosary. Traditions hold that Our Lady chose him because the confraternity had originally been started in the province in which he lived. It was also reported that Christ and St. Dominic spoke to him.

The Dominican began this new work in 1460. He promoted devotion to the Rosary in northern France and in Flanders and organized Rosary Confraternities.

Historians note that in his zeal to propagate the Rosary, it was Blessed Alan who attempted to attribute its invention to St. Dominic; he took this position based on a number of testimonies, including a treatise written by a certain John of Monte (d. 1442), a Dominican bishop and friend of the Carthusians. Blessed Alan wrote of St. Dominic's role in the origin of the Rosary in his book *De Dignitate Psalterii*.

Among the sayings attributed to Blessed Alan is: "The Holy Rosary is the storehouse of countless blessing." And, quoting Our Lady's words to him: "When you say your Rosary, the angels rejoice, the Blessed Trinity delights in it, my Son find joy in it too, and I myself am happier than you can possibly guess. After the Holy Sacrifice of the Mass, there is nothing in the Church that I love as much as the Rosary."

DESCENDIMIENTO — *See* Desolata.

DESOLATA

Good Friday service in honor of Mary as the Sorrowful Mother.

The devotion, whose name comes from the Italian for "desolate," can include prayers, songs, and processions. Also known as *Ora della Desolata* ("Hour of Our Lady of Sorrows"), it is held on Good Friday in some areas, on Holy Saturday in others.

In some parts of Colombia, the service is called the *Descendimiento* and the *Procesion de la Soledad de Maria*. A large image of Christ is taken down from the cross in the presence of Mary, all dressed in black as the Virgin of Soledad (Solitude). A long procession begins through the barrios, finally arriving at the tomb, where in the presence of Mary, Christ is buried. Then, Our Lady is enthroned and accompanied by the people in her mourning for several hours.

In some parishes a *Homenaje a María*, an hour of prayer before the image of Mary, recalls all the mothers who have lost their husbands or sons because of violence.

In Mexico, the service is known as *Peseme* and is celebrated on Good Friday, when the final ceremony of the day is a wake service for the dead Lord. Participants "accompany" Mary in her sorrow as images of Jesus (in a coffin) and Mary (dressed in black) are placed in the sanctuary. The service also includes prayers and singing.

In the province of Teramo, Italy, the tradition dates back to 1260. There, a Good Friday morning procession represents Mary desperately searching for her Son, who has been sentenced to death. A statue of the Sorrowful Mother is carried by veiled, mourning women, through an itinerary known as the "Seven Churches," starting from St. Augustine and ending at the Church of the Annunciation, where Mary finds Christ lying dead in an ornate coffin.

DEVOTIONS, MARIAN

Devotions to Mary center on Christ and present her as the archetype of faithful discipleship in the Church.

As the bishops at the Second Vatican Council wrote in their *Dogmatic Constitution on the Church* (*Lumen Gentium*):

Mary has by grace been exalted above all angels and men to place second only to her Son, as the most holy mother of God who was involved in the mysteries of Christ: she is rightly honored by a special cult in the Church (66).

That devotion "proceeds from true faith, by which we are led to recognize the excellence of the Mother of God, and by which we are moved to filial love toward our mother and to imitation of her virtues" (67).

From the Church's earliest centuries, there was devotion "in veneration and love, in invocation and imitation, according to her own prophetic words: 'all generations shall call me blessed, because he that is mighty has done great things to me' (Lk. 1:48)" (*Lumen Gentium*, 66). Other evidence found in Scripture includes Elizabeth's greeting to Mary as "Mother of my Lord" (Lk. 1:43), meaning the queen-mother of the Messiah king and, in John's Gospel, accounts of Mary at Cana and Calvary show her believing in Jesus, an example for all Christians.

In the second century, Mary was referred to as the "new Eve" associated with Christ, the "new Adam." Both the art in the catacombs and the writing of the time show an increasing veneration of the Mother of Christ. As early as the second century, "born of the Holy Spirit and the Virgin Mary" was used in baptismal creeds.

Historians note that Marian devotion spread throughout Christendom at a time when the truth about Christ — that he was God as well as human from the first instant of his human conception — was seen to depend on the revealed truth about her: that she is the *Theotokos*, the God-Bearer, the Mother of God.

The first evidence of a liturgical cult comes from the East and reflects the Council of Ephesus' teaching on *Theotokos*. This "remembrance of Mary" probably began as early as the fifth century and was part of the Christmas liturgy. From about A.D. 700 to 1400, there was greater concentration on Mary's role as queen of heaven, spiritual mother, and unique and powerful intercessor. During the High Middle Ages (1000–1200), Marian devotion was similar to devotion given to the saints, based on belief in the Communion of Saints, the community made up of the Church on earth and the souls in heaven and purgatory.

During this time, there was also a great deal of Marian literature, including sermons, prayers, liturgical offices, and Masses.

In the twelfth century, devotion was strongly influenced by two doctrinal trends. The first was a focus on Mary's compassion on Calvary and an interpretation of Christ's words "Woman, behold your son" (Jn 19:26), seen as signifying Mary's spiritual motherhood of all Christians. The second was the doctrine of the Assumption, promoting the availability of Mary's assistance to all Christians now.

In the thirteenth century, great cathedrals were dedicated to Our Lady, and prominent saints spoke and wrote of her influence on their lives. (Among these were Sts. Francis of Assisi, Dominic, Bonaventure, Albert the Great, and Thomas Aquinas.) Historians note that during this time, variations of the Hail Mary were in use (although it wasn't until the fifteenth century that this prayer took the form in which it is said today). Also, litanies that included lists of Marian titles were developed, among them the Litany of the Blessed Virgin Mary (the Litany of Loreto).

With advances in the development of the printing press in the fifteenth century, Marian devotion once again spread, with distribution of many editions of sermons on Mary composed by St. Bernardine of Sienna and promotion of confraternities of the Rosary.

Artistically, Mary was shown as the "mantle Virgin," under whose protection all — both nobles and common folk — were cared for. This image was later rejected by the Reformation, although neither Luther nor Calvin was totally opposed to veneration of Mary. Rather, they limited it to imitation of the obedient, humble Mary of the Gospels. Traditional devotion to Our Lady was rejected in the same way that calling upon the saints was. Giving Mary particular titles was seen as derogatory of Christ's unique role as mediator.

The Council of Trent defended both the cult of Mary and the other saints and the internal development of devotion within the Church continued. The Sodality of Our Lady was founded in 1563, followed by sodalities and associations based on this prototype.

Marian studies and devotions flourished in seventeenth- and eighteenth-century Spain and France. Practices included the "slavery of Mary," based on Mary's queenship and in imitation of the Christ Child's dependence on her in his formative years. There was also the "sanguinary vow," a pledge to defend to the death the Immaculate Conception during a time when that dogma was still being debated within the Church. Historians point out that during this era, some customs were carried to excess, and there were protests against them.

In France, devotion focused on Mary's role in the Word-made-flesh, Our Lady's place in one's interior life (especially for seminarians), and the Immaculate Heart of Mary. There was also a consecration to Mary, properly seen as a consecration to Jesus *through* Mary. Its best known form was that of the "holy slavery of Mary," promoted by St. Louis Marie de Montfort. Popular — but misplaced and exaggerated — piety in this area led to strong reactions. St. Alphonsus Liguori defended Marian devotion with careful arguments, particularly in his "Glories of Mary."

Following the Enlightenment and the French Revolution, both new and newly-restored religious orders demonstrated a concern for Mary's role in their apostolates. Apostolic zeal was seen as an authentic charism of Marian devotion, especially among missionary orders, including the Marists, the Oblates of Mary Immaculate, the Claretians, and the Scheut Fathers. There was also an effort among lay sodalities, a pattern that continued into the twentieth century and the founding of the Legion of Mary.

Nineteenth-century devotion was also influenced by reported apparitions and the shrines that developed around them, including: Lourdes, La Salette, Knock, and others. This, too, continued into the twentieth century with, most notably, Fatima in 1917.

From the mid-nineteenth through the twentieth, popes promoted Marian devotions, wrote encyclicals on Mary, and promulgated Marian dogma, including the Immaculate Conception and the Assumption. The twentieth century also saw local, national, and international Marian congresses and a popularity in pilgrimages to Marian shrines worldwide.

Our Lady of La Salette

After World War II, a renewal of biblical and patristic studies included placing attention on Mary and her example for the Church and her role in it. At Vatican Council II, Marian devotion was a topic in the *Dogmatic Constitution on the Church*, the *Decree on Ecumenism*, and the *Constitution on Sacred Liturgy*. The Council Fathers reassessed devotion in light of scriptural, pastoral, and ecumenical perspectives. Her role in the liturgy was proposed as the norm for devotion to Mary.

The Council was also careful to teach that even such special devotion differs essentially from that due Christ and the Trinity alone:

> This cult, as it has always existed in the Church, for all its uniqueness, differs essentially from the cult of adoration, which is offered equally to the Incarnate Word, and to the Father and the Holy Spirit, and it is most favorable to it (*Lumen Gentium*, 66).

In technical and traditional terms, devotion to Mary is a form of *dulia*, or the homage and honor owed the saints, both angelic and human, in heaven. It is not *latria*, or adoration and worship which can be given only to God. Because of her unique relationship to Christ in salvation history, the special degree of devotion due to Mary has traditionally been called *hyperdulia*.

DIVINA INFANTITA (MARIA NIÑA)

While this devotion and image of Mary as a child was originally called *Divina Infantita* (*Divine Infant*), the name was theologically incorrect. It was then changed to *Maria Niña* or *Maria Niña Immaculata* (*The Child Mary* or *The Immaculate Child Mary*).

It traces its origins to a mid-nineteenth-century Mexico City Conceptionist nun, Sr. Magdalena (d. 1859) who had a vision of Our Lady as a young girl. Later, miracles were attributed to the intercession of the Child Mary, and orders of nuns (Slaves of the Immaculate Child) and priests (Missionaries of the Nativity of Mary) were established in her honor.

The feast of *Maria Niña* is celebrated on September 8, the feast of the Nativity of Mary.

See also **Maria Bambina.**

DIVINE MOTHERHOOD — *See Mother of God.*

DIVINE PRAISES

Fourteen praises traditionally recited or sung to conclude the Benediction of the Blessed Sacrament, including four references to Mary. Today, the rite of Benediction makes their use optional, and they are sometimes prayed as a litany. The original form is attributed to Luigi Felici, an eighteenth-century Jesuit who promoted their use as a reparation for public blasphemy. The present form reads:

Blessed be God.
Blessed be his holy name.
Blessed be Jesus Christ, true God and true man.
Blessed be the name of Jesus.
Blessed be his most Sacred Heart.
Blessed be his most Precious Blood.
Blessed be Jesus in the most holy Sacrament of the Altar.
Blessed be the Holy Spirit, the Paraclete.
Blessed be the great Mother of God, Mary most holy.
Blessed be her holy and Immaculate Conception.
Blessed be her glorious Assumption.
Blessed be the name of Mary, Virgin and Mother.
Blessed be St. Joseph, her most chaste spouse.
Blessed be God in his angels and in his saints.

DIVINE PRIVILEGE

Term used to describe God's gift to Mary, that she was immaculately conceived and so never had original sin.

In a catechetical lesson during a general audience on September 3, 1997, Pope John Paul II noted:

> In fact, while the faithful receive holiness through Baptism, Mary was preserved from all stain of original sin and was redeemed antecedently by Christ. Furthermore, although the faithful have been freed "from the law of sin" (cf. Rom 8:2), they can still give in to temptation, and human frailty continues to manifest itself in their lives. "We all make many mistakes," says the Letter of James (3:2). For this reason the Council of Trent teaches: "No one can avoid all sins, even venial sins, through out his life" (DS 1573). By divine privilege, however, the Immaculate Virgin is an exception to this rule, as the Council of Trent itself recalls (ibid.).

The pontiff's lesson at the Wednesday general audience was part of his weekly catechetical series on Mary, which lasted more than a year.

DIVINE PROVIDENCE, OUR LADY, MOTHER OF

Devotion and image that originated in the thirteenth century.

The original image, an oil painting depicting Mary holding the sleeping Christ Child, was venerated by the Servants of Mary and other Italian religious orders. Its title is attributed to St. Philip Benizi (1233–1285), who served as superior of the Servants of Mary.

The devotion later became popular in Spain, where a shrine was built in Tarragona, Catalonia. Fr. Gil Estéve y Tomás (1798–1858), who was from that region, had become acquainted with devotion while he was in the seminary. When he was named bishop of Puerto Rico in 1848, he placed his diocese in the hands of Divine Providence.

At that time, his cathedral church and the diocese's finances were in ruins, but within five years, both had been restored — and devotion to Our Lady, Mother of Divine Providence, firmly established.

Bishop Estéve y Tomás ordered a statue to be carved in Barcelona, which according to a

Our Lady, Mother of Divine Providence

popular style of that time, was designed to be dressed. Featuring a seated Mary holding the Christ Child, it remained in the cathedral until it was replaced in 1920 by an all-wood carving, the image of Our Lady of Divine Providence, now most familiar and best known to the Puerto Rican communities. It shows a seated Mary leaning over the sleeping Child Jesus, who is on her lap. Mary's hands are folded in prayer as she gently supports her Son's left hand.

In 1969, Pope Paul VI declared Our Lady of Divine Providence the principal patroness of Puerto Rico. He also transferred her feast day from January 2 to November 19, the day on which Europeans first landed on the island.

In 1976, the older carving, the one ordered by Bishop Estéve y Tomás, was chosen to be solemnly crowned during the meeting of the Latin American Bishops Council (CELAM) in San Juan. On the eve of the event, the image was severely damaged by a fire; nevertheless, it was crowned the following day before thousands, including cardinals, archbishops, and bishops from throughout Latin America.

Later, the statue was sent to Spain to be restored, and then placed in a national shrine in Puerto Rico.

Our Lady, Mother of Divine Providence, is also patroness of the Barnabite Fathers, the Clerics Regular of St. Paul. That association dates back to 1611 and the order's first house in Rome, when members sought Mary's intervention for finding funding to complete the construction of the Church of St. Charles ai Catinari. The pastor placed in the order's archives a letter recommending that members always rely on Our Lady's unfailing help.

Later that century, the order found it necessary to vacate their second home in Rome but wanted to take with them an image of Mary that was painted on a wall and place it over an altar. When the image and wall were accidentally destroyed, the architect responsible for the mishap offered to replace it with a painting of Mary holding the Infant Jesus in her arms. It was the work of Raphael's student, Scipion Pulzone, known as Gaetan. This painting was placed on the altar of a chapel on the first floor of the St. Charles rectory, behind the main altar. It was there that the Barnabites gathered daily for the recitation of the Divine Office.

At this time, another member of the order came across the letter that had been placed in the archives, and devotion to Our Lady, Mother of Providence, was established. At the end of the nineteenth century, the order's superior general decreed every Barnabite was to have a copy of the painting *Our Lady, Mother of Divine Providence*, in his room.

A third well-known image of this Marian devotion is a Portuguese limestone statue in the Mother of Divine Providence Oratory in the Basilica of the National Shrine of the Immaculate Conception in Washington, DC. It depicts a standing Mary holding the Christ Child in her left arm. At the base of the sculpture by Theodore Barbarossa is the prayer: "Hear, Aid, and Console our Community and our Families."

The Sisters of Mary of Divine Providence of the North American Communities donated the oratory to commemorate the fiftieth anniversary of the religious profession of Mother Angela Cettini, who was the congregation's Superior General for eighteen years and had been a member of the North American community prior to her being elected Mother General.

Devotion to Our Lady under this particular title originated with the congregation's founder, Blessed Aloysius Guanella (1842–1915). Fr. Guanella often prayed to Mary as the Mother of Divine Providence in a parish church in Rome staffed by the Barnabite Fathers.

A prayer to Our Lady, Mother of Divine Providence reads:

> *O Mary, Mother of Divine Providence, you sit as Queen at the right hand of your Son. You aid the Church in her needs and, with maternal care, provide for the personal needs of us, her children, who were entrusted to you at the foot of the Cross by Jesus, our Lord. I implore you to remove from us whatever is harmful, evil, or destructive, and bestow on us only that which is helpful, holy, and loving. I ask you this through Christ, our Lord. Amen.*

DOCTORS OF THE CHURCH, MARIAN

Many of the theologian-saints who have been given the title Doctor of the Church have dealt with Marian themes in their writing and sermons. Marian Doctor is an informal title given to those whose devotion to Our Lady was a prominent feature of their spirituality and their writing.

The doctors most associated with Mary include Sts. Ephraem, Ambrose, Jerome, Augustine, Cyril of Alexandria, John of Damascus, Anselm, Bernard, Albert the Great, Thomas Aquinas, Peter Canisius, Lawrence of Brindisi, and Alphonsus Liguori.

St. Bernard

St. Thomas Aquinas

DOCTRINE, DEVELOPMENT OF

The concept that the truth of Divine Revelation cannot change but, under the continuing guidance of the Holy Spirit, the Church can constantly enter into a fuller awareness of what it possesses and come to "a better understanding of Revelation in matters of faith and morals" (*CCC*, 892).

Because God does not contradict himself, a truth cannot develop into its opposite. This is why a major rule governing development of doctrine is that the process must always follow a line of continuity in the same sense and with the same meaning. A so-called development that changed the meaning of a doctrine would in fact be a corruption, not a development. In the case of authentic development of doctrine, comprehension grows while revealed truth remains as always.

At times in the Church's history, a mystery that seemed implicit in Scripture was made explicit by a papal definition. A prime example of the development of doctrine is the Church's teaching on the Immaculate Conception.

DOCTRINES OF THE CHURCH, MARIAN

Teachings of the Church that particularly focus on the truths about Mary and her unique role in salvation history.

Marian doctrines include Mary as the Mother of God, her Immaculate Conception, her perpetual virginity, and her Assumption.

See also specific doctrines.

DOGMATIC CONSTITUTION ON THE CHURCH — *See Vatican Council II, Appendix B.*

DOLORS, SEVEN — *See Sorrows of Mary.*

DOMINICANS

Popular name for the Order of Preachers, a mendicant order founded by St. Dominic de Guzman (1170–1221).

The order's original purpose was to teach and preach against heresies that were rampant at the time. Among its early members were two of the Church's foremost theologians: Sts. Albert the Great and Thomas Aquinas.

The Dominican family also includes the Second Order of Dominican cloistered nuns and the Dominican Laity. There are also many congregations of Dominican sisters.

According to Dominican tradition, the order's Marian character is based on St. Dominic's own love for Our Lady. In material written between 1246 and 1248, the Roman Dominican, Constantine of Orvieto, says Dominic entrusted the entire care of the order to Mary as its special patron. In 1217, St. Dominic sent his small group of friars to Paris and to Spain from their first house in Toulouse on August 15, the feast of the Assumption.

St. Dominic also had a central role in the creation of the order's *Primitive Constitutions*, both in its initial version in 1216 and the refined edition of the first chapter at Bologna in 1220. In it, the formula for profession has the friar declaring: "I . . . make profession and promise obedience to God, to Blessed Mary . . . and to you brother N.N., Master of the Order of Friars Preachers . . . ."

The connection of St. Dominic with the beginning of the Rosary is a tradition that goes back many centuries and even has been

St. Dominic

The connection of St. Dominic with the beginning of the Rosary is a tradition that goes back many centuries and even has been accepted in the writings of many popes. Some historians now note that while documents from St. Dominic's day that expressly link him with the Rosary are lacking, the tradition has its basis in the founder's devotion to Mary, a trait he implanted in the young order. They credit Blessed Alan de la Roche (also known as de Rupe), a fifteenth-century Dominican, with first strongly promoting the Rosary as its known today.

See also de la Roche, Blessed Alan, O.P.; Queen of Preachers; Rosary; Rosary Sunday; Scapular of St. Dominic.

DORMITION OF MARY

Feast still celebrated in Eastern liturgies that commemorates Mary's peaceful journey to God in heaven and reaffirms the doctrine of the Assumption.

The term "dormition" figuratively refers to Mary's death and means "the falling asleep." The death of Mary is not mentioned in the New Testament, but apocryphal literature includes details about Mary's last hours.

See Assumption; Death of Mary.

DOWRY, OUR LADY'S

A title for England.

Some historians say it comes from an image of St. Edmund (d.c. 869), King of England, who is shown lifting his hands to Mary and asking that she "defend and preserve England, your dowry, and hold it in all prosperity." Others note that in 1399, Thomas Arundel, the Archbishop of Canterbury, wrote: "But we English, being the servants of her [Mary's] special inheritance and her own dowry, as we are commonly called, ought to surpass others in the fervor of our praises and devotions."

DRAGON IN APOCALYPSE — *See Scripture, Mary in.*

DULIA, HYPERDULIA, LATRIA — *See Devotions, Marian.*

EASTERN CHURCH, MARY IN THE

Mariologists note that since its earliest centuries, the Church in the East has shown an unwavering devotion to Our Lady in its liturgies, prayers, and art which has influenced the Church in the West.

(The Catholic Church in the East includes the Alexandrian, Antiochan, Armenian, Byzantine, and Chaldean rites. Of these, the Byzantine is by far the most widely used Eastern liturgical tradition.)

In the Byzantine calendar (with the liturgical year beginning on September 1), many of the major holy days coincide with those of the Roman calendar; among five Byzantine holy days of obligation is the Assumption (or Dormition).

A number of Marian feasts celebrated in the West originated in the East — for example, the Birth of Mary, the Immaculate Conception, and the Presentation of Mary.

The first evidence of a Marian liturgical cult comes from the East and reflects the Council of Ephesus' teaching on *Theotokos.*

An ancient Eastern hymn to Mary, still very much in use today, is the *Akathistos.* The name itself, applied by the fifth century, in Greek means "not seated." The Church stipulated that it be sung or recited standing (as when the Gospel is read) as a sign of reverence for Mary. The Latin translation, edited by Bishop Christopher of Venice around the year 800, greatly influenced the piety of the medieval West.

Art historians point out that within the wider genre of religious icons, particular forms of devotion to Mary (dating back to the fifth century) include the *Odigitria* (or *Hodegetria*) and *Eleousa.* Even today, in Byzantine (and Orthodox) churches, the central door of an iconstasis (a screen separating a church's sanctuary from its nave) through which Holy Communion is brought and offered to the faithful is always flanked by an image of Mary on the left and Christ on the right.

See also **Akathistos;** *Art, Mary in;* **Devotions, Marian;** *Eleousa and* **Oumilenie;** *Ephesus, Council of; Feasts of Mary.*

EGYPT, FLIGHT INTO — *See Scripture, Mary in.*

EINSIEDELN, OUR LADY OF

Image of the Madonna and Child located in the Abbey of Our Lady of the Hermits outside Zurich, Switzerland.

This popular pilgrimage destination dates back to St. Meinrad (d. 861), a Benedictine hermit and martyr, who had built his cell on the spot. Not long after he was clubbed to death by two thieves who believed he had treasures, a chapel was erected on the site and, later, a church and Benedictine abbey.

According to pious tradition, in 948, just before the dedication ceremony for the church, Our Lord appeared and was seen saying the words of consecration from the Mass. When a bishop arrived to perform the dedication, a voice was heard to say, "Stop, brother. The church has been consecrated by God." Historians note the resemblance between this and the events surrounding the church of Our Lady of Le Puy, France, in the fifth century.

Over the centuries, both the church and the abbey have been damaged by fire several times, but the image of Mary has not been harmed. It is believed that the present statue, also known as the *Black Madonna*, was carved in 1466, after the third major fire. It is probably from northern Switzerland or southern Germany and stands just under four feet in height. Because it has been darkened by centuries of candle and incense smoke, it is referred to as a Black Madonna.

See also Black Madonnas.

ELEOUSA AND *OUMILENIE*

Terms for the style of icon depicting Mary and the Christ Child in a loving embrace.

In the West, the *Virgin Eleousa* is known as the *Virgin of Loving-Kindness, Virgin of Compassion,* or *Virgin of Tenderness.* A more literal translation of the Greek term *Eleousa* (*Eleusa*) is "the merciful." Since the sixteenth century, in Russia, this type of painting has been called *Oumilenie* (that is, "of affectionate tenderness").

In both, the faces of the Mother and Child are touching affectionately, but the styles express two different aspects of the relationship. One pertains to Mary, the other to Jesus. *Eleousa* refers to the virtue of Mary: mercy. *Oumilenie* refers to the sentiment experienced by the Child following the intervention of his Mother: affectionate tenderness.

See also Art, Mary in.

ELIZABETH AND ZECHARIAH — *See Scripture, Mary in.*

EMBLEMS OF MARY — *See Art, Mary in; Litanies; Mary Garden; Symbols of Mary.*

EMMERICH, BLESSED ANNE CATHERINE

Augustinian nun, stigmatic, and ecstatic, whose private revelations were recorded in several volumes, including the apocryphal *The Life of the Blessed Virgin Mary.*

Emmerich was born in Flamsche, near Coesfeld, Westphalia, in 1774 and, while still a child, began to receive spiritual gifts from

Blessed Anne Catherine Emmerich

God. After entering the convent, she had an accident in 1806 that made it impossible for her to leave her room for the next six years.

Always suffering from frail health, Emmerich was bedridden from 1813 to the time of her death, in 1824. She died in Dulman, where her remains are preserved.

Historians note it is difficult to know the truth about many of her supernatural experiences, because the main source of information about them is the writings of the romantic poet Clemens Brentano (1778–1842), whose works were characterized by an excess of fantastic imagery.

Emmerich did not write any descriptions of her visions. Instead, she spoke about them to Brentano, who, in turn, wrote them in a sort of diary, which he published in book form several years after her death. His work frequently exaggerated and embellished the facts, so scholars today do not consider Brentano's work (including his best known, *The Dolorous Passion*) to be a reliable reporting of what Emmerich really experienced.

At the time when Pope John Paul II beatified her in 2004, the Vatican did not comment on the writing by Brentano except to say the author "visited Anne Catherine daily to record her visions which he later published." It did, however, note:

A striking characteristic of the life of Anne Catherine was her love for people. Wherever she saw need, she tried to help. Even in her sickbed she sewed clothes for poor children and was pleased when she could help them in this way. Although she could have found her many visitors annoying, she received all of them kindly. She embraced their concerns in her prayers and gave them encouragement and words of comfort.

See also Apocryphal writings, Mary in; Ephesus; Revelation, Divine and Private.

ENCYCLICALS, MARIAN

An encyclical is a pastoral letter written by the pope. In general, it concerns matters of doctrine, morals, discipline, or significant commemorations. Its formal title consists of the first few words of the official text.

The encyclicals that deal with a Marian theme are:

Leo XIII
1884 *Superiore anno* (on the recitation of the Rosary), August 30
1891 *Octobri Mense* (on the Rosary), September 22
1893 *Laetitiae sanctae* (commending devotion to the Rosary), September 8
1894 *Iucunda semper expectatione* (on the Rosary), September 8
1895 *Adiutricem* (on the Rosary), September 5
1896 *Fidentem piumque animum* (on the Rosary), September 20
1897 *Augustissimae Virginis Mariae* (on the Confraternity of the Holy Rosary), September 12
1898 *Diuturni temporis* (on the Rosary), September 5

Pius X
1904 *Ad diem illum laetissimum* (on the Immaculate Conception), February 2

Pius XI
1937 *Ingravescentibus malis* (on the Rosary), September 29

Pius XII

1946 *Deiparae Virginis Mariae* (To all bishops: on the possibility of defining the Assumption of the Blessed Virgin Mary as a dogma of faith), May 1

1951 *Ingruentium malorum* (on reciting the Rosary), September 15

1953 *Fulgens corona* (proclaiming a Marian Year to commemorate the centenary of the definition of the dogma of the Immaculate Conception), September 8

1954 *Ad Caeli Reginam* (proclaiming the Queenship of Mary), October 11

1957 *Le pelerinage de Lourdes* (warning against materialism on the centenary of the apparitions at Lourdes), July 2

John XXIII

1959 *Grata recordatio* (on the Rosary: prayer for the Church, missions, international, and social problems), September 26

John Paul II

1987 *Redemptoris Mater* (on the role of Mary in the mystery of Christ and her active and exemplary presence in the life of the Church), March 25

ENTREATY (OR SUPPLICATION) OF THE MOTHER OF GOD

A Byzantine Rite service which asks, in part, that Mary pour out her compassion.

The service, sung every evening on the fourteen days of fasting before the feast of the Assumption, includes litanies, chants, a Gospel reading, and petitions to Mary. It is also called the "Little Paraklesis" or "Little Canon of the Supplication to the Most Holy Mother of God."

EPHESUS

Ancient city in modern-day Turkey near Smyrna, where the Apostle John is thought to have died. Because, as he was dying on the cross, Jesus placed Mary under the care of St. John (Jn. 19:26–27), the tradition grew that Mary also lived and possibly died in Ephesus.

In the early 1820s, the German mystic nun Blessed Anne Catherine Emmerich reported seeing a vision of Mary's house in Ephesus. Years later, a priest, relying on what she had described, came upon the ruins of a building that — if intact — would have fit her description. It was determined the foundation dated to the first century. The house was restored and soon pilgrims — both Christian and Muslim — began to visit it. Today they number some one million annually.

A 1954 article in *L'Osservatore Romano* quotes Pope Pius XII saying:

> The holy House should be a Marian center which is unique throughout the world, a place where Christians and Moslems of all rites and denominations and of all nationalities can meet each other to venerate the Mother of Jesus, and make true the prophecy, "All Generations will call me blessed."

See also Emmerich, Blessed Anne Catherine; Islam, Mary in.

EPHESUS, COUNCIL OF

Third ecumenical council of the Church, held in Ephesus in 431. Attended by some 200 bishops, the council condemned Palagian and Nestorian heresies and endorsed the Marian title *Theotokos*, or Bearer of God.

Nestorianism denied the unity of the divine and human natures in the Person of Christ. Palagianism, proceeding from the assumption that Adam had a natural right to supernatural life, held that man could attain salvation through the efforts of his natural powers and free will; it involved errors concerning the nature of original sin, the meaning of grace, and other matters.

See also Mother of God.

EPHESUS, OUR LADY OF

Marian image depicting Our Lady with Middle Eastern features and having her head covered with a sheer, pale veil. The image is based on private revelations Elizabeth Fraser experienced during a 1959 pilgrimage to Mary's house in Ephesus.

In 2003 the Basilica of the National Shrine of the Immaculate Conception in Washington, DC, dedicated its Oratory of Our Lady of Ephesus in the crypt church. The mosaic of Mary displayed there is based on Fraser's description.

See also Revelation, Divine and Private.

ESCHATOLOGICAL ICON OF THE CHURCH

Title used in the *Catechism of the Catholic Church* (972) to describe Mary's role as the Church moves toward the end of time.

The *Catechism* explains what the title means by quoting *Lumen Gentium.* Between now and the end of the world, Mary...

> ... in the glory which she possesses in body and soul in heaven, is the image and beginning of the Church as it is to be perfected in the world to come. Likewise she shines forth on earth until the day of the Lord shall come, a sign of certain hope and comfort to the pilgrim People of God (*LG* 69).

In his general audiences on March 14, 2001, Pope John Paul II spoke of Mary as the eschatological icon of the Church:

> Let us fix our gaze, then, on Mary, the icon of the pilgrim Church in the wilderness of history but on her (the Church's) way to the glorious destination of the heavenly Jerusalem, where she will shine as the Bride of the Lamb, Christ the Lord. The Mother of God, as the Church of the East celebrates her, is the Hodegetria, she who "shows the way." That is, Christ, the only mediator for fully encountering the Father.

See also **Hodegetria.**

EVANGELICAL AND FUNDAMENTALIST CHURCHES, MARY IN

In evangelical and fundamentalist churches, commonly held beliefs about Marian doctrine and devotion include:

The "biblical" Mary is dramatically different from the Mary of Mariology. Mary was a simple girl, conscious of her humble status, who had none of the attributes or titles later given to her devotees. This view is based on their interpretation both of the overall scriptural message and of scriptural references to Mary in particular.

In Scripture, Mary is slighted and even rebuked by Christ. For example, when she and the relatives of Jesus come to see him, he uses that occasion to explain who his real brethren are (those who do the will of the Father) (Mt. 12:46–50). When a woman proclaims the blessedness of Mary for being his mother, Jesus points out that blessedness comes from hearing the word of God and doing his will (Lk. 11:27–28). When Mary asks for Jesus' help in Cana, he answer that his has not yet come (Jn. 2:1–4). Citing these three incidents, Evangelicals and fundamentalists maintain that Jesus did not have any special regard for Mary, and she had no special place in his mission of salvation.

Without exception, Marian doctrines are unscriptural. The doctrines of Mary's Motherhood of God, perpetual virginity, Immaculate Conception, and Assumption contradict or add to Scripture and obscure the uniqueness of Christ. Not only does Scripture says nothing of her Motherhood of God, Immaculate Conception, Assumption, or unique role as "mediatrix;" the Bible can even be interpreted as denying all these privileges and titles.

Marian mediation and intercession are contrary to the teaching of salvation by faith alone. Praying to Mary and asking for her intercession leads to a theology of salvation by works and denies the all-sufficiency of Christ's redemptive death and his unique mediatorship.

Marian devotion is a form of idolatry, which includes diabolic signs and wonders. By "worshiping" Mary, Marian devotees violate biblical prohibitions against worship of anyone but God. Statues and images of Mary violate the prohibition against idolatry. Claims of Marian apparitions are unacceptable on scriptural grounds, and the alleged signs and wonders associated with Marian apparitions can be attributed to the devil.

In contrast, Catholic apologists note that Marian doctrine and devotion are fundamental to the historic Christian Faith. They cite the clear witness of the Old and the New Testaments; the role of Mary in Scripture as the Daughter of Zion, the Ark of the Covenant, and the New Eve; the liturgies and devotion of the earliest Christian communities; the crucial link between Marian doctrine and Christological and Trinitarian doctrine; and the consistent experience of Mary in the lives of millions of Christians through the centuries, as they gave themselves to Christ.

See particular Marian doctrine; Doctrine, Development of; Devotions, Marian; Mediatrix; Reformation and Mary; Scripture, Mary in.

FAMILY ROSARY CRUSADE

An international promotion of the family praying the Rosary together.

Fr. Patrick Peyton, C.S.C., who came to be known as "the Rosary priest," began The Family Rosary, Inc., in 1942 and coined the phrase "The family that prays together stays together." Fr. Peyton used the media — films, radio, and television — to promote the family Rosary. The crusade has distributed more than three million rosaries worldwide.

Fr. Peyton died in 1992, at the age of 83. In 2001, the Vatican Congregation for Sainthood Causes formally opened the cause for his possible canonization and declared him a Servant of God.

FATIMA, OUR LADY OF

Image and devotion based on six apparitions in Fatima, Portugal. After three preliminary visitations by an angel, Mary first appeared on May 13, 1917, to three children: Lucia dos Santos, age ten; and her cousins, Jacinta and Francisco Marto, ages seven and nine.

Except for the visit in August, the apparitions took place at the Cova da Iria, a grazing area near the village of Aljustrel, within the parish of Fatima, north of Lisbon. The children reported seeing the Virgin monthly from May through October 13.

During the final visit in October, Mary identified herself as Our Lady of the Rosary, and her promised miracle — the appearance of the sun "spinning" — was witnessed by 50,000 people.

The children reported that Mary requested frequent recitation of the Rosary, penance, increased devotion to her Immaculate Heart, prayers for the conversion of Russia, and the building of a church in her honor.

Francisco died in 1919, followed by Jacinta in 1920. Lucia, who later became a Carmelite nun, received a seventh apparition in 1921. She died in 2005.

Patrick Peyton, C.S.C.

In 1930, Pope Pius XI authorized devotion to Our Lady of Fatima. The Marian shrine in Fatima is among the most famous in the world.

Fatima became especially prominent during the papacy of John Paul II. The 1981 attempt on his life took place on May 13, the anniversary of the first apparition. He attributed his survival to a direct intervention of Our Lady of Fatima, and in 1984, he formally consecrated Russia to the Immaculate Heart. In 2000, Pope John Paul II beatified Francisco and Jacinta and revealed the third prophecy (or "secret") given to the children by Mary.

Until then known only to the visionaries and a select few within the Church, it had been the subject of much speculation. The third secret spoke of an assassination attempt on the pope and the collapse of the Soviet Union.

See also Apparitions of Mary; First Saturday devotion.

FATIMA, WORLD APOSTOLATE OF
— See Blue Army.

Jacinta and Francisco Marto, Lucia dos Santos

FEASTS OF MARY

In strict liturgical language, a "feast" is a celebration of lesser rank than a "solemnity" but of higher rank than a "memorial." In popular usage, "feast" is applied to all the liturgical days on which the Church commemorates a mystery of the Lord or Our Lady, or keeps the memory of a saint.

Ultimately or primarily, the Church establishes each Marian feast; declares whether it should be observed locally, regionally, or universally; and says what degree of solemnity should be attributed to it, depending on the importance of the theme celebrated. Marian feasts can be classified into four categories:

Feasts based on events in scripture (the Annunciation)

Feasts that are the object of dogmatic statements (the Immaculate Conception)

Feasts that originated in a popular devotion and/or a special event (Our Lady of the Rosary)

Feasts with a geographical connection based on apparitions or other special events (Our Lady of Lourdes)

The earliest Marian feasts are believed to be Byzantine in origin and demonstrate how early Christological controversies influenced devotion to Mary. They are: Feast of the Presentation of Our Lord (February 2, sometimes called the "Purification of Mary"), Solemnity of the Annunciation (March 25), Solemnity of the Assumption (August 15), and the Feast of the Birth of Mary (September 8).

These came to the Roman liturgy through the Gelasian Sacramentary, a liturgical book dating back to the early Middle Ages. The oldest Marian feast in the West is the Solemnity of Mary, Mother of God (January 1).

Other feasts of later origin include: Immaculate Conception (December 8), Visitation (May 31), Queenship of Mary (August 22), Our Lady of Sorrows (September 15), and Our Lady of the Rosary (October 7).

Among optional memorials are: Our Lady of Lourdes (February 11), Our Lady of Mount Carmel (July 16), Dedication of the Basilica of St. Mary Major (August 5), Presentation of Mary (November 21), and Immaculate Heart of Mary (Saturday after the second Sunday after Pentecost)

FIAT IN THE NAME OF HUMANITY

Fiat ("Let it be") is the Latin translation of Mary's response to the angel Gabriel's announcement that God had chosen her to be the mother of the Messiah (Lk. 1:26–38). *Fiat in the Name of Humanity* refers to Mary's pronouncement representing not only her personal answer but all humankind's proper submission to the will of God and his plan for redemption.

See also Annunciation.

FIFTEEN SATURDAYS

A devout practice first encouraged in the seventeenth century by Dominicans.

The devotion consists of saying five decades of the Rosary over the fifteen Saturdays preceding the feast of Our Lady of the Rosary (October 7), going to confession, and receiving Holy Communion. The practice was popular in France, Belgium, and Italy.

FINDING IN THE TEMPLE — *See Joyful Mysteries of the Rosary; Scripture, Mary in.*

FIRST SATURDAY DEVOTION

Devotion that began after Mary's apparitions in Fatima, Portugal, in 1917.

It calls for receiving Holy Communion on the first Saturday of each month, celebrating the sacrament of Reconciliation within eight days before or after this day, reciting five decades of the Rosary, and making a fifteen-minute meditation on one of the mysteries of the Rosary.

Church historians note that although the practice became more popular after Fatima, its roots can be traced to St. John Eudes (1601–1680), considered the apostle of devotion to the Sacred Hearts of Jesus and Mary, and to Fr. Jean Jacques Olier (1608–1657), founder of the Society of St. Sulpice.

The devotion is seen as a form of reparation for the blasphemies and acts against Christ. Pope Benedict XV (r. 1914–1919) granted a plenary indulgence at the hour of death to all who make acts of reparation on eight consecutive Saturdays.

See also Fatima, Our Lady of.

FLORES DE MAYO

Spanish for "flowers of May," a month-long Filipino Marian celebration first introduced to that country by the Spaniards.

Parishioners gather flowers to decorate the church and, typically, the community meets in the afternoons to pray the Rosary, place flowers before a Marian image, and share home-made treats. In many parishes, the festivities include an evening Mass.

Over time, a second celebration called *Santacruzan* ("Festival of the Holy Cross") has come to conclude the *Flores de Mayo*. It commemorates of the finding of the Holy Cross in Jerusalem by St. Helena (d. 330), mother of Constantine the Great. Young women, called "Accolades of Our Lady," are chosen to represent various characters, including faith, hope, and charity.

FLOS CARMELI

Latin title of the prayer "Flower of Carmel." The prayer was written by St. Simon Stock (c.1165–1265), and in response, tradition holds, he received the scapular from Mary. It reads:

> *O Beautiful Flower of Carmel, most fruitful vine, splendor of heaven, holy and singular, who brought forth the Son of God, still ever remaining a pure virgin, assist us in our necessity! O Star of the Sea, help and protect us. Show us that you are our Mother.*

See also Scapular.

FLOWERS, PLANTS — *See Mary Garden.*

FOUNTAIN OF BEAUTY

Marian title from the Litany of Mary, Queen. — *See Litany of Mary, Queen.*

FOUNTAIN, OUR LADY OF THE
— *See Caravaggio, Our Lady of.*

FRANCISCAN CROWN ROSARY

— *See Rosary of the Seven Joys of Our Lady.*

FRANCISCANS

Popular name for the Order of Friars Minor, a mendicant order founded by St. Francis of Assisi (1181/82–1226).

See Immaculate Conception; Pontifical International Marian Academy; Portiuncula; Way of the Cross.

St. Francis of Assisi

FULLNESS OF GRACE, MARY'S

The concept that Mary's dignity is above that of all created persons and angels because of her role as the Mother of God.

In the opening paragraph of his 1854 encyclical on the Immaculate Conception, *Ineffabilis Deus*, Pope Pius IX declared:

> Far above all the angels and all the saints so wondrously did God endow her with the abundance of all heavenly gifts poured from the treasury of his divinity that this mother, ever absolutely free of all stain of sin, all fair and perfect, would possess that fullness of holy innocence and sanctity than which, under God, one cannot even imagine anything greater, and which, outside of God, no mind can succeed in comprehending fully.

See also Immaculate Conception.

GABRIEL — *See Angelic Salutation.*

GABRIEL BELL

Medieval English custom of designating a bell that would be used to mark the reciting of Hail Marys in the morning and evening. Bells dedicated to Our Lady were inscribed with sayings in her honor.

See also Angelus.

GARABANDAL

Mountain village in Spain where four young girls reported Mary appeared to them almost two thousand times between 1961 and 1965. Rome has made no statement on the authenticity of their claims.

See also Apparitions of Mary.

GATE, VIRGIN OF THE — *See Iviron, Our Lady of.*

GATE OF HEAVEN

Marian title used in the Litany of the Blessed Virgin Mary (also known as the Litany of Loreto), which was originally approved in 1587 by Pope Sixtus V.

The Father and Doctor of the Church St. Ambrose (340–397) wrote: "Who is this Gate if not Mary? Mary is the Gate through which Christ entered this world!" (*The Consecration of a Virgin and the Perpetual Virginity of Mary,* 8:52).

See Litany of the Blessed Virgin Mary.

GENEALOGY OF MARY — *See Ancestors of Mary.*

GIETRZWALD, POLAND

Polish town, founded in 1352, which is the site of Marian apparitions in the late nineteenth century. The oldest witness to Marian devotion in Gietrzwald is a *pietá* that dates from 1425, and since 1500, the town's patronal feast day has been the Birth of Mary, September 8.

A miraculous image revered there was first mentioned in 1505. It shows Mary and the Christ Child, surrounded by angels, holding a banner with the inscription: *Ave regina coelorum, ave domina angelorum* ("Hail, Queen of Heaven; hail, Our Lady of the Angels"). The image was crowned in 1717.

Between June 27 and September 16, 1877, Mary appeared there to two children, Justina Schaffrinski and Barbara Samulowski. She presented herself as the Immaculate Conception and stressed the importance of the Rosary. During the apparitions, some 2,000 people were on hand three times a day. On Sundays the number reached 10,000, and on the final day — on which a statue of Mary was blessed and placed in a small chapel — 50,000 were present.

The Church's recognition of these apparitions, to which a number of conversions and healings have been attributed, was not granted until 1977. Among those present for this event was Krakow's Cardinal Karol Wojtyla who, the following year, became Pope John Paul II.

GIRDLE OF OUR LADY, FEAST OF THE

A Byzantine Rite observance commemorating the enshrining of what was venerated as Mary's sash (or girdle) in a church in Constantinople. Our Lady's *Zona* was a theme for writers and poets.

See Relics of Mary.

GLORIES OF MARY, THE

Writing of St. Alphonsus Liguori, published in 1750, and later distributed in more than 800 editions in many languages. The work was meant to encourage devotion to Mary during a period when reason was seen as being more important than dependence on God.

The book is divided into two main sections. The first is a commentary on the Marian prayer *Salve Regina* ("Hail, Holy Queen"). The second discusses a number of Marian mysteries and feasts, such as the Annunciation and the Sorrows of Mary. St. Alphonsus used many sources (including, for example, Sts. Thomas Aquinas, Bernard, and Bridget of Sweden) to support his teaching.

This work remains in print today.

GLORIFIED BODY

The Church teaches that all persons will rise from the dead and their bodies will be "glorified," or spiritualized in a humanly unknown manner. Resurrected bodies will have four essential qualities:

- Impassibility: the inability to suffer pain and the absence of defects.
- Clarity: the brightness of glory, beauty, and splendor that overflows from the beatific vision (seeing God) and transforms all bodies.
- Subtlety: all bodies will be in their true nature, but will be entirely docile in a spiritual manner.
- Agility: the body, as a perfect instrument of the soul, will be in accord with, and have access to, the wonders of the universe by being able to understand the mysteries of creation.

In his 1950 apostolic constitution *Munificentissimus Deus,* which solemnly defined the dogma of the Assumption of Mary, Pope Pius XII wrote:

St. Alphonsus Liguori

We pronounce, declare and define it to be a divinely revealed dogma: that the Immaculate Mother of God, the ever Virgin Mary, having completed the course of her earthly life, was assumed body and soul into heavenly glory.

See also Assumption.

GLORIOUS MOTHER OF GOD

Marian title from the Litany of Mary, Queen.

See Litany of Mary, Queen.

GLORIOUS MYSTERIES — *See Rosary.*

GLORY OF THE HOLY SPIRIT

Marian title from the Litany of Mary, Queen.

See Litany of Mary, Queen.

GLORY OF THE HUMAN RACE

Marian title used in prayer by St. Bernadine of Siena (1380–1440).

One version reads:

O Lady, blessed among all women, you are the glory of the human race, the salvation of all our people. Your merits are limitless, and you have power over all creation. You are the Mother of God, the sovereign Lady of the world, and the Queen of Heaven. You are the dispenser of all graces, and the ornament of the Holy Church. You are the model of the just, the consolation of the pious, and the root of our salvation. You are the joy of paradise, the gate of heaven, the glory of God. We have been happy to sing your praises. We beg you,

O Mother of Mercy, to make up for our weakness, to excuse our presumption, to accept our devotion, to bless our labors. Imprint your love in the hearts of all of us, so that after having loved and honored your Son on earth, we may with you praise him and bless him forever in heaven. Amen.

GOLDEN HEART, VIRGIN WITH THE
— *See Beauraing, Our Lady of.*

GOLDEN SATURDAYS, THE

Popular medieval Marian devotion on the three Saturdays following the feast of St. Michael, at the end of October.

A document from 1387 found in the town of Bischofsdorf, near Mattighofen, Germany, sets its date for the "next three golden Saturdays," indicating the practice was well known by then and widespread in Austria, Bohemia, Bavaria, and Württemberg. The celebration included reception of the sacraments and festivities, particularly at places of pilgrimage. Traces of the custom can still be found in these areas today.

The origin of the three golden Saturdays is unknown, but a document from 1765 says it was based on a promise from Mary:

Whoever will honor me on three Saturdays after the Feast of the Archangel Michael — who always guarded my virginal pure conception, without stain of original sin — with a devotion of zealous prayer, especially with the holy Rosary . . . shall have the consolation of all my graces for a joyfully blessed little hour of death, without any struggle with evil powers and temptations.

Although the legend cannot be proven, it does demonstrate how the association between Mary and St. Michael was explained at the time. Earlier and more often than in the West, the art and popular devotion in the East showed St. Michael as the protector of Mary and the Child Jesus. Here, also, ancient legends make that association, including being Mary's protector at the time of her death and assumption; so, St. Michael was long considered the patron of the dying.

The term "golden" was used to identify the devotion as something especially valuable, important, and effective. The number three may indicate that the Masses were not celebrated all in one place, but at three different locations, to which the people could walk on a pilgrimage on three consecutive Saturdays.

GOOD COUNSEL, OUR LADY OF

Image and devotion based on an Albanian medieval icon known as *Our Lady of Shkodra*.

According to tradition, the painting was taken to Italy after Albania was invaded by Ottoman Turks and later placed in a shrine in Genazzano, Italy. Miracles and favors have been attributed to Our Lady of Good Counsel, the patroness of Albania.

Located some thirty miles from Rome, Genazzano had been a center for the cult of the Roman goddess Venus in pre-Christian times. About the fourth century, a church named St. Mary, Mother of Good Counsel, was built there.

A millennium later, in 1356, it was placed under the care of the Order of St. Augustine; by this time, however, the building was in ruins. The next century saw many efforts to

Our Lady of Shkodra

restore it. A devout widow named Pettrucia sold all her property to fund the project, but because there still was not enough money to complete it, she began to earnestly pray for the rest.

Pious tradition holds that on April 25, 1467, as the town celebrated the feast of its patron, St. Mark, a cloud moved through the village and came to rest on the walls of the half-finished structure. It was then the people found a fresco of the Madonna and Child there. They immediately came together and began to complete the restoration work.

As the townspeople wondered about the image, two pilgrims from Albania arrived and said they had been searching for that very picture, which was missing from its customary place in the Albanian town of Scutari. The image had been an object of great devotion there until the city came under siege by the Ottoman Turks — so, the visitors told the residents of Genazzano, Mary had moved to their city.

The fresco, about a foot wide and eighteen inches high, is now encased in a glass, metal, and marble framework. Art experts speculate it

Our Lady of Good Counsel

may be the work of the early fifteenth-century artist Gentile da Fabriano. Originally, it was part of a larger fresco that covered part of a wall but was later hidden by a baroque shrine altar. Later, it was covered with plaster, and a terra cotta image of Mary was hung on the wall. During the restoration by the Augustinians and the widow Pettrucia, a section of the outer wall may have cracked and broken off, revealing the painting beneath it.

Now, the upper portion of the fresco has separated from the back wall and is only a sheet of thin plaster. Even so, it has remained intact for centuries, even surviving the bombing of the town during World War II.

Approval of devotion to Our Lady of Good Counsel was given by Pope Paul II (r. 1464–1471), and the image was crowned by Pope Innocent XI in 1682.

During the Counter-Reformation, the Augustinians placed their order under the pro-

tection of Our Lady of Good Counsel and began to honor her wherever they were established. In Germany, for example, some 70,000 images were soon distributed. Today, copies of the image are found in Augustinian churches and cloisters.

The Jesuits also promoted the devotion worldwide, and many confraternities developed under her patronage. Pope Leo XIII added the invocation "Mother of Good Counsel, pray for us" to the Litany of Loreto.

A "Short Prayer to Mary Most Holy of Good Counsel to Implore Her Protection," dating back to 1796, reads:

O Mary of Good Counsel, inflame the hearts of all who are devoted to you, so that all of them have shelter in you, O great Mother of God. O most worthy Lady, let everyone choose

Our Lady of Good Counsel by Sarullo

you as teacher and wise counselor of their souls, since you are, as St. Augustine says, the counsel of the Apostles and counsel of all peoples. Amen.

See also Scapular of Our Lady of Good Counsel.

GOOD HEALTH, OUR LADY OF

Devotion popularly known as Our Lady of Vailankanni, which can be traced to mid-sixteenth-century India and is attributed to three apparitions.

In the first, Mary and the Infant Jesus appeared to a Hindu boy who had been carrying milk to a customer's home. As he rested under a tree near a pond (or "tank"), Mary asked for milk for her Son, and the boy gave some to her. When he later reached the customer's house, he apologized for his tardiness and the missing milk by telling the customer what had happened. The customer, also Hindu, discovered the milk pot was still full and decided a miracle had occurred. He asked to be shown where the event had taken place, and the boy took him there. Again, Mary appeared by the pond. When word of the occurrences spread, the local Catholic community was overjoyed, and the location became known as *Matha Kulam*, or "Our Lady's tank."

The second apparition was some years later. A lame child was selling buttermilk near a public square on the outskirts of the village when Mary appeared to him. Again, she asked for milk for the Infant Jesus, and the boy gave some to her. She also asked him to go to a certain wealthy Catholic man in a nearby town and tell him what had happened. The boy,

unaware that he had been cured of his disability, ran to do as she had requested.

Meanwhile, that rich man had had a vision the previous night in which Mary had asked him to build a chapel in her honor. After the boy told him of that day's occurrence, they returned to where Mary had appeared, and Our Lady appeared to both of them. The man erected a simple, thatched chapel on the site to "Mother of Good Health" (*Arokia Matha*).

A few years later, Mary appeared to some Portuguese merchant sailors and rescued them from a violent storm that had wrecked their ship. When the sailors reached the shore of Vailankanni, local fisherman took them to the thatched chapel. As a way to give thanks and pay tribute to Mary, they built a small permanent chapel on their return trip and, on subsequent visits, made improvements on it. The sailors dedicated the chapel to Our Lady on September 8 to celebrate the feast of her nativ-

Our Lady of Good Health, Vailankanni

ity and to mark the date of their safe landing to Vailankanni.

In 1933, the small chapel was replaced by a large church; in 1962, Pope John XXIII named it a basilica. Each September, the feast of Mary's birth is marked there with a nine-day festival, drawing nearly two million pilgrims, both Catholic and non-Catholic. Because of miraculous cures attributed to the intercession of Our Lady of Good Health, the basilica is known as "the Lourdes of the East."

In the United States, the Basilica of the National Shrine of the Immaculate Conception dedicated its Oratory of Our Lady of Good Health, Vailankanni, in 1997, in conjunction with the fiftieth anniversary of India's independence. A gold-gilded statue — a replica of the original image in the shrine — was crowned and consecrated in Vailankanni before being placed in the oratory. The oratory was a gift of the Indian American Catholic Association in Washington, DC.

On December 26, 2004, tsunamis triggered by a magnitude 9 earthquake deep in the Indian Ocean devastated coastlines throughout southern Asia, including Vailankanni, and took hundreds of thousands of human lives. More than 1,000 people were killed in the area surrounding the shrine, but the surging waves stopped at the gates of the shrine compound, and some 2,000 pilgrims attending Mass in the basilica were not injured.

GOOD HOPE, OUR LADY OF — See
Confidence, Our Lady of.

GOOD REMEDY, OUR LADY OF

Marian title promoted by St. John of Matha (1160–1213), founder of the Order of the Most Holy Trinity.

The Trinitarians raised large amounts of money to buy Christian slaves being sold by Muslims, and the order credited its success to Mary's intervention. Images of Our Lady of Good Remedy sometimes show Mary handing a bag of money to St. John. In recent times, the order has revived its original charism to free Christians enslaved in some Muslim countries.

Our Lady of Good Remedy

GRACE

The free and undeserved gift God gives to human beings to respond to their vocation to become his adopted children.

As sanctifying grace, God shares his divine life and friendship in a habitual gift, a stable and supernatural disposition that enables a soul to live with God and to act by his love. In actual grace, he gives a person help to conform one's life to God's will. Sacramental graces and special graces (charisms, the grace of one state of life) are gifts of the Holy Spirit to help a person live out his or her Christian vocation.

The Catholic Church teaches that Mary, "full of grace," was immaculately conceived (was never stained with original sin) and remained sinless.

See Immaculate Conception.

GRACE, OUR LADY OF

Title used to refer to at least two images.

One, depicting Mary and the Christ Child in a loving embrace (the *eleousa* style), is an icon of Italo-Byzantine origin brought from Rome and placed in the cathedral in Cambrai, France, in the mid-fifteenth century. There, it was given the title *Our Lady of Grace* and is still venerated as patroness of that city (also called the "Town of Our Lady"). Pious tradition holds it was painted by St. Luke.

About fourteen inches by ten inches, the painting was crowned in 1894 and is annually carried in procession through the streets of Cambrai on the feast of the Assumption.

The second is based on a picture found in 1610 by Venerable Dominic of Jesus and Mary, a Spanish Discalced Carmelite. The portrait shows Mary wearing a full veil, a blue mantle decorated on the right shoulder with a rosette-backed star, and a red gown. A jeweled crown and a necklace were added later.

Because the head tilts slightly to the left, the image is sometimes called *Our Lady of the Bowed Head.* The image has been enshrined in Vienna since the seventeenth century and is now in the Carmelites' Church of the Holy Family. Miracles have been attributed to the intercession of Our Lady of Grace.

See also Eleousa *and* Oumilenie.

GREAT RETURN, OUR LADY OF THE
— *See* Boulogne, Our Lady of.

GREEN SCAPULAR — *See Scapular of the Immaculate Heart (Green Scapular).*

GRITERÍA — *See* Immaculate Conception of El Viejo, Our Lady of the.

GUADALUPE, OUR LADY OF

Devotion and image based on apparitions seen by St. Juan Diego at Tepeyac, near Mexico City, in 1531.

Juan, a 57-year-old peasant, widower, and recent convert to Catholicism, was on his way to early morning Saturday Mass — said in honor of Mary — and catechism lessons when he heard music playing, which drew his attention to the base of the barren and rocky hill of Tepeyac. A radiantly beautiful young woman affectionately called to him by name — addressing him as "Little Juan" — and then

Our Lady of Guadalupe

not believe Our Lady had appeared in his diocese. Knowing that Tepeyac was the site of the temple of the Aztec corn goddess, Tonantzin, it was easy for him to assume this visitor was offering a jumble of local tradition and new-found Christian belief. Not wishing to offend, the bishop suggested Juan come back to see him a few days later.

Returning to Tepeyac, Juan again saw Mary and, after apologizing for failing in the task she had given him, suggested she choose someone else for her mission. In a later telling of the events to others, Juan described how warm her smile was as she offered consoling words and admitted that, yes, there were others she could send, but she had chosen him. She promised that her message — coming from him — would be accepted and acted upon.

The next day Juan again walked to Mass, this time wearing his coarse cloak, his *tilma,* because the weather had turned cooler, and then went back to the bishop's house, where he repeated his story. This time, before giving an answer, the bishop asked for some sort of proof of the events as Juan described them. His visitor was to bring the bishop some sign that this young woman was the Mother of God and that she wanted a church built on Tepeyac hill. Juan readily agreed to the bishop's request, which greatly surprised the prelate.

Again as Juan made his way home, Mary appeared to him and promised to provide a sign for Bishop Zumarraga the following day. Unfortunately, that night Juan's uncle, with whom he lived, became gravely ill. Thus, that day, Juan stayed with the man and was unable to visit the site where he had seen Mary.

A day later, his uncle's health had not improved, so Juan left to bring a priest to the

told him she was the "ever Virgin Mary, Mother of the true God." Next, she pointed out a spot on which she wanted a church built for the people where "I will hear their weeping, their complaints, and heal all their sorrows, hardship, and suffering."

She told Juan he would be her messenger to the local bishop, Don Juan de Zumarraga, who had only recently arrived from Spain and had a great devotion to Mary.

Juan immediately went to the bishop's house and — through an aide interpreting his native Nahuatl dialect into the bishop's Spanish — told him what had just happened. The bishop was cordial and understanding but did dying man. But, to avoid seeing the young woman and having to once more apologize for his failure, he circled around Tepeyac. Even so, Mary appeared to him a fourth time. She assured him his uncle's health would improve and instructed him to climb to the top of the barren hill. There he found and gathered fresh Castilian roses, which he placed in his cloak.

Mary then arranged the flowers and tied his cloak at the shoulder, telling him to open it only when he was meeting with the bishop. Because roses were out of season and Tepeyac was barren soil, he believed the flowers would provide the sign the bishop had requested two days earlier.

Finally, Juan was once more in the bishop's presence and told the prelate he had the sign. As Juan opened his cloak, the flowers tumbled to the floor and the bishop fell to his knees, joined by others who were also in the room. An image of Mary had miraculously appeared on the peasant's *tilma*.

The cloak was immediately enthroned in the bishop's chapel until a church could be built. Until his death in 1548, Juan remained the image's guardian.

Though made of natural fibers, the *tilma* is still remarkably preserved. It is now enshrined at the Basilica of Our Lady of Guadalupe in Mexico City. Around 1531, a small adobe chapel was erected on the spot Mary had pointed out to Juan. Later, a larger church was built there, and the present basilica was blessed in 1976.

At the time of the apparitions, Mary also appeared to Juan's uncle. She cured him and identified herself as "Holy Mary, ever Virgin of Guadalupe." The actual words in Nahuatl mean "she who crushes the stone serpent;" at that time, the primary god of the native religion in that area was a stone serpent, and its followers practiced human sacrifice. But to those who spoke Spanish, the Lady's words sounded like *Guadalupe*, the name of a favorite image of Our Lady in Spain.

Because the image depicts Mary as a young *mestiza* maiden — one who is of both Native American and European background — it is also called *La Morenita* (*The Little Brown One*). It is recognized as a version of the Immaculate Conception.

Pope Pius XII declared Our Lady of Guadalupe patroness of the Americas, and her feast is celebrated on December 12. Juan Diego was canonized in 2002, and his feast day is December 9.

See also Apparitions of Mary.

GUARD OF HONOR OF THE IMMACULATE HEART OF MARY

An archconfraternity begun by Franciscan Father Bonaventure Glattman in Munich, Germany in 1932. Approved by the Holy See, it promotes devotion to Mary, especially through a daily prayer.

See also Confraternity, Archconfraternity.

HAIL, HOLY QUEEN — *See Salve Regina.*

HAIL MARY — *See Ave Maria.*

HAIL MARY OF OUR SORROWFUL MOTHER

Prayer attributed to St. Bonaventure (d. 1274) used in the novena to Our Sorrowful Mother, a Servite devotion. It reads:

> *Hail! Mary, full of sorrows, the Crucified is with you; tearful are you among women, and tearful is the fruit of your womb, Jesus. Holy Mary, mother of the Crucified, give tears to us, crucifiers of your Son, now, and at the hour of our death. Amen.*

HAIL QUEEN OF THE HEAVENS — *See Ave Regina Caelorum.*

HAL, OUR LADY OF

Statue originally owned by St. Elizabeth of Hungary (1207–1231). The image was passed down to several members of the royal family until Princess Alice of Holland gave it to the church in Hal, Belgium, in 1267.

Made of dark walnut (a "Black Madonna"), the statue is dressed in royal robes with Mary and the Infant Jesus wearing papal crowns. The shrine that houses the statue became a favorite place of pilgrimage in the late thirteenth century. Miracles have been attributed to the intercession of Our Lady of Hal.

See also Black Madonnas.

HANDMAID OF THE LORD

Mary's description of herself when giving her assent to God's will at the Annunciation: "Behold, I am the handmaid of the Lord; let it be to me according to your word" (Lk. 1:38).

See Annunciation.

HANNAH'S HYMN OF PRAISE

Name given to 1 Sam. 2:1–10, a source and prototype for Mary's *Magnificat* in Lk. 1:46–55.

Hannah was the childless wife of Elkanah of Ephraim. In answer to her prayer and her vow to devote her child to Yahweh, she gave birth to Samuel, and later had three more sons and two daughters.

Scripture scholars note that the hymn was not written by her but was placed at the beginning of the book of 1 Samuel. It is a psalm and, as with most of the book of Psalms, contains no evidence for an exact date. The author exults in the safety that one feels in Yahweh's power. It is the Lord who defeats the powerful, impoverishes the rich, and raises up the poor and the needy. Yahweh's wicked adversaries are destroyed.

The Hymn of Praise reads:

My heart exults in the LORD, my strength is
*   exalted in the Lord.*
My mouth derides my enemies, because I
*   rejoice in thy salvation.*
There is none holy like the LORD,
*   there is none besides thee;*
*   there is no rock like our God.*
Talk no more so very proudly,
*   let not arrogance come from your mouth;*
for the LORD is a God of knowledge,
*   and by him actions are weighed.*
The bows of the mighty are broken, but the
*   feeble gird on strength.*
Those who were full have hired themselves
*   out for bread,*
*   but those who were hungry have ceased to*
*   hunger.*
The barren has borne seven,
*   but she who has many children is forlorn.*
The Lord kills and brings to life;
*   he brings down to Sheol and raises up.*
The Lord makes poor and makes rich;
*   he brings low, he also exalts.*
He raises up the poor from the dust;
*   he lifts the needy from the ash heap,*
to make them sit with princes and inherit a
*   seat of honor.*
For the pillars of the earth are the LORD's,
*   and on them he has set the world.*
He will guard the feet of the faithful ones;

but the wicked shall be cut off in
*   darkness;*
*   for not by might shall a man prevail.*
The adversaries of the LORD shall be broken to
*   pieces;*
*   against them he will thunder in heaven.*
The LORD will judge the ends of the earth;
*   he will give strength to his king,*
*   and exalt the power of his anointed.*

See **Magnificat.**

HEALTH OF THE SICK

Marian title used in the Litany of the Blessed Virgin Mary (also known as the Litany of Loreto), which was originally approved in 1587 by Pope Sixtus V.

See Litany of the Blessed Virgin Mary.

HELP OF CHRISTIANS, OUR LADY

Ancient Marian devotion.

More than 1,000 early Byzantine texts refer to Mary as "Empress Helper," and the ruins of

Our Lady, Help of Christians

Mary, Help of Christians

a fifth-century African basilica featured the inscription, "Holy Mary, help us." By the tenth century, the Greek liturgy had a special patronage of Mary, asking for her help because God gave her "the office of protecting the Christian people." The title "Mary, Help of Christians" has been found in the Litany of Loreto from the sixteenth century.

Victories attributed to the intercession of Our Lady at the Battle of Lepanto in 1571, and again at the Battle of Vienna in 1683, popularized the title, and it became historically entwined with the titles Our Lady of Victory and Our Lady of the Rosary.

In Passau, Bavaria, a painting of Mary dating back to the mid-sixteenth century was placed in a shrine built in 1624 in honor of Our Lady, Help of Christians. Pilgrims traditionally offered the short prayer *Maria, hilif* (Mary, help). Pope Urban VIII (r. 1623–1644) approved a confraternity of Mary, Help of Christians, of Passau.

In the early nineteenth century, after Napoleon Bonaparte imprisoned Pope Pius VII, the pontiff organized an intense Rosary campaign to Mary, Help of Christians. As a sign of thanksgiving for Mary's help, on the abdication of the French leader and his own release from incarceration, Pius instituted the Feast of Our Lady, Help of Christians, celebrated on May 24.

Since the time of their founder, St. John Bosco (1815–1888), Salesians have invoked Mary under this title as the patroness of their congregation.

Our Lady, Help of Christians, is also the patroness of Australia.

See also **Pompeii, Our Lady of the Rosary of.**

HELP OF THE SICK, OUR LADY — *See Scapular of St. Camillus.*

HERESY

The obstinate postbaptismal denial or doubt by a Catholic of any truth which must be believed as a matter of divine and Catholic faith (Canon 751, of the Code of Canon Law).

Formal heresy involves deliberate resistance to the authority of God, who communicates revelation through Scripture, Tradition, and the teaching authority of the Church. Heresies have been significant not only as disruptions of unity of faith but also as occasions for the clarification and development of doctrine, including teachings regarding Mary.

See **Ephesus, Council of.**

HERMITS, OUR LADY OF THE — *See* Einsiedeln, Our Lady of the.

HEROD

The name of many rulers mentioned in the New Testament and in history.

Herod I (c. 74 B.C.– 4 B.C.), also known as Herod the Great, was the Roman-appointed king of Judea at the time of Christ's birth. It was Herod the Great who, in an attempt to kill the Messiah, ordered the massacre of the innocents, sending the Holy Family into exile in Egypt.

His son, Herod Antipas (b. 20 B.C.), became ruler in 4 B.C. It was Herod Antipas who ordered the beheading of John the Baptist (Mt. 14:3–12; Mk. 6:17–29). He served as tetrarch at the time of the ministry and trial of Christ, who appeared before him and was mocked (Lk. 23:7–13).

Herod Agrippa (10 B.C.–A.D. 44), the grandson of Herod the Great and son of Herod Antipas, ruled at the time of the early Church and persecuted the followers of Christ, including having James killed and Peter imprisoned (Acts 12:1–24).

See Scripture, Mary in.

HEROINE OF THE QURAN

Islamic Marian title.

See Islam, Mary in.

HODEGETRIA

Variation of the word *Odigitria,* a type of ancient icon depicting Mary "showing the way."

See Art, Mary in.

HOLY FAMILY

Jesus, Mary, and Joseph.

The feast of the Holy Family is celebrated on the Sunday after Christmas and commemorates it as the model of domestic society, holi-

Rest on the Flight to Egypt

Holy Family by Batoni

Flight into Egypt

ness, and virtue. The devotional background of the feast was strong in the seventeenth century and in the eighteenth century, in prayers composed for a special Mass, Blessed François de Laval, the first Canadian bishop, likened the Christian family to the Holy Family. Pope Leo XIII consecrated families to the Holy Family and composed his own Office of the Holy Family. In 1921, Pope Benedict XV extended the office and Mass of the feast to the whole Church.

HOLY HEART OF MARY, MOST PURE HEART OF MARY — *See Immaculate Heart of Mary.*

HOLY HOUSE OF LORETO — *See Loreto, Holy House of.*

HOLY INNOCENTS

Feast celebrated on December 28 to commemorate the infants who suffered death at the hands of Herod's soldiers seeking to kill the child Jesus who, with Mary and Joseph, escaped to Egypt (see Mt. 2:13–23). The Holy Innocents have been venerated as martyrs since the early Church, and a feast has been observed since the fifth century.

See also Scripture, Mary in.

HOLY MARY

Traditional form of address (as in the *Ave Maria*, the Hail Mary) and title (as in the Litany of the Blessed Virgin Mary, also known as the Litany of Loreto).

See also Ave Maria and Litany of the Blessed Virgin Mary.

HOLY MOTHER OF GOD

Title used in many prayers, including the Litany of the Blessed Virgin Mary, also known as the Litany of Loreto.

See Litany of the Blessed Virgin Mary; Mother of God.

HOLY NAME OF MARY

Feast introduced by Pope Innocent XI after the victory of the Christian forces over the Turks at the city wall of Vienna on September 12, 1683.

The saving of the city was a pivotal point in the future of the Christian empire, and so the feast was votive, an act of thanksgiving for the intercession of Mary. Although it was expunged from the calendar in 1969, Pope John Paul II restored it in 2002 as an optional memorial.

HOLY SPIRIT AND MARY

The Catholic Church has always believed that though the Holy Spirit is inseparable from the other Persons of the Blessed Trinity, he intervened in a personal way in the work of humanity's salvation and made Mary his associate in that work.

The Church has also maintained that, acting in a manner consistent with his proper character as Personal Love of the Father and Son, he acted with both infinite power and infinite gentleness in perfectly adapting the person of Mary and her dynamic powers of body and spirit to the role assigned her in the plan of redemption.

Because of her privileges and the exceptional gifts of grace that the Holy Spirit gave her, Mary is addressed in the liturgy as "Temple of the Lord" and "Sanctuary of the Holy Spirit."

It was the Holy Spirit who filled Mary with grace in the very first moment of her conception and so redeemed her in a particular way in view of the merits of Christ, the Savior of humanity. It was the Holy Spirit who descended upon her, inspired her consent in the name of humanity to the virginal conception of the Son of God, and made her womb fruitful so that she might bring forth the Savior of her people and Lord of a kingdom that will never end (see Lk. 1:32–33). It was the Holy Spirit who filled her soul with jubilant gratitude and moved her to sing the Magnificat to God her Savior (see Lk. 1:45–55). It was the Holy Spirit who suggested to the Virgin that she faithfully remember the words and events connected with the birth and childhood of her only Son, events in which she played such an intimate, loving part (see Lk. 2:19, 33, 51).

The Church also teaches it was the Holy Spirit who urged the compassionate Mary to ask her Son to change water into wine at the wedding feast of Cana, which marked the beginning of his public ministry (see Jn. 2:11). And it was the Third Person of the Blessed Trinity who strengthened the soul of the Mother of

Christ as she stood beneath the cross, and inspired her once again, as he had at the Annunciation, to consent to the will of the heavenly Father, who wanted her to be associated as a mother with the sacrifice her Son was offering for humanity's redemption (see Jn. 19:25). It was the Holy Spirit who filled the Sorrowful Mother with immense love so that she might accept as a last testament from her Son her maternal mission with regard to John, the beloved disciple (see Jn. 19:26–27); a mission which, as the Church has always understood it, prefigured her spiritual motherhood toward humanity as a whole.

It was the Holy Spirit who inspired Mary to be a model intercessor during the hours in the Upper Room, when the disciples of Jesus "together . . . devoted themselves to constant prayer" along with "some women . . . and Mary the mother of Jesus" (Acts 1:14), and waited for the promised Paraclete. And, finally, it was the Holy Spirit who prepared her when, in the words of Pope Pius XII's apostolic constitution *Munificentissimus Deus*, "the Immaculate Mother of God, the ever Virgin Mary, having completed the course of her earthly life, was assumed body and soul into heavenly glory."

The Church also teaches the Assumption did not put an end to Mary's mission as an associate of the Holy Spirit in the mystery of salvation. Even though she is now in heaven, she continues to be spiritually present to all her redeemed children and at the heart of the pilgrim Church.

See also Annunciation; Assumption; Immaculate Conception; Scripture, Mary in; Mediatrix.

HOLY VIRGIN OF VIRGINS

Marian title used in the Litany of the Blessed Virgin Mary (also known as the Litany of Loreto), which was originally approved in 1587 by Pope Sixtus V.

See Litany of the Blessed Virgin Mary.

HOPE, OUR LADY OF

Ancient devotion.

One of the first shrines with that title was built in Mezières, France, in 930. It was reported that, in 1871, Our Lady of Hope appeared in the French village of Pontmain, revealed herself as the "Madonna of the Crucifix," and gave the world a message of hope through prayer and the cross.

See also Pontmain, Our Lady of.

HOSTYN, OUR LADY OF

Devotion dating back to tradition that Czech refugees sought protection from the Mongol invasion of 1241 along the hill of Hostyn Castle.

In the besieged fortress, as they prayed for Mary's intervention, a sudden violent storm hit and sent the enemy troops fleeing in terror. After that, the Shrine of Hostyn, on the hilltop in Moravia, became a place of pilgrimage and devotion to the Mother of God.

In the Basilica of the National Shrine of the Immaculate Conception, the Chapel of Our Lady of Hostyn (also known as the Czech National Chapel) was a gift of the Czech-American Catholics and was dedicated in June 1983 by Cardinal James Hickey.

Our Lady of Hostyn

The chapel's design illustrates the struggle of the Czech nation as witnessed through the nation's devotion to Mary. A life-size figure of carved wood recalls the rescue of the Czech nation in 1241. Mary is shown with the Christ Child atop rain clouds; a bolt of lightning is in hand. The translation of the inscription on the face of the arch above the statue reads, "Remain a Mother to your people."

A bronze statue of St. John Neumann, native of Bohemia, Bishop of Philadelphia, and the first American male to be canonized, is located at the entrance. The position of the statue facing the Blessed Mother, suggests that the bishop — as if entering the chapel — is leading the way to Our Lady of Hostyn.

HOURS OF OUR LADY

Another name for the Little Office of the Blessed Virgin Mary.

See Little Office of the Blessed Virgin Mary.

HOUSE, MARY'S — *See Ephesus; Loreto, Holy House of.*

HOUSE OF GOLD

Marian title used in the Litany of the Blessed Virgin Mary (also known as the Litany of Loreto). It refers to Mary as a "golden palace" for the Son and God, and to her wearing golden garments as she stood next to her Son after she was assumed into heaven.

See Litany of the Blessed Virgin Mary.

HYMNS, MARIAN

Songs that honor Mary and invoke her intercession. These works can be categorized as antiphons, sequences, canticles, or hymns.

One ancient song to Mary originated in the East, and by the fifth century, came to be known as the *Akathistos*. Both Christological and Marian, it was later translated into Latin and strongly influenced medieval piety in the West.

Antiphons of Our Lady are based on scriptural texts and have been sung at the conclusion of the Evening Prayer in the Liturgy of the Hours. The selection varies according to the time of the liturgical year and includes *Alma Redemptoris Mater, Ave Regina Caelorum, Regina Caeli* and *Salve Regina.*

The *Magnificat* is an example of a canticle, a liturgical song taken from the Bible. Among noted composers who have written music for the *Magnificat* are Johann Sebastian Bach, Wolfgang Amadeus Mozart, and Antonio Vivaldi.

Many others prominent classical composers have written Marian music. Among the best known are Johannes Brahms, Antonín Dvořák, Edvard Grieg, George Frederick Handel, Franz Joseph Haydn, Gustav Holst, Gustav Mahler, Sergei Rachmaninoff, Maurice Ravel, Franz Schubert, Piotr Ilych Tchaikovsky, and Richard Wagner. Schubert's *Ave Maria* is, perhaps, the most universally recognized classical Marian hymn.

Hymns to Mary have also been written in a popular contemporary style. These continue to be sung at Mass, particularly on Marian feasts, and during Marian events, such as May crownings or public recitations of the Rosary. Marian hymns often used at May crownings include *'Tis the Month of Our Mother; On This Day, O Beautiful Mother; Bring Flowers of the Rarest; Hail, Holy Queen Enthroned Above*; and *Immaculate Mary*. A service which is not primarily Marian, the Stations of the Cross, traditionally includes a Marian hymn, the *Stabat Mater* ("At the Cross Her Station Keeping").

See also **Akathistos**; *Antiphons of Our Lady;* **Magnificat; Stabat Mater.**

HYPAPANTE

Name of the February 2 Byzantine feast that corresponds to the Presentation of Our Lord in the Roman Rite. The name (which in English means "meeting") refers to the meeting of the Christ Child with Simeon.

See Presentation.

HYPERDULIA

The special veneration given to Mary because of her unique role in the mystery of Redemption, her exceptional gifts of grace from God, and her preeminence among the saints. *Hyperdulia* is not adoration (*latria*), which is given to God alone, but a form of *dulia*, the homage and honor given the saints and angels.

See Devotions, Marian.

ICONS

Images painted (or "written," in iconographic terms) according to strict religious rules and traditions in an attempt to capture an expression of the divine.

After Jesus, Mary is the most important subject for iconographers. Icons are sacramentals and have held a position of great importance in the tradition of the Eastern Church. In the West, the most prominent Marian icon is *Our Lady of Perpetual Help*.

See Art, Mary in.

ICONSTASIS

A screen separating a church's sanctuary from its nave.

In Byzantine and Orthodox churches, an iconstasis' central or royal door (though which Holy Communion is brought and offered to the faithful) is always flanked by an image of Mary on the left and Christ on the right.

IDOLATRY

Worship of any but the one true God. Idolatry is a violation of the first commandment. Marian devotion is not idolatry or adoration but *hyperdulia*.

See Hyperdulia.

IMITATION OF OUR LADY

Book by Francis Arias, S.J. (1533–1605) patterned after Thomas à Kempis' *Imitation of Christ*.

The author was highly regarded by St. John of Ávila, and St. Francis de Sales, in his *Introduction to a Devout Life*, recommended the reading of his works.

IMMACULATE CONCEPTION

The dogma proclaimed in Christian Tradition and defined 1854 in Pope Pius IX's apostolic constitution *Ineffabilis Deus,* which "holds that the most Blessed Virgin Mary, in the first instant of her conception, by a singular grace and privilege granted by almighty God in view of the merits of Jesus Christ, the Savior of the human race, was preserved free from all stain of original sin."

While there is no explicit revelation of the Immaculate Conception in the scripture, Pope Pius cited three references as the biblical basis defining the Immaculate Conception to be "doctrine revealed by God."

- "I will put enmity between you and the woman, and between your offspring and hers; he will strike at your head, while you strike at his heel" (Gen. 3:15).
- And coming to her, he [Gabriel] said, "Hail, favored one! The Lord is with you" (Lk. 1:28).

• [Elizabeth] cried out in a loud voice and said, "Blessed are you among women, and blessed is the fruit of your womb'" (Lk. 1:42).

Most Eastern and Western Church Fathers had taught that Mary was always free from even the slightest personal sin, but they were unclear about her being exempt from original sin. Some of the Church Fathers and, later, some Doctors of the Church were unable to accept the Immaculate Conception as a revealed truth of faith.

Among those with serious doubts were St. Bernard of Clairvaux (credited with writing the *Memorare*), St. Albert the Great, St. Thomas Aquinas, and St. Bonaventure. They argued the doctrine seemed to exempt Mary from being redeemed by her Son, the Savior of the whole world, including her.

Other theologians, especially Franciscans, challenged and reexamined that apparent stumbling block. The "theological breakthrough" was mainly the work of John Duns Scotus (1266–1308), who introduced the notion of "preservative" redemption.

As later proclaimed by Pope Pius IX, it meant that Mary was free from sin at the first moment of her conception by virtue of special grace from God. This made her free from original sin and so she was a recipient, in a foreseen manner, of the redemptive merits of Christ.

Theologians say her "preredemption" was the infusion of grace at the moment of her soul's entry into her body. This special exemption also made Mary free of concupiscence (desires and tendencies for sinful sense-pleasure) and free of all sin throughout her entire life.

Immaculate Conception

But the "theological path" from the time of Scotus (who came to be called the "Herald of the Immaculate Conception") until Pius IX's encyclical was not a straight or smooth one. It took centuries for the teaching to gain acceptance in the hearts of the faithful.

Five years before issuing *Ineffabilis Deus*, Pope Pius released an encyclical titled *Ubi Primum*, asking bishops around the world what they, their clergy, and the faithful believed concerning the Immaculate Conception. The pontiff also wanted to know whether or not these three groups wished it to be defined as dogma. The response to the latter was strong and positive.

Church historians say among the major influences in the historical development of the Immaculate Conception was *sensus fidelium* (the belief of the faithful), especially in the liturgical worship of the Church. It was this witness behind the gradual extension and elevation of the feast of the Immaculate Conception. And it was the Church at large that helped create the theological climate in which doctrinal difficulties could be addressed and definitively settled.

Four years after Pius' pronouncement, Mary appeared eighteen times to fourteen-year-old Bernadette Soubirous near the little town of Lourdes, France. On March 25, the feast of the Annunciation, the teen asked the visitor to identify herself. At that time, Our Lady declared, "I am the Immaculate Conception."

See also Doctrine, Development of; Lourdes, Our Lady of; Scripture, Mary in.

IMMACULATE CONCEPTION, ARCHCONFRATERNITY OF THE

An association which arose after the apparitions of Mary at Lourdes, France, in 1858. It later combined with the Blue Scapular.

See Confraternity; Fatima, Our Lady of; Scapular of the Immaculate Conception.

IMMACULATE CONCEPTION, BASILICA OF THE NATIONAL SHRINE OF THE

Preeminent Marian shrine of the Roman Catholic Church in the United States of America.

Bishop John Carroll, the country's first prelate, had placed the new nation under the protection of the Immaculate Conception. At the Sixth Provincial Council of Baltimore in 1846, the American hierarchy chose the Blessed Virgin Mary, under the title of the Immaculate Conception, as the patroness of the country, a choice proclaimed by Pope Pius IX the following year.

Immaculate Conception

In the early 1900s, Bishop Thomas J. Shahan, the fourth rector of The Catholic University of America, proposed building a national shrine in the nation's capital to honor Our Lady. When Bishop Shahan met Pope Pius X on the feast of the Assumption 1913, the pontiff offered the bishop his support and gave a personal contribution of $400 to the building fund.

After convincing the board of trustees of The Catholic University to donate land at the southwest corner of the campus for the shrine, Bishop Shahan recruited Catholic groups from across the country to collect contributions for the church's construction. In early 1914, he published the first issue of *Salve Regina*, a newsletter to promote national enthusiasm for building this "monument of love and gratitude, a great hymn in stone."

In 1915, Fr. Bernard McKenna of Philadelphia was named the shrine's first director, and five years later, the cornerstone was laid. The crypt level opened for services in 1924 and was completed by 1931. The center of the Crypt Church features a carved altar dedicated to Our Lady of the Catacombs. More than 30,000 women who held "even a remote kinship with the name Mary" contributed to or are remembered in this altar.

Basilica of the National Shrine of the Immaculate Conception

The Great Depression and World War II interrupted construction on the Byzantine-Romanesque-style upper church; but, after the war, Washington's Archbishop Patrick O'Boyle joined Archbishop John Noll of Fort Wayne, IN, to revive the project. In 1953, the country's bishops pledged their support to secure the funds needed to complete the Great Upper Church. Catholics from parishes nationwide responded overwhelmingly to this appeal, and construction resumed during the Marian Year of 1954.

The Great Upper Church was dedicated in 1959, the same year workers completed the shrine's bell tower, a gift from the Knights of Columbus. In 1990, Pope John Paul II named the shrine a minor basilica.

The shrine features the largest collection of contemporary ecclesiastical art in the United States, including mosaics, sculptures, and paintings. It has more than sixty-five chapels and oratories dedicated to Our Lady, under a variety of Marian devotions and images associated with the various nations and ethnic groups worldwide whose citizens and descendants now make their home in America.

See also Mary Garden.

IMMACULATE CONCEPTION, CHAPLET OF THE

Devotion written by St. John Berchmans (1599–1621), who recited it daily to obtain, through the intercession of Mary, the grace never to commit any sin against the virtue of purity. This sacramental consists of three sets of four beads with a medal of the Immaculate Conception at the end.

The prayer begins:

O God, come to my aid; O Lord make haste to help me in my time of need.

On the first set of beads:

I thank Thee, O Eternal Father, for having by Thy Almighty power preserved Mary, most holy, Thy blessed daughter from the stain of original sin.

This is followed by an Our Father and four Hail Marys. After each Hail Mary, this prayer is said:

Blessed be the pure, most holy and Immaculate Conception of the Blessed Virgin Mary.

On the second set of beads:

I thank Thee, O Eternal Son, for having by Thy wisdom preserved Mary, most holy, Thy blessed mother from the stain of original sin.

This is followed by an Our Father and four Hail Marys. After each Hail Mary, this prayer is said:

Blessed be the pure, most holy and Immaculate Conception of the Blessed Virgin Mary.

On the third set of beads:

I thank Thee, O Holy Spirit Eternal, for having by Thy love preserved Mary, most holy, Thy Blessed Spouse from the stain of original sin.

This is followed by an Our Father and four Hail Marys. After each Hail Mary, this prayer is said:

Blessed be the pure, most holy and Immaculate Conception of the Blessed Virgin Mary.

The chaplet concludes with a Glory Be.

IMMACULATE CONCEPTION, FEAST OF THE

This solemnity and holy day of obligation, celebrated on December 8, commemorates the fact that from the first moment of her conception, Mary was preserved from original sin and filled with grace.

The present form dates back to December 8, 1854, when Pope Pius IX defined the dogma of the Immaculate Conception.

An earlier feast which testified to the long-standing belief in this truth was observed in the East by the eighth century, in Ireland in the ninth, and, later, throughout Europe.

In 1846, Mary was proclaimed patroness of the United States under this title.

IMMACULATE CONCEPTION OF EL VIEJO, OUR LADY OF THE

Image and devotion which, tradition holds, has been venerated in El Viejo, Nicaragua, since the sixteenth century when the statue was brought to America by a relative of St. Teresa of Ávila.

Some maintain it was her brother, Rodrigo de Cepeda Ahumada, who — never traveling without it — had it with him when he arrived in the port city of Realejo and later moved to the Franciscan mission of El Viejo.

There, a room in his house became an oratory visited by neighbors, who were attracted by the beautiful expression on the statue's face. When Cepeda received orders to transfer to Peru, he planned on taking the image with him, but bad weather kept postponing the move until he realized it was God's will that he give up his beloved *Immaculata* and that she stay among the people who had also come to love her. The Virgin has never left Nicaragua and is now in a basilica that bears her name.

The image *Our Lady of the Immaculate Conception of El Viejo* is a woodcarving about thirty-three inches tall. Mary is dressed in beautiful robes, which are changed often. The statue is kept in a silver reliquary.

The sanctuary of the basilica is unique in that it holds a valuable collection of many different kinds of silver objects given in gratitude for favors received. Each year, on December 6, these items are taken out to the public plaza, where the people gather to clean and polish them. This is known as "The Washing of the Silver."

In Nicaragua, where *La Purísima* is patroness, the traditional image of the Immaculate Conception can be found in many churches and homes. Mary's December 8 feast is a national celebration. On its eve, the famous *Gritería* (shouting) takes place. Families build ornate home altars that can be seen from outside. People looking in yell, "Who is the cause of our joy?" and the residents answer, "Mary's Conception." Then, the visitors are treated to sweets and special dishes.

Immaculate Heart of Mary

IMMACULATE HEART OF MARY

Devotion that began in the Middle Ages, was fostered by St. John Eudes (1601–1680) in France through his book *The Admirable Heart of Mary,* and gained a renewed popularity after the apparitions of Mary in Fatima in 1917.

It recognizes the Heart of Mary as symbolic of her maternal love, which assented wholeheartedly to Jesus, to his coming, and to his redeeming humanity on the cross. It underscores that such love from Mary draws one ever closer to Christ.

St. John Eudes was the first to celebrate a Mass and Divine Office of Mary under this title. A feast — celebrated on different dates in various places — had been authorized in 1799. Now, the memorial is on the Saturday following the second Sunday after Pentecost, the day following the Feast of the Sacred Heart of Jesus. In 1942, Pope Pius XII consecrated the entire human race to Mary under this title; in 1944, he ordered the feast to be observed throughout the Church in order to obtain Mary's intercession for "peace among nations, freedom for the Church, the conversion of sinners, the love of purity, and the practice of virtue."

That prayer reads:

Most Holy Virgin Mary, tender Mother of men, to fulfill the desires of the Sacred Heart of Jesus and the request of the Vicar of Your Son on earth, we consecrate ourselves and our families to your Sorrowful and Immaculate Heart, O Queen of the Most Holy Rosary, and we recommend to you, all the people of our country and all the world.

Please accept our consecration, dearest Mother, and use us as you wish to accomplish your designs in the world.

O Sorrowful and Immaculate Heart of Mary, Queen of the Most Holy Rosary, and Queen of the World, rule over us, together with the Sacred Heart of Jesus Christ, Our King. Save us from the spreading flood of modern paganism; kindle in our hearts and homes the love of purity, the practice of a virtuous life, an ardent zeal for souls, and a desire to pray the Rosary more faithfully.

We come with confidence to You, O Throne of Grace and Mother of Fair Love. Inflame us with the same Divine Fire which has inflamed your own Sorrowful and Immaculate Heart. Make our hearts and homes Your shrine, and through us, make the Heart of Jesus, together with your rule, triumph in every heart and home. Amen.

See also Admirable Heart of Mary, The.

IMMACULATE HEART OF MARY, CHAPLET OF THE

A five-decade Rosary is used for this chaplet. The Sign of the Cross is made five times, in veneration of the Christ's five wounds. The prayer said on the five large beads is, "Sorrowful and Immaculate Heart of Mary, pray for those who seek refuge in you." On each set of ten smaller beads, this prayer is said: "Holy Mother, save us through your Immaculate Heart's flame of love." The devotion concludes with three recitations of the Glory Be.

IMMACULATE HEART OF MARY, CONSECRATION TO THE — *See Immaculate Heart of Mary.*

INCARNATION

The "coming-into-flesh," or taking of human nature, by the Second Person of the Trinity.

Jesus became human as the Son of Mary, being miraculously conceived by the power of the Holy Spirit, without ceasing to be divine. His divine Person hypostatically unites his divine and human natures.

The union of the divine and human natures in Christ is a permanent one. Starting from the moment of his human conception, it continues through his life on earth, his sufferings and death, his resurrection from the dead and ascension to glory with the Father, his sending the Holy Spirit upon the Apostles and the Church, and his unending mediation with the Father for the salvation of human beings.

INCOMPARABLE VIRGIN MARY, THE

Work written by St. Peter Canisius (1521–1597), a Jesuit theologian and Doctor of the Church, which first appeared in 1577.

It quotes more than 4,000 biblical texts in its defense of the Church's Marian doctrines against positions being promoted during the

St. Peter Canisius

Reformation that were challenging and discrediting those teachings.

INEFFABILIS DEUS

Papal bull in which Pope Pius IX solemnly defined the dogma of the Immaculate Conception. Its title in English is *The Ineffable God.* The term refers to the fact that God is indescribable.

The work begins:

> God ineffable — whose ways are mercy and truth, whose will is omnipotence itself, and whose wisdom "reaches from end to end mightily, and orders all things sweetly" — having foreseen from all eternity the lamentable wretchedness of the entire human race which would result from the sin of Adam, decreed, by a plan hidden from the centuries, to complete the first work of his goodness by a mystery yet more wondrously sublime through the Incarnation of the Word.

See Immaculate Conception.

INFANCY NARRATIVES

First two chapters of the Gospels of Matthew and Luke that describe Jesus' lineage and Mary's role in his conception, birth, infancy, and childhood.

See Scripture, Mary in.

INKPOT, OUR LADY OF THE — *See Star of the Sea.*

INSTITUTE OF THE BLESSED VIRGIN MARY

Religious community founded by Englishwoman Mary Ward in 1609.

Her goal was an independent self-governing congregation patterned after a model of the Society of Jesus, free of the confines of the cloister, and responding to the urgent needs of her time.

In 1847, five members from Ireland went to Canada to begin the work of educating the children of the many Irish immigrants who had gone there. By 1881, the long distance from Ireland, and difficulties in communication with a motherhouse on the other side of the Atlantic Ocean, warranted that the institute in North America become an independent generalate. In 2003, the two were reunited.

INTERCESSION OF MARY

Prayers and petitions by Mary to God on behalf of another.

As the bishops explained in their Vatican II document, *Dogmatic Constitution on the Church* (60–63):

There is but one Mediator as we know from the words of the apostle, "for there is one God and one mediator of God and men, the man Christ Jesus, who gave himself a redemption for all." The maternal duty of Mary toward men in no wise obscures or diminishes this unique mediation of Christ, but rather shows his power. For all the salvific influence of the Blessed Virgin on men originates, not from some inner necessity, but from the divine pleasure. It flows forth from the superabundance of the merits of Christ, rests on his mediation, depends entirely on it and draws all its power from it. In no way does it impede, but rather does it foster the immediate union of the faithful with Christ.

Predestined from eternity by that decree of divine providence which determined the incarnation of the Word to be the Mother of God, the Blessed Virgin was in this earth the virgin Mother of the Redeemer, and above all others and in a singular way the generous associate and humble handmaid of the Lord. She conceived, brought forth and nourished Christ. She presented him to the Father in the temple, and was united with him by compassion as he died on the cross. In this singular way she cooperated by her obedience, faith, hope and burning charity in the work of the Savior in giving back supernatural life to souls. Wherefore she is our mother in the order of grace.

This maternity of Mary in the order of grace began with the consent which she gave in faith at the Annunciation and which she sustained without wavering beneath the cross, and lasts until the eternal fulfillment of all the elect. Taken up to heaven she did not lay aside this salvific duty, but by her constant intercession continued to bring us

the gifts of eternal salvation. By her maternal charity, she cares for the brethren of her Son, who still journey on earth surrounded by dangers and cultics, until they are led into the happiness of their true home. Therefore the Blessed Virgin is invoked by the Church under the titles of Advocate, Auxiliatrix, Adjutrix, and Mediatrix. This, however, is to be so understood that it neither takes away from nor adds anything to the dignity and efficaciousness of Christ the one Mediator.

For no creature could ever be counted as equal with the Incarnate Word and Redeemer. Just as the priesthood of Christ is shared in various ways both by the ministers and by the faithful, and as the one goodness of God is really communicated in different ways to His creatures, so also the unique mediation of the Redeemer does not exclude but rather gives rise to a manifold cooperation which is but a sharing in this one source.

The Church does not hesitate to profess this subordinate role of Mary. It knows it through unfailing experience of it and commends it to the hearts of the faithful, so that encouraged by this maternal help they may the more intimately adhere to the Mediator and Redeemer.

By reason of the gift and role of divine maternity, by which she is united with her Son, the Redeemer, and with His singular graces and functions, the Blessed Virgin is also intimately united with the Church. As St. Ambrose taught, the Mother of God is a type of the Church in the order of faith, charity and perfect union with Christ. For in the mystery of the Church, which is itself rightly called mother and virgin, the Blessed Virgin stands out in eminent and singular fashion as exemplar both of virgin and mother. By her belief and obedience, not knowing man but overshadowed by the Holy Spirit, as the new Eve she brought forth on earth the very Son of the Father, showing an undefiled faith, not in the word of the ancient serpent, but in that of God's messenger. The Son whom she brought forth is He whom God placed as the first-born among many brethren, namely the faithful, in whose birth and education she cooperates with a maternal love.

See also Co-Redemptrix, Co-Redemptorist.

IRISH PENAL ROSARY

Rosary designed to be used inconspicuously during times of religious oppression in Ireland. Traditionally, it features a string of ten beads with a cross on one end and a ring on the other. The thumb is placed in the ring for the first decade, the index finger for the second decade, and so on.

ISLAM, MARY IN

Muslim scholars note that Mary is held in high esteem in Islam and the Koran, pointing out that an entire chapter of that holy book is titled *Maryam*, the Arabic for "Mary," a name that remains popular for daughters in Muslim families. They add that it was the Prophet Muhammad himself who said, "The best of the world's women is Mary" and, "Among women none attained perfection except Mary the daughter of `Imran, and Asiya the wife of Pharaoh."

The Koran speaks of Mary's miraculous pregnancy and the birth of Jesus. While not going into many details, it presents Mary as a chaste and pious woman who was chosen, purified, and preferred over all of the women of creation to be the one to give birth to the "Messenger Jesus" through the command of God.

The English translations of some verses from the Koran which speak of the story of Mary include:

Surah 66:12:

And Mary, daughter of `Imran, who attended to her private parts [guarded her chastity], and she sincerely believed in the Words of her Lord, and His Books; and she was one of the devout.

Surah 3:42–43:

And [remember] when the angels said: O Mary! Verily, Allah has chosen you, purified you, and chosen you above the women of the worlds. O Mary! Submit yourself with obedience to your Lord [Allah] and prostrate yourself, and bow down along with those who bow down [for Him].

Surah 19:16–31:

And mention in the Book Mary [the Book of Surah], when she withdrew in seclusion from her family to a place facing east. She placed a screen from them; then We sent to her Our Spirit [Gabriel], and he appeared before her in the form of a man in all respects. She said: Verily, I seek refuge with the Most Gracious [Allah] from you, if you do fear Allah. He said: I am only a messenger from your Lord, [to announce] to you the gift of a righteous son.

She said: How can I have a son, when no man has touched me, nor am I unchaste? He said: So [it will be], your Lord said: "That is easy for Me [Allah]." And [We wish] to appoint him as a sign to mankind and a mercy from Us [Allah], and it is a matter [already] decreed [by Allah].

So she conceived him, and she withdrew with him to a remote place. And the pains of childbirth drove her to the trunk of a date palm. She said: "Would that I had died before this, and had been forgotten and out of sight!" Then (one) cried from beneath her, saying: "Grieve not: your Lord has provided a water stream under you. And shake the trunk of date palm towards you, it will let fall fresh ripe dates upon you. So eat and drink and be glad. And if you see any human being, say: 'Verily, I have vowed a fast unto the Most Gracious [Allah] so I shall not speak to any human being this day.'"

Then she brought him [the baby] to her people, carrying him. They said: "O Mary! Indeed you have brought a fabricated thing. O sister [i.e., the like] of Aaron! Your father was not a man who used to commit adultery, nor your mother was an unchaste woman." Then she pointed to him. They said: "How can we talk to one who is a child in the cradle?" He (Jesus) said: "Verily, I am a slave of Allah, He has given me the Scripture and made me a Prophet; And He has made me blessed wheresoever I be, and has enjoined on me prayer, and zakat (alms), as long as I live."

In their Vatican II document *Nostra Aetate* (*Declaration on the Relation of the Church to Non-Christian Religions*), the bishops wrote:

The Church regards with esteem also the Muslims. They adore the one God, living and subsisting in himself; merciful and all-powerful, the Creator of heaven and earth, who has spoken to men; they take pains to submit wholeheartedly to even his inscrutable decrees, just as Abraham, with whom the faith of Islam takes pleasure in linking itself, submitted to God. Though they do not acknowledge Jesus as God, they revere him as a prophet. They also honor Mary, his virgin Mother; at times they even call on her with devotion. In addition, they await the day of judgment when God will render their deserts to all those who have been raised up from the dead. Finally, they value the moral life and worship God especially through prayer, almsgiving, and fasting.

Since in the course of centuries not a few quarrels and hostilities have arisen between Christians and Moslems, this sacred synod urges all to forget the past and to work sincerely for mutual understanding and to preserve as well as to promote together for the benefit of all mankind social justice and moral welfare, as well as peace and freedom.

Islamic devotion to Mary includes shrines in Muslim countries, such as Meryemana near Ephesus in Turkey.

See also Ephesus.

IVIRON, OUR LADY OF

Icon once kept in a small chapel at the gate to Moscow's Red Square and venerated as the special protectress of that city. The word "Iviron" means "of Georgian origin."

In pre-revolutionary Russia, it was traditional for the tsar to first visit this shrine when coming to the city. Miracles were attributed to the intercession of Our Lady of Iviron, and the icon was taken in a coach drawn by six horses to visit the houses of the sick and to be present at weddings, baptisms, and other religious celebrations. Whenever the original painting was removed from the shrine, it was replaced by a replica.

The icon itself is a reproduction of a famous icon in the Greek Orthodox monastery of Iviron on Mount Athos, a community founded in the tenth century by three Georgian monks. Pious tradition holds that the monks observed a flaming shape on the ocean and, at the same time, Mary appeared in the dream of an old Georgian hermit monk named Gabriel, who lived in the monastery of the Georgians in the Mount Athos community. Mary ordered the Georgian monk to go to the beach, walk on the waves, and retrieve the icon. He followed her instructions, as onlookers watched in won-der, and then placed the icon in the church of the Georgian monastery of the Iberians.

At the beginning of the seventeenth century, Tsar Alexis of Russia suddenly fell ill and felt compelled to ask that the "Virgin of the Gate" be brought from Athos to heal him. The monks were not willing to part with the image and decided to make and send a copy. This was taken to Moscow in 1648, and the tsar was instantly cured.

The image was placed in the small chapel on the square in front of the Kremlin. Following the 1917 revolution, the shrine was destroyed, but the Marian image was saved and, for many years, was hidden in a closed monastery. Later, it was moved to the Cathedral of Christ the Savior, in the Sokolniki section of Moscow.

JASNA GORA, OUR LADY OF — *See Czestochowa, Our Lady of.*

JESUS AND MARY — *See Mother of God; Scripture, Mary in.*

JESUITS

Popular name for the Society of Jesus, founded by St. Ignatius Loyola (1491–1556).

See Christian Life Community.

JOACHIM AND ANNE

Husband and wife who were the parents of Mary.

Anne is also called Ann, Anna, and Hannah (the Hebrew word for "grace"). Joachim is also listed as Cleophas, Eliacim, Heli, Jonachir, and Sadoc. No details of their lives are extant; information about them is taken from apocryphal sources.

The apocryphal *Protoevengelium of St. James* says that Joachim was born in Nazareth and married Anne while both were young. but they were childless. When he was ridiculed for this, Joachim fasted for forty days in the desert until an angel announced he and Anne would have a child. The writings also say both prayed for a child, and an angel appeared to Anne. telling her she would have a child who "shall be blessed by

St. Anne

all the world." It was reported that Joachim died after witnessing the presentation of Jesus in the Temple in Jerusalem.

Both St. Joachim and St. Anne were venerated in the Eastern Church since its earliest times. Anne became popular in the West in the thirteenth century, and Joachim in the sixteen century. July 26 is their feast day.

See also Apocryphal writing, Mary in.

JOHN XXIII, POPE

Pontiff from 1958 to 1963 who convoked the Second Vatican Council (the twenty-first ecumenical council) but died before it completed its work. He was beatified by Pope John Paul II in 2000.

In his 1959 encyclical *Grata Recordatio* (on the Rosary: prayer for the Church, missions, international, and social problems), Pope John wrote to Catholic bishops worldwide:

> These pleasant memories of our younger days [and encyclicals on the Rosary issued annually by Pope Leo XXIII] have not faded or vanished as the years of our life have passed. On the contrary, we want to declare in complete frankness and simplicity that the years have made Mary's rosary all the dearer to us. We never fail to recite it each day in its entirety and we intend to recite it with particular devotion during the coming month . . . Before we conclude this encyclical we also wish to ask you, Venerable Brethren, to recite Mary's rosary through the month of October with particular devotion, and to entreat the Virgin Mother of God in suppliant prayer, for another intention which is dear to our heart: that the Roman Synod may bring many blessings and benefits upon this city; that the forthcoming Ecumenical Council, in which you will participate by your presence and your advice, will add wondrous growth to the universal Church; and that the renewed vigor of all the Christian virtues which We hope this Council will produce will also serve as an invitation and incentive to reunion for Our Brethren and children who are separated from this Apostolic See.

Pope John XXIII

The council opened on October 11, the Feast of the Purification of Mary. The pontiff said he selected that date because it was the anniversary of what the Ecumenical Council of Ephesus on October 11, 431, declared and proclaimed: that Mary was *Theotokos,* or Mother of God. "Mary," he said, "God's Virgin Mother, on this feast day of her noble motherhood, gives it her gracious protection." And in his conclusion prayed: "Mary, help of Christians, help of bishops . . . prosper now this work of ours, and by your kindly aid bring it to a happy, successful conclusion."

A Marian prayer by Blessed John XXIII reads:

O Mary, your name has been on my lips and in my heart from my early infancy. When I was a child I learned to love you as a Mother, turn to you in danger, and trust your intercession. You see in my heart the desire to know the truth, to practice virtue, to be prudent and just, strong and patient, a brother to all.

O Mary, help me to keep to my purpose of living as a faithful disciple of Jesus, for the building up of the Christian society and the joy of the holy Catholic Church. I greet you, Mother, morning and evening; I pray to you as I go on my way; from you I hope for the inspiration and encouragement that will enable me to fulfill the sacred promises of my earthly vocation, give glory to God, and win eternal salvation. O Mary! Like you in Bethlehem and on Golgotha, I too wish to stay always close to Jesus. He is the eternal King of all ages and all peoples. Amen.

See also Vatican II.

JOHN PAUL II, POPE

Pontiff from 1978 to 2005 who, among his many accomplishments, was noted for the central role that devotion to Mary played in his life and ministry.

As a teen in his native Poland, he became a member of the Sodality of Mary in 1934, was twice elected to serve as the local chapter's president, and made his first pilgrimage to the Marian shrine at Czestochowa.

Ordained an auxiliary bishop of Krakow in 1958, he chose as his motto *Totus tuus,* a shortened version of St. Louis de Montfort's Marian consecration: "I am totally yours (*totus tuus*), and all that I possess is yours. I accept you in all that is mine. Give me your heart, O Mary."

Two decades later, the newly elected pontiff would include the letter M — for Mary — on his coat of arms and, during his pontificate, would fix April 28 as the feast for St. Louis in the Universal Church. He would also intro-

duce the Luminous Mysteries to the Rosary, a devotion that he noted in his 2002 apostolic letter, *Rosarium Virginis Mariae* (*Rosary of the Virgin Mary*):

Twenty-four years ago, on 29 October 1978, scarcely two weeks after my election to the See of Peter, I frankly admitted: "The Rosary is my favorite prayer. A marvelous prayer! Marvelous in its simplicity and its depth. [. . .]. It can be said that the Rosary is, in some sense, a prayer-commentary on the final chapter of the Vatican II Constitution Lumen Gentium, a chapter which discusses the wondrous presence of the Mother of God in the mystery of Christ and the Church. Against the background of the words Ave Maria the principal events of the life of Jesus Christ pass before the eyes of the soul. They take shape in the complete series of the joyful, sorrowful and glorious mysteries, and they put us in living communion with Jesus through — we might say — the heart of his Mother. At the same time our heart can embrace in the decades of the Rosary all the events that make up the lives of individuals, families, nations, the Church, and all mankind. Our personal concerns and those of our neighbor, especially those who are closest to us, who are dearest to us. Thus the simple prayer of the Rosary marks the rhythm of human life."

With these words, dear brothers and sisters, I set the first year of my Pontificate within the daily rhythm of the Rosary. Today, as I begin the twenty-fifth year of my service as the Successor of Peter, I wish to do the same. How many graces have I received in these years from the Blessed Virgin through the Rosary: *Magnificat anima mea Dominum*! I wish to lift up my thanks to the Lord in the words of his Most Holy Mother, under whose protection I have placed my Petrine ministry: *Totus Tuus!*"

Pope John Paul II

John Paul II credited Mary with saving his life from an assassination attempt in St. Peter's Square on May 13, 1981, which left him severely wounded. Pointing out that the attack had occurred on the feast of Our Lady of Fatima, he would say, "One hand fired, and another guided the bullet." A year later, in Fatima, he placed the bullet that doctors took from his body in the crown on Mary's statue there.

In his first encyclical, *Redemptor Hominis* (*Redeemer of Man*, 1979), John Paul II wrote of Mary's role in salvation history:

We can say that the mystery of the Redemption took shape beneath the heart of the Virgin of Nazareth when she pronounced her "fiat." From then on, under the special influence of the Holy Spirit, this heart, the

heart of both a virgin and a mother, has always followed the work of her Son and has gone out to all those whom Christ has embraced and continues to embrace with inexhaustible love. For that reason her heart must also have the inexhaustibility of a mother. The special characteristic of the motherly love that the Mother of God inserts in the mystery of the Redemption and the life of the Church finds expression in its exceptional closeness to man and all that happens to him.

In 1987, during a Marian Year to mark the 2,000th anniversary of the birth of Our Lady, John Paul II issued *Redemptoris Mater* (*Mother of the Redeemer*), his encyclical on the role of Mary in the mystery of Christ and her active and exemplary presence in the life of the Church. In it, he wrote of the "Marian Church" (the Church of disciples) which preceded and made possible the "Petrine Church" (the Church of office and authority*)*.

The pontiff wrote:

In the redemptive economy of grace, brought about through the action of the Holy Spirit, there is a unique correspondence between the moment of the Incarnation of the Word and the moment of the birth of the Church. The person who links these two moments is Mary: Mary at Nazareth and Mary in the Upper Room at Jerusalem. In both cases her discreet yet essential presence indicates the path of "birth from the Holy Spirit." Thus she who is present in the mystery of Christ as Mother becomes — by the will of the Son and the power of the Holy Spirit — present in the mystery of the Church. In the Church too she continues to be a maternal presence, as is shown by the words spoken from the Cross: "Woman, behold your son!"; "Behold, your mother." (24)

At Pope John Paul II's funeral Mass in April 2005, Cardinal Joseph Ratzinger (who later that month would be elected Pope Benedict XVI) concluded his homily by speaking of the pontiff's love of Our Lady:

> The Holy Father found the purest reflection of God's mercy in the Mother of God. He, who at an early age had lost his own mother, loved his divine mother all the more. He heard the words of the crucified Lord as addressed personally to him: "Behold your Mother." And so he did as the beloved disciple did: he took her into his own home . . . *Totus tuus*. And from the mother he learned to conform himself to Christ.
>
> None of us can ever forget how in that last Easter Sunday of his life, the Holy Father, marked by suffering, came once more to the window of the Apostolic Palace and one last time gave his blessing urbi et orbi. We can be sure that our beloved Pope is standing today at the window of the Father's house, that he sees us and blesses us. Yes, bless us, Holy Father. We entrust your dear soul to the Mother of God, your Mother, who guided you each day and who will guide you now to the eternal glory of her Son, our Lord Jesus Christ. Amen.

JOY OF ISRAEL

Marian title from the Litany of Mary, Queen which is also used in other liturgical prayers. The description was originally used by the high priest Joakim and the elders of the Israelites when they congratulated and blessed Judith, who played a crucial role in the Israelites' overcoming the Assyrians (See Jud. 15:8–10).

See Litany of Mary, Queen.

JOY, OUR LADY OF

Marian title.

The image of Our Lady of Joy (or Our Lady, the Joy of All Afflicted) has varied and has been depicted in a variety of media, from paintings and icons (such as an eighteenth-century piece located in Transfiguration Church at Ordynka, Moscow) to sculptures (including Jacques Lipchitz' work [*Notre Dame de Liese*] in New Harmony, IN) to stamps (including Brazil's 1983 Christmas issues).

See also Cause of Our Joy, Our Lady; Joys of Mary.

JOYFUL MYSTERIES OF THE ROSARY
— *See Rosary.*

JOYS OF MARY

Traditional devotion commemorating the principal joys of Mary.

Although originally only five events were noted, the number later grew to seven to match Mary's sorrows.

Devotion to the "Seven Joys of the Blessed Virgin Mary" was especially popular in medieval England up to the time of Henry VIII's breaking away from the Church. As part of the Franciscan Crown Rosary, the Seven Joys were propagated worldwide by members of the order.

JOYS OF MARY

Traditionally, the joys are: the Annunciation, the Visitation, the Nativity of Christ, the Adoration of the Magi, the Finding in the Temple, the Resurrection, and the Assumption.

See also Rosary of the Seven Joys of Our Lady (Franciscan Crown Rosary).

KATERI INDIAN ROSARY

A chaplet created in the twentieth century associated with Blessed Kateri Tekakwitha (1656–1680), the "Lily of the Mohawks," and promoted by the Tekakwitha League.

The Rosary's twenty-four beads represent the years of Kateri's life. The first eight-bead set is brown, the color of the earth, and an Our Father is recited on each. The second set is red, the color of blood, and a Hail Mary is prayed on each bead. And the third set is clear, like water. A Glory Be is recited on each.

Francis Tsonnatouan created a devotion known as "Catherine's Chaplet," shortly after Blessed Kateri's death. He and his wife had lived in the same mission village with the young Mohawk and, recognizing her holiness, had sought her advice. After her death, he kept some of her relics and a small chaplet consisting of a cross and five beads. The Creed was said on the cross, followed by an Our Father, a Hail Mary, and three Glory Bes.

See also Chaplet; Rosary.

KEVELAER, OUR LADY OF

Devotion associated with the image *Our Lady, Comforter of the Afflicted.*

On three separate occasions near Christmas 1641, as Heinrich Busman was praying in front of a crucifix in a field outside the town of Keve-laer, Germany, he heard a voice telling him, "Build here a little chapel for me."

Only a little while later, his wife had a vision and saw a picture similar to one she had seen on two small copper prints in the possession of two soldiers from the town. The two men were combatants in the Thirty Years' War between France and Germany and had visited the shrine of Our Lady of Luxembourg to pray for the safety of their captain, then a prisoner of war. Before leaving the shrine, they had bought small prints of the image known as *Our Lady, Comforter of the Afflicted.*

Busman purchased one of the three-by-four-inch prints and placed it in the small shrine he erected. In 1654, the Chapel of Mercy was built to house the image. Later, a basilica and facilities for pilgrims were added, but the picture remains in the Chapel of Mercy.

Today more than half a million people visit the shrine annually.

See also Consolation, Our Lady of.

KIBEHO (RWANDA), OUR LADY OF

Image and devotion based on apparitions reported by seven teenagers and young adults from 1981 to 1989.

On November 28, 1981, Alphonsine Mumureke, a boarding student at Kibeho College — a school in Kibeho, Rwanda, run by the Benebikira Sisters — was serving tables at the noon meal when she heard someone call to her as "my daughter." The young woman turned but saw no one addressing her. Curious, she left the dining room to find out who had spoken to her. No one else had heard the voice.

In the hallway, Alphonsine immediately saw a beautiful lady. The girl later reported the visitor's hands were folded in front of her and her skin was not the white often used to portray Mary in works of art; the student could not determine the color. But the woman had a beauty beyond compare. She wore a white veil and a seamless white dress and, as was the custom among Rwandan villagers, she was shoeless.

When Alphonsine asked her who she was, the woman answered, "I am the Mother of the Word," answering her in Kinyarwanda, the language of Rwanda's people. Mary said she had heard the teen's prayers and asked her to become a member of the Legion of Mary to help her realize her vocation.

After seeing Mary rise in the air and disappear, Alphonsine collapsed on the hallway floor and remained there for about a quarter of an hour. When a nun was finally able to rouse her, the teen told the others what had happened. Others had heard her talking but had not seen or heard the visitor, so her words were met with disbelief — and even scorn — until, over time, six others were also granted the privilege of seeing and speaking with Our Lady, who continued to call for reconciliation, penance, and prayer.

The seven visionaries were: Alphonsine Mumureke, Anathalie Mukamazimpaka, Marie-Claire Mukangang, Stephanie Mukamurenzi, Agnes Kamagaju, Emmanuel Segatashya, and Vestine Salina.

Several of the seers had visions for only a few months and a few for only six months to a year. Alphonsine continued to have apparitions until November 28, 1989.

From the time of the first apparition, news of the event spread, attracting the public's attention. A devotion to Our Lady of Kibeho, the Mother of the Word, developed. The apparitions received ecclesiastical approval in 1988. In 2001, the Holy See released a declaration by Bishop Augustin Misago of Gikongoro, Rwanda, on the apparitions witnessed by Alphonsine, Anathalie, and Marie-Claire that took place in 1982–83. He declared his belief that those apparitions were authentic, met the criteria established by the Church in the matter of private apparitions and revelations, and were a warning about attitudes that led to the 1994 ethnic genocide in the country.

It was reported that among those killed was Marie-Claire and all of Alphonsine's family, except the seer herself.

See also Apparitions of Mary.

KNOCK, OUR LADY OF

Image and devotion based on a reported apparition in Knock, Ireland, on the evening of August 21, 1879, when fifteen witnesses, ranging in age from six to seventy-five, saw Mary, St. Joseph, and St. John the Evangelist.

The three appeared in a tableaux in front of the parish church. A lighted area near the gable of the building was seen by all who were in the area. The visionaries reported the three figures were clothed in dazzling white. Mary's robe was covered by a large white cloak that fastened at the throat, and her head held a brilliant crown surmounted with glittering crosses. There was a rose where the headpiece fitted to her brow. She looked up and seemed to be praying. St. Joseph stood to her right; St. John, at an angle, stood to her left. Behind them was an altar with a large cross; in front of the altar stood a young lamb.

The scene lasted for a little more than ninety minutes, and neither Mary nor the saints spoke. Thus, the image is sometimes referred to as *Our Lady of Silence.*

Within two months of the apparitions, a commission was set up to study the event. Evidence was taken from fourteen witnesses, and their testimony was later found to be "trustworthy and satisfactory" by the priests delegated to examine them on behalf of the Church.

The parish church became a pilgrimage site, with miracles attributed to the intercession of Our Lady of Knock. In 1976, a new church was dedicated there, and Pope John Paul II visited Knock in 1979.

Today, the shrine has about one million pilgrims annually.

See also Apparitions of Mary.

KNOTS, THE VIRGIN WHO UNTIES

An ancient motif or theme.

The *Knotenlöserin* (a woman who loosens knots) dates back to St. Irenaeus, a second-century theologian who saw the relationship between Eve and Mary as similar to that between Adam and Christ. The second unties (or undoes) what the first one knotted (or did).

This traditional German Marian devotion is particularly popular in Argentina under its Spanish equivalent: *La Virgen Desatanudos.* The devotion was brought to that country in the early 1980s by Archbishop Jorge Mario Bergoglio, S.J., who at that time was rector at the Jesuit University of El Salvador in Buenos Aires. The archbishop had come upon the image at the Church of St. Peter am Perlach (where it is known under its German name) during a visit to Augsburg.

That painting, attributed to Baroque German artist Johann Melchior Georg Schmittdner, dates back to the early seventeenth century. Mary is shown with an angel on her left side handing her a white ribbon full of knots. As the ribbon continues through Mary's hands, it falls to her right side, with the knots untied, into the hands of a second angel.

KROLOWA POLSKI (QUEEN OF POLAND) — *See* Czestochowa, Our Lady of.

LA CHAPELLE, OUR LADY OF

Ancient Marian image in a shrine in the Church of La Chapelle in Brussels, Belgium.

LA CONQUISTADORA

Devotion and image.

Around Christmas 1625, Fr. Alonso Benavides, the Franciscan superior of the New Mexico missions, brought a small wooden statue of Mary to the church of the Assumption in Santa Fe. A representation of the Assumption of Our Lady, it was decorated with bright arabesques over gold leaf. The statue became the focus of a Marian confraternity, and her devotees dressed her to look like a Spanish queen in the style of that era.

The image was given the official title *Our Lady of the Rosary*, but was popularly referred to as *La Conquistadora* because she had come in the days of the conquistadors. When fighting erupted between the Pueblos and Spaniards in 1680, the statue was moved to what is now Juarez, Mexico, and enshrined in a chapel dedicated to her. In 1693, the colonists set out to reconquer Santa Fe and placed their efforts under her protection. After meeting with success, they began an annual thanksgiving observance in 1694, carrying the image in procession to a shrine of boughs and singing a novena of Masses.

The image was crowned in 1954 with an Episcopal Coronation and with a Papal Coronation in 1960.

La Conquistadora

LA LECHE, OUR LADY OF

Image and devotion.

A depiction of Mary nursing the Infant Jesus was drawn on the walls of Rome's catacombs. The devotion was particularly popular in Spain toward the end of the sixteenth century; among its promoters was King Philip II, who erected a shrine to Our Lady of La Leche in Madrid. Unfortunately, the building was destroyed in 1937, during the Spanish Civil War.

In the early seventeenth century, Spanish settlers built the New World's first shrine to Mary in St. Augustine, FL. The chapel was dedicated to *Nuestra Señora de La Leche y Buen Parto* (*Our Nursing Mother of Happy Delivery*) and featured a small statue depicting Mary holding the Infant Child with her right arm and offering him her breast.

The original Marian image and chapel were destroyed during battles in the region, but the present chapel was begun in 1915, with a statue of Our Lady of La Leche that replicates the original.

Recent excavations, however, have revealed what are believed to be the foundation for the first stone chapel, and the shrine remains a center of devotion, most notably for mothers and mothers-to-be.

LA MORENITA, THE LITTLE BROWN ONE — *See Guadalupe, Our Lady of.*

LA NAVAL

Devotion and image also known as *Our Lady of the Rosary of the Philippines*.

The hardwood statue, with the faces of Mary and the Child Jesus carved from ivory, depicts a Filipina in royal clothes typical of seventeenth-century Spain. The piece was commissioned by the Spanish governor general on the death of his father in 1593. Because victories at sea became associated with the

October 7 feast of Our Lady of the Rosary, the title *La Naval* came to be used for Mary in her role as helper of navies. Miracles have been attributed to her intercession.

Almost five feet in height, the statue was presented to the Manila Dominicans and enshrined in the old St. Domingo Church. During World War II, the shrine was bombed and, after being hidden in the church's vault, the statue was moved to the chapel at the University of St. Thomas. In 1952, the cornerstone was laid for a new shrine at the St. Domingo Church in Quezon City.

LA SALETTE, MISSIONARIES OF OUR LADY OF — *See La Salette, Our Lady of.*

LA SALETTE, OUR LADY OF

Image and devotion based on an apparition of Mary to two children in the French village of La Salette on September 19, 1846.

As Maximim Giraud, eleven, and Melanie Matthieu, almost fifteen, were herding cows in a meadow outside town, the pair saw a glowing orb of light. As they stared, it opened to reveal a woman seated inside who held her face in her hands, as if she were weeping. The visitor then stood and crossed her hands across her chest. The children could see that the beautiful lady was wearing a long white dress that seemed to glisten with pearls of light. A luminous white headdress covered her head, topped by a tall crown. She wore a shawl trimmed with roses across her shoulders and had a large yellow apron tied around her waist. On her feet were white slippers with pearls and gold buckles. A crucifix on a chain hung around her neck. A pair of pliers was on its horizontal beam to the right of Christ; a hammer to his left.

The visitor told the children prayer, penance, and humility were needed, and a disaster would strike the people unless they repented of their sins. She also said Sundays were not being observed, and blasphemy was rampant.

First speaking in French, the lady then switched to the local dialect, which the children understood. After telling Maxim and Melanie to make her message known, the woman disappeared.

That night, the children told their families what had happened, and the news quickly spread. The next day, they reported to the parish priest, prompting the local bishop to begin a very detailed investigation. Miraculous cures followed, as people in that region began to heed Mary's warning and become more fervent in the practice of their Catholicism.

On September 19, 1851, the fifth anniversary of the apparition, the bishop signed a doctrinal pronouncement on La Salette. Examined by Rome and then distributed in the area, it said the apparition had all the marks of truth and authorized the cult of Our Lady of La Salette.

The message Mary confided to the two visionaries regarding the necessity of penance was communicated to Pope Pius IX that same year and has since been known as the "secret" of La Salette.

A basilica was built in Our Lady's honor on the site of the apparition, which remains a major pilgrimage shrine.

An order of priests dedicated to Mary under this title began in 1852 to care for pilgrims visiting the shrine. Later, these Missionaries of Our Lady of La Salette (M.S.) expanded their ministry to conduct missions and retreats as well as parish and social work, always with the underlying charism of promoting reconciliation. They have spread devotion to Our Lady of La Salette worldwide.

LA VANG, OUR LADY OF

Image and devotion based on apparitions reported by the Catholic community in Hué, Vietnam, in 1798; also known as *Duc Me La Vang.*

The history of Catholicism in that country dates back to missionaries arriving in 1533; within a century after their arrival, there were

Our Lady of La Vang

more than 100,000 Catholics. Seminaries were established, and a group of women religious formed in 1670 remains active today.

Then, in 1798, the king issued an anti-Catholic edict and ordered all churches and seminaries destroyed. Many fleeing from the town of Quang Tho took refuge in the deep forest of La Vang, enduring harsh weather, sickness, and starvation, as well as the threat of wild animal attacks. At night, they frequently met in small groups to say the Rosary and offer other prayers.

It was on one of those evenings, in a grassy spot near an ancient banyan tree, that a beautiful lady appeared to them. She wore a long cape and was holding a child in her arms. There were two angels at her side. The people recognized the visitor as the Blessed Mother. All those present saw and heard the apparition.

She offered them comforting words and told them to boil the leaves from the surrounding trees to use as medicine. She also said that from that day on, all those coming to this place to pray would have their prayers heard and answered.

The people built a small chapel there in her honor and, over the following years, news of the event spread among those in the region to other places. Despite its isolated location in the high mountains, the site drew pilgrims willing to make their way through the thick, dangerous jungle to pray to Our Lady of La Vang. These pilgrimages went on, even as the ongoing persecution campaign continued.

Attacks on Vietnamese Catholics and missionaries continued until 1886; then, a local bishop ordered a church built in honor of Mary under this title. Because of both the rugged and remote location and limited funding, it took fifteen years for the building to be completed. More than 12,000 people attended its dedication, celebrated from August 6 to 8, 1901. In 1928, a larger church was constructed to accommodate the increasing number of pilgrims.

Throughout the years, those with a devotion to Our Lady of La Vang spoke of prayers answered. In 1961, the Council of Vietnamese Bishops selected the shrine as the National Sacred Marian Center. The following year, Pope John XXIII elevated the church to the status of basilica, but subsequently it was destroyed in the summer of 1972, during the Vietnam War.

In 1988, during the canonizing ceremony of 117 Vietnamese martyrs, Pope John Paul II repeatedly recognized the importance and significance of Our Lady of La Vang and expressed a desire for the rebuilding of the La Vang Basilica to commemorate the 200th anniversary of the apparition. That rebuilding has not yet happened; at present, an outside altar remains a place of pilgrimage.

LADDER ROSARY

Rosary on which the beads are strung between dual chains, like rungs on a ladder.

There are two traditions associated with the Ladder Rosary. One is a vision by St. Dominic, in which he saw souls climbing to heaven on the Rosary. The other says St. Francis de Sales had a vision of two ladders leading to heaven. The first, rather steep, led directly to Jesus. The second, far less steep, led to Mary. Jesus told St. Francis, "Tell your sons to come by the other ladder" — meaning that the easiest way to Jesus was through Mary.

LADY ALTAR

Traditionally, the altar with the most prominent position in a church, after the main altar.

LADY CHAPEL

A chapel dedicated to Mary. Traditionally, Our Lady's Chapel is behind or near the main altar.

LADY DAY

Another name for the Feast of the Annunciation. Lady Day was also the first day of the year in the British Empire until 1752.

See Annunciation.

LAUDESI

Members of guilds or confraternities in medieval Italy who met in the evening to sing canticles or praises before a statue of Mary. One group of *Laudesi* brought together the Seven Holy Founders, who became the Servants of Mary, or Servites.

See also Servants of Mary.

LEGENDS OF MARY

Collections of stories, principally originating in medieval times, about miracles attributed to Mary.

Even though some of these pious tales had no basis in fact, the stories helped spread Marian devotion in a number of ways, including the Little Office of the Blessed Virgin Mary, the Joys of Mary, and the concept of Mary as the Mother of Mercy. Among the more impor-tant collections are the *Miracles of the Blessed Virgin* by Dominic of Evesham; the *Miracles of the Blessed Virgin Mary* by William of Malmesburg; and the *Miracles of the Blessed Virgin Mary* by Johannes Herolt.

LEGION OF MARY

International apostolate founded in Dublin, Ireland, in 1921 by Frank Duff (1889–1980) on principles based on the teaching of the Mystical Body of Christ and those presented by St. Louis de Montfort in his book, *True Devotion to Mary*. With some three million members, it is the largest apostolic organization of lay people in the world.

St. Louis de Montfort

The Legion's purpose is for members to give glory to God through prayer and service. Among its works are door-to-door evangelization, parishioner visitation, prison ministry, and visitation of the sick or aged. Legionaries are under the guidance of a spiritual director named by the pastor.

The Legion of Mary is organized on a pattern following the military divisions of ancient Rome. The smallest group is called a *praesidium;* two or more praesidia make up a *curia.* The regional governing body is a *senatus,* and the general headquarters in Dublin is known as the *concilium.*

In a 1982 address to Italian Legionaries, Pope John Paul II noted:

> Yours is an eminently Marian spirituality, not only because the Legion glories in carrying Mary's name as its unfurled banner, but above all because it bases its method of spirituality and apostolate on the dynamic principle of union with Mary, on the truth of the intimate participation of the Virgin Mary in the plan of salvation.
>
> In other words, you intend to render your service to every person, who is the image of Christ, with the spirit and the solicitude of Mary.

LEO XIII, POPE

Pontiff from 1878 to 1903 who, among his eighty-six encyclicals, wrote eleven letters on Mary and the Rosary, including annual messages from 1891 to 1898. He became known as "the pope of the Rosary."

In *Octobri Mense* (1891), for example, Pope Leo taught:

The Eternal Son of God, about to take upon Him our nature for the saving and ennobling of man, and about to consummate thus a mystical union between Himself and all mankind, did not accomplish His design without adding there the free consent of the elect Mother, who represented in some sort all human kind, according to the illustrious and just opinion of St. Thomas, who says that the Annunciation was effected with the consent of the Virgin standing in the place of humanity. [III. q. xxx, a. 1]

With equal truth may it be also affirmed that, by the will of God, Mary is the intermediary through whom is distributed unto us this immense treasure of mercies gathered by God, for mercy and truth were created by Jesus Christ. [Jn 1.17] Thus as no man goeth to the Father but by the Son, so no man goeth to Christ but by His Mother.

How great are the goodness and mercy revealed in this design of God! . . . Mary is this glorious intermediary; she is the mighty Mother of the Almighty; but — what is still sweeter — she is gentle, extreme in tenderness, of a limitless loving-kindness. As such God gave her to us. Having chosen her for the Mother of His only begotten Son, He taught her all a mother's feeling that breathes nothing but pardon and love. Such Christ desired she should be, for He consented to be subject to Mary and to obey her as a son a mother.

Such He proclaimed her from the cross when he entrusted to her care and love the whole of the race of man in the person of His disciple John. Such, finally, she proves herself by her courage in gathering in the heritage of the enormous labors of her Son, and in accepting the charge of her maternal duties towards us all.

LE PUY, OUR LADY OF

Marian image and devotion. Le Puy, just south of Lyon, France, features one of the most ancient Marian shrines in the world. A fifty-five-foot statue, *Our Lady of France,* holding the Christ Child, stands on a hill overlooking the valley.

In the city, the cathedral features a Black Madonna, a replica of an ancient statue which was subjected to a mock trial, burned, and beheaded during the French Revolution. Tradition says it was brought to Le Puy by St. Louis, who received it during his imprisonment by the Sultan of Egypt. The present statue, made of black marble, depicts a seated Mary holding the Child Jesus on her knees.

Popes and French kings, as well as prominent saints such as Dominic, Vincent Ferrer, and Anthony of Padua, made pilgrimages to Le Puy. Unable to make the visit herself, St. Joan of Arc sent her mother as her representative.

See also Black Madonnas.

LIESSE, OUR LADY OF

Ancient image and devotion also referred to as *Our Lady, Cause of Our Joy.*

In medieval times, three Crusaders who had been captured by the Saracens, then released, brought the statue of Our Lady and the Christ Child from Egypt to northern France. The original image was destroyed during the French Revolution, but the medieval basilica at Liesse remained a center of Marian devotion and pilgrimage destination. A replacement was installed and crowned in 1857.

St. John Baptist de la Salle (1651–1719), founder of the Congregation of Christian Brothers, had a special devotion to Our Lady of Liesse.

St. John Baptist de la Salle

LILY — *See Symbols of Mary.*

LITANY

A prayer in the form of series of invocations, each of which is followed by a petitionary response.

A litany typically also includes introductory and concluding prayers. In addition to Marian litanies, there are litanies of the Holy Name, the Sacred Heart, the saints, and more. Some litanies have been approved by the Church for liturgical use while others have been written for private use.

See also title of particular litany.

LITANY OF THE BLESSED VIRGIN MARY

Also known as the Litany of Loreto, a prayer in the form of responsive petition that dates back to medieval times and was first approved in 1587 by Pope Sixtus V.

The most popular of the Marian litanies, it may have been first published in a book of prayers in 1551, under the influence of St. Peter Canisius. An earlier and much longer version seems to have been printed in a missal of the mid-fourteenth century.

The prayer reads:

Lord, have mercy.
Christ, have mercy.

Lord, have mercy. Christ, hear us.
Christ, graciously hear us.

God the Father of heaven, have mercy on us.
God the Son, Redeemer of the world, have mercy on us.
God the Holy Spirit, have mercy on us.
Holy Trinity, one God, have mercy on us.

Holy Mary, pray for us.
Holy Mother of God,
Holy Virgin of Virgins,
Mother of Christ,
Mother of divine grace,
Mother most pure,
Mother most chaste,
Mother inviolate,
Mother undefiled,
Mother most amiable,

Mother most admirable,
Mother of good counsel,
Mother of our Creator,
Mother of our Savior,
Virgin most prudent,
Virgin most venerable,
Virgin most renowned,
Virgin most powerful,
Virgin most merciful,
Virgin most faithful,
Mirror of justice,
Seat of wisdom,
Cause of our joy,
Spiritual vessel,
Vessel of honor,
Singular vessel of devotion,
Mystical rose,
Tower of David,
Tower of ivory,
House of gold,
Ark of the covenant,
Gate of heaven,
Morning star,
Health of the sick,
Refuge of sinners,
Comforter of the afflicted,
Help of Christians,
Queen of angels,
Queen of patriarchs,
Queen of prophets,
Queen of apostles,
Queen of martyrs,
Queen of confessors,
Queen of virgins,
Queen of all saints,
Queen conceived without original sin,

Queen assumed into heaven,

Queen of the most holy Rosary,

Queen of families,

Queen of peace,

Lamb of God, who takes away the sins of the world,

Spare us, O Lord.

Lamb of God, who takes away the sins of the world,

Graciously hear us, O Lord.

Lamb of God, who takes away the sins of the world,

Have mercy on us.

Pray for us, O holy Mother of God.

That we may be made worthy of the promises of Christ.

Let us pray. Grant, we beseech You, O Lord God, that we your servants may enjoy perpetual health of mind and body, and by the glorious intercession of Blessed Mary, ever Virgin, may we be freed from present sorrow, and rejoice in eternal happiness. Through Christ our Lord.

Amen.

The litany also features a number of variations for the final prayer, depending on the liturgical season, including:

Advent:

Father, in your plan for our salvation your Word became man, announced by an angel and born of the Virgin Mary. May we who believe that she is the Mother of God receive the help of her prayers. We ask this through our Lord Jesus Christ, your Son, who lives and reigns with you and the Holy Spirit, one God, for ever and ever. Amen.

Christmas Season:

Father, you gave the human race eternal salvation through the motherhood of the Virgin Mary. May we experience the help of her prayers in our lives, for through her we received the very source of life, your Son, our Lord Jesus Christ, who lives and reigns with you and the Holy Spirit, one God, for ever and ever. Amen.

Lent:

Lord, fill our hearts with your love, and as you revealed to us by an angel the coming of your Son as man, so lead us through his suffering and death to the glory of his resurrection, for he lives and reigns with you and the Holy Spirit, one God for ever and ever. Amen.

Easter Season:

God our Father, you give joy to the world by the resurrection of your Son, our Lord Jesus Christ. Through the prayers of his mother, the Virgin Mary, bring us to the happiness of eternal life. We ask this through our Lord Jesus Christ, your Son, who lives and reigns with you and the Holy Spirit, one God for ever and ever. Amen.

LITANY OF THE IMMACULATE HEART OF MARY

Marian prayer written by Venerable John Henry Newman, shortly after he joined the Catholic Church in 1845.

A version without author attribution was featured in the *Golden Manual* of 1851 under the title "The Sacred Heart of Mary." Later, a

Venerable John Henry Newman

"Litany of the Heart of Mary" was published in *Help of Christians* (1863, 1875). One version of the prayer reads:

Lord, have mercy on us.
Christ, have mercy on us.
Lord, have mercy on us. Christ, hear us.
Christ, graciously hear us.

God the Father of Heaven,
Have mercy on us.
God the Son, Redeemer of the world,
Have mercy on us.
God the Holy Spirit,
Have mercy on us.
Holy Trinity, One God,
Have mercy on us.

Heart of Mary, pray for us.
Heart of Mary, like unto the Heart of God,
Heart of Mary, united to the Heart of Jesus,
Heart of Mary, instrument of the Holy Spirit,
Heart of Mary, sanctuary of the Divine Trinity,

Heart of Mary, tabernacle of God Incarnate,
Heart of Mary, immaculate from your creation,
Heart of Mary, full of grace,
Heart of Mary, blessed among all hearts,
Heart of Mary, throne of glory,
Heart of Mary, most humble,
Heart of Mary, holocaust of Divine Love,
Heart of Mary, fastened to the cross with Jesus crucified,
Heart of Mary, comfort of the afflicted,
Heart of Mary, refuge of sinners,
Heart of Mary, hope of the agonizing,
Heart of Mary, seat of mercy,

Lamb of God, who takes away the sins of the world,
Spare us, O Lord.
Lamb of God, who takes away the sins of the world,
Graciously hear us, O Lord.
Lamb of God, who takes away the sins of the world,
Have mercy on us.

Christ hear us,
Christ, graciously hear us.
Immaculate Mary, meek and humble of heart,
Make our hearts like unto the Heart of Jesus.

Let us pray: O most merciful God, who, for the salvation of sinners and the refuge of the miserable, was pleased that the Most Pure Heart of Mary should be most like in charity and pity to the Divine Heart of your Son,

Jesus Christ, grant that we who commemorate this sweet and loving Heart may by the merits and intercession of the same Blessed Virgin, merit to be found like to the Heart of Jesus, through the same Christ Our Lord. Amen.

LITANY OF LORETO — *See Litany of the Blessed Virgin Mary.*

LITANY OF MARY, ELEVENTH CENTURY IRISH

Medieval prayer that reads:

Great Mary, pray for us.
Greatest of Marys,
Greatest of women,
Mother of Eternal Glory,
Mother of the Golden Light,
Honor of the Sky,
Temple of the Divinity,
Fountain of the Gardens,
Serene as the Moon,
Bright as the Sun,
Garden enclosed,
Temple of the Living God,
Light of Nazareth,
Beauty of the world,
Queen of Life,
Ladder of heaven,
Mother of God, pray for us. Amen.

LITANY OF MARY, QUEEN

Prayer from the Church's rite for *Crowning an Image of the Blessed Virgin Mary.*

It reads:

Lord, have mercy.
Lord, have mercy.
Christ, have mercy.
Christ, have mercy.
Lord, have mercy.
Lord, have mercy.

God, our Father in Heaven,
have mercy on us.
God the Son, Redeemer of the world,
have mercy on us.
God, the Holy Spirit,
have mercy on us.
Holy Trinity, one God,
have mercy on us.

Holy Mary, pray for us.
Holy Mother of God,
Most honored of virgins,
Chosen daughter of the Father,
Mother of Christ the King,
Glory of the Holy Spirit,
Virgin daughter of Sion,
Virgin humble and poor,
Virgin gentle and obedient,
Handmaid of the Lord,
Mother of the Lord,
Helper of the Redeemer,
Full of grace,
Fountain of beauty,
Model of virtue,
First fruit of the redemption,
Perfect disciple of Christ,
Untarnished image of the Church,

Woman transformed,

Woman clothed with the sun,

Woman crowned with stars,

Gentle Lady,

Gracious Lady,

Our Lady,

Joy of Israel,

Splendor of the Church,

Pride of the human race,

Advocate of grace,

Minister of holiness,

Champion of God's people,

Queen of love,

Queen of mercy,

Queen of peace,

Queen of angels,

Queen of patriarchs and prophets,

Queen of apostles and martyrs,

Queen of confessors and virgins,

Queen of all saints,

Queen conceived without original sin,

Queen assumed into heaven,

Queen of all the earth,

Queen of heaven,

Queen of the universe,

Lamb of God, you take away the sins of the world; spare us, O Lord.

Lamb of God, you take away the sins of the world; spare us, O Lord.

Lamb of God, you take away the sins of the world; have mercy on us.

Pray for us, O glorious Mother of the Lord, that we may become worthy of the promises of Christ.

God of mercy, listen to the prayers of your servants who have honored your handmaid as

mother and queen. Grant that by your grace we may serve you and our neighbor on earth and be welcomed into your eternal kingdom. We ask this through Christ our Lord. Amen.

LITANY OF OUR LADY OF HOPE (OUR LADY OF PONTMAIN)

Prayer that reads:

Lord, have mercy.

Lord, have mercy.

Christ, have mercy.

Christ, have mercy.

Lord, have mercy.

Lord, have mercy.

Our Lady of hope, pray for us.

Our Lady of the way,

Our Lady of light,

Fullness of Israel,

Prophecy of the new age,

Dawn of the new world,

Mother of God,

Mother of the liberating Messiah,

Mother of the redeemed,

Mother of all people,

Our Lady of hope, Light up our way.

Virgin of silence, pray for us.

Virgin who listens,

Virgin who sings,

Servant of the Lord,

Servant of the Word,

Servant of the redemption,

Servant of the kingdom,

Our Lady of hope, light up our way.

Disciple of Christ, pray for us.

Witness of the Gospel,
Sister of humanity,
Beginning of the Church,
Mother of the Church,
Model of the Church,
Image of the Church,
Our Lady of hope, light up our way.

Mary, blessed among women, pray for us.
Mary, dignity of women,
Mary, greatness of women,
Woman faithful in waiting,
Woman faithful in her task,
Woman faithful in discipleship,
Woman faithful to the cross,
Our Lady of hope, light up our way.

First fruit of Easter, pray for us.
Splendor of Pentecost,
Star of evangelization,
Shining presence,
Prayerful presence,
Welcoming presence,
Active presence,
Our Lady of hope, light up our way.

Hope of the poor, pray for us.
Trust by the humble,
Strength of the marginalized,
Relief of the oppressed,
Defender of the innocent,
Courage of the persecuted,
Comforter of the exiled,
Our Lady of hope, light up our way.

Voice of freedom, pray for us.

Voice of communion,
Voice of peace,
Sign of God's maternal aspect,
Sign of the Father's nearness,
Sign of the Son's mercy,
Sign of the Spirit's fruitfulness,
Our Lady of hope, light up our way.

Christ, Savior of history,
have mercy on us.
Christ, Savior of humanity,
have mercy on us.
Christ, Hope of creation,
have mercy on us.
Let us pray:
Almighty and eternal God, the blessed Virgin Mary, glorious Mother of your Son, helps and defends all those who call upon her. By her intercession may we be strong in faith, steady in hope, and persevere in your love. We ask this through Christ our Lord. Amen.

LITANY OF OUR LADY OF LOURDES

Prayer that reads:

Lord, have mercy. Lord, have mercy.
Christ, have mercy. Christ, have mercy.
Lord, have mercy. Lord, have mercy.
Christ, hear us. Christ, graciously hear us.
God the Father of Heaven, have mercy on us.
God the Son, Redeemer of the world, have
mercy on us.
God the Holy Spirit, have mercy on us.
Holy Trinity, one God, have mercy on us.

Holy Mary, pray for us.

Holy Mother of God,

Mother of Christ,

Mother of our Savior,

Our Lady of Lourdes, help of Christians,

Our Lady of Lourdes, source of love,

Our Lady of Lourdes, mother of the poor,

Our Lady of Lourdes, mother of the handicapped,

Our Lady of Lourdes, mother of orphans,

Our Lady of Lourdes, mother of all children,

Our Lady of Lourdes, mother of all nations,

Our Lady of Lourdes, mother of the Church,

Our Lady of Lourdes, friend of the lonely,

Our Lady of Lourdes, comforter of those who mourn,

Our Lady of Lourdes, shelter of the homeless,

Our Lady of Lourdes, guide of travelers,

Our Lady of Lourdes, strength of the weak,

Our Lady of Lourdes, refuge of sinners,

Our Lady of Lourdes, comforter of the suffering,

Our Lady of Lourdes, help of the dying,

Queen of heaven,

Queen of peace,

Lamb of God, you take away the sins of the world. Spare us, O Lord.

Lamb of God, you take away the sins of the world. Graciously hear us, O Lord.

Lamb of God, you take away the sins of the world. Have mercy on us.

Christ, hear us; Christ, graciously hear us.

Let us pray: Grant us, your servants, we pray you, Lord God, to enjoy perpetual health of mind and body. By the glorious intercession of Blessed Mary ever Virgin, may we be delivered from present sorrows, and enjoy everlasting happiness. Through Christ our Lord. Amen.

LITANY OF OUR LADY OF SEVEN SORROWS

Prayer that reads:

Lord, have mercy on us.

Christ, have mercy on us.

Lord, have mercy on us. Christ, hear us.

Christ, graciously hear us.

God, the Father of heaven, have mercy on us.

God the Son, Redeemer of the world, have mercy on us.

God the Holy Spirit, have mercy on us.

Holy Mary, Mother of God, pray for us.

Holy Virgin of virgins,

Mother of the Crucified,

Sorrowful Mother,

Mournful Mother,

Sighing Mother,

Afflicted Mother,

Forsaken Mother,

Desolate Mother,

Mother most sad,

Mother set around with anguish,

Mother overwhelmed by grief,

Mother transfixed by a sword,

Mother crucified in your heart,

Mother bereaved of your Son,

Sighing dove,

Mother of dolors,

Fount of tears,
Sea of bitterness,
Field of tribulation,
Mass of suffering,
Mirror of patience,
Rock of constancy,
Remedy in perplexity,
Joy of the afflicted,
Ark of the desolate,
Refuge of the abandoned,
Shield of the oppressed,
Conqueror of the incredulous,
Solace of the wretched,
Medicine of the sick,
Help of the faint,
Strength of the weak,
Protectress of those who fight,
Haven of the shipwrecked,
Calmer of tempests,
Companion of the sorrowful,
Retreat of those who groan,
Terror of the treacherous,
Standard-bearer of the martyrs,
Treasure of the faithful,
Light of confessors,
Pearl of virgins,
Comfort of widows,
Joy of all saints,
Queen of your servants,
Holy Mary, who alone are unexampled,

Pray for us, most Sorrowful Virgin,
That we may be made worthy of the promises of Christ.
Let us pray.

O God, in whose Passion, according to the prophecy of Simeon, a sword of grief pierced through the most sweet soul of your glorious Blessed Virgin Mother Mary: grant that we, who celebrate the memory of her Seven Sorrows, may obtain the happy effect of your Passion, who lives and reigns world without end. Amen.

See also Sorrows of Mary.

LITTLE COMPANY OF MARY, SISTERS OF THE

International congregation of women religious founded in England by Mary Potter (1847–1913) in 1877, with the fundamental mission to evangelize.

In explaining the work of the Little Company of Mary, Mother Potter — an advocate of the spirituality promoted by St. Louis Marie de Montfort — explained: "We shall love with our whole hearts, our whole minds. . . . When we do this, we shall be real Christians."

Long associated with health care services, the congregation's ministries now also include pastoral, parish, and retreat work; and the care of the aged, the infirm, and the dying in their homes.

In 1988 Pope John Paul II declared Mother Potter "venerable," the first of three steps leading to canonization.

See also Company of Mary.

LITTLE CROWN OF THE BLESSED VIRGIN MARY — *See Crown of the Blessed Virgin Mary, Little.*

LITTLE FLOWER ROSARY

Chaplet of twenty-five beads associated with devotion to St. Thérèse of Lisieux, the Little Flower, and traditionally recited between nine and twenty-four days in a row.

The prayer on the first bead is, "St. Thérèse of the Infant Jesus, Patroness of Missions, pray for us!" On each of the remaining twenty-four beads, a Glory Be is recited in honor of the Blessed Trinity and in thanksgiving for St. Thérèse, who lived only twenty-four years.

On successive days, the chaplet adds: "St. Thérèse, the Little Flower, please pick me a rose from the heavenly garden and send it to me with a message of love. Ask God to grant me the favor I implore and tell Him I will love Him each day more and more."

This is followed by five Our Fathers, five Hail Marys, and five Glory Bes. On the fifth day, an additional set of five each is added.

LITTLE OFFICE OF THE BLESSED VIRGIN MARY

Marian prayer patterned on the Divine Office (the Liturgy of Hours), containing the usual divisions, but much shorter.

Historians note that it first appeared in the ninth or tenth century; perhaps it was originally collected to be prayed in conjunction with the Votive masses of Our Lady on Saturday, written by the liturgical master of Charlemagne's court, Alcuin.

St. Peter Damian (1007–1072) revised it and recommended its use, and subsequently the prayer was adopted by two religious communities, the Cistercians and the Camaldulen-

sians. Later, secular clergy (those not belonging to a religious order) also used it.

The prayer varied among communities and locations but was standardized by Pope Pius V in 1585. It was included in the Book of Hours in Mary's honor and used by the laity. Women's congregations and third orders frequently made its recitation mandatory for members.

In a 1952 revision, prayers corresponding to the periods of the liturgical season were added. The Second Vatican Council designated the revised office as part of the public prayer of the Church.

LITTLE OFFICE OF THE IMMACULATE CONCEPTION

Prayer that follows the Divine Office (the Liturgy of the Hours) attributed to St. Alphonsus Rodriguez (1531–1617).

A lay brother in the Society of Jesus, for decades he served as a doorkeeper at the College of Majorca (Spain), where students and visitors came to seek his advice and spiritual direction.

The devotion was patterned after the Little Office of the Blessed Virgin Mary, with a series of tributes taken from titles in Scripture.

LITTLE ROSARY OF ST. ANNE

A chaplet named for St. Anne, the mother of the Virgin Mary.

The prayer, which dates back to the late nineteenth century and was devised by devotees of St. Anne, is divided into three parts, each with one Our Father, five Hail Marys, and one Glory Be. The first section is said in honor of Jesus, the second in honor of Mary, and the third in honor of

St. Anne. After each Hail Mary, the petitioner prays: "Jesus, Mary, and Anne, grant me the favor I ask."

See also Chaplet.

LITURGICAL COLORS FOR MARIAN FEASTS

A white chasuble and stole, the color symbolic of purity and life in the faith, are worn for feasts and commemorations of the Blessed Virgin Mary.

On solemn occasions, better than ordinary vestments may be used, even though their color (gold, for example) does not match the requirements of the day. While some parishes and communities have white or gold vestments with blue trim or featuring Marian themes, blue is not a liturgical color in the Catholic Church.

LIVING ROSARY

Public prayer service in which participants arrange themselves in the form of a Rosary. Each person takes a turn reciting the first part of an Our Father or Hail Mary, with the rest of the group offering the concluding second part. The term is also used when decades are assigned to individuals who agree to say the prayers at some time during the day.

LIVING ROSARY, ASSOCIATION OF THE

Worldwide confraternity founded in 1826 in France by Pauline Jaricot (1799–1862), who

Our Lady of Loreto

also began the Society for the Propagation of the Faith.

The association was placed under the spiritual guidance of the Dominicans. Members agree to pray an assigned decade of the Rosary daily.

LORETO, HOLY HOUSE OF
LORETO, OUR LADY OF

Pilgrimage site in Loreto, Italy, along the shore of the Adriatic Sea.

According to pious legend, Mary's house at the time of the Annunciation was transported by angels in 1291 from Nazareth to Tersato in Dalmatia, and then, in 1294, to Loreto. The earliest recorded pilgrimage to the site dates back to 1313. From that time, the holy house became one of the major pilgrimage sites of Europe.

The house is a small rectangular building, encased in marble, but originally constructed from materials not found in the vicinity of the domed basilica that now surrounds it.

In addition to the house itself, there is a much-venerated Marian image. The original statue of the Virgin, destroyed by fire in 1921, was replaced by a replica — a Black Madonna depicting the Virgin and Christ Child in dark wood.

Pope Benedict XV (r. 1914–1922) declared Our Lady of Loreto the patron of all those involved in flying.

LORETO SISTERS

Popular name of the Institute of the Blessed Virgin Mary.

See Institute of the Blessed Virgin Mary.

St. Bernadette and Our Lady of Lourdes

LOURDES, OUR LADY OF

Marian image, shrine and optional memorial celebrated on February 11.

Between February 11 and July 16, 1858, fourteen-year-old Bernadette Soubirous reported seeing eighteen visions of a woman dressed in white in a grotto near Lourdes, France. The woman's head and shoulders were covered with a white veil which fell to the full length of her robe. She wore a plain blue sash around her waist, and a golden rose was on each foot. She carried a white Rosary with a cross and chain of gold over her right arm.

During the ninth visit, the woman instructed the teen to "drink from the fountain and bathe in it." Bernadette was confused because there had never been a water source at the spot. As she scraped the gravel away from the ground where she knelt, a previously unknown spring began to flow. It still provides water for the healing baths at the shrine at Lourdes today.

During the visitor's last appearance, Bernadette asked the woman who she was and was told, "I am the Immaculate Conception." A basilica was dedicated at the site in 1901, and it has been estimated as many as six million pilgrims visit Lourdes annually. The shrine has been the sight of many reported miracles.

See also Immaculate Conception; Lourdes water.

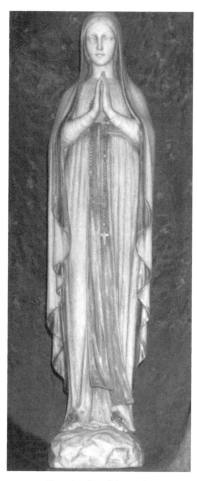

Our Lady of Lourdes

LOURDES WATER

Sacramental associated with Marian shrine in Lourdes, France. The water comes from a spring discovered by St. Bernadette while she was having a vision of Mary in 1858. Miracles have been attributed to its use.

See also Lourdes, Our Lady of.

LUJAN, OUR LADY OF

Image and devotion.

This two-foot-tall terracotta statue of the Immaculate Conception was made in Brazil and sent to Argentina in 1630. While originally similar to the work of Spanish Baroque painter Bartolomé Esteban Murillo (c. 1617–1682), the image was given a solid silver covering in 1887 to keep it from decaying. It is usually clothed in a white robe and a light blue cloak, the colors of the Argentina's flag. Only the dark face with large blue eyes and the hands folded in prayer are now visible.

Tradition holds that the ox-drawn wagon taking the statue from Buenos Aires to Santiago del Estero stopped for some unknown reason by the Lujan River, near the home of Don Rosendo Oramas. The oxen were replaced and the wagon was unloaded but the new team still refused to cross the river. That was when those trying to goad the animals across the water noticed that two small boxes that had been left in the back of the wagon. Each contained a Marian image; one was the Immaculate Conception and the other was the Blessed Mother holding the Christ Child.

The statue of Mary and her Son was unloaded, but still the ox could not be moved. It was returned to the wagon and the box containing the other statue was taken out. Immediately the animals began to pull forward. The amazed witnesses repeated the transfers several times with the same result until they came to realize Our Lady wished to stay in Lujan.

At first, the statue was taken to Oramas' home. He built a primitive chapel for it there, where Our Lady was venerated for forty years. A bigger and more beautiful shrine was completed in 1685, and the final sanctuary was built in the nineteenth century. The image was crowned in 1887 and, in 1930, Pius XII gave the church the title of basilica.

Our Lady of Lujan is the patron of Argentina, Uruguay, and Paraguay, and devotion to her is strong throughout South America.

LUX VERITATIS

Latin for "Light of Truth," the title of the encyclical Pope Pius XI issued in 1931 to mark the 1,500th anniversary of the Council of Ephesus which affirmed Mary as the Mother of God.

See Ephesus, Council of.

MADONNA

Italian for "my lady," a term for Mary, usually in images in which she is holding the Christ Child. Painters have titled their works using the term, such as Raphael's *Madonna of the Chair* or Boticelli's *Madonna of the Magnificat.*

See also Art, Mary in.

MADONNA DEL GHISALLO

Image and devotion based on a medieval legend that said Count Ghisallo was traveling near the village of Magreglio, Italy, when bandits attacked him. Seeing an image of Mary in a roadside shrine, he broke free of the robbers and ran to it where he took refuge, begged for Mary's help, and, miraculously, was spared from further harm. As news of the event spread, the Madonna del Ghisallo became known as the patroness of local travelers.

More recently, her chapel, located at the top of a steep hill, became a landmark and resting place for bicyclists. After World War II, the shrine's pastor, Father Ermelindo Vigano, suggested it become a shrine for cyclists and in 1949 Pope Pius XII named her their patroness. The chapel is now part shrine and part cycling museum, with photos and artifacts from the sport. It features an eternal flame in memory of cyclists who have died and who are remembered at services on All Souls' Day and Christmas Eve.

MADONNA DELLA FIDUCIA — *See* Confidence, Our Lady of.

MADONNA DELLA STRADA

Painting in the Church of the Gesu in Rome. Also known as *Our Lady of the Wayside,* the image dates back to the fourteenth century and was originally kept in the Church of the Astalli. There are also a number of religious houses of formation and local sanctuaries throughout Western Europe known by the name of *Our Lady of the Street.* The title is sometimes used in representations of Mary intended to symbolize poverty and homelessness. The chapel at Loyola University Chicago, built in 1938, is named for her.

A second popular image by Italian artist Roberto Ferruzzi (1854–1934) also came to be known as *Our Lady of the Street* although it was originally called *Little Madonna (La Madonnina).* It shows a girl of about eleven holding her baby brother in her arms. Although Ferruzzi never intended the painting to depict Our Lady, the young girl looked like a young Mary with the Infant Jesus.

MADONNA OF MERCY — *See Casa Santa Maria.*

MADONNA OF MILK, SHRINE OF THE — *See Caravaggio, Our Lady of.*

MADONNA OF THE CRUCIFIX — *See Pontmain, Our Lady of.*

MAGI — *See Scripture, Mary in.*

MAGNIFICAT

Mary's canticle or hymn of praise and thanksgiving on the occasion of her visitation to her cousin Elizabeth (Lk. 1:46–55).

The *Magnificat,* which gets it name from the first word of the prayer in Latin, is reminiscent of the song of Hannah (1 Sam. 1–10) and is an acknowledgment of the great blessing given by God to Mary as the Mother of the Second Person of the Blessed Trinity made human. It is recited in the Liturgy of the Hours as part of the Evening Prayer. One version reads:

My soul magnifies the Lord,
and my spirit rejoices in God my savior;
for he has regarded the low estate of his
*	handmaiden.*
For behold, henceforth all generations will
*	call me blessed:*
for he who is mighty has done great things
*	for me,*
and holy is his name.
And his mercy is on those who fear him
from generation to generation.
He has shown strength with his arm,
he has scattered the proud in the
*	imagination of their hearts,*
he has put down the mighty from their
*	thrones,*
and exalted those of low degree;
he has filled the hungry with good things,
and the rich he has sent empty away.
He has helped his servant Israel
in remembrance of his mercy,
as he spoke to our fathers,
to Abraham and to his posterity for ever.

See also Scripture, Mary in.

MARIA BAMBINA

Italian for "Infant Mary," a devotion that dates back at least to the early eleventh century, when Santa Maria Fulcorina Church in Milan, Italy, was dedicated to the Nativity of Mary. Later, it was named the cathedral.

Today, the center of devotion to Mary as an infant is based in the mother house chapel of the Sisters of *Maria Bambina,* Milan. The sisters have a wax image of the Infant Mary made in 1735, a time when the modeling of wax images of the Infant Jesus and Infant Mary was popular. Miracles have been attributed to the intercession of *Maria Bambina,* and the image was solemnly crowned in 1904.

The devotion spread from Milan throughout Italy and traveled to the United States with Italian immigrants. It became customary to give newlyweds a small wax image of the *Maria Bambina.*

MARIA NIÑA — See Divina Infantita.

MARIA STEIN

Shrine and monastery near Basel, Switzerland. According to tradition, in the fourteenth century, after a child fell down a cliff there but was unharmed, grateful residents placed a statue of

Mary in a nearby cave. It became a pilgrimage destination. After a similar accident had the same result in 1540, the number of visitors increased, and a monastery was established to care for them.

MARIALIS CULTUS

Apostolic exhortation issued by Pope Paul VI in 1974. Its title in English is *For the Right Ordering and Development of Devotion to the Blessed Virgin Mary.*

The document's purpose was developing devotion to Mary within the context of the renewal resulting from the Second Vatican Council. Beginning with the revised Roman Liturgy, it notes the central place Mary has within the liturgical year and how Marian

Pope Paul VI

themes relate to the mysteries of Christ and the Church. It points out Mary is "a model of the spiritual attitude with which the Church celebrates and lives the divine mysteries" in that "she is recognized as a most excellent exemplar of the Church in the order of faith, charity and perfect union with Christ."

The document calls for a renewal of devotion to Our Lady that is respectful of tradition but "open to the legitimate requests of the people of our time." Such devotion, it says, must reflect the proper Trinitarian and Christological aspects that form its foundation and show the legitimate place Mary has in the Church. It warns against those who would "scorn, *a priori*, devotions of piety which, in their correct forms, have been recommended by the Magisterium, who leave them aside and in this way create a vacuum which they do not fill" and includes a section on the *Angelus* and the Rosary.

Its conclusion notes:

> The Church's devotion to the Blessed Virgin is an intrinsic element of Christian worship. The honor which the Church has always and everywhere shown to the Mother of the Lord, from the blessing with which Elizabeth greeted Mary (cf. Lk. 1:42–45) right up to the expressions of praise and petition used today, is a very strong witness to the Church's norm of prayer and an invitation to become more deeply conscious of her norm of faith. And the converse is likewise true. The Church's norm of faith requires that her norm of prayer should everywhere blossom forth with regard to the Mother of Christ. Such devotion to the Blessed Virgin is firmly rooted in the revealed word and has solid

dogmatic foundations. It is based on the singular dignity of Mary, "Mother of the Son of God, and therefore beloved daughter of the Father and Temple of the Holy Spirit — Mary, who, because of this extraordinary grace, is far greater than any other creature on earth or in heaven" [*Lumen Gentium*, 53].

See also Devotions, Marian.

MARIAM —*See Name of Mary.*

MARIAN CONGRESS, MARIAN CONFERENCE — *See Congress, Marian.*

MARIAN DEVOTIONS — *See Devotions, Marian.*

MARIAN HELPERS, ASSOCIATION OF

Spiritual benefit society founded in 1944 to prayerfully and financially support the priests and brothers of the Congregation of Marians of the Immaculate Conception (founded in 1673).

The association, which has some 1.5 million members, produces and distributes Catholic literature and informational material, including a quarterly magazine, *Marian Helper*. It also promotes devotion to Divine Mercy, as encouraged by St. Faustina Kowalska. The National Shrine of the Divine Mercy is on the grounds of the association's headquarters in Stockton, MA.

See also Marians of the Immaculate Conception.

MARIAN LIBRARY/INTERNATIONAL MARIAN RESEARCH INSTITUTE

Located at the University of Dayton in Dayton, OH, the Marian Library/International Marian Research Institute is a center of study and research on Mary. It holds the world's largest collection of printed materials on the Blessed Virgin and serves as the headquarters of the Mariological Society of America.

In 1943, the Marianists of the University of Dayton founded The Marian Library to commemorate the triple centennial to be celebrated in 1949–1950: the arrival of the Marianists in the United States (1849); the death of Fr. William Joseph Chaminade, founder of the Society of Mary (1850); and the founding of the University of Dayton (1850).

The Marian Library offers its resources to all qualified students and scholars who need an extensive collection of books, periodicals, and other materials centered on studies related to Mary. It has more than 150,000 items in more than fifty languages, dating from the beginning of printing to the present day. It includes a general reference collection with resources in patristics, biblical studies, Christology, ecclesiology, spirituality, church history, hymnography, iconography, general and specialized bibliography.

There are also more than 63,000 clippings from newspapers and magazines, nearly

Marian Library Medal

100,000 cards depicting Mary in the art of all ages and numerous Marian shrines, collections of statues from around the world, Marian postage stamps, recordings of Marian music, Marian medals, rosaries, more than 10,000 slides on Marian art (especially from the twentieth century), and video and audio recordings on Marian themes and related topics.

The library issues a multilingual journal, *Marian Library Studies* (New Series), devoted to the publication of original and scholarly research in all aspects of the field of Marian Studies: editions of early texts, historical research and its documentation, historical bibliography, as well as comparative studies in such areas as religion, archaeology, iconography, symbolism, theological anthropology, and psychology.

In 1975, an institute of graduate studies in theology was founded in affiliation with the Pontifical University Marianum, directed by the Servants of Mary (Servites) in Rome. The Sacred Congregation for Catholic Education approved the International Marian Research Institute (IMRI) on November 5, 1975. Since 1975, IMRI has organized annual summer schools at the graduate level to promote the programs of Marian Studies established by the Marianum and adapted to the needs of students in the United States and abroad. Students can prepare for a licentiate and doctorate in theology, with a concentration in Marian studies, earn a certificate in Marian studies, or gain credit hours toward a master's degree granted in conjunction with the Department of Religious Studies at the University of Dayton.

IMRI is incorporated into the Faculty of Theology Marianum and is empowered to grant the Licentiate of Sacred Theology (S.T.L.) and Doctorate of Sacred Theology (S.T.D.) degrees, following the prescribed courses of study.

Other services offered by The Marian Library/International Marian Research Institute include a speakers bureau, religious art exhibitions, and related publications. A Web site offers online access to Marian teachings, homiletic helps, meditations, a calendar of Marian events, a bibliography, book reviews, news, virtual exhibits of contemporary artists, music, shrines, resources, frequently asked questions, and more.

The library also has an art gallery devoted to contemporary religious art, especially Marian art, and a museum focused on the display of Nativity scenes from the Crèches Collection of the Marian Library (numbering more than 900 sets).

See also Mariological Society of America, Society of Mary.

MARIAN MEDAL

Award available for Catholic members of the Girl Scouts and Camp Fire Girls.

The Marian Program is designed to help girls learn more about Mary and themselves as they read about Mary in Scripture and follow her journey as she grows into the woman known as the Mother of God.

MARIAN MOVEMENT OF PRIESTS

An international organization with the purpose of spiritual renewal through consecration to the Immaculate Heart of Mary.

The movement was founded by Fr. Stefano Gobbi, a priest from Milan, Italy, based on his interior locutions (a form of private revelation), which began on a 1972 pilgrimage to Fatima. At that time, he was praying for a group of priests who had abandoned their vocations and were attempting to form an association in rebellion against the authority of the Roman Catholic Church.

The following year, Fr. Gobbi began to write down these interior locutions that he was receiving. Messages dating from July 1973 to December 1997 are published in a book titled *To the Priests, Our Lady's Beloved Sons.*

In September 1973, the organization's first national gathering took place, with twenty-five of the eighty priests already enrolled taking part. Beginning in 1974, the first cenacles of prayers were held. The term for these times of prayer refers to the upper room in which the Last Supper was held and where Mary and the apostles awaited the coming of the Holy Spirit on Pentecost. They include an invocation to the Holy Spirit; the recitation of the Rosary; prayers for the pope; a reading and meditation on one of more of the messages in *To the Priests, Our Lady's Beloved Sons*; and an act of consecration to the Immaculate Heart of Mary.

Worldwide membership has grown to some 400 cardinals and bishops, more than 100,000 priests, and millions of professed religious and laity.

See also Revelation, Divine and Private.

MARIAN YEAR

A period of twelve or more months dedicated to encouraging devotion to Mary. The first Marian Year was proclaimed by Pope Pius XII in 1954 to mark the centenary of the definition of the dogma of the Immaculate Conception. The second, called by Pope John Paul II and running from Pentecost 1987 to the feast of the Assumption 1988, was observed in preparation for the start of the third millennium of Christianity in the year 2000.

Marian Years have also been celebrated on the national and diocesan level.

MARIANISTS — *See Society of Mary.*

MARIANITES OF THE HOLY CROSS

One of three orders tracing its foundation back to Fr. Basil Moreau, a priest of the Diocese of Le Mans, France.

In 1837, he began the Congregation of the Holy Cross (C.S.C.) for priests and brothers and, the following year, gave a rule of life to a group of devout laywomen who assisted them, first by doing domestic work. Later, because of so many requests for help, the sisters were trained to teach and nurse. They became the Marianites of Holy Cross, and in 1841, the first members received the religious habit.

The Marianites were dedicated to Mary, and in particular to Mary as Our Lady of Sorrows, also known as Our Lady of Seven Dolors. The first woman in leadership for the Marianites, Leocadie Gascoin, received the religious name Mother Mary of Seven Dolors.

Today, members form three distinct congregations: Marianites of Holy Cross, Sisters of the Holy Cross, and Sisters of Holy Cross. The men and women religious of Holy Cross minister in Europe, North and South America,

Africa, and Asia. In 2003, Pope John Paul II declared Father Moreau "venerable."

MARIANNHILL MISSIONARIES

Congregation of the Missionaries of Mariannhill, a Religious order of priests and brothers founded in 1909 by Abbot Francis Pfanner, dedicated to Mary and St. Anne.

A monastic community involved in intense missionary work in Africa, Papua New Guinea, Europe, Canada, and the United States, it has an apostolate of prayer and labor.

MARIANS OF THE IMMACULATE CONCEPTION

Religious order founded by John Papczynski (later known as Fr. Stanislaus of Jesus Mary Papczynski) in 1673 when the first Marian monastery was established in the *Puszcza Korabiewska* (Korabiew Forest) near Skierniewice, Poland. Today it is called *Puszcza Marianska* (the Marian Forest).

Biographers note that, as a Pole, Father Stanislaus had a devotion to Mary deeply rooted in his familial, religious, and cultural heritage. They point out he was also strongly influenced by the miraculous defense of the Jasna Gora Monastery in Czestochowa (which saved the historic site from the destruction of a Swedish invasion) and by the consecration of Poland to Mary by King John Casimir in Lwow (present-day L'viv, Ukraine). It was at this event that the Polish nation was publicly entrusted to Mary's care and Our Lady was given the title "Queen of Poland."

Fr. Stanislaus determined his new religious order would focus on religious education to deepen the faith of the common people. Members were to act with missionary zeal in bringing knowledge of the faith to those whose religious education had been most neglected. The order received the approval of Pope Innocent XII in 1699.

Today, the Congregation of the Marians is organized in seven provinces with more than one hundred locations worldwide. In 1992, the Holy See declared Fr. Stanislaus "venerable."

See also Marian Helpers, Association of.

MARIAPOLIS

Name of annual meeting of members of the Focolare movement, an association of men and women founded by Chiara Lubich in Trent, Italy, in 1943.

The purposes of the association include personal spiritual benefit, promoting a deeper prayer life, and bringing about spiritual good through the everyday conditions of work and service to others.

MARIAZELL, OUR LADY OF

Image and pilgrimage site.

According to pious tradition, in 1157, a Benedictine monk named Magnus left the Abbey of St. Lambrecht to retire into the wilderness of the Austrian Alps and took a wooden statue with him. About twenty-two inches high, it depicted the Madonna and Christ Child. When he reached a point in the forest where thick growth and rocks blocked his way, he prayed to Mary and the stones opened. Soon after that, he stopped and set up

Our Lady of Mariazell

his new hermitage, placing the statue on a white branch of a linden tree. Later, shepherds and hunters living in the area came to him, and he became their priest. After some years had passed, they and others helped him build a small chapel around the tree.

Miracles were attributed the intervention of Our Lady of Mariazell, and the first church was built around 1200. In the middle of the next century, it was replaced by a larger one. A still larger and more ornate structure was constructed in the late seventeenth century. Tradition holds that during this last project, the linden tree, the original site of the statue, was found. One of the curiosities of the church is the fact that it has three spires, one of Gothic design between two that are Baroque.

Over the last six centuries, Hungarian and Austrian royalty have donated a large number of gifts to the pilgrimage site and to Our Lady of Mariazell, almost rivaling the collection in Altötting.

Members of the royal families, as well as aristocracy, rulers, and high officials, who came to the church, took off their official robes and other symbols of power and wealth before entering. Traditionally, pilgrims going into the church still do so while performing the same act of penance. They advance, kneeling, up the main stairway with arms outstretched, or they carry heavy stone blocks as acts of penance in memory of those who, centuries ago, helped to build the church. Some stop for a time to lie prostrate on the ground. Those with a devotion to Our Lady of Mariazell but who cannot travel to the site write letters to Mary, which are preserved in the church's archives.

See also **Altötting, Our Lady of.**

MARIOLATRY

The sin of idolatry in the form of giving to Mary the worship that belongs to God alone. The term is sometimes used to refer to errors and excesses in devotion to Our Lady.

See **Hyperdulia.**

MARIOLOGICAL SOCIETY OF AMERICA

A theological society dedicated to the study of Mary, with an interest in encouraging Marian catechetics and spirituality.

The society was founded by Fr. Juniper B. Carol, O.F.M., in October 1949, and charter members gathered for the first meeting in Washington, DC, in January 1950. Since that time, the society has met annually in various cities throughout the United States.

Since 1979, the office of the executive secretary has been located at the Marian Library at the University of Dayton, OH.

MARIOLOGY

The part of dogmatic theology which, since the seventeenth century, concerns Mary in her relation to God and her fellow creatures under God.

Scriptural Mariology limits itself to the study of New Testament texts that refer to Mary (cf. Mt. 1:16–2:23; 12:46–50; 13:55; Mk. 3:31–35; 6:3; Lk. 1:26–2:52; 8:19–21; 11:27–28; Jn. 1:14; 2:1–12; 19:25–27; Acts 1:14; Rom. 1:3; Gal. 4:4). The study also concerns itself with defined Marian dogmas: her divine motherhood, her perpetual virginity, her Immaculate Conception, and her Assumption.

In its final chapter (8), Vatican II's *Dogmatic Constitution on the Church* offered the first official Mariology of the Roman Church. It presented Mary in biblical, patristic, ecclesial, and ecumenical perspectives.

MARISTS —*See Society of Mary.*

MARTYRS, OUR LADY OF

Church in Rome originally built by Marcus Agrippa in 25 B.C. as a temple for the gods. It was consecrated as a church by Pope Boniface IV (r. 608–615) in honor of Mary and all martyrs. The church holds the tomb of the painter Raphael.

MARY ALTAR —*See Lady Altar.*

MARY GARDEN

Medieval custom of planting small gardens featuring flowers, herbs and shrubs associated with Mary by legend. In the mid-twentieth century the practice was revived in Europe and the United States. Most simply, a Mary Garden is a portion of a larger garden set aside in honor of Mary.

Hundreds of plants are traditionally associated with Our Lady. Among them, for example (using their common, botanical, and religious names), are:

Baby's Breath, *Gypsophila paniculata,* Our Lady's Veil

Bleeding Heart, *Dicentra spectabilis,* Mary's Heart

Canna Lily, *Canna indica,* Rosary Bead Plant

Canterbury Bells, *Campanula medium,* Our Lady's Nightcap

Columbine, *Aquilegua vulgaris,* Our Lady's Shoes

Cowslip Primrose, *Primula veris,* Our Lady's Keys

Daffodil, *Narcissus psuedo-Nar,* Mary's Star

English Daisy, *Bellis perennis,* Mary-Loves

Forget-me-not, *Myosotis scorpoides,* Eyes of Mary

Foxglove, *Digitalis purpurea,* Our Lady's Gloves

Marigold, *Tagetes sp.,* Mary's Gold

Morning Glory, *Ipomoea purpurea,* Our Lady's Mantle

Pansy, *Viola tricolor,* Our Lady's Delight

Petunia, *Petunia hybr.,* Our Lady's Praises

Rose, *Rosa* gen., Emblem of Mary

Sunflower, *Helianthus annus,* Mary's Gold

Sweet Pea, *Lathyrus odoratus,* Our Lady's Flower

Sweet William, *Dianthus barbatus,* Our Lady's Cushion

Tulip, *Tulipa gesneriana,* Mary's Prayer

The first Mary Garden in the United States is believed to be that at St. Joseph's Church in Woods Hole, MA. In 1932, Frances Crane Lillie, a summer resident of the town, researched herbs and plants with old religious names that symbolized Mary. Later, she planted a selection of them in a Garden of Our Lady at the parish church.

All the major plantings in the Mary's Garden at the Basilica of the Shrine of the Immaculate Conception in Washington, DC, are selected for their white blossoms, representing Our Lady's purity. Perennials, ground covers, and spring-flowering bulbs occur at intervals, and include anemone, aster, cornflower, cranesbill, hosta, and lamb's ear. They provide flowers throughout the growing seasons and many species were selected for their traditional association with Mary.

See also Immaculate Conception, Basilica of the National Shrine of the.

MARY HELP OF CHRISTIANS — *See Help of Christians, Our Lady.*

MARY IMMACULATE — *See Immaculate Conception.*

MARY MAJOR — *See St. Mary Major, Basilica of.*

MARY REPARATRIX (RESTORER)

Title that is rarely used.

There is a religious congregation of St. Mary Reparatrix, founded by Blessed Emily d'Oultremont, who died in 1978. The term is also related to the La Salette spirituality where Mary is featured as the one who attempts to reconcile the human race with God but *reparatrix* is not explicitly used. There is also the tradition and devotion of "the Virgin who unties knots" in contrast to Eve who tied them. Again, the title is not explicitly used.

The title was used by a number of writers, including Eadmar (1055–c.1141) who refers to Mary as *reparatrix perditi orbis* (restorer of the ruined world). In his 1904 encyclical *Ad diem illum laetissimum* (*On the Immaculate Conception*), Pope Pius X uses that version to illustrate Mary's role in the mediation of grace. Pope Pius XI used the title in his 1928 encyclical *Miserentissimus Redemptor* (*On Reparation of the Sacred Heart*).

See also Knots, the Virgin Who Unties; **La Salette, Our Lady of.**

MARYKNOLL

Catholic mission movement, established in 1911 as the Catholic Foreign Mission Society of America by the bishops of the United States. In 1912, it moved its headquarters to a hilltop farm above Ossining, NY, and the hill was dedicated to the Blessed Virgin as Mary's Knoll.

Responsibility for the society's development was given to two diocesan priests, Fr. James Anthony Walsh of Boston and Fr. Thomas Frederick Price of North Carolina, with the commission to recruit, send and support U.S. missioners in areas around the world.

On June 29, 1911, Pope Pius X blessed the founding of Maryknoll and its missioners left for China in 1918. Today there are more than five hundred Maryknoll priests and brothers serving in countries around the world, principally in Africa, Asia, and Latin America.

The Maryknoll Sisters of St. Dominic was founded in 1912 by Mary Josephine Rogers (Sister Mary Joseph). It was the first group of Catholic sisters in the United States to devote their lives in service overseas. Today some seven hundred members from more than twenty nations serve in thirty countries worldwide.

Maryknoll Lay Missioners are members of the laity (single men and women, couples, and families) who work with the poor, oppressed, and marginalized in a number of countries. Members make a three-and-a-half-year renewable commitment.

Maryknoll Affiliates are persons joined in a special relationship with Maryknoll through local chapters committed to a global vision, spirituality, community, and action.

MARYMAS

A term that can be used to refer to any Marian feast. The suffix *mas* comes from the Latin *mittere* "to send" and is the origin of the term Mass. Most often Marymas refers to the feast of the Annunciation. The choice of March 25 for that feast is directly related to the feast of the Nativity nine months later, on December 25, and so the word Marymas was used in the same way as Christmas.

In medieval England, the term was used for the Mass said in the Lady chapel or in honor of Mary.

MATER DOLOROSA

Latin for "Sorrowful Mother."

See Sorrows, Our Lady of.

MAY

Month dedicated to Marian devotion, a popular tradition dating back the sixteenth century. Although May is a form of "Mary," the name comes from the Latin for the "month of Maia," the Roman goddess of grain. The people of ancient Rome celebrated the first day of May by honoring Flora, the goddess of flowers, who was represented by a small statue wreathed in garlands. A procession of singers and dancers carried the statue past a sacred tree decorated with blossoms. Later, festivals of this kind spread to other parts of Europe, reaching their height of popularity in England during the Middle Ages. Dances around a May pole were common and, often, a May queen was chosen as part of the festivities.

St. Philip Neri

Devotions to Our Lady on the first days of May date back to St. Philip Neri (1515–1595) who began the custom of decorating the statue of Mary with spring flowers.

Annibale Dionisi, an Italian Jesuit, proposed devotions to Mary throughout the entire month. As happened with other pre-Christian customs and festivals, the Church incorporated the earlier May celebrations and gave them a Christian dimension. May began to be celebrated in honor of Mary with many of the same type of festivities, including floral tributes, processions, and the crowning of a statue. Those customs continue, as does another: the May altar, a Marian shrine set up in the church or at home. Typically, it features an image of Mary and is decorated with flowers. In some households, it is the focal point for evening prayer during the month.

See also Coronation of the Blessed Virgin Mary.

MAY CROWNING —*See Coronation of the Blessed Virgin Mary; May.*

MEDAL

Sacramental; a flat, metal, wood, or plastic disc with a religious image and/or inscription on one or both sides.

The custom of wearing medals is an ancient one, traced back as far as the time of the catacombs.

Religious medals are enormously varied and are used to commemorate persons (Christ, the Blessed Mother, the saints), places such as famous shrines (e.g., Lourdes, Fatima, St. Peter's Basilica), past historical events (e.g., dogmatic definitions, miracles, dedications), or personal graces (e.g., baptism, First Communion, ordination). Medals may include symbols that relate to the mysteries of our faith, and some serve as badges of pious associations.

See also Marian Medal; Miraculous Medal.

MEDIATOR DEI

Encyclical (*On the Sacred Liturgy*) promulgated by Pope Pius XII in 1947.

In four paragraphs addressing honoring Mary, the pontiff noted:

> Among the saints in heaven the Virgin Mary, Mother of God, is venerated in a special way. Because of the mission she received from God, her life is most closely linked with the mysteries of Jesus Christ, and there is no one who has followed in the footsteps of the Incarnate Word more closely and with more merit than she: and no one has more grace and power over the most Sacred Heart of the Son of God, and through him, with the Heavenly Father. Holier than the Cherubim and Seraphim, she enjoys unquestionably greater glory than all the other saints, for she is "full of grace," she is the Mother of God, who happily gave birth to the Redeemer for us. Since she is therefore, "Mother of mercy, our life, our sweetness and our hope," let us all cry to her "mourning and weeping in this vale of tears," and confidently place ourselves and all we have under her patronage. She became our Mother also when the divine Redeemer offered the sacrifice of himself; and hence by this title also, we are her children. She teaches us all the virtues; she gives us her Son and with him all the help we need, for God "wished us to have everything through Mary." (169)

Throughout this liturgical journey which begins anew for us each year under the sanctifying action of the Church, and strengthened by the help and example of the saints, especially of the Immaculate Virgin Mary, "let us draw near with a true heart, in fullness of faith having our hearts sprinkled from an evil conscience, and our bodies washed with clean water," let us draw near to the "High Priest" that with him we may share his life and sentiments and by him penetrate "even within the veil," and there honor the heavenly Father for ever and ever. (170)

When dealing with genuine and solid piety, we stated that there could be no real opposition between the sacred liturgy and other religious practices, provided they be kept within legitimate bounds and performed for a legitimate purpose. In fact, there are certain exercises of piety which the Church recommends very much to clergy and religious. (173)

It is our wish also that the faithful, as well, should take part in these practices. The chief of these are: meditation on spiritual things, diligent examination of conscience, enclosed retreats, visits to the blessed sacrament, and those special prayers in honor of the Blessed Virgin Mary among which the rosary, as all know, has pride of place. (174)

MEDIATRIX

Title used in reference to Mary's role as a mediator. The *Catechism of the Catholic Church* notes the motherhood of Mary in the order of grace continues without interruption from her consent which she gave at the Annunciation and sustained beneath the cross,

"until the eternal fulfillment of all the elect." After being taken up to heaven, she continued this saving office, but also "by her manifold intercession continues to bring us the gifts of eternal salvation. . . . Therefore the Blessed Virgin is invoked in the Church under the titles of Advocate, Helper, Benefactress, and Mediatrix"(*Lumen Gentium*, 62).

The *Catechism* goes on to explain that Mary's function as mother of all people in no way obscures or lessens this unique mediation of Christ, but shows its power. Her "salutary influence" on humanity "flows forth from the superabundance of the merits of Christ, rests on his mediation, depends entirely on it, and draws all its power from it" (*LG* 60).

While no creature could ever be counted along with the Incarnate Word and Redeemer, just as the priesthood of Christ is shared in various ways both by his ministers and the faithful — and as the one goodness of God is radiated in different ways among his creatures — so, too, the unique mediation of the Redeemer does not exclude but rather gives rise to a manifold cooperation which is but a sharing in this one source (*LG* 62, *CCC* 970).

In the words of Pope Paul VI: "We believe that the Holy Mother of God, the new Eve, Mother of the Church, continues in heaven to exercise her maternal role on behalf of the members of Christ" (*Creed of the People of God*, 15).

See also Co-Redemptrix, Co-Redemptorist; Intercession of Mary.

MEDJUGORJE, OUR LADY OF

Title and devotion associated with Bosnia-Herzegovina site of the reported apparitions of Mary to eight children, beginning in 1981.

The children said that Mary referred to herself as the Queen of Peace and that she continued to appear to them even after they were adults. Many pilgrims have been attracted to the spot.

MEMORARE

Prayer attributed to St. Bernard of Clarvaux (c. 1090–1153).

It reads:

Remember, O most gracious Virgin Mary, that never was it known that anyone who fled to your protection, implored your help, or sought your intercession was left unaided. Inspired by this confidence, I fly unto you, O Virgin of Virgins, my Mother. To you I come, before you I stand, sinful and sorrowful. O, Mother of the Word Incarnate, despise not my petitions, but in your mercy hear and answer me. Amen.

MENSE MAIO — *See Paul VI.*

MERCEDARIANS —*See* Mercy, Our Lady of.

MERCY, MOTHER OF

Image and devotion based on visions reported by Antonio Botta on a hillside near Savona, Italy, in 1536. Botta said Mary told him, "I want mercy and not justice." A shrine was built on the spot and later was replaced by a basilica.

MERCY, OUR LADY OF

Image and devotion dating back to the thirteenth century.

Tradition says that around 1218, St. Peter Nolasco and James I, King of Aragon and Catalonia, each separately had a vision of Mary, who asked them to found a religious order dedicated to rescuing the many Christian captives held by the Muslims. St. Peter reported Mary was dressed all in white and the shield of the order was imprinted on a scapular she wore over a long tunic. A cloak covered her shoulders and her long hair was covered by a lace mantilla.

Some images of Our Lady of Mercy have her standing with the Christ Child in her arms, and others depict her with her arms extended showing a royal scepter in her right hand and open chains, a symbol of liberation, in her left.

St. Peter and St. Raymond of Peñafort began the Order of Our Lady of Ransom — the Mercedarians, now called the Order of Our Lady of Mercy. In addition to the usual three vows, the Mercedarians took a fourth vow: to give themselves up, if necessary, in exchange for a slave.

In 1235, Pope Gregory IX approved of the order, which went on to free thousands of Christian prisoners. Later, its ministry shifted to teaching and social work.

In the sixteenth century, Mercedarians who came to Peru with Spanish conquistadors brought the devotion and built the first chapel and later, church, in the city of Lima. There, in what became the Basilica of Mercy, an image of *Our Lady of Mercy* (*La Virgen de la Merced*) was enthroned at the beginning of the seventeenth century, and that Marian image was considered the patroness of the capital. In 1730, she was proclaimed "Patroness of the Peruvian Lands" and, in 1823, "Patroness of the Armies of the Republic."

See also Crown of Twelve Stars; Seven Saturdays in Honor of Our Lady of Ransom.

MERITXELL, OUR LADY OF

Image and devotion based on tradition dating back to the late twelfth century.

Pious legend holds that as townspeople from Meritxell, located in the Pyrenees Mountains, were going to Mass in nearby Canillo they found a wild rose in bloom by the roadside, even though it was winter. At the foot of the shrub was a statue of Mary and the Christ Child. They placed the statue in a chapel in the church in Canillo but found it back at the rose bush the following day. Residents from Encamp took the statue to their church; again, it was back at the rose bush on the next day. Although snow was falling at the time, an area the size of a chapel was completely bare, and the townspeople of Meritxell took that as a sign that they should build a chapel to house the statue. Centuries later, in September 1972, the chapel burned down and the statue was destroyed. The new Meritxell chapel holds a replica of the original image.

MESSAGES AND COMMUNICATIONS FROM MARY — *See Revelation, Divine and Private.*

MILITIA OF THE IMMACULATE CONCEPTION

Canonically established pious association whose purpose is evangelization and catechesis, beginning with members' own consecration to Immaculate Mary. Association membership is open to men and women.

The militia was established by St. Maximilian Kolbe and six fellow Franciscans in Rome in 1917, the seventy-fifth anniversary of the conversion of Alphonse Ratisbonne, a renowned anti-Catholic and agnostic of Jewish lineage. Inspired by the story of Ratisbonne's conversion through the mediation of Our Lady, St. Maximilian and his companions asked for Mary's intercession for anti-Christians of their time.

St. Maximilian Kolbe

MIRACLE

An observable event or effect in the physical or moral order of things, with reference to salvation, that cannot be explained by the ordinary operation of the laws of nature and which, therefore, is attributed to the direct action of God.

A miracle makes known, in an unusual way, the concern and intervention of God in human affairs for the salvation of humanity. A miracle can be related to the intercession of Mary (such as cures at Marian shrines) but all miracles are an act of God.

MIRACULOUS MEDAL

Devotion and image associated with visions of Our Lady reported by St. Catherine Labouré (1806–1876) at Rue du Bac, Paris.

The first Miraculous Medal was made in 1832, based on Mary's instructions to the young French Vincentian nun. Because many

St. Catherine Labouré

cures and conversions were soon attributed to Mary's intercession in association with the medal, it soon became popularly known as the Miraculous Medal.

The front of the oval medal depicts Mary standing on a globe as the Queen of Heaven and Earth, crushing the head of a serpent — representing Satan — beneath her foot. The year of the vision, 1830, is at the bottom of the medal; around the circumference is "O Mary, conceived without sin, pray for us who have recourse to thee." The reference supports the dogma of the Immaculate Conception, proclaimed twenty-four years later in 1854.

The back of the medal has twelve stars around the circumference, which can refer to the apostles representing the entire Church as it surrounds Mary. They also recall the vision of St. John in the Book of Revelation (12:1), in which "a great sign appeared in heaven, a woman clothed with the sun, and the moon under her feet, and on her head a crown of twelve stars." There is a cross in the upper center with a bar under it symbolic of the earth. Entwined in the bar is a large "M" for Mary, representing her association with her son, Jesus; with her part in salvation; and with her role as the mother of the Church. Beneath the "M" are two hearts: the Sacred Heart of Jesus on the left and the Immaculate Heart of Mary on the right.

See Miraculous Medal, Association of the.

MIRACULOUS MEDAL, ASSOCIATION OF THE

Organization formed soon after the first Miraculous Medals were distributed. Established at the motherhouse of the Congregation of the Mission in Paris, its purpose was to spread devotion to Mary.

In appearing to St. Catherine Labouré (1806–1876), Mary entrusted to the Daughters of Charity and the priests of the Congregation of the Mission the work of promoting Marian devotion through her medal.

Over time, other associations were established elsewhere in the world. Pope Pius X recognized these in 1905 and approved a charter in 1909.

In 1918 an association was established by the Western Province of the Congregation of the Mission in the United States, headquartered in Perryville, Missouri. At first operated by the students at St. Mary's Seminary under the direction of their religious superior, it soon expanded and was given its own director, staff, and office space. The National Shrine of Our Lady of the Miraculous Medal is located there. The association has more then one million enrolled members and 65,000 promoters. There are about 350,000 contributors to the association.

See also Miraculous Medal.

MIRIAM —*See Name of Mary.*

MIRROR OF JUSTICE

Marian title used in the Litany of the Blessed Virgin Mary (also known as the Litany of Loreto), which was originally approved in 1587 by Pope Sixtus V.

Mary is referred to as "the mirror of justice" because she reflects the sanctity, holiness, and supernatural goodness of her son, Christ.

MIRROR OF OUR LADY — *See Brigettine Office.*

MISSIONARY OBLATES OF MARY IMMACULATE — *See Oblates of Mary Immaculate.*

MISSIONARY ROSARY

Multicolored Rosary promoted by members of the Society of the Divine Word (SVD) to

Our Lady of the Miraculous Medal

encourage prayer for the missions worldwide. The beads are:

Red for the Americas (both North and South), green for Africa, white for Europe, blue for Oceania, and yellow for Asia.

MISSIONARIES OF OUR LADY OF AFRICA — *See* **Africa, Our Lady of.**

MODEL OF FAITH AND CHARITY

Description of Mary used in the *Catechism of the Catholic Church*:

> By her complete adherence to the Father's will, to his Son's redemptive work, and to every prompting of the Holy Spirit, the Virgin Mary is the Church's model of faith and charity. Thus she is a "preeminent and . . . wholly unique member of the Church"; indeed, she is the "exemplary realization" (typus) [LG 53; 63] of the Church. (967)

MONTH OF MARY — *See May.*

MONTH OF THE ROSARY — *See October.*

MONTHLY DEVOTIONS

Custom of dedicating a particular month to a specific devotion.

Traditionally they are: January, the Holy Name; February, the Passion of Our Lord; March, St Joseph; April, the Holy Eucharist; May, Our Lady; June, the Sacred Heart; July, the Most Precious Blood; August, the Immaculate Heart of Mary; September, Our Lady of Sorrows; October, the Most Holy Rosary; November, the Holy Souls; December, the Divine Infancy.

MONTSERRAT

Benedictine monastery and a shrine to Our Lady near Barcelona, Spain.

The image of Mary there dates back to the twelfth or thirteenth century. It is polychrome wood and has black features and so is called *La Morenita* or "the little dark one." The monastery began in the eleventh century and was rebuilt in the nineteenth century. This particular Black Madonna is the patron of Catalonia. Her feast day is on April 27.

See also **Black Madonnas.**

MORNING OFFERING

Prayer recited each morning, offering the day in union with Christ's self-offering

The most common form in the United States is that used by the Apostleship of Prayer, an association begun in 1844 by Fr. Francis Xavier Gautrelet, S.J. in the seminary in Le Puy, France. Now worldwide, it promotes the glory of God and the salvation of souls through constant prayer, particularly to the Sacred Heart. It is headquartered in Rome with secretariats in most countries. Members daily make an offering and pray for the particular intentions of the pope.

The prayer reads:

O Jesus, through the Immaculate Heart of Mary, I offer You all my prayers, works, joys

and sufferings of this day, for all the intentions of Your Sacred Heart, in union with the Holy Sacrifice of the Mass throughout the world, in reparation for my sins, for the intentions of all our associates, and for the general intention recommended this month.

See also Immaculate Heart of Mary.

MORNING STAR

Marian title used in the Litany of the Blessed Virgin Mary (also known as the Litany of Loreto), which was originally approved in 1587 by Pope Sixtus V.

Mary is referred to as "the morning star" because as the morning star precedes the sun, announcing the dawn of the day, she precedes Christ, the "Sun of Justice," announcing the day of salvation.

MOST BLESSED SACRAMENT, OUR LADY OF THE

Title and devotion associated with St. Peter Julian Eymard (1811–1868), founder of the Congregation of the Blessed Sacrament.

In 1865, while on a long retreat in Rome and meditating on Mary, Peter wrote:

> I owe to her my preservation, my vocation and above all the grace of the Most Blessed Sacrament. She gave me to her Son as his servant, his child of predilection.

And later:

> How she has led me by the hand, all by herself, to the priesthood! And then to the Most Blessed Sacrament! From Nazareth Jesus went to the Cenacle and Mary there made her dwelling place.

Biographers note that the priest's consecration to Mary led him to consecrate himself to the Eucharist, and from that point his Marian devotion was opened up to a new dimension: with Mary, from Nazareth to the Cenacle. They add that in the nineteenth century, when Marian devotion was strongly influenced by the revelations of Mary of Agreda (a seventeenth-century Franciscan mystic), Peter could imagine Our Lady receiving communion from the hand of St. John and in continuous adoration before the tabernacle. It was reasonable to assume that after the Ascension, Mary lived in the heart of the Christian community, both as a member and as a symbol of the Church. She was present, even if not named, at a time when "they devoted themselves to the apostles' teaching, and to fellowship, and to the breaking of bread and prayer."

By 1864, Peter had planned the bold project of acquiring the Cenacle of Jerusalem and making it into a chapel of eucharistic adoration. During his lengthy stay at Rome in 1864–1865, in order to follow through with his plan, he spent nine weeks on retreat while waiting for the reply from the Vatican. During this time, he discovered that what really mattered was not the shrine of the Cenacle or the creation of a community at Jerusalem but "the Cenacle in me — the glory of God in me." He received this grace in a special way with the vow he made, on March 21, 1865, of the gift of his personality.

His meditation on Mary in the Incarnation carries traces of this:

> The adoration of the Most Holy Virgin of the incarnate Word. Here is my model, my mother Mary! First adorer of the incarnate Word. I have made a great request to our

Lord, that of giving me to the Most Holy Virgin, adorer, as my true mother, and of making me part . . . of her act of continual adoration while she carried the incarnate Word in her womb.

Tradition says that shortly before his death, on May 1, 1868, while inaugurating the month of Mary at the novitiate of Saint-Maurice, near Paris, Peter invited order members to honor Mary under the title of Our Lady of the Most Blessed Sacrament, as a final testimony of his Marian devotion.

See also Agreda, Venerable Mary of; Cenacle.

MOST EXCELLENT FRUIT OF REDEMPTION

Description of Mary given in the Second Vatican Council's *Constitution on the Sacred Liturgy* (*Sacrosanctum Concilium*):

In celebrating this annual cycle of Christ's mysteries, holy Church honors with especial love the Blessed Mary, Mother of God, who is joined by an inseparable bond to the saving work of her Son. In her the Church holds up and admires the most excellent fruit of the redemption, and joyfully contemplates, as in a faultless image that which she herself desires and hopes wholly to be. (103)

MOTHER OF CHRIST, OF DIVINE GRACE, MOST PURE, MOST CHASTE, INVIOLATE, UNDEFILED, MOST AMIABLE, MOST ADMIRABLE, OF GOOD COUNSEL, OF OUR CREATOR, OF OUR SAVIOR — *See Litany of the Blessed Virgin Mary.*

MOTHER OF EMMANUEL

Title that refers to Mary being the mother of Jesus under his messianic title "God with us." After learning that Mary was pregnant, Joseph was told by an angel in a dream:

Behold, a virgin shall conceive and bear a son and his name shall be called Emmanuel (which means, God with us) (Mt. 1:23, quoting Is. 7:14).

In his 1987 encyclical, *Redemptoris Mater* (*On the Blessed Virgin Mary in the life of the Pilgrim Church*), Pope John Paul II noted:

Through the faith and piety of individual believers; through the traditions of Christian families or "domestic churches," of parish and missionary communities, religious institutes and dioceses; through the radiance and attraction of the great shrines where not only individuals or local groups, but sometimes whole nations and societies, even whole continents, seek to meet the Mother of the Lord, the one who is blessed because she believed is the first among believers and therefore became the Mother of Emmanuel. (28)

MOTHER OF GOD

Doctrine and title dogmatically defined at the Council of Ephesus in 431.

As the Second Vatican Council points out in its *Dogmatic Constitution on the Church* (*Lumen Gentium*):

From the earliest times the Blessed Virgin is honored under the title of "Mother of God" (*Theotokos*), under whose protection the faithful take refuge together in prayer in all their perils and needs (66).

Theotokos — "bearer of God"— is Mary's principal title in the Greek Church. It dates back to the third century and was probably first used by Origen (185–254) and then accepted by the Greek Fathers of the Church. It has been translated into Latin at *Mater Dei* (Mother of God), *Dei Genitrix* (She who has borne God), and *Deipera* (Birthgiver of God).

Although *Theotokos* is not a biblical title for Mary, the New Testament's revelation regarding the human origins (*tokos*) of Jesus from the Virgin Mary began a line of development in the tradition. Over time, that led to the Church calling her the Mother of God (*Theos*) to safeguard the mystery of the Incarnation (the Second Person of the Blessed Trinity being born a human being).

What the New Testament does offer are portraits of Christ (or "Christologies") of conception and preexistence. He was born of Mary, *and* he existed and was divine before that birth.

Matthew and Luke write of the birth of Jesus. In Luke's infancy narrative, Mary is told:

> "And behold, you will conceive in your womb and bear a son, and you shall call his name Jesus. He will be great, and will be called the Son of the Most High; and the Lord God will give to him the throne of his father David, and he will reign over the house of Jacob for ever; and of his kingdom there will be no end. . . . therefore the child to be born will be called holy, the Son of God" (Lk. 1:31–33, 35).

St. Paul writes "for us there is one God, the Father, from whom are all things and for whom we exist, and one Lord, Jesus Christ, through whom are all things and through whom we exist" (1 Cor. 8:6). And the Prologue of John's Gospel speaks explicitly of the same Word (*Logos*) who became a human being is also God (*Theos*).

At the end of the New Testament era, the conception and preexistence Christologies combined in Sacred Tradition. (It is another example of how Tradition may develop dogmas that are rooted, but not explicitly affirmed, in Scripture.)

Theotokos

A most ancient prayer to Mary, the *Sub Tuum Praesidium*, begins "We fly to your patronage, O Holy Mother of God." Some historians date the Greek version going back as early as the third century. Alexander, the Patriarch of Alexandria, was the first to use the title in his writing in 325. His successor, St. Athanasius (c. 295–373) used it often in his writing as did St. Cyril of Jerusalem (died c. 386) and Eusebius of Caesarea (c. 260–c. 340) in early Christian Palestine. In the last half of the fourth century in what is now Turkey, St. Basil the Great (c. 330–379), St. Gregory Nazianzus (c. 329–c. 390), and St. Gregory of Nyssa (c. 335–c. 394) used the title.

In the fifth century, the Nestorian controversy led to *Theotokos* being dogmatically defined. The dispute focused primarily on the Incarnation. Nestorius, Patriarch of Constantinople (died c. 451) had been asked to make a pronouncement on whether or not it was accurate to give Mary the title Mother of God. Although *Theotokos* had been used for at least a century and probably longer, he ruled in favor of *Christokos,* "Christ-Bearer." In making his decision, he noted concern that *Theotokos* would make Mary appear to be a goddess who gives birth to divinity. Then, too, he added, it presented the risk of reducing Jesus to a mere creature, as the Arian heresy had done in the previous century (a position condemned by the Council of Nicaea in 325 and the Council of Constantinople in 381). And, a third concern, giving Mary the title of Mother of God could make the human nature of Christ seem incomplete — as had the heresy of Apollinarius, who denied that Jesus had a human soul (a position also condemned at Constantinople).

See also Ephesus, Council of; Solemnity of Mary, Mother of God.

MOTHER OF THE CHURCH

Title proclaimed by Pope Paul VI in 1964 at the close of the third session of the Second Vatican Council. The pontiff declared Mary as "Mother of the Church," meaning mother of the whole people of God, in response to requests from bishops at the council. Though this was an explicit affirmation in the idea of Mary in this role, it had been accepted by popes before Paul VI.

Later, Pope John Paul II inserted the title in the Litany of the Blessed Virgin Mary.

MOTHER OF REFUGEES —*See* Bai Dau, Our Lady of.

MOTHER THRICE ADMIRABLE

Title given to Marian image at Ingolstadt, Germany. Fr. James Rem, S.J., (1546–1618) believed the title "Mother most admirable" in the Litany of Loreto (later called the Litany of the Blessed Virgin Mary) was a summary of all of Mary's privileges and of her whole being. He came to this conclusion during a mystical experience while the students of the *Colloquium Marianum* (Marian congregation) were singing the litany and he had them repeat the petition three times, in the form of a *trishagion*, meaning each was given greater emphasis. The custom developed, and the image of Mary and the Christ Child in the school chapel was named thrice blessed, wonderful, or admirable.

This title was adopted in 1915 by future members of the Schoenstatt Movement who venerate her as *Mother thrice admirable, Queen and Victoress of Schoenstatt.*

See also **Schoenstatt, Our Lady of.**

MYSTERIES OF THE ROSARY —*See Rosary.*

MYSTERY PLAYS AND MARY

Religious dramas performed during the Middle Ages. Some honoring Mary were held on Marian feasts, such as the Assumption on August 15.

MYSTICAL ROSE

Marian title used in the Litany of the Blessed Virgin Mary (also known as the Litany of Loreto), which was originally approved in 1587 by Pope Sixtus V.

It compares the rose as the queen of flowers with Mary as the queen of saints. She is also seen as the greatest mystic, because she kept all these things "in her heart" (Lk. 2:19, 51).

In ancient times, the rose was a symbol of mystery; in the the early Christian community, it was used to symbolize both martyrdom and paradise.

See also **Litany of the Blessed Virgin Mary.**

Mystical Rose

NAME OF MARY

Mary is the English translation of the Latin *Maria* or Greek *Maria* or *Mariam*, which comes from the Hebrew *Miriam*.

The meaning and etymology of *miryam* is uncertain but perhaps may be derived from the Egyptian *mrjt* meaning "beloved." Miriam was also the name of the sister of Moses and Aaron.

NAME OF MARY, MOST HOLY

September 12 feast day that began in Spain in 1513 and in 1671 was extended to all of that country and the Kingdom of Naples. In 1683, King John Sobieski of Poland — who had entrusted himself to Mary — brought his troops to Vienna where they stopped the advance of Turks loyal to Mohammed IV in Constantinople. In gratitude to Our Lady, Pope Innocent XI made the feast universal.

See also **Piekary, Our Lady of.**

NATIVITY — *See Scripture, Mary in.*

NATIVITY OF MARY — *See Birth of Mary.*

NAZARETH — *See Scripture, Mary in.*

NEED, OUR LADY IN

Reference to Mary entrusted by Jesus to the care of St. John the Evangelist at the foot of the cross (Jn. 19:26–27).

John and Mary

NEW EVE

Title that refers to Mary's role at the re-creation of humanity through the Redemption.

The concept date backs to the writing of the Church Fathers who noted that Paul had portrayed Christ as the New Adam. For example, in comparing Mary to Eve, St. Irenaeus (130–202) wrote: "It was right and necessary that Adam be restored in Christ . . . that Eve be restored in Mary. . . ."

In their *Dogmatic Constitution on the Church* (*Lumen Gentium*), the bishops at Vatican II noted:

> By her belief and obedience, not knowing man but overshadowed by the Holy Spirit, as the new Eve she brought forth on earth the very Son of the Father, showing an undefiled faith, not in the word of the ancient serpent, but in that of God's messenger (63).

NEW MILLENNIUM, OUR LADY OF THE

Thirty-three-foot, 8.5-ton statue of Mary commissioned by Carl Demma of Oak Lawn, IL, to fulfill his lifelong dream of bringing Our Lady to all the people of the Chicago area. Made of steel ribbons by Charles Cooper Parks of Wilmington, DE, the statue was blessed by Pope John Paul II during his visit to St. Louis in 1999 and by Chicago's Cardinal Francis George, O.M.I., outside Holy Name Cathedral that same year.

A "pilgrim statue," it is moved from parish to parish on a flatbed truck fitted with hydraulic lifts and leather straps for positioning. The statue remains on the truck for viewing.

A prayer to Our Lady of the New Millennium, written by Pope John Paul II reads:

Mother of the Redeemer,
with great joy we call you blessed.

In order to carry out His plan of salvation,
God the Father chose you before the creation
of the world.
You believed in His love and obeyed His
word.

The Son of God desired you for His Mother
when He became man to save the human
race.
You received Him with ready obedience and
undivided heart.

The Holy Spirit loved you as His mystical
spouse
and filled you with singular gifts.
You allowed yourself to be led
by His hidden and powerful actions.

On the eve of the third Christian
Millennium,
we entrust to you the Church
which acknowledges you and invokes you as
Mother.

To you, Mother of the human family and of
the nations,
we confidently entrust the whole of
humanity,
with its hopes and fears.

Do not let it lack the light of true wisdom.
Guide its steps in the ways of peace.
Enable all to meet Christ,
the Way, the Truth, and the Life.

Sustain us, O Virgin Mary, on our journey
of faith
and obtain for us the grace of eternal
salvation.
O clement, O loving, O sweet Mother of
God and our Mother, Mary!

NICENE CREED

Profession of faith recited at Sunday Mass. The original Nicene Creed was written and issued by the Council of Nicaea in 325 in response to the Arian heresy. The prayer known today as the Nicene Creed is, more accurately, the Nicene-Constantinople Creed, issued by the First Council of Constantinople in 381. It is more sophisticated than the Apostles' Creed or the original Nicene Creed and makes reference to Christ's being "born of the Virgin Mary."

The prayer reads:

We believe in one God, the Father, the
Almighty, maker of heaven and earth, of
all that is seen and unseen.

We believe in one Lord, Jesus Christ, the
only Son of God, eternally begotten of
the Father, God from God, Light from
Light, true God from true God,
begotten, not made, one in Being with
the Father. Through him all things were
made. For us men and for our salvation
he came down from heaven: by the
power of the Holy Spirit he was born of
the Virgin Mary, and became man. For
our sake he was crucified under Pontius
Pilate; he suffered, died, and was buried.
On the third day he rose again in
fulfillment of the Scriptures; he ascended
into heaven and is seated at the right
hand of the Father. He will come again
in glory to judge the living and the dead,
and His kingdom will have no end.

We believe in the Holy Spirit, the Lord, the
giver of life, who proceeds from the
Father and the Son. With the Father
and the Son he is worshiped and
glorified. He has spoken through the
Prophets.

We believe in one holy catholic and
apostolic Church. We acknowledge one
baptism for the forgiveness of sins. We
look for the resurrection of the dead, and
the life of the world to come. Amen.

NOTRE DAME DU CAP — *See Cape, Our Lady of the.*

NOVENA

Public or private devotional practices over a period of nine consecutive days or, by extension, over nine weeks in which one day a week is set aside for the devotions. The word novena is derived from the Latin word *novem,* meaning "nine."

Traditionally, the nine days between the Ascension of Our Lord and the descent of the Holy Spirit on Mary and the apostles on Pentecost Sunday have been considered the first novena.

Novenas feature prayers for a particular intention, and are in honor of a particular saint, or a particular facet of the life of Jesus or Mary. The person making the novena is often praying to obtain special graces or favors. Any suitable prayers may be used in making a novena, but it is preferable to attend Mass and receive Holy Communion daily as practices of the novena.

Public novenas are made in churches, often in preparation for a specific feast. Other elements of the novena services may include the Stations of the Cross, litanies, and hymns.

Many of today's novenas first gained popularity in the seventeenth century, but the spirit of the novena stretches further back in history. The exact origin of this custom is unknown.

A novena in honor of Our Lady of Perpetual Help is known worldwide. Other Marian novenas include the Immaculate Conception, Mount Carmel, and the Sorrowful Mother.

See also particular Marian novenas.

NOVENA IN HONOR OF THE IMMACULATE CONCEPTION

One version of the prayer reads:

Almighty Father, we offer this novena to honor the Blessed Virgin Mary. She occupies a place in the Church which is highest after Christ and yet very close to us, for you chose her to give to the world that very Life which renews all things, Jesus Christ Your Son and Our Lord.

And so we praise you, Mary, Virgin and mother. After the Savior himself, you alone are all holy, free from all stain of sin, gifted by God from the first instant of your conception with a unique holiness.

R. We praise and honor you.

Mary, free from all sin and led by the Holy Spirit, you embraced God's saving will with a full heart, and devoted yourself totally as a

handmaid of the Lord to the fulfillment of his will in your life, and to the mystery of man's redemption.

R. We thank you and love you.

Mary, your privileged and grace-filled origin is the Father's final step in preparing humanity to receive its Redeemer in human form. Your fullness of grace is the Father's sign of his favor to the Church and also his promise to the Church of its perfection as the Bride of Christ, radiant in beauty. Your holiness in the beginning of your life is the foreshadowing of that all embracing holiness with which the Father will surround his people when his Son comes at the end of time to greet us.

R. We bless you among all women.

Mary, we turn with confidence to you who are always ready to listen with a mother's affection and powerful assistance. Consoler of the Afflicted, Health of the Sick, Refuge of Sinners, grant us comfort in tribulation, relief in sickness, and liberating strength in our weakness.

You who are free from sin, lead us to combat sin. Obtain for us the victory of hope over anguish, of fellowship over alienation, of peace over anxiety, of joy and beauty over boredom and disgust, of eternal visions over temporal ones, of life over death. Mary, conceived without sin, pray for us who have recourse to you. (Mention your request here.)

Let us pray:

God Our Father, we make these petitions through Mary. We pray most especially for the coming of your Kingdom. May you, together with your Son and Holy Spirit, be known, loved and glorified and your law of love faithfully followed. We pray in faith through Jesus Christ, your Son and Our Lord, in whom all fullness dwells, now and forever. Amen.

See also Immaculate Conception.

NOVENA TO OUR LADY OF GOOD REMEDY

One version of the prayer reads:

O Queen of heaven and earth, Most Holy Virgin, we venerate you. You are the beloved Daughter of the Most High God, the chosen Mother of the Incarnate Word, the Immaculate Spouse of the Holy Spirit, the Sacred Vessel of the Most Holy Trinity.

O Mother of the Divine Redeemer, who under the title of Our Lady of Good Remedy comes to the aid of all who call upon you, extend your maternal protection to us. We depend on you, Dear Mother, as helpless and needy children depend on a tender and caring mother.

Hail, Mary . . .

Our Lady of Good Remedy, source of unfailing help, grant that we may draw from your treasury of graces in our time of need. Touch the hearts of sinners, that they may seek reconciliation and forgiveness. Bring comfort to the afflicted and the lonely; help the poor and the hopeless; aid the sick and the suffering. May they be healed in body and strengthened in spirit to endure their sufferings with patient resignation and Christian fortitude.

Hail, Mary . . .

Dear Lady of Good Remedy, source of unfailing help, your compassionate heart knows a remedy for every affliction and misery we encounter in life. Help me with your prayers and intercession to find remedy for my problems and needs, especially for: (mention your petition).

On my part, O loving Mother, I pledge myself to a more intensely Christian lifestyle, to a

more careful observance of the laws of God, to be more conscientious in fulfilling the obligations of my state in life, and to strive to be a source of healing in this broken world of ours.

Dear Lady of Good Remedy, be ever present to me, and through your intercession, may I enjoy health of body and peace of mind, and grow stronger in the faith and in the love of your Son, Jesus.

Hail, Mary . . .

V. *Pray for us, O Holy Mother of Good Remedy.*

R. *That we may deepen our dedication to your Son, and make the world alive with his Spirit. Amen.*

See also Good Remedy, Our Lady of.

NOVENA TO OUR LADY OF MOUNT CARMEL

One version of the prayer reads:

First Day

O Beautiful Flower of Carmel, most fruitful vine, splendor of heaven, holy and singular, who brought forth the Son of God, still ever remaining a pure virgin, assist us in our necessity! O Star of the Sea, help and protect us! Show us that you are our Mother!

(pause and mention petitions)

Our Father, Hail Mary, and Glory Be.
Our Lady of Mount Carmel, pray for us.

Second Day

Most Holy Mary, Our Mother, in your great love for us you gave us the Holy Scapular of Mount Carmel, having heard the prayers of your chosen son St. Simon Stock. Help us now to wear it faithfully and with devotion. May it be a sign to us of our desire to grow in holiness.

(pause and mention petitions)

Our Father, Hail Mary, and Glory Be.
Our Lady of Mount Carmel, pray for us.

Third Day

O Queen of Heaven, you gave us the Scapular as an outward sign by which we might be known as your faithful children. May we always wear it with honor by avoiding sin and imitating your virtues. Help us to be faithful to this desire of ours.

(pause and mention petitions)

Our Father, Hail Mary, and Glory Be.
Our Lady of Mount Carmel, pray for us.

Fourth Day

When you gave us, Gracious Lady, the Scapular as our Habit, you called us to be not only servants, but also your own children. We ask you to gain for us from your Son the grace to live as you children in joy, peace and love.

(pause and mention petitions)

Our Father, Hail Mary, and Glory Be.
Our Lady of Mount Carmel, pray for us.

Fifth Day

O Mother of Fair Love, through your goodness, as your children, we are called to live in the spirit of Carmel. Help us to live in charity with one another, prayerful as Elijah of old, and mindful of our call to minister to God's people.

(pause and mention petitions)

Our Father, Hail Mary, and Glory Be.
Our Lady of Mount Carmel, pray for us.

Sixth Day

With loving provident care, O Mother Most Amiable, you covered us with your Scapular as a shield of defense against the Evil One. Through your assistance, may we bravely struggle against the powers of evil, always open to your Son, Jesus Christ.

(pause and mention petitions)

Our Father, Hail Mary, and Glory Be.
Our Lady of Mount Carmel, pray for us.

Seventh Day

O Mary, Help of Christians, you assured us that wearing your Scapular worthily would keep us safe from harm. Protect us in both body and soul with your continual aid. May all that we do be pleasing to your Son and to you.

(pause and mention petitions)

Our Father, Hail Mary, and Glory Be.
Our Lady of Mount Carmel, pray for us.

Eighth Day

You give us hope, O Mother of Mercy, that through your Scapular promise we might quickly pass through the fires of purgatory to the Kingdom of your Son. Be our comfort and our hope. Grant that our hope may not be in vain but that, ever faithful to your Son and to you, we may speedily enjoy after death the blessed company of Jesus and the saints.

(pause and mention petitions)

Our Father, Hail Mary, and Glory Be.
Our Lady of Mount Carmel, pray for us.

Ninth Day

O Most Holy Mother of Mount Carmel, when asked by a saint to grant privileges to the family of Carmel, you gave assurance of your Motherly love and help to those faithful to you and to your Son.

Behold us, your children. We glory in wearing your holy habit, which makes us members of your family of Carmel, through which we shall have your powerful protection in life, at death and even after death.

Look down with love, O Gate of Heaven, on all those now in their last agony!

Look down graciously, O Virgin, Flower of Carmel, on all those in need of help!

Look down mercifully, O Mother of our Savior, on all those who do not know that they are numbered among your children.

Look down tenderly, O Queen of All Saints, on the poor souls!

(pause and mention petitions)

Our Father, Hail Mary, and Glory Be.
Our Lady of Mount Carmel, pray for us.

See also **Carmel, Our Lady of Mount.**

NOVENA TO OUR LADY OF PERPETUAL HELP

Popular devotion long associated with the Redemptorist Congregation.

Fifty years after the icon *Our Lady of Perpetual Help* was given to the Redemptorist by Pope Pius IX (r. 1846–1878), the Redemptorists of St. Louis, Missouri, commemorated the event by having a Solemn Novena in her honor in their church. Later, monthly novenas were held, and in 1916 a perpetual novena, held weekly, was established.

One version of the prayer reads:

Behold at your feet, O Mother of Perpetual Help, a wretched sinner who has recourse to you. O Mother of Mercy, have pity on me. I hear you called by all, the Refuge and the Hope of sinners; be, then, my refuge and my hope. Assist me, for the love of Jesus Christ; stretch forth your hand to a miserable fallen creature who recommends himself to you, and who devotes himself to your service forever. I bless and thank Almighty God, who in his mercy has given me this confidence in you, which I hold to be a pledge of my eternal salvation. It is true, dearest Mother, that in the past I have miserably fallen into sin because I had not turned to you. I know that with your help I shall conquer. I know, too, that you will assist me, if I recommend myself to you; but I fear, dear Mother. that in time of danger, I may neglect to call on you, and thus lose my soul. This grace, then, I ask of you with all my soul, that, in all the attacks of hell, I may ever have recourse to you. O Mary, help me; O Mother of Perpetual Help, never suffer me to lose my God.

Three Hail Marys.

Mother of Perpetual Help, grant that I may ever invoke your most powerful name, which is the safeguard of the living and the salvation of the dying. O Purest Mary, O Sweetest Mary, let your name henceforth be ever on my lips! Delay not, O Blessed Lady, to help me whenever I call on you; for, in all my temptations, in all my needs, I shall never cease to call on you, ever repeating your Sacred Name, Mary! O, what consolation, what sweetness, what confidence what emotion fills my soul when I utter your Sacred Name, or even only think of you! I thank the Lord for having given you, for my good, so sweet, so powerful, so lovely a name. But I will not be content with merely uttering your name; let my love for you prompt me ever to hail you, Mother of Perpetual Help.

Three Hail Marys.

Mother of Perpetual Help, you are the dispenser of all the gifts which God grants to us miserable sinners; and for this end he has made you so powerful, so rich, and so bountiful in order that you may help us in our misery. You are the advocate of the most wretched and abandoned sinners who have recourse to you; come to my aid, dearest Mother, for I recommend myself to you. In your hands I place my eternal salvation, and to you I entrust my soul. Count me among your most devoted servants; take me under your protection and it is enough for me. For, if you protect me, dear Mother, I fear nothing; not from my sins, because you will obtain for me the pardon of them from Jesus your Divine Son. But one thing I fear, that in the hour of temptation I may through negligence fail to have recourse to you and thus perish miserably. Obtain for me, therefore, the pardon of my sins, love for Jesus, final perseverance, and the grace to have recourse to you and (mention your request here), *O Mother of Perpetual Help.*

Three Hail Marys.

Pray for us, O Mother of Perpetual Help, that we may be made worthy of the promises of Christ.

Let us pray: Lord Jesus Christ, who gave us your Holy Mother, Mary, whose renowned image we venerate, to be a Mother ever ready to help us, grant, we beseech you, that we who constantly implore her maternal aid may merit to enjoy perpetually the fruits of your redemption, who lives and reigns with God forever and ever. Amen.

See also Perpetual Help, Our Lady of.

NOVENA TO OUR LADY OF THE ROSARY

Said along with the Rosary, one version of the prayer reads:

My dearest Mother Mary, behold me, your child, in prayer at your feet. Accept this Holy Rosary, which I offer you in accordance with your requests at Fatima, as a proof of my tender love for you, for the intentions of the Sacred Heart of Jesus, in atonement for the offenses committed against your Immaculate Heart, and for this special favor which I earnestly request in my Rosary Novena: (mention petitions).

I beg you to present my petition to your Divine Son. If you will pray for me, I cannot be refused. I know, dearest Mother, that you want me to seek God's holy will concerning my request. If what I ask for should not be granted, pray that I may receive that which will be of greater benefit to my soul.

I offer you this spiritual "Bouquet of Roses" because I love you. I put all my confidence in you, since your prayers before God are most powerful. For the greater glory of God and for the sake of Jesus, your loving Son, hear and grant my prayer. Sweet Heart of Mary, be my salvation. Amen.

NOVENA TO OUR SORROWFUL MOTHER

One version of the prayer reads:

1. For a Particular Grace

Most blessed and afflicted Virgin, Queen of Martyrs, who did stand generously beneath the cross, beholding the agony of your dying Son; by the sword of sorrow which then pierced your soul, by the sufferings of your sorrowful life, by the unutterable joy which now more than repays you for them; look down with a mother's pity and tenderness, as I kneel before you to contemplate your sorrows, and to lay my petition with childlike confidence in your wounded heart. I beg of you, O my Mother, to plead continually for me with your Son, since he can refuse you nothing, and through the merits of his most sacred Passion and Death, together with your own sufferings at the foot of the cross, so to touch his Sacred Heart, that I may obtain my request: (mention your requests and let your secondary intention be to pray for the intentions of all the people making this novena anywhere in the world).

Sorrowful Mother by Kaulbach

For to whom shall I fly in my wants and miseries, if not to you, O Mother of mercy, who, having so deeply drunk the chalice of your Son, can most pity us poor exiles, still doomed to sigh in this vale of tears? Offer to Jesus but one drop of his Precious Blood, but one pang of his adorable Heart; remind him that you are our life, our sweetness, and our hope, and you will obtain what I ask, through Jesus Christ our Lord. Amen.

Hail Mary. Virgin Most Sorrowful, pray for us. (Repeated seven times each.)

2. *Prayer for a Happy Death*

Mary, Refuge of Sinners, my sweet Mother, by the sorrow you did experience, when you did witness the agony and death of your divine Son on the cross, mercifully intercede for me, I entreat you, when my soul is about to leave this world; drive away all evil spirits, come to take my soul, and to present it to the eternal Judge. O Queen of Heaven, do not abandon your child; next to Jesus you will be my comfort in that dread hour. Ask your Son to grant, in his infinite mercy, that I may die embracing his holy feet, kissing his sacred wounds, saying with my last breath: "Jesus, Mary and Joseph, I give you my heart and my soul." Amen.

3. *The Hail Mary of Our Sorrowful Mother*

(Prayer of St. Bonaventure)

Hail! Mary, full of sorrows, the Crucified is with you; tearful are you among women, and tearful is the fruit of your womb, Jesus. Holy Mary, Mother of the Crucified, give tears to us, crucifiers of your Son, now, and at the hour of our death. Amen.

4. *For Our Sick Relatives and Friends*

Queen of Martyrs and Mother of Consolation by that sword of sorrow which pierced your soul, when you did see your Son Jesus Christ our Lord raised upon the cross, pierced with nails and covered with His own Blood; pray for these sick persons (mention names here) that they may by your powerful intercession be cured of their illness, and thus we may both in time and eternity give you heartfelt thanks.

5. For Our Beloved Dead

Most Blessed Virgin Mary, my Mother, I turn to you in supplication, and by that sword which pierced your sorrowful heart, when you did behold your beloved Son Jesus Christ bow down his head and give up the ghost, I pray and beseech you to help the holy souls in purgatory, and particularly those for whom I now pray. (Mention names here.)

Mother of Sorrows, Queen of Martyrs for the love of your divine Son, whose precious blood was shed for us, help us with your powerful intercession, who are in danger not only of falling into purgatory, but of losing our souls forever in hell. O Mary, Mother of Grace; Mother of mercy, pray for us now and at the hour of our death.

Eternal Father, through the most precious Blood of Jesus and the Sorrows of Mary, have pity upon the holy souls in purgatory. Amen.

6. An Act of Consecration to Our Sorrowful Mother

Holy Mary, Mother of God and Queen of Martyrs, I do this day choose you as my model, protectress, and advocate. In your Immaculate Heart, pierced with so many swords of sorrow, I place my poor soul forever. Receive me as your special servant as a partaker in your sufferings. Give me strength always to remain close to that Cross on which your only Son died for me. All that I am and have, I consecrate to your service. Accept every good work that I may perform and offer it to your Son for me. Dear Mother, help me to be worthy of the title: "Servant of Mary." Stand by me in all my actions that they may be directed to the glory of God. As you were close to Christ, your Son, on the cross, be near to me, your child, in my last agony. Obtain for me, that I may invoke your and his sweet Name saying with my lips and my heart: "Jesus, Mary, and Joseph, assist me in my last agony. Jesus, Mary, and Joseph, may I die in peace in your holy company."

See also Servites.

NOVENA TO THE IMMACULATE CONCEPTION

One version of the prayer reads:

Immaculate Virgin! Mary, conceived without sin! Remember, you were miraculously preserved from even the shadow of sin, because you were destined to become not only the Mother of God, but also the mother, the refuge, and the advocate of man; filled therefore, with the most lively confidence in your never-failing intercession, we most humbly implore you to look with favor upon the intentions of this novena, and to obtain for us the graces and the favors we request.

You know, O Mary, how often our hearts are the sanctuaries of God, who abhors iniquity. Obtain for us, then, that angelic purity which was your favorite virtue, that purity of heart which will attach us to God alone, and that purity of intention which will consecrate every thought, word, and action to his greater glory. Obtain also for us a constant spirit of prayer and self-denial, that we may recover by penance that innocence which we have lost by sin, and at length attain safely to that *blessed abode of the saints, where nothing defiled can enter.*

O Mary, conceived without sin, pray for us who have recourse to you.

V. You are all fair, O Mary.

R. You are all fair, O Mary.

V. And the original stain is not in you.

R. And the original stain is not in you.

V. You are the glory of Jerusalem.

R. You are the joy of Israel.

V. You are the honor of our people.

R. You are the advocate of sinners.

V. O Mary, Virgin, most prudent.

R. O Mary, Mother, most tender.

V. Pray for us.

R. Intercede for us with Jesus our Lord.

V. In your conception, Holy Virgin, you were immaculate.

R. Pray for us to the Father whose Son you did bring forth.

V. O Lady!, aid my prayer.

R. And let my cry come unto you.

Let us pray: Holy Mary, Queen of Heaven, Mother of Our Lord Jesus Christ, and mistress of the world, who forsakes no one, and despises no one, look upon me, O Lady!, with an eye of pity, and entreat for me of your beloved Son the forgiveness of all my sins; that, as I now celebrate, with devout affection, your holy and immaculate conception, so, hereafter I may receive the prize of eternal blessedness, by the grace of him whom you, in virginity, did bring forth, Jesus Christ Our Lord: Who, with the Father and the Holy Spirit, lives and reigns, in perfect Trinity, God, world without end. Amen.

See also Immaculate Conception.

NUNC DIMITTIS

The canticle, or hymn, that Simeon proclaimed when seeing Jesus with Mary and Joseph in the Temple at the Presentation. The name comes from the first two words of the prayer in Latin.

Recorded in the Gospel of Luke (Lk. 2: 29–32), it is an expression of joy and thanksgiving for the blessing of having lived to see the Messiah. It is used in the Night Prayer of the Liturgy of the Hours.

Luke notes that Joseph and Mary were amazed at what was said about Jesus. And after Simeon blessed them, he foretold to Mary that "this child is destined for the fall and rise of many in Israel, and to be a sign that will be contradicted (and you yourself a sword will pierce) so that the thoughts of many hearts may be revealed."

One version of the prayer reads:

Now, Master, you may dismiss your servant in peace, according to your word, for my eyes have seen your salvation, which you prepared in sight of all the peoples, a light for revelation to the Gentiles, and glory for your people Israel.

OBLATES OF MARY IMMACULATE

Religious order of men founded by St. Eugene De Mazenod.

Born in France in 1782, Eugene grew up in a wealthy family, but his home life was troubled. His parents came from very different backgrounds, and they eventually divorced — a rare occurrence for Catholics in the eighteenth century.

During the French Revolution, the De Mazenods went into exile, and at different periods, the boy was separated from his mother or father for years at a time.

After years of trying to find his place in life, Eugene experienced a conversion at the age of twenty-five and entered the seminary. He was ordained a priest in 1811. Five years later, he invited others to join him in his ministry to the poor and founded the Oblates of Mary Immaculate. He died in 1861 and was canonized in 1995.

Although the Oblates were established in the United States in 1847, it wasn't until 1941 that the members first introduced the devotion to Our Lady of the Snows to North America. Fr. Paul Schulte, O.M.I. — known as the "Flying Priest of the Arctic" — promoted this devotion to Mary during his mercy flights to the Eskimos in isolated missions. A painting of the priest bringing the Eucharist to an Eskimo community was placed in the chapel of St. Henry's Seminary in Belleville, IL. It depicted Mary, holding the Christ Child, surrounded by the Northern Lights.

Fr. Edwin J. Guild, O.M.I., the director of the Missionary Association of Mary Immaculate, was also instrumental in cultivating the devotion. A nine-day novena of prayer services to Mary as Our Lady of the Snows, begun in 1943, continues to this day.

As the devotion gained popularity, the seminary chapel was no longer large enough to handle the number of visitors, so the Oblates searched for a new location to develop a shrine. In 1958, after they purchased eighty acres of farmland on the bluffs overlooking the Mississippi River Valley, construction began on the National Shrine of Our Lady of the Snows. Development continued with a series of additions over the next three decades and, in 1991, the Church of Our Lady of the Snows was completed. An eighty-five-foot-tall Millennium Spire was dedicated in 1998.

Today, members of the order serve worldwide.

See also St. Mary Major, Basilica of; Pontmain, Our Lady of.

OBLATES OF THE VIRGIN MARY

Religious order founded in Italy by Ven. Bruno Lanteri (1759–1830).

Fr. Lanteri and three fellow priests began a diocesan congregation in 1816 named the Oblates of Mary Most Holy. It soon disbanded, but while on retreat, Fr. Lanteri felt inspired by the Holy Spirit to begin it again. The Oblates of the Virgin Mary received papal approval in 1827.

The order came to the United States in 1976. Today its apostolates include preaching the Spiritual Exercises of St. Ignatius Loyola, formation of the clergy, propagation of the truth against current errors, social communications, the missions, and formation of the laity.

As did the order's founder, members foster a tender love for Mary.

OCOTLAN, OUR LADY OF

Marian devotion and image based on apparition reported by Juan Diego Bernardino in Tlaxcala, Mexico, in 1541.

The visionary said Mary brought him to an unknown spring by a ravine of oak trees. On the following day, the people noticed an ocote (a type of pine tree) burning, and an image of Mary was found inside the charred trunk. It is now housed in a basilica there, named in honor of Our Lady of Ocotlan. Miracles have been attributed her intercession, and the spring continues to flow.

OCTOBER

Traditional month dedicated to the Rosary.

Historians say the custom dates back to devotions held to mark the October 1572 victory of Lepanto and the institution of the feast of the Holy Rosary by Pope Gregory XIII in 1563. The practice became more widespread when, in the nineteenth century, Pope Pius IX granted indulgences to those who attended the services.

See also Rosary Sunday.

OFFICE OF OUR LADY — *See Little Office of the Blessed Virgin Mary.*

ORIGINAL SIN

The act by which the first humans disobeyed God's commandment and chose to follow their own will rather than God's. As a consequence, they lost the grace of original holiness and became subject to the law of death, and sin became universally present in the world.

In addition to the personal sin of Adam and Eve, the term describes the fallen state of human nature, which affects every person born into the world and from which Jesus, the "new Adam," came to redeem humanity.

Our Lady of Ocotlan

The dogma of the Immaculate Conception teaches that Mary, like Christ, was born without the stain of original sin.

See Immaculate Conception.

ORTHODOX CHURCH, MARY IN THE

The Orthodox Church teaches that Mary is the woman God chose to bear his Son in this world and that she remained a virgin. She is called "All Holy" because God chose her to manifest his presence among humanity and is considered the bridge between God and people.

For these reasons, Mary is highly praised and venerated in the Orthodox Church. Members ask her to intercede for them to God, but this devotion is not worshiping; worship is due to God alone. The Orthodox make a distinction between worship and intercessory prayer, noting that just as one asks other people to pray for him or her, so a person asks that of Mary because she has found favor in God's eyes and has a unique relationship with God.

OUR LADY — *See Titles of Mary.*

OUR LADY'S ALTAR — *See Lady Altar.*

OUR LADY'S CHAPEL — *See Lady Chapel.*

OUR LADY'S DAY — *See Lady Day.*

OUR LADY OF . . . — *See (Name), Our Lady of; Titles of Mary.*

OUR LADY'S PSALTER

Early name for the Rosary.

The custom of praying all 150 Psalms (a "psalter" is a book of psalms) evolved into reciting that number of Our Fathers and, later, Hail Marys.

See Rosary.

OUR LADY'S ROSARY MAKERS

Organization that produces and supplies free rosaries to missionaries around the world. The ministry was established in Louisville, Kentucky, in 1949 by Br. Sylvan, C.F.X., a high school teacher. Today, individuals and guilds of rosary makers are in more than a dozen countries.

OUR LADY'S TANK — *See* **Good Health, Our Lady of.**

PALESTINE

Country in which Mary lived. Nazareth, the site of the Annunciation, and Cana, where — at Mary's request — Christ performed his first miracle, were in the north, in Galilee. Jerusalem, and Bethlehem were in the south, in Judea.

See also Scripture, Mary in.

PALOMA, VIRGIN DE LA — *See* Atocha, Our Lady of.

PANAGHIA KAPOLI

Location on a hill some ten miles from Ephesus. The remains of a house in which Mary was supposed to have lived was discovered here. It was located following indications given by Blessed Anne Catherine Emmerich in her writings on the life of Mary.

See also Emmerich, Blessed Anne Catherine; Ephesus.

PANAGIA

Orthodox title for Mary, which translates into English as "The All-Holy."

The word is also used for a triangular loaf of bread lifted up in Orthodox monasteries with the words, "Great is the name of the Holy Trinity, All-Holy God-Bearer, help us." The "lifting of the *Panagia*" is thought to recall the Dormition and Assumption of Mary and is sometimes used as an intercession for travelers.

Panagia (or *Platytera*, "more spacious than the heavens," a depiction of the Queen of Heaven) is also the term for a particular type of icon of the *Theotokos*, in which she is facing front and usually depicted full-length with her hands in the *orans* position and with the image of Christ Child in front of her chest. In icons of *Panagia*, the Greek letters for "Mother of God" are usually placed on the left and right sides of the icon. A *panagia* can also be an *engolpion* (a medallion) with an icon of the *Theotokos*, worn by an Orthodox bishop.

See also Art, Mary in; Orthodox Church, Mary in the.

Platytera Mary and the Child Jesus

PATRONESS, MARY AS

An image, devotion, or title under which Mary is acknowledged to be a special protector and intercessor for persons, churches, dioceses, and the universal Church, as well as for schools, organizations, guilds, professions, regions, cities, countries, and continents.

PAUL VI, POPE

Pontiff from 1963 to 1978 who, in 1974, issued *Marialis Cultus*, an apostolic exhortation "for the right ordering and development of devotion to the Blessed Virgin Mary."

Six years earlier, he had published *Solemnis Professio Fidei* (*Creed of the People of God*), which included four main Marian teachings: the ancient Creed's "born of the Virgin Mary"; the Council of Ephesus' teaching on the *Theotokos*; and the dogmas of the Immaculate Conception and Assumption. It also expressed beliefs in Mary's continued maternal role and belief in her as one who cooperates with Christ.

Other Marian teachings from Pope Paul VI include material in:

Mense Maio (*The Month of May,* 1966 encyclical): This call to pray for peace in the world during the month of May was published only five months after the promulgation of the Apostolic Constitution *Lumen Gentium* and is the first magisterial document after the council to contain Marian teaching. The text includes the title given to Mary by Paul on November 21, 1964 (the day of *Lumen Gentium's* promulgation): Mother of the Church.

Christi Matri (*On Prayers for Peace During October,* 1966 encyclical): Issued one year after Pope Paul VI's historic trip to the United Nations, the pontiff urges the nations to acquire an attitude of peace like that of Christ, the Prince of Peace. After describing the evils of war and calling for peace and justice, Pope Paul encourages the bishops and all the faithful to turn to Mary in prayer and recommends the Rosary. He confirms the Second Vatican Council's support of the devotion and calls it "a solemn custom of the faithful during the month of October to weave with the prayers of the Rosary a spiritual garland to the Mother of Christ" (1).

Signum Magnum (*On Venerating and Imitating the Virgin Mary, Mother of the Church and Model of All Virtues,* 1967 apostolic exhortation): Presented during Pope Paul VI's visit to Fatima to commemorate the fiftieth anniversary of the Marian apparitions there, it calls for and repeats the consecration of the world to the Immaculate Heart of Mary. The document also addresses a growing pastoral concern regarding Marian devotion.

After beginning by asserting that honor is accorded to Mary throughout history, it establishes the basis for Marian devotion, as well as its value for Christian unity, and clarifies that Marian devotion is consistent with liturgical reform.

The document repeatedly quotes *Lumen Gentium* and extends the teaching on Mary, Mother of the Church. Specifically treated are: Mary as mother and model, and active imitation of her: "To Jesus through Mary" (24). Mary's intimate union with her Son as his educator is also addressed: "No human mother can limit her task solely to the procreation of new human beings; she must also undertake the task of nourishing them and educating them. So it is with the Blessed Virgin Mary" (9).

The document notes that Mary's motherly duty continues in teaching members of his Church as she taught Christ in his childhood. She is mother of all, and spiritual Mother of the Church, because Christ "designated her [as] the mother not only of John the Apostle," but also *of the human race,* which he somehow represented" (Leo XIII, *LG* 58, *SM* 10). She carries on this role in heaven and "her spiritual motherhood transcends the boundaries of time and space. It is part of the Church's history for all times, because she never ceases to exercise her maternal office or to help us" (33). Even as she enjoys the vision of the Blessed Trinity, she "does not forget her children who now are engaged in the pilgrimage of faith" (11). Her serving of the whole human race began from the moment of the Annunciation, and her entire life, then and now, was and is one of loving service. The term, "pilgrimage of faith" (based on *Lumen Gentium* 58) became a frequent theme in subsequent documents and is a major development in post-Vatican II Marian thought.

Though also scriptural, the exhortation is first based on doctrine and devotion. In contrast to *Lumen Gentium,* which does not quote this particular verse, the passage from the Book of Revelation (12:1), the "great sign," the "woman clothed with the sun," is referenced to Mary, as the title of the document also indicates. It is the duty of the Christian to honor her and praiseworthy to imitate her for she is the Great Sign of the Church in the contemporary world, the Great Sign fully consecrated to Christ and participant in his work of redemption by her close association with him and cooperation with grace. The pope also explains that there are many ways to venerate Mary and offers numerous suggestions (29). The solemn consecration of the human race to the Immaculate Heart of Mary is also discussed, and a link is drawn between Lourdes and Fatima (37).

Recurrens Mensis October (*On the Recurrence of the Month of October,* 1969 apostolic exhortation): This was written to mark the fourth centenary of *Consueverunt Romani,* an apostolic letter from St. Pius VI, who explained and fostered the traditional form of the Rosary. The purpose of Paul VI's document is to encourage the Rosary devotion. The three parts discuss the intercession of Mary as a way to turn to God. The first section calls on all people to be peacemakers; the second centers on the obligation of every Christian to pray; and the third lists the prayer intentions. The document is pastoral and devotional in nature, and does not incorporate a broad range of doctrinal concepts.

See also **Marialis Cultus.**

PEACE AND GOOD VOYAGE, OUR LADY OF — *See* **Antipolo, Our Lady of.**

PEACE, OUR LADY OF

Image and devotion dating back to 1682 when, pious tradition holds, merchants found an abandoned box on the shore of El Salvador's *Mar del Sur*.

Unable to open the tightly sealed container, they assumed it contained something of value, and decided to take it to San Miguel where they would find a way to get into it. They tied the box to a donkey's back and, after reaching the city on November 21, planned on telling the local authorities of their find. But when they went past the parish church, the animal lay down on the ground and then the merchants were able to open the box. They were amazed to discover it contained a wooden statue of Our Lady holding the Christ Child.

Legend says they never found out for whom the box was intended or how it came to be on the beach, but when warring locals learned of the event, they ceased their fighting. Tradition also holds that some century and a half later, in 1833 — after one faction had defeated the other — instead of the victorious side completely destroying their opponents, as was expected, it had the blessed image placed in the atrium of the parish church. At the feet of Our Lady, the members made a solemn vow to harbor no more grudges and to eliminate hatred from their hearts. For this reason, the image was given the name *Our Lady of Peace*.

Today, the statue is dressed in a white robe with the national shield of El Salvador embroidered on the front. Mary holds a gold palm leaf in her right hand in memory of the 1787 eruption of a local volcano, which threatened to destroy the city. Frightened citizens brought the statute to the main door of the cathedral, and, legend says, at that precise moment the flowing lava changed direction, moving away from the city. As this happened, the people also saw a white palm leaf in the clouds; it seemed to sprout from the crater of the volcano. Interpreting this as a sign of Our Lady's protection, they decided to place in her hand a gold palm like the one they had seen in the sky.

At the location where the lava shifted, there is a town called *Milagro de la Paz* (Miracle of Peace).

Pope Benedict XV authorized the crowning of the image. On November 21, 1921, a crown of gold and precious stones was placed on Mary's head, and a new shrine dedicated to Our Lady of Peace was completed in 1953. The feast of Our Lady of Peace is November 21.

PEKING, OUR LADY OF — *See* **China, Our Lady of.**

PELLEVOISIN, OUR LADY OF

Title based on a series of Marian apparitions in 1876 reported by Estelle Faguette in a village in the diocese of Bourges, France.

Estelle was a domestic servant who had been dying of consumption — then made a remarkable recovery and went on to live for more than another half century. She associated her return to good health with five visions of Our Lady, which she claimed were followed by ten more in that same year.

St. Margaret Mary Alacoque

The bishops of Bourges have never made a pronouncement on the reputed visions, and it was forbidden to make statues or pictures of Mary wearing the scapular. Still, pilgrims come to a commemorative chapel in the town.

There is a shrine of Our Lady of Pellevoisin in New York City's St. Paul Church.

See also Scapular.

Pentecost

She reported that Mary told her, "If you want to serve me, be simple, and let your words and deeds agree," and that she said she was very distressed by people's neglect of her Son in prayer and in the Blessed Sacrament. She also showed the maid a white scapular with an image of the Sacred Heart on it and told her to ask her bishop to encourage its use in reparation to Jesus.

The scapular was later approved and a confraternity of Mary, Mother of Mercy, was instituted to spread its use. Although no mention was made of Pellevoisin in connection with its approval, St. Margaret Mary Alacoque (1647–1690) was referred to.

(This French religious spread devotion to the Sacred Heart in accordance with revelations made to her in 1675.)

PENTECOST

Events recorded in Acts 2:1–41 that tell of the descent of the Holy Spirit on the apostles, Mary (Acts 1:14), and others gathered in the upper room fifty days after Easter and ten days after the Ascension. It is regarded as the birthday of the Church.

See Scripture, Mary in.

PERFECT FOLLOWER OF CHRIST

Title for Mary.

It is used, for example, in Pope Paul VI's 1974 apostolic exhortation *Marialis Cultus*: Mary "is worthy of imitation because she was the first and the most perfect of Christ's disciples" (35).

PERFECT SANCTITY

Reference to Mary's Immaculate Conception. For example, on his meditation on the Immaculate Conception *Blessed Be Christ the King*, St. Pio of Pietrelcina (1887–1968) wrote:

> The Eternal Father created her pure and immaculate and is well pleased in her for

St. Pio of Pietrelcina

she is the worthy dwelling of his only Son. Through the generating of his Son in his bosom from all eternity, he forecasts the generation of his Son as Man in the pure womb of this mother, and he clothed her from her conception in the radiant snowy garment of grace and of most perfect sanctity; she participates in his perfection.

PERPETUAL HELP, OUR LADY OF

Image and devotion.

Perhaps the best known Marian icon in the world, the original painting is on a wood panel about 17 by 21 inches in size and is located in the Church of St. Alphonsus in Rome. It has been under the care of the Redemptorist Order since the mid-nineteenth century when Pope Pius IX instructed the order to promote the devotion worldwide. The image itself is at least four centuries older.

The Byzantine-style painting depicts Mary holding the Christ Child; his sandal dangles from his right foot. On either side of them are the archangels Gabriel and Michael holding instruments of the Passion.

Tradition holds that a merchant stole the image from a church in Crete and took it with him to Rome around the year 1495. After he became fatally ill, he asked a friend to put it in a church as a form of restitution. Instead, his wife kept it; but later, Mary appeared to the couple's young daughter and asked that the painting be placed in the Church of St. Matthew, between the Basilicas of St. Mary Major and St. John Lateran, where it could be venerated by the faithful. During the apparition, Our Lady also referred to herself as "Holy Mary of Perpetual Help."

Our Lady of Perpetual Help

On March 27, 1499, the picture was solemnly enthroned on the high altar in the Church of St. Matthew, placed under the protection of the Augustinian Fathers, and venerated there for almost three centuries until 1798. Then, the French army seized the city, took Pope Pius VI (r. 1774–1799) into captivity, and leveled thirty churches in Rome — including St. Matthew's. Fortunately, the painting was removed from the church before the building's destruction and kept in a private chapel of the Augustinians at St. Mary in Posterula, near the Tiber River.

In 1863, while preaching in Rome's Church of the Gesu, Fr. Francis Blosi, S.J., told the history of Our Lady of Perpetual Help with the hope that the image could be located and be placed in veneration for the faithful once again.

A member of the Redemptorist Order, Fr. Michael Marchi, had served Mass in the private Augustinian Chapel when he was a child and knew where the icon was.

When Pope Pius IX heard the story, he decreed that the miraculous image be given to the Redemptorists and be venerated in their Church of St. Alphonsus, now located between the Basilicas of St. Mary Major and St. John Lateran. The order had bought the land in 1855 to build a church, including the site on which St. Matthew's Church had stood.

The painting *Our Lady of Perpetual Help* was exposed for public veneration above the high altar on April 26, 1866. The image was solemnly crowned the following year. Although not celebrated on the Church's universal calendar, the Redemptorist Order observes the Feast of Our Lady of Perpetual Help on June 27.

Devotion to Our Lady of Perpetual Help became so popular that its confraternity soon was granted the status of archconfraternity.

PERPETUAL ROSARY FOR THE DEAD

Custom established in seventeenth-century Italy by the Dominicans Petronis Martini (Bologna) and Timothy Ricci (Florence). Records of the Perpetual Rosary at the Dominican Basilica in Krakow, Poland, date from 1902.

Members pray the entire Rosary at a specific time of day, once a month, or once a year. The Joyful Mysteries are recited for the conversion of sinners; the Sorrowful to ask help for the dying; and the Glorious Mysteries to aid the souls in purgatory.

Membership in this Rosary fraternity is worldwide. Members are asked to attempt to receive the Sacraments of Reconciliation and the Eucharist on their chosen day of prayer.

PERPETUAL VIRGINITY — *See Virginity of Mary, Perpetual.*

PEYTON, C.S.C., FR. PATRICK — *See Family Rosary Crusade.*

PIEKARY, OUR LADY OF

Image and devotion centered in Piekary, Poland. The painting *Our Lady of Piekary*, which is of unknown origin, depicts a seated Mary holding the Christ Child in her left arm and an apple in her right hand. It has been the focus of Marian devotion since the beginning of the seventeenth century. Miracles have been attributed to Our Lady of Piekary's intercession.

In 1683, Polish king John Sobieski stopped to pray in the Piekary shrine and ask for Mary's help before leaving with his army for Vienna to battle the Turks.

In 1702, to keep the image safe during wartime, it was moved to Opole, where it remains in the Church of the Holy Cross. But the painting itself was not seen as something special, and at that site, it never attracted crowds of pilgrims. Rather, in Piekary where only a replica of the painting was located, pilgrims continued to gather to honor Our Lady.

In the nineteenth century, an increase in visitors prompted the building of a new, larger church. While it was being constructed, four chapels at each corner of the church were erected between 1844 and 1849, dedicated to St. Teresa, St. Sebastian, St. Francis, and Our Lady-Healer, in which a replica of the Piekary Madonna (also known as "the healer") is kept. In the twentieth century it became customary for men to make a pilgrimage to Our Lady of Piekary on the last Sunday of May. In 1967, then-Cardinal Karol Wojtyla (later Pope John Paul II), first attended the event and regularly took part in the pilgrimages from that time on until his election as pontiff in 1978.

During the pope's visit home to Poland in 1983, the Piekary painting was temporarily moved to Katowice, and he gave the image the title *Mother of Justice and Social Love.*

See also Name of Mary, Most Holy.

PIETÀ

From the Italian for "pity," an artistic representation of Mary holding the dead body of Christ after he has been taken down from the cross.

Pietà by Michelangelo

This depiction became common toward the end of the Middle Ages, when devotion to Our Lady of Sorrows increased. The most famous *Pietà* is Michelangelo's marble sculpture, in St. Peter's Basilica in Rome.

See Art, Mary in.

PILAR, OUR LADY OF

Also known as *Our Lady of the Pillar* (*Nuestra Señora del Pilar*), an image and shrine near Zaragoza, Spain.

The simple wooden statue features Our Lady holding the Christ Child, who holds a bird in his hand. It stands on a stone pillar about six feet high. An ancient tradition says that in the year 40, St. James the Apostle journeyed to Spain to spread the Gospel, and that as he paused to pray beside the River Ebro, Our Lady — who was still in Jerusalem — appeared on a pillar to him and seven companions. She offered words of encouragement and requested a chapel be built at that spot. The present church dates from the seventeenth century.

Although there is no evidence for the devotion before the twelfth century, it holds a treasured place in Spanish piety. The feast of Our Lady of Pilar is celebrated there on October 12.

PILGRIM VIRGIN

Practice that refers to statues, icons, and other images of Mary being transported from home to home, parish to parish, and country to country to promote devotion. Among the best known are the images of Our Lady of Fatima, which travel throughout the world visiting parishes and homes, a practice promoted by the Knights of Columbus and the Blue Army.

PILGRIMAGE

In relation to devotion to Mary, a journey to a Marian apparition site, image, or shrine that is made to venerate a sacred object or relic, seek increased spiritual or physical health, do penance, or offer thanksgiving for graces received or favors granted through Mary's intercession.

In general, pilgrims in the early Church traveled to the Holy Land, Rome, and Compostella, Spain (where relics said to be those of St. James the Greater were discovered).

During medieval times, Marian shrines throughout Europe became destinations for pilgrims. Some sites, for the most part, were known only regionally or nationally (Piekary, Poland, for example) but others had international appeal (such as Loreto, Italy).

After the Reformation, the popularity of pilgrimages to Marian shrines and other sites fell off but regained favor in the nineteenth century after reported apparitions in several locations, such as Lourdes in 1858 and Pontmain in 1871. The trend continued throughout the twentieth century after Mary's appearance in Fatima in 1917. Medjugorje became a pilgrimage site after reported apparitions began in 1981.

Although the majority of Marian pilgrimage destinations have been in Europe, the custom is universal. Two examples are Our Lady of Guadalupe in Mexico and Our Lady of La Vang in Vietnam.

Today the most popular sites worldwide each have millions of visitors annually.

PITY, OUR LADY OF — *See* Pietà.

PIUS IX, POPE (BLESSED)

Pontiff from 1846 to 1878 who, in 1854, promulgated the apostolic constitution *Ineffabilis Deus,* which "holds that the most Blessed Virgin Mary, in the first instant of her conception, by a singular grace and privilege granted by almighty God in view of the merits of Jesus Christ, the Savior of the human race, was preserved free from all stain of original sin."

See Immaculate Conception.

Blessed Pope Pius IX

PIUS X, POPE (ST.)

Pontiff from 1903–1914, whose writing on Mary includes his 1904 encyclical, *Ad Diem Illum Laetissimum* (*On the Immaculate Conception*), marking the fiftieth anniversary of Pope Pius IX's apostolic constitution *Ineffabilis Deus.* Pius X wrote:

For is not Mary the Mother of Christ? Then she is our Mother also. And we must in truth hold that Christ, the Word made Flesh, is also the Savior of mankind. He had a physical body like that of any other man: and again as Savior of the human family, he had a spiritual and mystical body, the society, namely, of those who believe in Christ. 'We are many, but one sole body in Christ' (Romans 12:5). Now the Blessed Virgin did not conceive the Eternal Son of God merely in order that He might be made man taking His human nature from her, but also in order that by means of the nature assumed from her He might be the Redeemer of men. For which reason the Angel said to the Shepherds: 'Today there is born to you a Savior who is Christ the Lord' (Luke 2:11). Wherefore in the same holy bosom of his most chaste Mother Christ took to Himself flesh, and united to Himself the spiritual body formed by those who were to believe in Him. Hence Mary, carrying the Savior within her, may be said to have also carried all those whose life was contained in the life of the Savior. Therefore all we who are united to Christ, and as the Apostle says are members of His body, of His flesh, and of His bones (Ephesians 5:30), have issued from the womb of Mary like a body united to its head. Hence, though in a spiritual and mystical fashion, we are all children of Mary, and she is Mother of us all. Mother,

Pope St. Pius X

spiritually indeed, but truly Mother of the members of Christ, who are we (S. Aug. *L. de S. Virginitate*, c. 6). (10)

PIUS XI, POPE

Pontiff from 1922 to 1939, whose writing on Mary includes his 1937 encyclical *Ingravescentibus Malis* (*On the Rosary*).

The Holy Father wrote:

Among the various supplications with which we successfully appeal to the Virgin Mother of God, the Holy Rosary without doubt occupies a special and distinct place. This prayer, which some call the Psalter of the Virgin or Breviary of the Gospel and of Christian life, was described and recommended by Our Predecessor of happy memory, Leo XIII, with these vigorous passages:

'Very admirable is this crown interwoven with the angelic salutation which is interposed in the Sunday prayer, and unites with it the obligation of interior meditation. It is an excellent manner of prayer . . . and very useful for the attainment of immortal life' (*Acta Leonis,* 1898, Vol. XVIII, pp. 154, 155). (9)

And this can well be deduced from the very flowers that form this mystic garland. What prayers in fact can be found more adaptable and holy? This first is that which our Divine Redeemer Himself pronounced when His disciples asked Him: 'Lord, teach us to pray' (Luke 11:1); a very holy supplication which both offers us the way — as far as it is possible for us — to render glory to God, and also takes into account all the necessities of our body and soul. How can the Eternal Father, when prayed to with the very words of His Son, refuse to come to our aid? (10)

The other prayer is the Angelic Salutation, which begins with the eulogies of the Archangel Gabriel and of St. Elizabeth, and ends with that very pious supplication by which we beg the help of the Blessed Virgin now and at the hour of our death. To these invocations, said aloud, is added the contemplation of the sacred mysteries, through which they place, as it were, under our eyes the joys, sorrows and triumphs of Jesus Christ and of His Mother, so that we receive relief and comfort in our sorrows. Following those most holy examples, we ascend to the happiness of the heavenly country by steps of ever higher virtue. (11)

This practice of piety, Venerable Brethren, admirably diffused by St. Dominic, not without the heavenly suggestion and inspiration of the Virgin Mother of God, is without doubt easy for all, even for the ignorant and the simple. But those wander from the path of truth who consider this devotion merely an annoying formula repeated with monotonous singsong intonation, and refuse it as good only for children and silly women! (12)

In this regard, it is to be noted that both piety and love, though always renewing the same words, do not always repeat the same thing but always express something new issuing from the intimate sentiment of devotion. And besides, this mode of prayer has the perfume of evangelic simplicity and requires humility of spirit; and, if we disdain humility, as the Divine Redeemer teaches, it will be impossible for us to enter the heavenly kingdom: 'Amen, I say to you, unless you become as little children you shall not enter the kingdom of heaven' (Mt. 18:3). (13)

Nevertheless, if men in our century, with its derisive pride, refuse the Holy Rosary, there is an innumerable multitude of holy men of every age and every condition who have always held it dear. They have recited it with great devotion, and in every moment they have used it as a powerful weapon to put the demons to flight, to preserve the integrity of life, to acquire virtue more easily, and in a word to attain real peace among men. (14)

PIUS XII, POPE

Pontiff from 1939–1958 who, in 1950, solemnly defined the Assumption of Mary as a dogma of the Faith. In his apostolic constitution *Munificentissimus Deus*, he wrote: "We pronounce, declare and define it to be a divinely revealed dogma: that the Immaculate Mother of God, the ever Virgin Mary, having completed the course of her earthly life, was assumed body and soul into heavenly glory."

Pope Pius XII also wrote five Marian encyclicals:

1946, *Deiparae Virginis Mariae* (To all bishops: on the possibility of defining the Assumption of the Blessed Virgin Mary as a dogma of faith)

1951, *Ingruentium Malorum* (On reciting the Rosary)

1953, *Fulgens Corona* (Proclaiming a Marian Year to commemorate the centenary of the definition of the dogma of the Immaculate Conception)

1954, *Ad Caeli Reginam* (Proclaiming the Queenship of Mary)

1957, *Le pelerinage de Lourdes* (Warning against materialism on the centenary of the apparitions at Lourdes)

Among the saints he canonized were three who were particularly linked with Marian devotion: St. Catherine Labouré, St. Louis Marie de Montfort, and St. Anthony Mary Claret.

See also Assumption.

POMPEII, OUR LADY OF THE ROSARY OF

Image and devotion dating back to the late nineteenth century and Blessed Bartolo Longo (1841–1926), who noted: "There is something about that picture which impresses the soul not by its artistic perfection but by a mysterious charm which impels one to kneel and pray with tears."

While visiting the valley of Pompeii on business in 1872, the Dominican brother was shocked and saddened when he saw the ignorance, poverty, and lack of religion among the people, and vowed to Mary to do all he could to promote devotion to the Rosary there.

To encourage the people, he decided to buy an image of Our Lady with the Rosary that could be used for veneration. A Dominican sister offered him a large painting that had been bought at a junk shop for three francs. But, in his own words:

> Not only was it worm eaten, but the face of the Madonna was that of a coarse, rough country-woman . . . A piece of canvas was missing just above her head . . . [and] her mantle was cracked. Nothing can be said of the hideousness of the other figures. St. Dominic looked like a street idiot. To Our Lady's left was a St. Rose. This latter I had changed later into a St. Catherine of Siena. . . . I hesitated whether to refuse the gift or to accept.

Noting his lack of enthusiasm, the sister urged him to accept it, predicting miracles would be associated with it. He took the artwork and made arrangements with a wagon driver to deliver it. It arrived at the chapel door in a sheet after being carried on the top of a load of manure being delivered to a nearby field.

Because others' first reaction to the painting was disappointment, Brother Bartolo had an artist refurbish the canvas, and he decorated it with diamonds donated by the faithful. A crown was placed on Mary's head, and the painting was solemnly mounted on a throne of marble imported from Lourdes.

As the sister had foretold, this Marian devotion soon had miracles associated with it. In less than ten years, almost one thousand cures were reported at the shrine. Today, many pilgrims still visit the shrine, around which one of the largest centers of social work in the world flourishes.

Our Lady of the Rosary of Pompeii

PONTIFICAL INTERNATIONAL MARIAN ACADEMY

Institute whose roots date back to 1946 and a commission formed to promote devotion to Mary and studies about her.

That year, the minister general of the Order of Friars Minor created the *Commissio Marialis Franciscana* at the International College of St. Anthony in Rome. Its task was to coordinate and promote studies in favor of Marian doctrine and devotion within the Franciscan order. Initially, the studies especially dealt with the dogma of the Immaculate Conception — which was about to mark its first centenary — and the dogma of the Assumption, which was about to be defined.

Later, the organization evolved into the *Academia Mariana Internationalis,* which, in 1950, was presented to the theological world with the celebration of the first International Mariological Congress and the eighth International Marian Congress. Because special permission from the Vatican had been needed each time that there was a celebration of an international congress, the Holy See was asked to institute a permanent institute for the promotion and moderation of the Mariological-Marian congresses. The *Academia Mariana* was proposed for this responsibility.

On December 8, 1959, Pope John XXIII gave the academy the title of "Pontifical."

See also Congress, Marian.

PONTMAIN, OUR LADY OF

Title and devotion to Our Lady of Hope based on a Marian apparition reported by six children near an old barn in Pontmain, France, in 1871.

They said Mary called herself the "Madonna of the Crucifix" and gave the world a message of hope through prayer and the cross. The youngsters ranged in age from two to twelve years.

Although some sixty adults who had also gathered there were unable to see anything supernatural, they said the demeanor of the children made it clear the youngsters were wit-nessing something. The children later reported Mary wore a blue robe decorated with golden stars. Her hair was covered with a black veil, and she wore a golden crown with a red line around the middle of it.

During the several phases of the three-and-a-half-hour apparition, writing appeared, which the oldest children spelled out to the adults. The first sentence: "But pray, my children." The next: "God will hear you in a short time." Finally, the message was "My Son permits himself to be moved."

The children reported that then the Lady looked sad and pensive as a large bloody cross with the words "Jesus Christ" appeared in front of her. She took it in her hands and seemed to pass it to the children. The red crucifix disappeared, and small white crosses appeared on both of her shoulders. Then Mary lowered her hands and smiled at the children. At this point the children joyfully shouted, "Look, she is smiling — she is smiling." Then, slowly, the apparition dissolved.

The following year, the local bishop acknowledged the apparition as authentic. Today, the church of Our Lady of Hope is on the site. Consecrated in 1900, it was raised to the status of a minor basilica by Pope Pius X.

One of the visionaries, Joseph Barbadette, later became a priest of the Oblates of Mary Immaculate; in the United States, the devotion was placed under the custody of that order.

See also Hope, Our Lady of; Oblates of Mary Immaculate.

POPES, STATEMENTS ABOUT MARY BY — *See name of particular pope.*

POPULAR PIETY

Term that designates those diverse cultic expressions of a private or community nature that, in the context of the Christian faith, are inspired predominantly not by the Sacred Liturgy but by forms deriving from a particular nation, people, or culture.

In its 2001 document *Directory on Popular Piety and the Liturgy*, the Congregation for Divine Worship and the Discipline of the Sacraments noted that "some of the earliest forms of veneration of the Blessed Virgin Mary also reflect popular piety, among them the *Sub tuum praesidium* and the Marian iconography of the catacombs of St. Priscilla in Rome" (23).

In Chapter Five, titled "Veneration of the Holy Mother of God," the authors say that "popular devotion to the Blessed Virgin Mary is an important and universal ecclesial phenomenon" and discuss many of its specific forms, including observances, prayers, the Rosary, litanies, scapulars, consecrations, and more.

See Devotions, Marian; Appendix A: Excerpt from the Directory on Popular Piety and the Liturgy.

PORTIUNCULA

A small portion (*portiuncula*) of land given to St. Francis of Assisi (1181/82–1226) by a local Benedictine monastery to be used for the fledgling Franciscan community.

A small chapel on the property was restored by the friars and now sits in the middle of the basilica of Our Lady of the Angels.

The Portiuncula Indulgence dates back to St. Francis' vision of Mary. She told him a plenary indulgence could be obtained for the dead as often as a person visited the chapel on August 2. Pope Honorius III (r. 1216–1227) granted the indulgence, under the condition that the Our Father, Hail Mary, and Glory Be are recited six times per visit for the pontiff's intentions. Now, the Portiuncula Indulgence can be transferred to any parish church, as long as certain requirements are met.

See also Franciscans.

PRAISERS OF OUR LADY — *See* Laudesi.

PRAYERS TO MARY — *See name of particular prayer; Devotions, Marian.*

PREDESTINATION OF MARY

From all eternity, God's choosing Mary to be the mother of his Son, and so the Mother of God. Though immaculately conceived without the stain of original sin, Mary retained full freedom of person and choice.

In the words of Vatican II's *Dogmatic Constitution on the Church (Lumen Gentium)*:

> The Father of mercies willed that the incarnation should be preceded by the acceptance of her who was predestined to be the mother of His Son, so that just as a woman contributed to death, so also a woman should contribute to life. That is true in outstanding fashion of the mother of Jesus, who gave to the world Him who is Life itself and who renews all things, and who was

enriched by God with the gifts which befit such a role. It is no wonder therefore that the usage prevailed among the Fathers [of the Church] whereby they called the mother of God entirely holy and free from all stain of sin, as though fashioned by the Holy Spirit and formed as a new creature. Adorned from the first instant of her conception with the radiance of an entirely unique holiness, the Virgin of Nazareth is greeted, on God's command, by an angel messenger as "full of grace," and to the heavenly messenger she replies: "Behold the handmaid of the Lord, be it done unto me according to thy word." Thus Mary, a daughter of Adam, consenting to the divine Word, became the mother of Jesus, the one and only Mediator. Embracing God's salvific will with a full heart and impeded by no sin, she devoted herself totally as a handmaid of the Lord to the person and work of her Son, under Him and with Him, by the grace of almighty God, serving the mystery of redemption. Rightly therefore the holy Fathers see her as used by God not merely in a passive way, but as freely cooperating in the work of human salvation through faith and obedience. For, as St. Irenaeus says, she "being obedient, became the cause of salvation for herself and for the whole human race." Hence not a few of the early Fathers gladly assert in their preaching, "The knot of Eve's disobedience was untied by Mary's obedience; what the virgin Eve bound through her unbelief, the Virgin Mary loosened by her faith." Comparing Mary with Eve, they call her "the Mother of the living," and still more often they say: "death through Eve, life through Mary" (56).

PREFACES OF OUR LADY

Formal proclamations of praise in the Eucharistic Prayer.

Although the number of prefaces was limited by the Council of Trent in the sixteenth century, Vatican II's revised Missal for the universal Church increased the number to more than eighty. It also left national conferences of bishops free to request more. The publication of the *Collection of Masses for the Blessed Virgin Mary Approved for Use in the Dioceses of the United States of America* in 1992 added more than forty additional prefaces to the Roman rite for English speakers.

See also **Collection of Masses of the Blessed Virgin Mary.**

PRESENTATION OF JESUS IN THE TEMPLE, FEAST OF THE

February 2 feast commemorating the presentation of Jesus in the Temple, according to prescriptions of Mosaic law (Lv. 12:2–8; Ex. 13:2; Lk. 2:22–32), and the purification of Mary forty days after his birth. In the East, where the feast began before the fourth century, it was marked primarily as a commemoration of Our Lord; in the West, where it was later adopted, it was regarded more as a Marian celebration until the revision of the liturgical calendar in 1970.

The Law of Moses prescribed that every Jewish mother was to be excluded from attendance at public worship for forty days after giving birth to a boy child. At the end of that period, she had to present a yearling lamb for a holocaust and a pigeon for a sin offering, thus purifying herself from ritual uncleanliness. In the case of poor people, two pigeons were used as an offering. Lk. 2:22–38 tells how Mary, after the birth of Jesus, fulfilled this command of the law, and how on the same occasion Simeon and Anna met the newborn Savior.

Originally, the feast was marked on February 14, because Christ's birth was celebrated on January 6. Because Jesus himself was present at Mary's purification, it came to be celebrated quite early as a festival of the Lord. The first historical description of the feast is given in the diary of Aetheria, about 390. From Jerusalem, the feast spread into the other churches of the East. The Armenians call it the Coming of the Son of God into the Temple. In the Coptic Rite, it was termed Presentation of the Lord in the Temple. In the Greek Church, it was known as the Meeting of the Lord, commemorating the meeting with Simeon and Anna. The Chaldeans and Syrians called it the Feast of the Old Man Simeon. In the Western Church, it appeared first in the liturgical books of the seventh and eighth cen-

turies under the title the Purification of Mary. In 701, Pope Sergius prescribed the procession with candles for this and the other three feasts of Mary that were at that time annually celebrated in Rome. The ceremony of blessing the candles originated in the eighth century, in the Carolingian Empire.

See also Scripture, Mary in.

PRESENTATION OF MARY

Feast celebrated on November 21, which was derived from a reference in the apocryphal *Protoevangelium of James* describing the Presentation of Mary in the Temple when she was three years old.

The beginnings of the feast can be traced in the East to the eighth century and, in the West, to the later Middle Ages. In 1585, Pope Sixtus V made it a feast in the universal Church. In the present form of the liturgy, it is ranked as a memorial, containing a special Collect.

One translation of the event in the *Protoevangelium of James* reads:

> And the child was two years old, and Joachim said: Let us take her up to the temple of the Lord, that we may pay the vow that we have vowed, lest perchance the Lord send to us, and our offering be not received. And Anna said: Let us wait for the third year, in order that the child may not seek for father or mother. And Joachim said: So let us wait. And the child was three years old, and Joachim said: Invite the daughters of the Hebrews that are undefiled, and let them take each a lamp, and let them stand with the lamps burning, that the child may

Presentation of Jesus in the Temple

not turn back, and her heart be captivated from the temple of the Lord. And they did so until they went up into the temple of the Lord. And the priest received her, and kissed her, and blessed her, saying: The Lord has magnified thy name in all generations. In thee, on the last of the days, the Lord will manifest His redemption to the sons of Israel. And he set her down upon the third step of the altar, and the Lord God sent grace upon her; and she danced with her feet, and all the house of Israel loved her.

See also Apocryphal Writing, Mary in.

PRIVILEGES OF MARY

Attributes of Mary that distinguish her from all other human beings. These include her immaculate conception; her freedom from all sin; and her resulting fullness of grace. Others are her virginity, her lack of ignorance, her spiritual maternity, her role in the God's plan of salvation, her role in the Church, and her right to the devotion of the Church's members.

PRO MARIA COMMITTEE — *See Beauraing, Our Lady of.*

PROCESSIONS, MARIAN

Form of popular piety that honors Mary on a particular feast, such as the Assumption or the Presentation of Jesus in the Temple. Other Marian processions take place in the context of public ceremonies at shrines, such as Lourdes, or as part of a celebration associated with the Marian months of May and October.

PROMPT SUCCOR, OUR LADY OF

Image and devotion; principal patroness of New Orleans and Louisiana.

The history of Our Lady of Prompt Succor (or, in more contemporary language, Fast Help) dates back to the Ursuline Monastery of New Orleans, which was founded under the auspices of Louis XV of France by a band of French Ursulines in 1727.

For a time when the area came under Spain's rule, Spanish sisters helped the Ursulines carry on their work of running a boarding school, day school, and orphanage; teaching Native Americans and blacks; and providing nursing care to the sick. But in 1800, the territory again fell under French jurisdiction and the Spanish sisters left for Cuba, fearing scenes from the recent French Revolution would be repeated in the colonies.

By 1803, only seven Ursulines remained, and the superior appealed to a cousin in France, Mother St. Michel, for aid and staff. She had been driven from her convent by the Reign of Terror but had since opened a boarding school for girls, and her bishop did not want to lose her. So, when she asked the prelate for permission, he answered that authorization could come only from the pope. But at the time, though in Rome, the pope was a virtual prisoner of Napoleon, and his jailers were under strict orders not to allow him to correspond with anyone. Then, too, there was no reliable way of sending messages to him.

Even so, Mother St. Michel wrote her request and, at prayer, felt inspired to ask Our Lady for help. In her prayer she pledged, "O Most Holy Virgin Mary, if you obtain a prompt and favorable answer to my letter, I promise to have you honored in New Orleans under the title of Our Lady of Prompt Succor." Her letter received a fast, positive response.

Mother St. Michel and her companions arrived in New Orleans in December 1810, bringing with them a statue of Mary that she had had commissioned in fulfillment of her vow. The image, which depicts a standing Mary holding the Christ Child, was installed in the convent chapel. From there, the devotion spread throughout the city, region and country.

The intercession of Our Lady of Prompt Succor is credited with both saving the convent from a fire in 1812 and with Andrew Jackson's victory over British forces in the Battle of New Orleans, three years later.

In 1851, Pope Pius IX authorized the celebration of the feast of Our Lady of Prompt Succor. In 1828, a shrine was consecrated in her honor.

PROPHECIES IN THE OLD TESTAMENT, MARY IN

Passages in which, while Mary is not mentioned by name, she is prophetically prefigured as the Mother of the Messiah.

While many Scripture scholars dispute whether any verses from the Old Testament can be called Marian, in a larger sense, the verses are supported by Tradition and the faith of the people of God, read in the light of Christ's life, death, Resurrection, and Ascension in the New Testament.

Three passages traditionally seen as prophesies are:

Gen. 3:15: "I will put enmity between you and the woman and between your seed and her seed; he shall bruise your head, and you shall bruise his heel."

Is.7:14–16: Therefore the Lord himself will give you a sign. Behold, a young woman shall conceive and bear a son, and shall call his name Emmanuel. He shall eat curds and honey when he knows how to refuse the evil and choose the good. For before the child knows how to refuse the evil and choose the good, the land before whose two kings you are in dread will be deserted.

Micah 5:1–2: But you, O Bethlehem Ephrathah, who are little to be among the clans of Judah, from you shall come forth for me one who is the ruler of Israel, whose origin is from old, from ancient days. Therefore, he shall give them up until the time when she who is in travail has brought forth; then the rest of his brethren shall return to the people of Israel.

In their *Dogmatic Constitution on the Church* (*Lumen Gentium*), when discussing Old Testament prophesies about Mary — and those three passages in particular — the bishops at Vatican II say:

The Sacred Scriptures of both the Old and the New Testament, as well as ancient Tradition, show the role of the Mother of the Savior in the economy of salvation in an ever clearer light and draw attention to it. The books of the Old Testament describe the history of salvation, by which the coming of Christ into the world was slowly prepared. These earliest documents, as they are read in the Church and are understood in the light of a further and full revelation, bring the figure of the woman, Mother of the Redeemer, into a gradually clearer light.

When it is looked at in this way, she is already prophetically foreshadowed in the promise of victory over the serpent which was given to our first parents after their fall into sin. (Cf. Gen. 3:15) Likewise she is the Virgin who shall conceive and bear a son, whose name will be called Emmanuel. (Cf. Is. 7:14; cf. Mich. 5:1–2; Mt. 1:22–23) She stands out among the poor and humble of the Lord, who confidently hope for and receive salvation from Him. With her the exalted Daughter of Sion, and after a long expectation of the promise, the times are fulfilled and the new Economy established, when the Son of God took a human nature from her, that He might in the mysteries of His flesh free man from sin.

See Scripture, Mary in.

PROTESTANT CHURCHES, MARY IN MAINLINE — *See Reformation and Mary.*

PROTOEVANGELIUM OF JAMES — *See Apocryphal Writing, Mary in.*

PSALTER, MARIAN — *See Our Lady's Psalter.*

PURIFICATION OF THE BLESSED VIRGIN MARY, FEAST OF THE

Previous title for feast celebrated on February 2, the Presentation.

See Presentation of Jesus in the Temple, Feast of the.

QUEEN OF ANGELS, OF PATRIARCHS, OF PROPHETS, OF APOSTLES, OF MARTYRS, OF CONFESSORS, OF VIRGINS, OF ALL SAINTS, CONCEIVED WITHOUT ORIGINAL SIN, ASSUMED INTO HEAVEN, OF THE MOST HOLY ROSARY, OF FAMILIES, OF PEACE —

See Litany of the Blessed Virgin Mary.

QUEEN OF LOVE, OF MERCY, OF PEACE, OF ANGELS, OF PATRIARCHS AND PROPHETS, OF APOSTLES AND MARTYRS, OF CONFESSORS AND VIRGINS, OF ALL SAINTS, CONCEIVED WITHOUT ORIGINAL SIN, ASSUMED INTO HEAVEN, OF ALL THE EARTH, OF HEAVEN, OF THE UNIVERSE — *See Litany of Mary, Queen.*

QUEEN OF ALL HEARTS, CONFRATERNITY OF MARY

Pious union established in 1899 in Ottawa, Canada, and erected as an archconfraternity by Pope Pius X in 1913.

The group's purpose is to help the members live and publicize the Marian Way of Life as explained in the writings of St. Louis de Montfort, to sanctify themselves, and to restore the reign of Christ through Mary.

Members wear a heart-shaped Queen of All Hearts medal. On the front is a design of the Queen of All Hearts Statuary group found in the Regina Dei Cuori Chapel in Rome. Mary is seated, holding the Child Jesus. St. Louis and an angel kneel at her feet. The book *True Devotion to Mary* is depicted under the group. On the other side of the medal is a shield with a monogram of Mary surmounted by a crown. The shield is circled with a Rosary entwined with a lily, symbolizing Mary's purity.

QUEEN OF ANGELS, OUR LADY —
See Angels, Our Lady of the.

QUEEN OF MERCY — *See Mother of Mercy.*

QUEEN OF THE AMERICAS

Title and devotion referring to Our Lady of Guadalupe as a patroness of all of North and South America.

See Guadalupe, Our Lady of.

QUEEN OF THE AMERICAS GUILD

Organization founded in 1979 by Bishop Jerome J. Hastrich of Gallup, NM, assisted by Bishop Thomas Drury of Corpus Christi, TX, to establish an English-information center and retreat center near the Basilica of Our Lady of Guadalupe in Mexico City and to promote devotion to Our Lady of Guadalupe.

QUEEN OF PEACE, OUR LADY

Title and devotion.

The statue *Our Lady, Queen of Peace* dates back to sixteenth-century France and is located in the chapel of the Religious of the Sacred Hearts of Jesus and Mary in Paris. Eleven inches high and carved from brown wood, it shows Mary holding the Christ Child in her left arm. In her right hand is an olive branch, a symbol of peace. Jesus holds a cross.

Documents trace the statue to the possession of a noble French family of the sixteenth century whose members displayed a deep devotion to Mary and were entrusted with the custody of the sacramental. It was while praying before the statue that one member, Duke de Joyeuse, felt called to religious life and joined the Capuchin Order, taking the name Fr. Ange. He had a chapel built in her honor in the order's house in Paris, later opened to the public. The oratory became the center of prayer and veneration of Our Lady, Queen of Peace.

Eventually, the statue was placed in a niche outside the door of the monastery, where it remained for some six decades. For several years, a clear light illuminated it during the night. Miracles began to be attributed to the intercession of Our Lady of Peace.

After Fr. Ange's death, the statue was moved to the chapel where he had been buried and the reports of miracles continued. A new, large chapel was built to hold the crowds who came to pray before the statue, which remained there until 1790.

During the French Revolution, the Capuchins were forced to abandon the monastery and gave the image to a pious lady named Madame Pepin, who willed it to her widowed sister, Mme. Violet Coipel. After the image had passed through a number of hands, Mme. Coipel presented it to Fr. Peter Coudrin, who was her spiritual director and the founder of the Congregation of the Sacred Hearts of Jesus and Mary. Following her suggestion, he gave all rights of possession to the order.

The statue was placed in the chapel of the Religious in the Rue de Piepus in Paris in 1806. Through the efforts of Fr. Coudrin's order, devotion to Mary under the title "Our Lady, Queen of Peace" has spread worldwide. The image was given a papal crown by Pope Pius X in 1906.

In the late twentieth century, visionaries who reported seeing Mary at Medjugorge said she introduced herself as the Queen of Peace.

QUEEN OF PREACHERS

Title and devotion that refers to Mary's role in St. Dominic's establishing the Order of Preachers, the Dominicans.

See Dominicans.

QUEENSHIP OF MARY

Memorial celebrated on August 22, commemorating Mary as queen of heaven, angels, and humanity. The universal observance was ordered by Pope Pius XII in his encyclical *Ad Caeli Reginam* on October 11, 1954. The original date of the memorial was May 31.

See Ad Caeli Reginam.

QUINCHE, OUR LADY OF

Image and devotion.

Our Lady of the Presentation of Quinche, Ecuador, is a two-foot-tall cedar sculpture carved in the sixteenth century by Don Diego de Robles, an artist credited with other popular and venerated images of Mary. Tradition holds that the people who commissioned the piece could not or would not pay the sculptor for it, and so he traded it to the Oyachi tribe for some cedar boards he needed.

A popular tradition had Mary appearing in a cave to local tribespeople and promising to deliver them from the dangerous bears that ate their children. Later, they were astounded when they saw Diego de Robles arrive carrying his statue: it had the same features as the Lady who had appeared to them.

The statue remained under the care of the Indians for fifteen years, until the local bishop ordered it moved to the village of Quinche, from which it finally took its name in 1604. Since then, the Marian image has been clothed in regal garments covered with jewels and embroidered with gold and silver threads. Mary holds a scepter in her right hand; in her left is the Christ Child, who lifts his right hand in blessing and in his left holds a gold globe crowned with a cross. Both Mary and Jesus wear jeweled crowns made of precious metal. The pedestal on which the statue stands is pure silver.

The face of the Child has features resembling those of the *mestizo* children of the area. Mary has a delicate oval face with a slender nose, thin lips, and a small mouth. Her slanted eyes and her sorrowful gaze with half-closed eyelids give her a unique gentleness. Ecuadorians affectionately refer to her as *La Pequehita* ("the little one").

There are a large number of songs in honor of the Virgin of Quinche, in many local dialects of the region, as well as in Spanish. Some have been sung for centuries.

The image was crowned in 1943, and her feast is celebrated each year on November 21. The present shrine was declared a national sanctuary in 1985.

R

RANSOM, OUR LADY OF — *See Crown of Twelve Stars; Mercy, Our Lady of.*

RECURRENS MENSIS OCTOBER — See Paul VI.

REDEMPTORIS MATER — *See John Paul II.*

REDEMPTORISTS

Popular name for the Congregation of the Most Holy Redeemer, founded by St. Alphonsus Maria Liguori (1696–1787).

See **Perpetual Help, Our Lady of.**

REFORMATION AND MARY

Although neither Martin Luther nor John Calvin totally rejected veneration of Mary, both limited it to imitating the obedient, humble Mother of Jesus presented in the Gospels, even as an example of a believing Church.

Early Reformers rejected calling on saints for assistance; particular titles (such as Queen of Heaven or spiritual mother) were considered derogatory to the unique role of Christ as mediator and as blasphemous of God, the one source of all grace.

Devotion to the saints, especially to Our Lady, continues to be a point of division between Roman Catholicism and Protestantism, a difference in an understanding of the Communion of Saints.

See also Trent, Council of.

REFUGE OF SINNERS

Title and image.

The Franciscan missionary Francisco Diego Garcia y Moreno, the first Bishop of the Californias, proclaimed *Nuestra Señora del Refugio, Patrona de las Ambas Californias.*

The official proclamation was made by Bishop Garcia Diego on January 4, 1843, at Mission Santa Clara in Alta California. He

Refuge of Sinners by Crosio

Refuge of Sinners

noted, "If through the centuries this most worthy Mother of God has shown goodness and compassion to all peoples and nations . . . will she not do likewise for those peoples who bind themselves to her as their refuge and special patroness?"

The entire coat of arms of Bishop Garcia Diego included only the image of Our Lady of Refuge. Paintings of this image depict Mary and the Infant Jesus leaning toward each other with no background between them. Both wear crowns. The original painting *Our Lady of Refuge* came to the Franciscan College of Zacatecas in Mexico from Italy.

The patronal feast was marked in all California missions and the parishes established later. Today, it is observed on July 4 in Baja California and July 5 in Alta California. The feast of Our Lady of Refuge (sometimes called Our Lady, Refuge of Sinners) has its own proper prayers for the Eucharistic Liturgy and the Liturgy of the Hours.

REGINA CAELI

Marian antiphon sung at the end of the Evening Prayer in the Liturgy of the Hours for the Easter season and recited in place of the *Angelus* at noon during that period. The title is the first line of the hymn, which, in English, is "Queen of heaven, rejoice."

The most recent of the four evening antiphons, its written form can be traced to the twelfth century. It was probably an adapted Christmas antiphon, and the author is unknown. In 1742, Pope Benedict XIV decreed that it was to be prayed in the Easter season during the ringing of the *Angelus* bell.

One version of the hymn reads:

Queen of heaven, rejoice, alleluia.
For He whom you merited to bear, alleluia.
Has risen, as He said, alleluia.
Pray for us to God, alleluia.
Rejoice and be glad, O Virgin Mary,
  Alleluia.
For the Lord has truly risen, Alleluia.

Let us pray: O God, who by the resurrection of your Son, our Lord Jesus Christ, has been pleased to fill the world with joy, grant, we beseech you, that through the intercession of the Virgin Mary, His Mother, we may receive the joys of eternal life, through the same Christ our Lord. Amen

See also Antiphons of Our Lady; Angelus.

REIMS, TAPESTRY OF OUR LADY OF

Marian tapestry in the cathedral in Reims, France, among those donated by Archbishop Robert de Lenoncourt in 1530.

Tapestry of *Our Lady of Reims*

Although the piece's origin is unknown, it may have been woven in the studios of Arras or Tournai. Many scenes are taken from the apocryphal gospels, and the symbols attempt to link the Old and New Testament. One of the most important themes is Mary's purity and perfection, probably in reaction to Protestant critics.

The fifteen tableaux relating the life of Mary begin with the tree of Jesse, tell the story of Joachim and Anne, and then move to Mary's life, concluding with her death and assumption.

RELICS OF MARY

Major relics associated with Mary.

In general, relics are the physical remains and effects of saints, items considered worthy of veneration inasmuch as they are representative of persons in glory with God. In line with norms laid down by the Council of Trent and subsequent enactments, discipline concerning relics is subject to control by the Congregations for the Causes of Saints and for Divine Worship and the Discipline of the Sacraments.

The word *relic* comes from the Latin for "remains." There are three categories of relics. First class is a part of a saint's body. Second class is an item worn or used by a saint during his or her lifetime. Third class is an item that has been touched to a first-class relic. Usually, it is a bit of cloth.

The earliest reference to relics is an account of the martyrdom of St. Polycarp who was killed in 156. By the fifth century, dismembering a body and dividing up the bones was considered an acceptable practice because, in the East, Christians believed the soul was totally present everywhere in the body, and so every part was of equal worth. By the tenth century, relics were being placed in shrines and in receptacles (called "reliquaries") in churches, which became centers of pilgrimage.

Some relics, even some that are well known, are of dubious origin. The veneration of a traditional relic can continue even if it cannot be authenticated. Some are almost certainly spurious; however, there is no need to assume deliberate fraud. Rather, honor given in good faith to a false relic is nevertheless profitable to the worshipper and in no way dishonors the saint. However, relics proven and known to be false must be withheld from the people.

No Catholic is formally bound to the positive veneration of relics; Catholics are, however, forbidden by the Council of Trent to say that such veneration ought *not* to be given.

In regard to what are considered among major Marian relics: The cathedral in Prado, Italy, keeps in a crystal and gold reliquary a strip of green ribbon said to have been worn by Our Lady as a belt. A relic claimed to be her veil has been kept in the Cathedral of Chartres for more than a thousand years. What some believe to be her shroud is kept at the cathedral in Aachen, Germany. And a blue velvet chair is venerated as a Marian relic in the chapel of the mother house of the Daughters of Charity in Paris, France. St. Catherine Labouré reported it was the chair in which the Blessed Mother sat during an apparition in 1803. Other churches have claimed to have strands of her hair and vials of her breast milk.

See also Chartres, Our Lady of; Girdle of Our Lady, Feast of the.

RESURRECTION — *See Scripture, Mary in.*

REVELATION, BOOK OF — *See Scripture, Mary in.*

REVELATION, DIVINE AND PRIVATE

God's communication of himself.

It is through revelation that God makes known the mystery of his divine plan, a gift of self-communication that is realized over time by deeds and words, and most fully by the sending of his Son, Jesus.

Divine revelation is transmitted through two sources: Sacred Tradition and Sacred Scripture. The 1965 *Dogmatic Constitution on Divine Revelation* (*Dei Verbum*) notes: "Sacred Tradition and Sacred Scripture make up a single deposit of the Word of God, which is entrusted to the Church."

It also states:

There exists a close connection and communication between sacred tradition and Sacred Scripture. For both of them, flowing from the same divine wellspring, in a certain way merge into a unity and tend toward the same end. For Sacred Scripture is the word of God inasmuch as it is consigned to writing under the inspiration of the divine Spirit, while sacred tradition takes the word of God entrusted by Christ the Lord and the Holy Spirit to the Apostles, and hands it on to their successors in its full purity, so that led by the light of the Spirit of truth, they may in proclaiming it preserve this word of God faithfully, explain it, and make it more widely known. Consequently it is not from Sacred Scripture alone that the Church draws her certainty about everything which has been revealed. Therefore both sacred tradition and Sacred Scripture are to be accepted and venerated with the same sense of loyalty and reverence.

The Church makes a strong distinction between divine revelation and private revelation. Private revelation is given by God to a person for his or her own benefit and the benefit of others, as opposed to the universal revelation for all given to Israel and the apostles.

Some private revelations have been approved by the Church. This only means they contain nothing contrary to faith and morals and that, in addition, there is sufficient evidence to justify belief in their authenticity. Even so, the Church does not — and cannot — impose belief in a private revelation and its contents, either on an individual or on the faithful at large.

RIVERS, OUR LADY OF THE

Image and devotion dating back to mid-twentieth century and Fr. Edward Schlattmann, pastor of St. Francis Church in Portage des Sioux, in the area just north of St. Louis, MO. Members of the Legion of Mary built a shrine to Our Lady of the Rivers as part of their invoking her aid to protect their area from flooding.

ROCKIES, OUR LADY OF THE

Marian image and devotion.

The statue of Our Lady of the Rockies is 90 feet tall and is located outside Butte, MT. The idea originated as an *ex voto* by Bob O'Neill in 1979. The base is 3,500 feet above the city and 8,510 feet above sea level.

ROSA MYSTICA — *See Mystical Rose.*

ROSARY

Extra-liturgical or private Marian devotion.

A form of mental and vocal prayers that focus on events ("mysteries") in the lives of Jesus and Mary, it has been a central devotion for clergy, religious, and the laity. Its appeal has spanned age, class, nationality, and ethnicity.

Sts. Peter Canisius (1521–1597), Louis Marie de Montfort (1673–1716), Alphonsus Liguori (1696–1787), Pope Pius V (1504–1572), and the popes from Leo XIII (r. 1878–1903) to the present have significantly contributed to its spread.

The historical development of the Rosary dates back toward the end of the twelfth century when the first half of the Hail Mary, as known today, began to assume the spiritual significance of the Our Father and the Creed and was seen as a prayer all Catholics should know. At that time, the Rosary began to take shape in the form of Our Lady's Psalter, one hundred fifty Hail Marys. To these were added meditations on mysteries in the lives of Mary and Jesus, from the Annunciation to their glorification.

In the first half of the fifteenth century, Dominic of Prussia, a Carthusian monk, helped make the devotion more popular by linking fifty Hail Marys with fifty such phrases. *Rosarium* (a rose garden) was used to mean this collection of fifty points of meditation, and so, the name *Rosary* became the official title of the devotion. Another Carthusian, Henry of Kalkar, divided the fifty Hail Marys into decades, with an Our Father between each.

By the early fifteenth century, the essential elements of the Rosary were established, but it did not become popular until it was simplified. In 1483, *Our Dear Lady's Psalter*, a book on the Rosary written by a Dominican, refers to the same fifteen mysteries as today, with one exception: the fourteenth combines Mary's coronation in heaven with the Assumption, and the fifteenth is the Last Judgment.

Blessed Alan de la Roche, another Dominican, founded the Confraternity of the Psalter of Jesus and Mary in 1470. It was a forerunner of the Rosary Confraternity, through which the devotion spread to the universal Church. It was Blessed Alan who particularly promoted the traditional association of St. Dominic with the Rosary.

Pope St. Pius V's papal bull of 1569, *Consueverunt Romani Pontifices* (sometimes referred to as the "Magna Carta" of the Rosary), firmly established both the devotion in the Church and its traditional form, which has been called the "Dominican Rosary." Four centuries later, in 1974, Pope Paul VI issued *Marialis Cultus*, an apostolic exhortation for the right ordering and development of Marian devotions. In it, he referred to the Rosary as a "compendium of the entire Gospel" (42). He also noted:

— As a Gospel prayer, centered on the mystery of the redemptive Incarnation, the Rosary is therefore a prayer with a clearly Christological orientation (46).

— By its nature the recitation of the Rosary calls for a quiet rhythm and a lingering pace, helping the individual to meditate on the mysteries of the Lord's life as seen through the eyes of her who was closest to the Lord. In this way the unfathomable riches of these mysteries are unfolded (47).

— The Rosary is an exercise of piety that draws its motivating force from the liturgy and leads naturally back to it, if practiced in conformity with its original inspiration. It does not, however, become part of the liturgy. In fact, meditation on the mysteries of the Rosary, by familiarizing the hearts and minds of the faithful with the mysteries of Christ, can be an excellent preparation for the creation of those same mysteries in the liturgical action and an also become a continuing echo thereof. However, it is a mistake to recite the Rosary during the celebration of the liturgy, though unfortunately this practice still persists here and there (48).

When "praying the Rosary," the ordinary practice has been to recite one of the three cycles (or sets) of mysteries.

Its essential elements are meditation on the mysteries and the recitation of a number of decades of Hail Marys, each beginning with the Lord's Prayer. Introductory prayers may include the Apostles' Creed, an initial Our Father, three Hail Marys and a Glory Be to the Father; each decade is customarily concluded with a Glory be to the Father; at the end, it is customary to say the Hail, Holy Queen and a prayer from the liturgy for the feast of the Blessed Virgin Mary of the Rosary.

The traditional mysteries of the Rosary, which are the subject of meditation, are:

Joyful Mysteries: Annunciation, Visitation, Nativity, Presentation, and Finding in the Temple.

Sorrowful Mysteries: Agony in the Garden, Scourging at the Pillar, Crowning of Thorns, Carrying of the Cross, and the Crucifixion.

Glorious Mysteries: Resurrection, Ascension, Descent of the Holy Spirit, Assumption, and Coronation.

In customary practice, only five decades are usually said at one time. Rosary beads are used to aid in counting the prayers without distraction.

In 2002, Pope John Paul marked the twenty-fourth anniversary of his election by signing the apostolic letter *Rosarium Virginis Mariae* (*The Rosary of the Virgin Mary*). In it he suggested the five new "mysteries of light."

> *Luminous Mysteries: Christ's Baptism in the Jordan, the Wedding at Cana, the Proclamation of the Kingdom, Transfiguration, and Institution of the Eucharist.*

See also de la Roche (de Rupe), O.P., Blessed Alan.

ROSARY CONFRATERNITY

Pious association organized in the fifteenth century. Some four centuries later, Pope Leo XIII gave the Dominican master general the right to promulgate the confraternity and all its devotions.

A person becomes a member by having his or her name inscribed in the membership register wherever the confraternity is accorded canonical status. Members strive to say all the decades of the Rosary each week. There are no meetings or dues.

ROSARY, DOMINICAN

The traditional Rosary, prayed using the Joyful, Sorrowful, and Glorious Mysteries.

ROSARY IN HONOR OF ST. JOSEPH

Chaplet using a standard Rosary, but replacing the Hail Mary with the following prayer:

> *Hail, Holy Joseph, spouse of the ever virgin Mary, foster father of God the Son, whom our Father in Heaven chose to be head of the Holy Family, pray for us sinners now and at the hour of our death. Amen.*

The mysteries for this chaplet are:

Joyful
1. *The Annunciation of Joseph*
2. *The Birth of Jesus*
3. *The Circumcision and Naming of Jesus*
4. *The Presentation of the Baby Jesus in the Temple*
5. *The Finding of the Boy Jesus in the Temple*

St. Joseph

Sorrowful

1. *Joseph's Spouse Mary is Found to Be With Child*
2. *The Journey to Bethlehem*
3. *Joseph Flees to Egypt with Mary and Jesus*
4. *Jesus is Lost in Jerusalem*
5. *The Death of Joseph*

Glorious

1. *The Glorification of St. Joseph*
2. *St. Joseph, Patron of the Universal Church*
3. *St. Joseph, Protector of Families*
4. *St. Joseph, Patron of the Sick and Suffering*
5. *St. Joseph, Patron of a Holy Death*

ROSARY OF THE DEAD

Chaplet dating back to the mid-nineteenth century and promoted by the Archconfraternity of Notre Dame du Suffrage. It is also referred to as "Beads of the Dead."

The chaplet consists of four decades of ten beads commemorating the forty hours between Jesus' death and his Resurrection. It features a cross and a medal of the archconfraternity, representing the souls in purgatory. There may also be five introductory beads, as on the Dominican Rosary.

Either the *De Profundis* (Psalm 130) or the Our Father and Hail Mary are said on the cross and the beginning and end of the chaplet. The Eternal Rest and the Acts of Faith, Hope, and Love are said on the large beads separating the decades, and "Sweet Heart of Mary, be my salvation" is said on decade beads.

ROSARY OF OUR LADY OF SORROWS (SERVITE)

Chaplet focusing on the traditional Seven Sorrows of Mary.

Promoted by the Servite Order, it features seven groups of seven beads with each group separated by a medal depicting one of the sorrows. At the end of the sacramental is a medal of Our Lady with her heart pierced by seven swords. Most often, a crucifixion scene is on the other side of the medal.

Each septet is introduced by a meditation to guide reflection as an Our Father and seven Hail Marys are prayed. The chaplet concludes with three Hail Marys as an added petition for true sorrow and a desire to model one's life on the example of the life and faith of Mary.

See also Seven Sorrows, Chaplet of the.

ROSARY OF OUR LADY OF TEARS

Chaplet promoted by the Institute of the Missionaries of the Scourged Jesus since 1930. The devotion is based on visions of Mary reported by the institute's co-founder, Sister Amelia.

The chaplet features seven sets of seven beads with each group separated by a larger bead, similar to the Rosary of the Seven Sorrows of Mary. At the end, there are three additional small beads and a medal of Our Lady of Tears.

One version of the devotion begins:

O crucified Jesus, we fall at your feet and offer you the tears of the one, who with deep compassionate love accompanied you on your sorrowful way of the cross. O good Master, grant that we take to heart the lessons which the tears of your most holy Mother teach us,

*so that we may fulfill your holy will on earth,
that we may be worthy to praise and exalt
you in heaven for all eternity. Amen.*

The prayer on the large beads is:

*V. O Jesus, look upon the tears of the one
who loved You most on earth,*

R. And loves you most ardently in heaven.

And the prayer on the small beads is:

V. O Jesus, listen to our prayers,

*R. For the sake of the tears of your most
Holy Mother.*

The prayer on the medal is:

*O Mary, Mother of love, sorrow and mercy,
we beseech you to unite your prayers with ours
so that Jesus, your Divine Son, to whom we
turn, may hear our petitions in the name of
your maternal tears, and grant us, not only
the favors we now ask, but the crown of everlasting life. Amen.*

ROSARY, OUR LADY OF THE

Popular title and image; "Queen of
Guatemala."

The Guatemalan image is a pure silver
statue completed by an unknown artist in
1592. It had been commissioned by Lopez de
Montoya, a Dominican priest. Mary holds a
large Rosary in her right hand and the sleeping
Christ Child — who faces forward — is in her
left arm.

Later, the statue's pedestal and Mary's robes
were covered with elaborate garments and
ornaments.

Devotees claim that the coloring of Our
Lady's face changes from bright pink to a
much more faded shade whenever there is a
conflict or some national misfortune is immi-
nent. Popular tradition holds that she had
gone traveling throughout the Americas and
that the Child fell asleep when they reached
Guatemala, which is why she stayed there.

In 1821, the leaders of the independence
movement proclaimed her patroness of the
new nation and took an oath before her image
that they would not rest until they freed
Guatemala.

The Virgin of the Rosary was solemnly
declared "Queen of Guatemala" in 1833 and
was crowned canonically on January 26, 1934,
in a huge ceremony at the principal plaza of
Guatemala City, in front of the cathedral. The
ceremony had to be held in the open because
there was no church large enough to accommodate the huge crowd.

The church and convent of St. Dominic,
current shrine of the Virgin of the Rosary, was
begun in 1788 and completed in 1808. October, the month dedicated to the Rosary, is
marked with celebrations and pilgrimages to
the Sanctuary of the Virgin of the Rosary.

ROSARY OF THE SEVEN JOYS OF OUR LADY

Marian devotion made up of seventy-two Hail
Marys; also known as the Franciscan Crown
Rosary and the Crown of the Seven Decades.

According to pious tradition, this chaplet
dates back to a young man who entered the
Franciscan Order in Assisi in 1422. Before
that, every day he had decorated a statue of
Our Lady with a wreath of flowers. Because he
was not able to continue the practice once he
entered the novitiate, he was considering leaving the order. While he was kneeling at Mary's
altar and explaining to Our Lady what he

planned to do and why, Mary appeared to him and instructed him to stay in the novitiate. She said would teach him how to weave a crown of roses that would not wither and would be more pleasing to her and more meritorious for him. She then taught him to pray the seven-decade Rosary with two additional Hail Marys in honor of the seventy-two years she lived on this earth.

Among those who strongly promoted the prayer was St. Bernadine of Siena (1380–1444), who entered the Confraternity of Our Lady at age seventeen and joined the Franciscans five years later.

The seven decades are: the Annunciation, the Visitation, the Nativity, the adoration of the Magi, the finding of the Child Jesus in the Temple, the Resurrection, and Mary's Assumption and coronation in heaven.

"ROSARY PRIEST, THE" — *See Family Rosary Crusade.*

ROSARY SUNDAY

Popular name for the feast of the Most Holy Rosary (October 7) in Dominican churches. One this day, roses are blessed and distributed in honor of Our Lady.

See also Feasts of Mary; Rose.

ROSE

Symbol of Mary.

The Church began using this flower as a symbol of Our Lady during the Middle Ages,

and a number of pious legends concerning Mary and roses date back to those times.

Our Lady of Guadalupe placed rare Castilian roses in St. Juan Diego's cloak as a sign of her presence. At Lourdes, France, St. Bernadette reported Mary appeared to her standing on a rosebush and had golden roses on her feet. Visionaries at LaSalette, France, also said Mary wore roses.

Roses and rose petals have often been blessed as sacramentals, a pious custom in Dominican churches on the Feast of the Holy Rosary.

ROSEMARY

Herb associated with Mary since the Middle Ages.

In ancient Greece, students wore sprigs of rosemary in their hair to stimulate the memory. Later, the plant became symbolic of remembrance. Along with many other plants and herbs, during medieval times the rosemary was rededicated to Mary.

One Spanish tradition holds that rosemary bushes gave shelter to Our Lady on the flight to Egypt and she dried her cloak on the plant, which is why its flowers are blue. Because of its association with Mary, it gained a role as protector against evil and was laid in cradles to prevent nightmares.

RUE DE BAC PARIS, OUR LADY OF — *See Miraculous Medal.*

SABBATINE PRIVILEGE

Reference to Mary's intercession associated with the Brown Scapular.

It says Mary will aid the souls of members of the Confraternity of the Blessed Virgin of Mount Carmel after their death by her continual intercession, by her suffrages and merits, and by her special protection, especially on Saturday (the original Sabbath and the day the Church has especially dedicated to Our Lady).

The Sabbatine privilege has often been misinterpreted to mean scapular wearers, simply because they are wearing this sacramental at the time of death, will go to heaven on the first Saturday after their deaths. But the Church teaches, and the Carmelite Rule affirms, that Jesus Christ is the only one who liberates a person from his or her sin.

See **Carmel, Our Lady of Mount.**

SACRAMENTALS, MARIAN

A sacramental is a sacred sign that resembles a sacrament and by which, through the prayers of the Church, spiritual effects are signified or obtained. A sacramental can be an object (such as holy water) or an action (such as a blessing). Among the sacramentals associated with Our Lady are rosaries, scapulars, and medals.

SACRED HEART, OUR LADY OF THE

Title used at shrine erected by Fr. Jules Chevalier (1824–1907), who founded the Missionaries of the Sacred Heart of Jesus (a religious congregation of priests and lay brothers) in Issoudun, France, in 1855.

The origin of the congregation is closely associated with Pope Pius IX's defining the dogma of the Immaculate Conception in 1854, at which time Fr. Chevalier made a pledge to himself to honor Our Lady in a special way. The following year he fulfilled that vow by building a shrine to Mary under the title "Our Lady of the Sacred Heart."

See also Immaculate Conception.

Our Lady of the Sacred Heart

SACRED HEARTS OF JESUS AND MARY, CONGREGATION OF THE —
See Queen of Peace, Our Lady.

SAINT

A "holy one" who, through the grace of Christ, leads a life in union with God and receives the reward of eternal life. More commonly, a deceased member of the faithful solemnly declared by the pope (canonized) as a model and intercessor to the Christian faithful and venerated on the basis of the fact that he or she has lived a life of heroic virtue or remained faithful to God through martyrdom.

Many "holy ones" as well as canonized saints have had a particular and prominent devotion to Mary.

ST. ALBERT THE GREAT — *See Assumption, Immaculate Conception.*

ST. ALPHONSUS LIGUORI — *See* Ad Caeli Reginam; *Assumption; Child of Mary;* Glories of Mary, The; *Redemptorists; Three Hail Marys;* True Devotion to the Blessed Virgin Mary, A Treatise on.

ST. ALPHONSUS RODRIGUEZ — *See Little Office of the Immaculate Conception.*

ST. ANNE — *See Apocryphal Writing, Mary in; Birth of Mary; Joachim and Anne; Scripture, Mary in.*

ST. ANSELM OF CANTERBURY — *See Child of Mary;* Daily, Daily Sing to Mary.

ST. ANTHONY CLARET — *See Claretians.*

ST. AUGUSTINE — *See Consolation, Our Lady of; Virginity of Mary, Perpetual.*

ST. BERNADETTE SOUBIROUS — *See Lourdes, Our Lady of.*

ST. BERNADINE OF SIENA — *See Assumption; Glory of the Human Race; Rosary of the Seven Joys of Our Lady.*

ST. BERNARD OF CLAIRVAUX — *See Immaculate Conception,* Memorare.

ST. BONAVENTURE — *See Assumption, Hail Mary of Our Sorrowful Mother, Immaculate Conception.*

ST. BRIDGET OF SWEDEN — *See Brigettine Office, Brigettine Rosary.*

ST. CASIMIR — *See* Daily, Daily Sing to Mary.

ST. CATHERINE LABOURÉ — *See Miraculous Medal.*

ST. CAMILLUS OF LELLIS — *See Scapular of St. Camillus.*

ST. DOMINIC — *See de la Roche (de Rupe) O.P., Blessed Alan; Dominicans; Pius X; Queen of Preachers.*

ST. ELIZABETH — *See Scripture, Mary in.*

ST. EUGENE DE MAZENOD — *See Oblates of Mary Immaculate.*

ST. FRANCIS DE SALES — *See Assumption;* Imitation of Our Lady.

ST. FRANCIS OF ASSISI — *See Franciscans; Portiuncula.*

ST. GREGORY NAZIANZEN — *See* Ad Caeli Reginam.

ST. IGNATIUS LOYOLA — *See Arantzazu, Our Lady of; Christian Life Community; Jesuits.*

ST. IGNATIUS OF ANTIOCH — *See Consolation, Our Lady of; Virginity of Mary, Perpetual.*

ST. IRENAEUS — *See Knots, the Virgin Who Unties.*

ST. ISIDORE — *See Almudena, Our Lady of.*

ST. JEROME — *See* Ad Caeli Reginam; *Virginity of Mary, Perpetual.*

ST. JOACHIM — *See Apocryphal Writing, Mary in; Joachim and Anne; Scripture, Mary in.*

ST. JOHN — *See Caregiver, Our Lady's; Scripture, Mary in; Tomb of Mary.*

ST. JOHN BOSCO — *See Daughters of Mary, Help of Christians; Our Lady, Help of Christians.*

ST. JOHN DAMASCENE — *See* Ad Caeli Reginam.

ST. JOHN EUDES — *See* Admirable Heart of Mary, The; Ave Maria *Salutation; Immaculate Heart of Mary.*

ST. JOHN OF ÁVILA — *See* Imitation of Our Lady.

ST. JOHN OF MATHA — *See* Good Remedy, Our Lady of.

ST. JOHN NEUMANN — *See Our Lady of Hostyn.*

ST. JOHN THE BAPTIST — *See Scripture, Mary in.*

ST. JOSEPH — *See Scripture, Mary in; Spouses of the Blessed Virgin Mary.*

ST. JUAN DIEGO — *See Guadalupe, Our Lady of.*

ST. LEO THE GREAT — *See Virginity of Mary, Perpetual.*

ST. LEONARD OF PORT MAURICE — *See Three Hail Marys.*

ST. LOUIS MARIE DE MONTFORT — *See Company of Mary; Consecration to Jesus through Mary; Crown of the Blessed Virgin Mary, Little; Legion of Mary; Queen of All Hearts, Confraternity of Mary; Secret of the Rosary, The; Slavery of Mary, Slave of Mary.*

ST. LUKE — *See Art, Mary in; Salus Populi Romani; Scripture, Mary in.*

ST. MARGARET MARY ALACOQUE — *See* Ave Maria *Salutation; Pellevoisin, Our Lady of.*

ST. MARIA MAZZARELLO — *See Daughters of Mary, Help of Christians.*

ST. MARY MAGDALENE — *See Scripture, Mary in.*

ST. MATTHEW — *See Scripture, Mary in.*

ST. MAXIMILIAN KOLBE — *See Militia of the Immaculate Conception.*

ST. MECHTILDE OF HELFTA — *See Three Hail Marys; Trinity, Our Lady of the.*

ST. MICHAEL THE ARCHANGEL — *See Golden Saturdays, The.*

ST. MONICA — *See Consolation, Our Lady of.*

ST. PETER CANISIUS — *See Assumption; Incomparable Virgin Mary, The.*

ST. PETER CHRYSOLOGUS — *See Virginity of Mary, Perpetual.*

ST. PETER JULIAN EYMARD — *See Most Blessed Sacrament, Our Lady of the.*

ST. PETER NOLASCO — *See Crown of Twelve Stars; Mercy, Our Lady of; Seven Saturdays in Honor of Our Lady of Ransom.*

ST. PHILIP BENIZI — *See Divine Providence, Our Lady, Mother of.*

ST. PHILIP NERI — *See May.*

ST. PIO OF PIETRELCINA — *See Perfect Sanctity.*

ST. PIUS X — *See Pius X; Queen of All Hearts, Confraternity of Mary.*

ST. RAYMOND OF PEÑAFORT — *See Crown of Twelve Stars; Mercy, Our Lady of.*

ST. ROBERT BELLARMINE — *See Assumption.*

ST. SIMON STOCK — *See* Carmel, Our Lady of Mount; Flos Carmeli; *Novena to Our Lady of Mount Carmel.*

ST. TERESA OF ÁVILA — *See* Immaculate Conception of El Viejo, Our Lady of the.

ST. THÉRÈSE OF LISIEUX — *See Little Flower Rosary; Smile, Our Lady of the.*

ST. THOMAS AQUINAS — *See Assumption; Immaculate Conception; Virginity of Mary, Perpetual.*

SALUS POPULI ROMANI

Image and devotion, Latin for "Protectress of the Roman People."

Considered by some to be the best-loved and most-honored Marian icon in Rome, it is housed in the *Cappella Paolina* — the Lady Chapel — of St. Mary Major Basilica in Rome.

Some historians claim the image can be traced to the post-iconoclastic period of the eighth century, but others believe it dates from

Salus Populi Romani

the thirteenth. By the fifteenth century, it was being honored, and miracles were attributed to Mary's intercession under this devotion, including sparing the city from plague during the pontificate of Pope St. Gregory the Great (r. 590–604).

The image itself is a type of iconography known as *Odigitria*. It depicts Our Lady holding the Christ Child in her arms. It is five feet high by three-and-a-quarter feet wide and painted on a thick slab of cedar. Mary wears a gold-trimmed dark blue mantle over a red tunic. It is also a "Lucan image" — that is, an icon which pious tradition holds was painted by St. Luke.

See also Art, Mary in.

SALVE REGINA

A Marian antiphon said or sung at various times of the Liturgy of the Hours. It is also a concluding prayer of the Rosary.

Beloved since the Middle Ages, the hymn is attributed to Hermann of Reichenau, a Benedictine monk who died in 1054. In English, the hymn's title and opening words are "Hail, Holy Queen."

In medieval times, laity joined monks and friars in singing the *Salve Regina* at the end of the day. Because sailors did likewise, it was the first hymn sung in the New World by the men who traveled with Christopher Columbus in 1492.

In English, the hymn reads:

Hail Holy Queen, Mother of mercy, our life, our sweetness and our hope. To you do we cry, poor banished children of Eve. To you do we send up our sighs, mourning and weeping in this valley of tears. Turn then, most gracious advocate, your eyes of mercy towards us; and after this our exile, show onto us the blessed fruit of your womb, Jesus. O clement, O loving, O sweet Virgin Mary.

When recited as a prayer, the following is sometimes added:

Pray for us, O holy Mother of God.
That we may be made worthy of the
promises of Christ. Amen.

See also Antiphons of Our Lady.

SAN JUAN, OUR LADY OF

Devotion, image, and pilgrim statue.

The Virgin of San Juan de los Lagos dates back to the early seventeenth century when Fr.

Antonio of Segovia, a Spanish Franciscan missionary, took a small statue of the Immaculate Conception to the town of San Juan Bautista Mezquetitlan, Mexico (later, named San Juan de los Lagos). By 1623, many of the Nochixlecas Indians venerated her under the title of *Cichaupilli,* meaning "Lady." Since that time, miracles have been attributed to the intercession of Mary under this title.

The statue depicts Our Lady with her hands folded in prayer. She stands on a half moon and two stars. The base is made of silver. Behind her, over her crown, are two angels holding a scroll with the inscription "Immaculate Mother, pray for us."

Today, the image is kept in a church dedicated to the Immaculate Conception and is known as Our Lady of St. John of the Lakes.

SATURDAY DEVOTION TO MARY

Tradition that appears to date back to the tenth century as a commemoration of Mary's sorrow at Jesus' death and at most of his disciples abandoning her on the day after his crucifixion.

From the 900s, Saturday became associated with Our Lady in other ways, and it became customary to celebrate a Mass in her honor on that day.

The Little Office of the Blessed Virgin Mary came to be recited on Saturdays, a practice especially followed by the Benedictines of Monte Cassino and Cluny. Later, the custom spread to other religious orders.

The Second Vatican Council maintained the commemoration of Mary on Saturdays. The revised Roman Missal from that period gives three common forms of the Mass of the

Blessed Virgin, plus one each for the seasons on Advent, Christmas, and Easter.

See also Little Office of the Blessed Virgin Mary.

SCAPULAR

Sacramental; part of religious habit.

The scapular began in the Middle Ages as a narrow piece of cloth, about the width of the shoulders, with an opening in the center so that it could be slipped over the head and hang in equal lengths. Originally, this was a work garment meant to protect the tunic; through the years, it became part of the habit. (The word itself comes from the Latin for shoulder blades [*scapula*]. A scapular was seen as a symbol of the yoke of Christ.)

Later, an abbreviated form came into use and was given to the laity so the wearer could share in the merits and good works of the particular group of which it served as a badge. Approved by the Church as sacramentals, these scapulars typically consist of two small squares of woolen cloth joined by strings and are worn about the neck. They are presented in a ceremony of investiture or enrollment. There are nearly twenty scapulars for devotional use, including many associated with Mary.

See particular scapular by name.

SCAPULAR MEDAL

Medallion with a representation of the Sacred Heart on one side and of the Blessed Virgin Mary on the other. Authorized by St. Pius X in 1910, it may be worn or carried in place of a scapular by persons already invested with a scapular.

SCAPULAR OF OUR LADY OF GOOD COUNSEL (WHITE SCAPULAR)

Sacramental associated with devotion to Our Lady of Good Counsel.

In 1753, Pope Benedict XIV established the Pious Union of Our Lady of Good Counsel. Later, Pope Leo XIII, a union member, instituted the white scapular of Good Counsel, added the title Mother of Good Counsel into the Litany of Loreto, and placed a copy of the image over the altar in the Pauline chapel in the Vatican.

The front panel of the white scapular is based on this image. It shows the Madonna with her eyes closed and the Christ Child's right arm around her neck. His left hand is at the neck of her garment.

The back panel features the papal coat of arms — the tiara and the keys of Peter. Underneath it are written the words of Pope Leo XIII: "Son, follow Her counsel." It is worn by members of the Pious Union of Our Mother of Good Counsel.

See also **Good Counsel, Our Lady of**; *Scapular.*

SCAPULAR OF OUR LADY OF MOUNT CARMEL (BROWN SCAPULAR)

Sacramental associated the Carmelite Order.

See **Carmel, Our Lady of Mount**; *Scapular.*

SCAPULAR OF OUR LADY OF RANSOM (WHITE SCAPULAR)

Sacramental associated with the Mercedarian Order and the confraternity it established. This white scapular features an image of Our Lady of Ransom on the front and the order's coat of arms on the back.

See also Ransom, Our Lady of; Scapular.

SCAPULAR OF ST. CAMILLUS (OUR LADY, HELP OF THE SICK; BLACK SCAPULAR)

Sacramental associated with the order founded by St. Camillus of Lellis (1550–1614) and its confraternity, established in 1860 by member Br. Ferdinand Vicari, under the invocation of Our Lady, Help of the Sick.

The front of the black woolen scapular depicts that image of Mary, and the back features a small red cross. The scapular is no longer available, and the confraternity has ceased to exist.

See also Scapular.

SCAPULAR OF ST. DOMINIC

Sacramental associated with the Order of Preachers, the Dominicans.

Blessed Reginald of Orleans (1183–1220) reported receiving this scapular from the hands of Mary. Made of white wool, it was approved by the order as the usual form of affiliation with the community. No images are necessary, but the scapular given in the house of the order's master general in Rome shows St. Dominic kneeling before a crucifix on one side and Blessed Reginald receiving the scapular from Mary on the other.

See also Scapular.

St. Camillus

SCAPULAR OF THE IMMACULATE CONCEPTION (BLUE SCAPULAR)

Scapular associated with Venerable Ursula Benincasa (1547–1618), foundress of the Theatines of the Immaculate Conception and promoted by the Order of Marians.

The small scapular is worn in honor of the Immaculate Conception for the conversion of sinners. It usually bears a symbol of the Immaculate Conception on one side and the name of Mary on the other.

The scapular was approved by Pope Clement X in 1671. In 1894, a confraternity of the Immaculate Conception of the Blessed Virgin and Mother of God, Mary, was erected in the Theatine church of St. Andrea della Valle in Rome. Members are invested with the blue scapular.

See also Archconfraternity; Confraternity; Scapular.

SCAPULAR OF THE IMMACULATE HEART (GREEN SCAPULAR)

Sacramental which is not properly a scapular because it does not have a front and back square, but is made up of a single square and single string (both of which are green).

One side of the square features an image of Mary, the other her Immaculate Heart, circled by an inscription of oval shape surmounted by a gold cross. The inscription reads, "Immaculate Heart of Mary, pray for us now and at the hour of our death."

The green scapular is not the habit of any confraternity, and its use is based on the private revelations of Daughter of Charity Sister Justine Bisqueyburu (1817–1903). She understood that this new scapular, and the prayers of those who used it, would be a means that God would use to bring to himself those who had no faith and to reconcile those who had strayed from their faith, so they would be assured of a happy death.

See also Scapular.

SCAPULAR OF THE IMMACULATE HEART OF MARY

Scapular that traces its history to 1877 and the Missionary Sons of the Immaculate Heart of Mary and the order's co-founder, Bishop Joseph Xifre, C.M.F. Pope Pius IX sanctioned it that same year

The scapular is made of white woolen cloth. The front features the image of the burning heart of Mary, out of which grows a lily. The heart is circled with a wreath of roses and pierced with a sword.

See also Scapular.

SCAPULAR OF THE MOST SACRED HEART OF JESUS

Sacramental based on Marian apparitions reported by Estelle Faguette in Pellevoisin, France, in 1876.

One side of the scapular has in image of Mary Immaculate. The other shows Jesus' pierced heart ringed with thorns and flames burning from the top. The heart is surmounted with a cross.

See Pellevoisin, Our Lady of; Scapular.

SCAPULAR OF THE SACRED HEARTS OF JESUS AND MARY

Sacramental approved by the Sacred Congregation of Rites in 1900.

One side shows an image of the two Sacred Hearts in their traditional representations, the Heart of Jesus with the cross and fire, wreathed with thorns; and the Heart of Mary pierced with a sword. Beneath these are the instruments of the Passion. The other side usually has a red cross. The Missionaries of the Sacred Heart and the Oblate Missionaries have custody of this scapular.

See also Scapular.

SCAPULAR OF THE SEVEN SORROWS (BLACK SCAPULAR)

Sacramental associated with the Servite Order. The scapular is made of black cloth and typically shows Our Lady of Sorrows on the front. The back may also have a Marian image.

See also Scapular, Servites.

SCAPULAR PROMISE — *See* Mount Carmel, Our Lady of; *Sabbatine Privilege.*

SCHOENSTATT, OUR LADY OF

Marian title and image associated with International Apostolic Movement of Schoenstatt, which traces its roots to 1914 and a German priest, Fr. Joseph Kentenich, and the members of the Marian Sodality under his care.

Members strive for everyday sanctity and try to serve the universal apostolate of the Church in the world today. The eighteenth of each month is celebrated as "covenant day," a reference to their covenant of love with the Mother of God. An image of Our Lady with the Christ Child is venerated in all Schoenstatt shrines worldwide. The original painting by Luigi Crosio (1835–1915) is titled *Refuge of Sinners* but is more commonly known as *Mother Thrice Admirable, Queen and Victoress of Schoenstatt.*

See also Mother Thrice Admirable.

SCHROCKEN ROSARY

Chaplet named for an Austrian Alpine village.

The angelic salutation of the Hail Mary is said on each of sixty-three beads, and a meditation is read aloud as the congregation concludes the prayer. There are no Our Fathers in this form of the devotion.

SCOTUS, JOHN DUNS — *See Immaculate Conception.*

SCRIPTURAL ROSARY

Form of Rosary combining customary prayers with passages from Scripture before each Hail Mary. The verses progress so that the story of each mystery is told as the decade is prayed.

The scriptural Rosary dates back to the Middle Ages, when the beads were prayed with a short thought or meditation for each, rather than a decade-long meditation for each mystery. In 1961, a nonprofit organization first known as the Scriptural Rosary Center (renamed the Christianica Center) was founded in Chicago to introduce the scriptural Rosary.

See also Rosary.

SCRIPTURE, MARY IN

Though there are no explicit references to Mary in the Old Testament (*see Prophecies in the Old Testament, Mary in*), the New Testament includes Mary's role as the Mother of the Messiah and Mother of the Church.

Ancient tradition says Mary's parents were St. Joachim and St. Anne. The authors of the New Testament include nothing about them, but they are featured in an apocryphal book titled the *Protoevangelium of James*, also known as the *Book of the Nativity of Mary* (*see Apocryphal Writing, Mary in*).

Scripture scholars note that a verse in the Gospel of John can be seen to indicate Mary had a sister (or at least a close blood relative, similar to references to Jesus' "brothers" and "sisters" elsewhere): "But standing by the cross of Jesus were his mother, and his mother's sister, Mary the wife of Clopas, and Mary Magdalene" (19:25).

as the *Book of the Nativity of Mary (see Apocryphal Writing, Mary in)*.

Scripture scholars note that a verse in the Gospel of John can be seen to indicate Mary had a sister (or at least a close blood relative, similar to references to Jesus' "brothers" and "sisters" elsewhere): "But standing by the cross of Jesus were his mother, and his mother's sister, Mary the wife of Clopas, and Mary Magdalene" (19:25).

The evangelists say that Mary's betrothed was named Joseph (Mt. 1:18) but, again, it is apocryphal writing that led to the tradition of his being an older man and, perhaps, a widower. Luke's list of genealogies say that he was a descendant of David (Mt. 1:1–17; Lk. 3:23–38) (*see Ancestors of Mary*). The Gospels also say he worked as a carpenter (Mt. 13:55, Mk. 6:3). The second chapter of Luke says that Joseph was Mary's betrothed — a first step which, according to Jewish law and custom at that time, was the equivalent to marriage in modern times. Later, Mary and Joseph would be formally married.

Luke gives an account of the Annunciation, the angel Gabriel visiting Mary in Nazareth, and her accepting God's invitation to be the mother of the Savior (Lk.1:26–28) (*see Annunciation*).

The evangelist includes her relationship to Zechariah and Elizabeth (her kinswoman) and the birth of their son, John, and her visitation to them. Soon after the Annunciation, Mary travels to a town in Judea (often identified as Ain Karin) only a few miles from Jerusalem. There Elizabeth, now six months pregnant, feels her unborn child leap with joy (Lk. 1:41, 44) and she greets Mary with "Blessed are you among women, and blessed is the fruit of your womb" (Lk. 1:42). Mary responds with a song of praise and thanksgiving to God, the *Magnificat* (Lk. 1:46–55) (*see* **Magnificat**). She stays with Elizabeth for three months (perhaps helping at the birth of John the Baptist) and then returns home (Lk. 1:56).

It's the evangelist Matthew who writes of Joseph's concern about Mary's becoming pregnant "before they lived together" (Mt. 1:18). But, "being a just man and unwilling to put her to shame, [he] resolved to send her away quietly" (Mt. 1:19). Before he can do that, an angel appears to him in a dream "saying, 'Joseph, son of David, do not fear to take Mary your wife, for that which is conceived in her is of the Holy Spirit; she will bear a son, and you shall call his name Jesus, for he will save his people from their sins'" (Mt. 1:20–21).

Matthew continues:

All this took place to fulfill what the Lord had spoken by the prophet: "Behold, a virgin shall conceive and bear a son, and his name shall be called Emmanuel" (which means, God with us). When Joseph woke from sleep, he did as the angel of the Lord commanded him; he took his wife, but knew her not until she had borne a son; and he called his name Jesus.

(See Virginity of Mary, Perpetual.)

The infancy narratives (the first two chapters of Matthew and Luke that describe Jesus' lineage and Mary's role in his conception, birth, infancy, and childhood) explain that, following a decree from the Roman Emperor Augustus, Joseph and Mary must travel ninety miles south from Nazareth to Bethlehem to register for a census. Once they arrive, there is no place for them to stay. It is possible they were shown one of the caves outside town, the location where, tradition says, Jesus was born. Luke also says Mary "wrapped him in swaddling cloths, and laid him in a manger" (Lk. 2:7).

An angel announces the birth of the Messiah to shepherds who are nearby and then a choir of angels appear, singing a song of praise (Lk. 2:10, 14). The shepherds immediately go to see Mary, Joseph, and the Infant, and discover it is as the angel had told them. They return home and tell others of what has happened and what they have seen. Luke says that Mary "kept all these things, pondering them in her heart" (Lk. 2:19).

At the end of eight days, the Infant is circumcised, and Joseph and Mary call him Jesus, the name given by the angel at the Annunciation (Lk. 2:21). And after forty days, Mary and Joseph go the Temple in Jerusalem and offer sacrifices. According to the Law of Moses, Mary is purified and Jesus is presented. It is here, Luke says, that the Holy Family encountered a devout man named Simeon, who had been promised by the Holy Spirit that he would not die until he had seen the Messiah (Lk. 2:25–27). Recognizing who the Infant is, he holds the young child and prays the *Nunc Dimittis* (*see* **Nunc Dimittis**). Giving the baby back to his parents, he adds that Mary, too, will suffer greatly (Lk. 2:34–35). It is during this visit to the Temple that the Holy Family also meets the prophetess Anna, who also recognizes the Messiah (Lk. 2:36–38).

It is the evangelist Matthew who writes of the visit of the Magi (Mt. 2:1–12), of Joseph taking Mary and Jesus to Egypt to avoid Herod's slaughter of the innocents (the flight into Egypt) and, after Herod's death, of the return of the Holy Family to Nazareth (Mt. 2:13–23).

The only passages from the "hidden life" of Jesus — that is, from the time of returning to Nazareth until his "public life" began when he was about thirty years old — is Luke's account of Mary and Joseph traveling with Jesus when he was twelve to observe the Passover in Jerusalem (Lk. 2:41–42) and his getting "lost in the Temple." It was after the homeward-bound caravan has traveled a day that Mary and Joseph realize Jesus is not with it. They return to the city and spend three days searching, only to find him "sitting among the teachers, listening to them and asking them questions; and all who heard him were amazed at his understanding and his answers" (Lk. 2:46–47).

When Mary asks, "Son, why have you treated us so? Behold, your father and I have been looking for you anxiously," Jesus answers, "How is it that you sought me? Did you not know that I must be in my Father's house?"

Luke says Mary and Joseph "did not understand the saying which he spoke to them" but the boy "went down with them and came to Nazareth, and was obedient to them." The author adds, "And his mother kept all these things in her heart." The section concludes with Luke telling the reader, "Jesus increased in wisdom and in stature, and in favor with God and man" (Lk. 2:48–52).

The public life of Jesus begins with the wedding feast at Cana, a city about three miles from Nazareth. It is after the first disciples have begun following Jesus, but before he goes to Jerusalem to cleanse the Temple. When Mary discovers the newlyweds have run out of wine, she asks Jesus to help. He responds, "O woman, what have you to do with me? My hour has not yet come." Mary says to the servants, "Do whatever he tells you." What follows is Christ's first miracle: the changing of water into wine.

Scripture scholars note that Jesus' overtone of refusing to help, or at least get involved in whatever is being asked, could represent a Hebrew expression. Then, too, persistence after apparently being rejected is an element of the other Cana miracle as well (the cure of the official's son; Jn. 4:47–50). It reminds the reader that no human, only the Father's will, guides Jesus in his ministry. At that same time, although the "hour" is determined by the Father, the miracle worked through the intervention of Mary is prophetic of it.

John goes on to say that after the miracle, Jesus "went down to Capernaum, with his mother and his brethren and his disciples; and there they stayed for a few days" (2:12) (*see Virginity of Mary, Perpetual*).

Mary is also mentioned when the crowds seem to overwhelm Jesus, and some people are saying he has lost his mind or is possessed. Then:

> . . . his mother and his brethren came; and standing outside they sent to him and called him. And a crowd was sitting about him; and they said to him, "Your mother and your brethren are outside, asking for you." And he replied, "Who are my mother and my brethren?" And looking around on those who sat about him, he said, "Here are my mother and my brethren! Whoever does the will of God is my brother, and sister, and mother" (Mk. 3:31–35).

What can be misinterpreted as an attempt to belittle his mother is really Jesus emphasizing the idea of a spiritual family. The same holds true for Lk. 11:27–28:

> A woman in the crowd raised her voice and said to him, "Blessed is the womb that bore you, and the breasts that you sucked!" But he said, "Blessed rather are those who hear the word of God and keep it!"

The next time Mary is mentioned in the Gospels is at the foot of the cross.

> When Jesus saw his mother, and the disciple whom he loved standing near, he said to his mother, "Woman, behold, your son!" Then he said to the disciple, "Behold, your mother!" And from that hour the disciple took her to his own home (Jn. 19:26–27).

It is Luke, the author of the Acts of the Apostles, who says Mary was present with the apostles in the upper room after the Ascension (1:14) and so, must have been with them on Pentecost when the Holy Spirit descended on them (2:1–4). (There is no mention in the Gospels or in Acts of Jesus appearing to Mary after his Resurrection.)

In his letter to the Galatians, Paul writes:

> But when the time had fully come, God sent forth his Son, born of woman, born under the law, to redeem those who were under the law, so that we might receive adoption as sons (4:4–5).

In the book of Revelation, John writes of what he saw in a vision:

> And a great portent appeared in heaven, a woman clothed with the sun, with the

moon under her feet, and on her head a crown of twelve stars (12:1).

She gives birth to a son "who is to rule all the nations with a rod of iron, but her child was caught up to God and to his throne" (12:5). When a dragon — that is, Satan — who has been lying in wait to kill the boy pursues the woman into the desert and tries to destroy her, she gets away with God's help and lives there in safety for three-and-a-half years.

Although this "woman clothed in the sun" has often been identified as Mary, the description of events does not match what the Gospels say.

In the early Church, the birth of the child was seen as symbolic of the Israel of the Old Testament and, after the boy is born and ascends into heaven, the woman is seen as representative of the Israel of the New Testament, that is, the Church.

In more recent times, there is the opinion that the vision has dual meanings. The woman clothed in the sun is the Church, but that does not exclude Mary, who also is representative of the Church.

SECRET OF THE ROSARY, THE

A book of reflections on the three sets of traditional mysteries of the Rosary, written by St. Louis de Montfort. A series of introductions addresses priests (white rose), sinners (red rose), devout souls (mystical rose tree), and little children (rosebud).

The saint tells priests:

I beg of you to beware of thinking of the Rosary as something of little importance — as do ignorant people and even several great but proud scholars. Far from being insignificant, the Rosary is a priceless treasure which is inspired by God.

Almighty God has given it to you because He wants you to use it as a means to convert the most hardened sinners and the most obstinate heretics. He has attached to it grace in this life and glory in the next. The saints have said it faithfully and the Popes have endorsed it.

When the Holy Spirit has revealed this secret to a priest and director of souls, how blessed is that priest! For the vast majority of people fail to know this secret or else they know it superficially. If such a priest really understands this secret he will say the Rosary every day and encourage others to say it. God and His Blessed Mother will pour abundant grace into his soul, so that he may become God's instrument for His glory; and his word, though simple, will do more good in one month than that of other preachers in several years.

In an early section discussing the origin of the devotion, St. Louis wrote:

The Rosary is made up of two things: mental prayer and vocal prayer. In the Holy Rosary mental prayer is none other than meditation of the chief mysteries of the life, death and glory of Jesus Christ and of His Blessed Mother. . . . Since the Holy Rosary is composed principally and in substance, of the Prayer of Christ and the Angelic Salutation, that is the Our Father and the Hail Mary, it is without doubt the first prayer and the first devotion of the faithful and has been in use all through the centuries from the time of the apostles and disciples down to the present.

See also Rosary.

Sedes Sapientiae

and seated it on her lap in his first years. An image of *Sedes Sapientiae* depicts a crowned, standing Mary with the Christ Child nestled in her arms.

See also Litany of the Blessed Virgin Mary.

SERVANTS OF MARY — *See Servites.*

SERVITES

Religious order, the Friar Servants or Mary.

Founded in 1233 by seven prominent citizens of Florence who had been meeting regularly as members of a religious society established in honor of Mary, it was approved as a religious order by the bishop of Florence sometime between the years 1240 and 1247 and by the Holy See in 1304. The order includes priests, brothers, contemplative nuns, and tertiaries.

An original intention of the Servites was devotion to Mary, particularly Our Lady of Sorrows. Members promote the Scapular of Our Lady of Sorrows, the Chaplet of the Seven Sorrows of Our Lady, and the Way of the Cross for the Sorrowful Mother (*Via Matris*).

See also Scapular of Our Lady of Sorrows; Seven Sorrows, Chaplet of the; Our Sorrowful Mother, National Sanctuary of; Via Matris.

SEVEN JOYS OF MARY — *See Joys of Mary.*

SEVEN SATURDAYS IN HONOR OF OUR LADY OF RANSOM

Custom associated with Marian title and the founding of the Mercedarian religious order by St. Peter Nolasco in 1218. Traditionally, the faithful took part in public exercises for seven Saturdays in honor of the Virgin. On one they were to visit a church associated with the Mercedarians. In recent time, the name was changed to Our Lady of Mercy.

See Mercy, Our Lady of.

SEVEN SORROWS OF MARY — *See Sorrows of Mary.*

SEVEN SORROWS, CHAPLET OF THE

Chaplet featuring seven sets of seven beads. A Hail Mary is said on each bead, and the mysteries for each set are:

1. *The Prophecy of Simeon.*
2. *The Flight into Egypt.*
3. *The Loss of the Child Jesus in the Temple.*
4. *Mary Meets Jesus carrying His Cross.*
5. *The Crucifixion.*
6. *Mary Receives the Body of Jesus from the Cross.*
7. *The Body of Jesus is Placed in the Tomb.*

The concluding prayer reads:

V. *Pray for us, O most sorrowful Virgin.*

R. *That we may be made worthy of the promises of Christ.*

Sorrowful Mother

Let us pray:
Lord Jesus, we now implore, both for the present and for the hour of our death, the intercession of the most Blessed Virgin Mary, your
Mother, whose holy soul was pierced at the time of your passion by a sword of grief. Grant us this favor, O Savior of the world, Who lives and reigns with the Father and the Holy Spirit forever and ever. Amen.

SEVEN WORDS

Reference to what Jesus said from the cross, including asking Mary to accept John's care and John to accept responsibility for taking care of Mary (Jn. 19:26–27). Traditionally, these two verses are seen as Jesus declaring that Mary is the spiritual mother of all the faithful, represented there by the apostle.

See Scripture, Mary in.

SHEPHERDS — *See Scripture, Mary in.*

SHRINE OF THE IMMACULATE CONCEPTION, BASILICA OF THE NATIONAL — *See Immaculate Conception, Basilica of the National Shrine of the.*

SIGNUM MAGNUM — *See Paul VI.*

SILENCE, OUR LADY OF — *See Knock, Our Lady of.*

SILENCE, VIRGIN OF — *See Litany of Our Lady of Hope.*

SILUVA, OUR LADY OF

Image and devotion dating back to early seventeenth century.

A reported apparition of Mary in Siluva, Lithuania, led to the discovery of a deed to a church that had been buried for safekeeping some four decades earlier when the building had been confiscated by anti-Catholic forces. The deed's recovery led many to return to their lost practice of the Faith.

The image of *Our Lady of Siluva* typically depicts a standing Mary holding the Christ Child.

SIMEON AND ANNA — *See Scripture, Mary in.*

SIN

Offense against God as well as reason, truth, and right conscience; a deliberate thought, word, deed, or omission, contrary to the eternal law of God. The Church teaches that Mary was born without original sin and remained sinless.

See Immaculate Conception.

SINGULAR VESSEL OF DEVOTION

Marian title used in the Litany of the Blessed Virgin Mary (also known as the Litany of Loreto), which was originally approved in 1587 by Pope Sixtus V.

The image refers to Mary as both dwelling place of the Spirit and his "agent" in the Incarnation. "With and through the Holy Spirit,

Our Lady of Siluva

the Virgin conceives and gives birth to the Son of God" (*CCC* 723).

See also Litany of the Blessed Virgin Mary.

SINJ, OUR LADY OF — *See* Velika Gospa.

SLAVERY OF MARY, SLAVE OF MARY

Metaphor used to describe devotion to Mary.

It is used, for example, by members of the Legion of Mary. "The Duty of Legionaries" reads, in part:

It is desirable that the practice of the Legionary devotion to Mary should be rounded off and given the distinctive character which has been taught by St. Louis de Montfort under the titles of "The True Devotion" or the "Slavery of Mary" and which is enshrined in his two books, the "True Devotion to the Blessed Virgin" and the "Secret of Mary." . . .

That devotion requires the formal entry into a compact with Mary, whereby one gives to her one's whole self, with all his thoughts, and deeds and possessions, both spiritual and temporal, past, present, and future, without the reservation of the smallest part or slightest little thing. In a word, the giver places himself in a condition equivalent to that of a slave possessing nothing of his own, and wholly dependent on, and utterly at the disposal of Mary . . .

But the earthly slave is far freer than the slave of Mary. The former remains master of his thoughts and inner life, and thus may be free in everything that matters to him. But the surrender to Mary bears with it everything: each thought, the movements of the soul, the hidden riches, the inmost self. All — on to the final breath — is committed to her that she may expend it all for God.

See also Legion of Mary.

SMILE, OUR LADY OF THE

Reference to statue associated with St. Thérèse of Lisieux (1873–1897).

Prior to her mother's death in 1877, Thérèse was described as lively and precocious. After her mother passed away, she became more sullen, introverted, and prone to tears.

The young girl suffered from a case of emotional illness in 1882, with symptoms such as nervous trembling, headaches, insomnia, and hallucinations. Then, on Pentecost Sunday, May 13, 1883, she had a miraculous experience: "seeing" the Smiling Face of Our Lady.

Years later, in her *Story of a Soul,* Thérèse described what happened:

Finding no help on earth, poor little Thérèse had also turned towards the Mother of heaven, and prayed with all her heart that

St. Thérèse of Lisieux

she take pity on her. All of a sudden the Blessed Virgin appeared beautiful to me, so beautiful that never had I seen anything so attractive; her face was suffused with an ineffable benevolence and tenderness, but what penetrated to the very depths of my soul was the "ravishing smile of the Blessed Virgin." At that instant, all my pain disappeared, and two large tears glistened on my eyelashes, and flowed down my cheeks silently, but they were tears of unmixed joy. Ah! I thought, the Blessed Virgin smiled at me, how happy I am. (SS 65–66)

The statue in the family home had the same posture and outstretched hands as the Miraculous Medal, but without the twelve stars, the globe, and Mary's foot crushing the head of the serpent.

SMOOTH DELIVERY, OUR LADY OF

Image and devotion in the Church of St. Augustine in Rome.

The marble statue of *Madonna del Parto,* carved in 1521 by Florentine sculptor Jacopo ("il Sansovino") Tatti, depicts a seated Mary with the Christ Child standing on her lap. Since the sixteenth century, Roman women have asked for her intercession for safe deliveries and healthy babies.

SNOWS, OUR LADY OF — *See St. Mary Major, Basilica of.*

SOCIETY OF MARY

Worldwide congregation of priests and brothers (the Marists) founded by Blessed William Joseph Chaminade at Bordeaux, France, in 1817.

Its mission is marked by total consecration to Mary. The Marianist "family" also includes the Daughters of Mary Immaculate, Marianist Lay Communities, and the Marian Alliance.

In addition to establishing schools, Marianists work in parishes, lead retreats, and are involved in special ministries, such as the Marian Library at the University of Dayton, OH.

See also Daughters of Mary Immaculate; Marian Library.

SOCIETY OF OUR LADY OF THE MOST HOLY TRINITY

Religious community founded by Fr. James Flanagan in 1958 and officially recognized by Bishop Rene Gracida of Corpus Christi, Texas, in 1994.

SOLT consists of priests, religious brothers and sisters, deacons, and both married and single lay persons, called apostles. "Committed" members have completed their initial formation, and have decided to commit their lives, within their respective vocations, to the Society of Our Lady. "Definitive" members have been committed members for a period of time. With the approval of their respective superiors, they perpetually profess public vows or promises. Lay members contract with SOLT to commit themselves to the Society of Our Lady. "Corporate" members serve the society on special projects. They assist or continue the work of SOLT members. "Auxiliary" members support SOLT members spiritually by their services, prayers and offerings. "Missionaries of Mercy" offer their sufferings, prayers, and friendship for the missions of the Society of Our Lady.

SODALITIES OF OUR LADY — *See Christian Life Community.*

SOLEDAD, VIRGEN DE (OUR LADY OF SOLITUDE)

Image and devotion dating back to the early seventeenth century.

Pious tradition offers various versions of a story involving a pack mule that entered the town of Oaxaca, Mexico, and died. No one knew who owned it, where it was from, or what is was carrying. When townspeople opened the packs, they discovered a statue of *Our Lady of Solitude*, an image depicting Mary dressed in black, representing the sorrowful and lonely time between the Crucifixion and the Resurrection. The statue features a standing Mary with her hands folded in prayer. She wears a crown of diamonds with a large pearl drop in the center, and a black velvet robe with semiprecious stones.

The locals interpreted the event to mean Mary wanted a shrine built on the spot, so they complied. The simple structure was later enlarged to become a church, then a basilica.

Our Lady of Soledad is the patron of the city and state, and of mariners who sail to and from the ports in that region.

In Columbia, there is a Good Friday devotion known as the *Descendimiento* and the *Procesion de la Soledad de Maria*. A large image of Christ is taken down from the cross in the presence of Mary, who is dressed in black as the *Virgen de Soledad*. A procession then leads both to a tomb where, in Mary's presence, Christ is buried. Mary is then enthroned and, for several hours, accompanied by the people in her mourning.

See also Desolata.

SOLEMNIS PROFESSIO FIDEI — *See Paul VI.*

SOLEMNITY OF MARY, MOTHER OF GOD

Solemnity (the highest rank of liturgical celebration) and holy day of obligation celebrated on January 1, the octave of Christmas. The Western liturgical calendar that took effect in 1970 reinstated the Marian character of the feast; that emphasis has always been a part of the Eastern tradition.

Prior to 1970, January 1 had been the Feast of the Circumcision. That commemoration dated back to at least the first half of the sixth century and marked Jesus' initiation into Judaism (see Lk. 2:21). By analogy, the feast focused attention on the initiation of persons into Christianity and their incorporation in Christ through baptism.

The Solemnity of Mary also supplanted the Feast of the Motherhood of Mary, which had been observed on October 11. In 1751, at the request of King Joseph Emmanuel, Pope Benedict XIV approved that feast for Portugal and composed the first Mass himself. In 1931, Pope Pius XI made the Feast of the Motherhood of Mary a universal observance to mark the 1,500[th] anniversary of the Council of Ephesus. It was that council that defended Mary's title of *Theotokos* (Greek for "God-bearer").

See also Ephesus, Council of; Mother of God; Pius XI.

SOLITUDE, OUR LADY OF — *See* Soledad, Virgen de.

SORROWFUL AND IMMACULATE HEART OF MARY

Devotion based on private revelations of Berthe Petit (1879–1943), a Franciscan tertiary and mystic from Belgium.

The image of the *Sorrowful and Immaculate Heart of Mary* shows Our Lady holding a lily in her left hand and the index of her right hand pointing to her sorrowful heart, which is surrounded by flames and pierced by a sword.

SORROWFUL MOTHER, NATIONAL SANCTUARY OF OUR

Shrine and botanical garden located in Portland, OR.

Commonly called "The Grotto," it was established by the Servite Friars in 1924 as a memorial to Christ's dying appeal from the cross, "Behold your Mother." Hundreds of thousands of tourists and pilgrims visit each year.

The central attraction, Our Lady's Grotto, was carved from solid basalt in the cliff wall in 1925. Above its natural rock altar is a white marble replica of Michelangelo's *Pietà*.

Above the grotto's cliff there is a bronze statue of *Our Sorrowful Mother,* designed especially for the sanctuary and blessed in the Vatican by Pope Pius XI in 1934 to commemorate the 700th anniversary of the Servite Order.

See also Servites.

SORROWS OF MARY, SEVEN SORROWS OF MARY

Also called the Seven Dolors of Our Lady, and seen as an expansion of the five sorrowful mysteries, they are:

1. Mary accepts in faith the prophecy of Simeon (see Lk. 2:34–35).
2. Mary flees into Egypt with Jesus and Joseph (see Mt. 2:13–14).
3. Mary seeks Jesus lost in Jerusalem (see Lk. 2:43–45).
4. Mary meets Jesus on the way to Calvary (see Lk. 23:26–27).
5. Mary stands near the cross of her Son (see Jn. 19:25–27).
6. Mary receives the body of Jesus taken down from the cross (see Mt. 27:57–59).
7. Mary places the body of Jesus in the tomb, awaiting the Resurrection (see Jn. 19:40–42).

In Central Europe, there is a feast known as *Schmerzensfreitag.* On this day, popular devotions are held, and a special soup is served for dinner. The soup is made of seven bitter herbs (watercress, parsley, leek, nettle, sour clover, primrose, and spinach) and is called *Siebenkrautersuppe.*

Particular devotions of Our Mother of Sorrows, including the Scapular and the Rosary of the Seven Sorrows, are proper to the Servite order.

The Church marks the memorial of Our Lady of Sorrows on September 15, the day following the Feast of the Triumph of the Cross.

SORROWS, OUR LADY OF

Title especially propagated by the Servite order.

See Servites, Sorrows of Mary.

SOUL

The spiritual essence of human beings and the subject of human consciousness and freedom.

Together, body and soul form one unique human nature. Every human soul is individual and immortal, immediately created by God. The soul does not die with the body but, rather, is separated from the body by death and will be reunited with it in the final resurrection. The soul of Mary was never stained by sin, including original sin. Mary, body and soul, was assumed into heaven.

See Assumption; Immaculate Conception.

SPIRITUAL VESSEL

Marian title used in the Litany of the Blessed Virgin Mary (also known as the Litany of Loreto), which was originally approved in 1587 by Pope Sixtus V.

Vas (vessel) is used to translate the Greek term *skeuos,* which means both *vessel* and *instrument* or *tool.* Mary is an "instrument of the Holy Spirit" because she is both the dwelling place of the Spirit and his agent in the Incarnation.

The Catechism of the Catholic Church explains that with and through the Spirit, Mary conceives and gives birth to the Son of God (*CCC* 723).

See also Litany of the Blessed Virgin Mary.

SPLENDOR OF THE CHURCH

Title from the Litany of Mary, Queen.

See Litany of Mary, Queen.

SPOUSES OF THE BLESSED VIRGIN MARY

St. Joseph and the Holy Spirit.

As the betrothed of Mary, Joseph is described in Scripture as "her husband . . . a just man and unwilling to put her to shame" (Mt. 1:18–19; cf. Lk. 1:27, 2:5) after learning she was pregnant. Rather, he decided "to send her away quietly."

An angel made it clear to him that the child was conceived "by the Holy Spirit" (Mt. 1:20). Joseph then lived with Mary in a chaste and virginal relationship. (The devotion known as the Divine Praises includes "Blessed be St. Joseph, her most chaste spouse.")

By reason of the Annunciation and Incarnation, the Holy Spirit is also considered the Spouse of the Blessed Virgin Mary, as it was by him that she conceived her child, Jesus.

ST. MARY MAJOR, BASILICA OF

Most prominent church in Rome dedicated to the Blessed Mother.

It was built around 352, during the reign of Pope Liberius, and so was first known as the Liberian Basilica. Along with Rome's St. Peter, St. John Lateran, and St. Paul-Outside-the-Walls, St. Mary Major is a papal (or "major") basilica.

The title "basilica" was originally applied to an official building in Roman Empire times; it is now assigned to churches because of their antiquity, dignity, historical importance, or significance as centers of worship. Major basilicas have a papal altar (used only by the pontiff or his delegate) and a holy door which is opened at the beginning of a Jubilee Year. Visiting all four patriarchal basilicas is prescribed as part of the condition for gaining a Jubilee Year indulgence.

Pope Sixtus II rebuilt the Liberian Basilica soon after the Council of Ephesus (432) affirmed Mary's title of *Theotokos* (God-bearer, the Mother of God). Since the seventh century, the building has been known as St. Mary Major (although customarily, the Blessed Virgin is seldom referred to with the title of "saint"). Through repeated restorations over the centuries, the structure has retained its character as an early Roman basilica. Its imposing façade was built in the mid-twelfth century, during the reign of Pope Eugene III; its interior walls feature mosaics dating back to the fifth century.

Among its treasured art is a painting of the Madonna and Child known as *Salus Populi Romani* — the Protector of the People of Rome — which, pious tradition holds, was painted by St. Luke.

The feast of the dedication of St. Mary Major is celebrated on August 5. Customarily on that day at the end of Mass, a shower of white rose petals is released from the dome of the Chapel of Our Lady to mark the tradition of Our Lady of the Snows. The church is popularly known as the first shrine to Mary under that title.

According to pious legend, the basilica traces its history back to an elderly, childless, aristocratic couple who asked the pope for advice concerning the distribution of their estate after their deaths. He recommended they pray about it before making a decision. On the night of August 4, A.D. 352, Mary appeared to them in their dreams and told them she wished a church to be built in her honor on the Roman hill covered with snow. The following morning, despite the warm summer weather, Esquiline Hill was blanketed in snow.

Or, according to a variation on the tradition, in the dreams Mary asked the church be built on Rome's Esquiline Hill and the sign to accompany the vision would be that the precise location would be marked by snow. The pontiff had a similar dream. The following morning a snowfall had traced the form of the basilica on the hill and the dimensions were staked out before the snow melted.

Both versions of the story say the couple's money was used to build the church, which was completed in two years and consecrated by Pope Liberius.

See also Apparitions of Mary; Ephesus, Council of; Oblates of Mary Immaculate; **Salus Populi Romani.**

STABAT MATER, STABAT MATER DOLOROSA

Traditional Marian prayer and hymn. *Stabat Mater* can be translated from the Latin as "the mother was standing."

Though its authorship is disputed, the prayer is commonly attributed to Jacopone da Todi (c. 1228–1306). It was well known in Europe by the end of the fourteenth century and included in several local missals in the fifteenth. In the eighteenth century it was inserted as a sequence into the Roman Missal and as a hymn into the Breviary for recitation on the Feast of the Seven Sorrows of the Virgin Mary (the Friday before Good Friday). After changes were introduced by Pope Pius XII, it now appears on the Feast of Our Lady of Sorrows (September 15). It is also used during the praying of the Stations of the Cross. One version reads:

At the Cross her station keeping,
stood the mournful Mother weeping,
close to Jesus to the last.

Through her heart, His sorrow sharing,
all His bitter anguish bearing,
now at length the sword has passed.

O how sad and sore distressed
was that Mother, highly blest,
of the sole-begotten One.

Christ above in torment hangs,
she beneath beholds the pangs
of her dying glorious Son.

Is there one who would not weep,
whelmed in miseries so deep,
Christ's dear Mother to behold?

Can the human heart refrain
from partaking in her pain,
in that Mother's pain untold?

Bruised, derided, cursed, defiled,
she beheld her tender Child
All with bloody scourges rent.

For the sins of His own nation,
saw Him hang in desolation,
Till His spirit forth He sent.

O thou Mother! fount of love!
Touch my spirit from above,
make my heart with thine accord.

Make me feel as thou hast felt;
make my soul to glow and melt
with the love of Christ my Lord.

Holy Mother! pierce me through,
in my heart each wound renew
of my Savior crucified.

Let me share with thee His pain,
who for all my sins was slain,
who for me in torments died.

Let me mingle tears with thee,
mourning Him who mourned for me,
all the days that I may live.

By the Cross with thee to stay,
there with thee to weep and pray,
is all I ask of thee to give.

Virgin of all virgins blest!
Listen to my fond request,
let me share thy grief divine.

Let me, to my latest breath,
in my body bear the death
of that dying Son of thine.

Wounded with His every wound,
steep my soul till it hath swooned,
in His very Blood away;

Be to me, O Virgin, nigh,
lest in flames I burn and die,
in His awful Judgment Day.

Christ, when Thou shalt call me hence,
be Thy Mother my defense,
be Thy Cross my victory;

While my body here decays,
may my soul Thy goodness praise,
safe in paradise with Thee. Amen.

STABAT MATER SPECIOSA

Companion hymn to the *Stabat Mater Dolorosa* which, unlike the sorrowful version, is not used in the liturgy.

Just as the *Stabat Mater Dolorosa* focuses on Mary at Calvary, the *Stabat Mater Speciosa* features our Lady in Bethlehem and parallels the phrasing of the better known hymn. The *Speciosa* contains thirteen double stanzas of six lines; the *Dolorosa* has ten.

Although an edition of the Italian poems of Jacopone da Todi (c.1228–1306) published at Brescia in 1495 contained both *Stabats*; the *Speciosa* became largely unknown until Frederick Ozanam (founder of the Society of St. Vincent de Paul) transcribed it from a fifteenth-century manuscript in the mid-nineteenth century for a work that was published in Paris.

One version of the hymn begins:

By the crib wherein reposing,
with His eyes in slumber closing,
lay serene her Infant-boy.

Stood the beauteous Mother feeling
bliss that could not bear concealing,
so her face o'erflowed with joy.

Oh, the rapture naught could smother
of that most Immaculate Mother
of the sole-begotten One;

When with laughing heart exulting,
she beheld her hopes resulting
in the great birth of her Son.

STAMPS

The first postage stamp featuring an image of Mary is dated February 14, 1920. It was issued in Bavaria and shows the Marian column standing on Munich's Marienplatz, which commemorates Maximilian I's victory over the Turks in 1620 near Prague, and especially Mary's patronage of the then-Kingdom of Bavaria.

On October 5, 1920, Liechtenstein issued a stamp depicting Mary, patroness of the principality. The first stamp to present a Nativity scene was issued in Estonia on June 10, 1936.

The United States began printing its stamps in 1846, but stamps of Mary were not begun until 1966. Today, postage stamps with Marian themes and images are issued by many countries.

Belize stamp, 1980

STAR OF THE SEA

Title. The hymn *Ave Maris Stella* ("Hail, Star of the Sea") presents Mary as the Gate of Heaven and also has her guiding travelers into port. It has been known from the ninth century, but may have been written earlier. From that time the image of Mary as the Star of the Sea became a popular one in Western devotion.

A wooden statue of Our Lady, Star of the Sea, has been venerated in Maastricht, Netherlands, since the late Middle Ages. About four feet tall, it was given to the Franciscan church there in 1400 by Nicholas von Harlaer when he joined the order. The image depicts Mary holding the infant Jesus in her left hand and a small vase in her right hand. The vase was originally intended as an inkpot — a remnant of a devotion popular in Flanders known as Our Lady of the Inkpot — but the vase is now used to hold a lily. The child, sculpted without clothes, is usually dressed in a brocade outfit while Mary wears a matching cloak.

STAR OF THE SEA, CHAPLET OF OUR LADY

Chaplet featuring a medal of Our Lady of Carmel, three separate beads, and twelve additional beads. The devotion begins while holding the medal and praying:

Most beautiful Flower of Mount Carmel, Fruitful Vine, Splendor of Heaven, Blessed Mother of the Son of God, Immaculate Virgin, assist me in this my necessity. O Star of the Sea, help me and show me herein that you are my Mother.

Holy Mary, Mother of God, Queen of Heaven and Earth, I humbly beseech you from the bottom of my heart, to help me in this necessity; there are none that can withstand your power.

The first three beads are for one Our Father, one Hail Mary, and one Glory Be. On each of the twelve beads, representing the twelve stars on Our Lady's crown, one Hail Mary is said, followed by the invocation: "Our Lady, Star of the Sea, help and protect us! Sweet Mother, I place this cause in your hand."

STATIONS OF THE SEVEN SORROWS
— *See* Via Matris.

SUB TUUM PRAESIDIUM

Earliest known prayer to the Virgin Mary whose text has survived; from the Latin for "under your protection."

The earliest text is written in Greek on an Egyptian papyrus and is the first documentary evidence of the existence of devotion to Mary. The papyrus, discovered in Egypt in 1917, dates to the second half of the third century. The date of the composition of the prayer is unknown. The *Sub Tuum* is used in Litanies to the Blessed Mother and as a concluding prayer in the Liturgy of the Hours. One translation reads:

We fly to thy patronage, O holy Mother of God; despise not our petitions in our necessities, but deliver us always from all dangers, O glorious and blessed Virgin. Amen.

SUYAPA, OUR LADY OF

Image and devotion.

Pious tradition holds that the little statue *Our Lady of the Conception of Suyapa* (Honduras) was found by a young peasant in January 1747. Alejandro Colindres and Lorenzo Martinez were on their way home to the village after harvesting corn. Halfway back to Suyapa as night fell, they decided to spend the night in a ravine. As soon as they lay down, however, Colindres felt something under him and assumed it was a stone. He picked it up and tossed it aside, but when he lay back down, the object was under him once again. Wondering what it was, he stuffed it into his pack and decided to examine it in the daylight. The next morning he saw that it was a statue of Mary.

The cedar carving, thought to be the work on an amateur artist, measures only about two-and-a-half inches high. It depicts Mary standing with her hands folded in front of her in prayer.

For some two decades, members and friends of the Colindres family venerated the image in the Colindres' home. Miracles were attributed to the intercession of Our Lady of Suyapa, and a chapel was built to house the statue. Later, a large church replaced the small shrine. Pius XII declared Our Lady of Suyapa patroness of the Republic of Honduras, and February 3 was chosen as her feast day. A festival in her honor is celebrated there from February 1 to 3.

SYMBOLS OF MARY

Emblems that represent a truth about the Blessed Virgin Mary.

Symbols in Church art date back as early as the third century; Marian symbols would include, for example, the lily (purity), a heart pierced by a sword (seven sorrows and the prediction of Simeon (Lk. 2:34–35), and a star (morning star). Litanies to our Lady often feature a list of symbolic titles.

See Art, Mary in; specific litanies; Mary Garden.

SYRACUSE, OUR LADY OF

Title and devotion also known as Our Lady of Tears, based on reports of tears flowing from the eyes of a small plaster plaque depicting the Immaculate Heart of Mary.

The event took place between August 29 and September 1, 1953, in the home of a young couple, Angelo Iannuso and Antonina Giusto, who lived in Syracuse, Sicily. On August 30, an amateur film maker recorded the event; on September 1, a commission of doctors and analysts went to the Iannuso home, sent by the chancery of the Archdiocese of Syracuse, and collected a sample of the liquid that flowed from the image's eyes. Analysis of the fluid revealed that it was human tears. On December 12 of that year, the Sicilian Bishops Conference declared the lachrymation of Mary in Syracuse authentic.

On October 17, 1954, Pius XII concluded the Marian Convention of Sicily with a radio message in which he noted:

> It is not without lively commotion that we are aware of the unanimous declaration of

273

the Episcopate of Sicily upon the reality of this event. Without a doubt, Mary is in heaven eternally happy and suffers neither pain [n]or sorrow; but she cannot remain insensitive, rather she always nourishes love and pity for the poor human race, which was given to her as their Mother, when sorrowful and tearful she remained at the foot of the Cross, where her Son was affixed. Will humanity understand the mysterious language of those tears? Oh, the tears of Mary! Upon Golgotha they were tears of compassion for her Jesus and of sadness for the sins of the world. Does she cry again for the renewed wounds produced in the Mystical Body of Jesus? Or does she cry for so many sons, in which error and sin have extinguished the life of grace, and who gravely offend the Divine Majesty? Or are they tears awaiting the belated return of her other sons, once faithful, and now dragged down by the false mirage of the legions of the enemies of God?

During a pastoral visit to Syracuse on November 6, 1994, John Paul II said:

The tears of Mary belong to the order of signs: They testify to the presence of our Mother in the Church and in the world. A mother weeps when she sees her children threatened by evil, be it spiritual or physical.

See also Apparitions of Mary.

Weeping Madonna of Syracuse

TAPER, OUR LADY OF THE

Image and devotion.

Pious legend holds that a statue of the seated Mary was found next to the Teifi River in Wales in the twelfth century. The Christ Child was seated on her lap and being held by her left arm. A lit candle — or taper — was in her right hand.

During the Reformation, the statue and the shrine which had housed it, were destroyed. A new church was completed in 1970, and in 1986, a new image of *Our Lady of the Taper* was blessed and placed there. Since then, it has been designated the Welsh National Shrine of Our Lady.

TEARS OF OUR LADY CHAPLET — *See Rosary of Our Lady of Tears.*

TEARS, OUR LADY OF — *See* Syracuse, Our Lady of.

TEMPLE, FINDING IN THE — *See Scripture, Mary in.*

TENDERNESS, OUR LADY OF — *See* Vladimir, Our Lady of.

THEOTOKOS — *See Ephesus, Council of; Mother of God.*

THIRTY DAYS, OUR LADY'S

Traditional name for August 15 to September 15 in some areas of central Europe.

See also Assumption.

THIRTY-THREE, OUR LADY OF THE

Image and devotion; patroness of Uruguay.

The *Virgin of the Thirty-Three* is a wood carving dating back to the Jesuit missions in Paraguay in the mid-eighteenth century. It was made in one of the Guarani workshops that flourished there. Only about fourteen inches high, it is a baroque carving of the Assumption on which Mary's cloak and robes seem to move because of their many pleats.

Around 1779, the statue was placed in the Jesuit-administered chapel in the village of Pintado (which would become Uruguay). Later — when the entire village moved to what is now the city of Florida, Uruguay — the residents took it with them.

On April 19, 1825, thirty-three Uruguayan patriots landed on the beaches of the Agraciada to begin the liberation of their country. When they reached Florida, they went to the small church and prayed before the statue.

National independence was proclaimed on August 25; at that time, the members of the Constitutional Court — having signed the Act of Independence — presented themselves once more before the Marian statue and placed their new country under her protection.

Since then, the image has been known as *La Virgen de los Treinta y Tres* (*The Virgin of the Thirty-Three*). On August 25, 1975, on the 150th anniversary of its independence, the Uruguayan nation officially declared this image, and the church in which it was venerated, historic monuments.

Since 1857, "The Liberator of Uruguay" has had a gold crown with precious stones, a gift of the second leader of the Thirty-Three, who later became president of the republic. The disproportionately large crown has become the distinctive feature of this Marian image.

The image was crowned canonically in 1961 by a representative of Pope John XXIII. The following year, the pontiff proclaimed her officially "Patroness of Uruguay."

The solemnity of Our Lady of the Thirty-Three is celebrated on the second Sunday of November, with a pilgrimage to her shrine from every part of the country.

THREE HAIL MARYS

Devotion.

The praying of three Hail Marys, one each in honor of the Father, Son, and Holy Spirit, is based on private revelations of St. Mechtilde of Helfta (d. 1298).

The Franciscan preacher St. Leonard of Port Maurice (d. 1751) recommended the devotion mornings and evenings, in honor of Mary Immaculate, to obtain the grace to avoid mortal sin both day and night.

St. Alphonsus Liguori (1696–1787) advised the devotion be said kneeling and wrote a short prayer to be recited after each Hail Mary. The devotion was also promoted by Fr. John

Baptist du Bois, founder of the Confraternity of the Three Hail Marys.

THREE PRIVILEGES — *See Trinity, Our Lady of the.*

TITLES OF MARY

Expressions of love, reverence, honor, and dignity for Mary, used in liturgies, litanies, devotions, hymns, and theological writings.

Some Marian titles have their origin in scripture (such as Handmaid of the Lord), while others refer to feasts, images, shrines, and places associated with Mary (such as Our Lady of Fatima).

See also particular title.

TOMB OF MARY

Mary's grave.

There are two traditions concerning Our Lady's tomb; one says it is in Jerusalem, and the other claims it's located in Ephesus, Turkey.

The Jerusalem tradition, based on apocryphal writing, dates back to the sixth century and says Mary was assumed into heaven after resting three days in the tomb. In recent times, some archeological remnants have revealed a possible site for Mary's tomb.

The tradition of Ephesus is based on the presumption that Mary spent the last years of her earthly life there in the company of St. John, to whom she had been entrusted by Jesus from the cross. It is based on the visions of Blessed Anne Catherine Emmerich (1774–1824).

Neither location claims to have Mary's bodily remains.

See also Dormition of Mary; Emmerich, Blessed Anne Catherine.

TOTUS TUUS

Motto of Pope John Paul II; an abbreviated version of the Marian consecration of St. Louis Marie de Montfort.

Karol Wojtyla made the total consecration to Mary at the age of fifteen, vowing, "I am totally yours (*totus tuus*), and all that I possess is yours. I accept you in all that is mine. Give me your heart, O Mary."

See John Paul II.

TOWER OF DAVID, TOWER OF IVORY

Marian titles used in the Litany of the Blessed Virgin Mary (also known as the Litany of Loreto), originally approved in 1587 by Pope Sixtus V.

Like a tower in ancient times, Mary is seen as a sure defense against one's enemy, the devil. The first title compares her to the towers built into the walls of Jerusalem. The second alludes to the beauty of her soul.

See Litany of the Blessed Virgin Mary.

TRENT, COUNCIL OF

Nineteenth ecumenical council, held between 1545 and 1563.

Its aim was the refutation of the errors of Protestant Reformers (Martin Luther, Huldrych

Zwingli, and John Calvin), the clarification of Catholic teaching in the wake of the spread of Protestant teaching, and the advancing of authentic and genuinely needed reform for the entire Church.

Trent defended the tradition of praying to Mary and the saints and asking for their intercessory prayers, as well as admiring and imitating their example. It also explicitly declared that Mary was exempt from the taint of original sin. From then on, the belief was embraced generally and defended by all schools of theology, although it would not be defined dogmatically until 1854.

Devotion to Mary, like the doctrine of the Real Presence, remained a central subject for controversy between Catholics and Protestants.

See also Reformation and Mary.

TRINITY AND MARY

Mary is the daughter of God the Father, the Mother of the Son of God, and the temple of the Holy Spirit. Despite her unique role in God's plan of salvation, she is not a divine person. Throughout the year, Mary's relation to the Trinity is celebrated in various feasts, liturgical seasons, and commemorations.

TRINITY, OUR LADY OF THE

Image and devotion.

The Church of Our Lady of the Trinity was built in Blois, France, in 1937. Its main sculpture, in the narthex of the building, depicts Mary with three rings intertwined on her chest and the three "privileges." The rings symbolize the distinctive unity of the Father, Son, and

Mary and the Trinity

Holy Spirit and are reminiscent of the so-called "privileges" of Mary, based on private revelations of St. Mechtilde of Helfta (d. 1298). The visionary reported Mary was endowed by the Trinity with power, wisdom, and love. These three privileges led to the devotion of the Three Hail Marys.

See also Three Hail Marys.

TRUE DEVOTION TO THE BLESSED VIRGIN MARY, A TREATISE ON

Major work by St. Louis Marie de Montfort. It outlines the characteristics of true devotion to Our Lady which, he said, consists of "giving oneself entirely to the Blessed Virgin in order to belong entirely to Jesus Christ though her." He characterized true devotion as having five qualities: being inward in spirit and heart; tender, with a childlike confidence; holy in imitation of Mary's virtues; loving because Mary is worthy of love; and unwavering in its perseverance.

TRUST, OUR LADY OF — *See* Confidence, Our Lady of.

UNDERGROUND, OUR LADY — *See Chartres, Our Lady of.*

UPPER ROOM — *See Cenacle, Our Lady of the.*

VATICAN II

Twenty-first ecumenical council, held in Rome between 1962 and 1965.

The documents of the Second Vatican Council and their Marian references are:

Sacrosanctum Concilium (*Constitution on the Sacred Liturgy*), 1963.

103. In celebrating this annual cycle of Christ's mysteries, holy Church honors with especial love the Blessed Mary, Mother of God, who is joined by an inseparable bond to the saving work of her Son. In her the Church holds up and admires the most excellent fruit of the redemption, and joyfully contemplates, as in a faultless image, that which she herself desires and hopes wholly to be.

Inter Mirifica (*Decree on the Means of Social Communication*), 1963.

No references to Mary.

Lumen Gentium (*Dogmatic Constitution on the Church*), 1964.

15. The Church recognizes that in many ways she is linked with those who, being baptized, are honored with the name of Christian, though they do not profess the faith in its entirety or do not preserve unity of communion with the successor of Peter. For there are many who honor Sacred Scripture, taking it as a norm of belief and a pattern of life, and who show a sincere zeal.

They lovingly believe in God the Father Almighty and in Christ, the Son of God and Savior. They are consecrated by baptism, in which they are united with Christ. They also recognize and accept other sacraments within their own Churches or ecclesiastical communities. Many of them rejoice in the episcopate, celebrate the Holy Eucharist and cultivate devotion toward the Virgin Mother of God.

46. All men should take note that the profession of the evangelical counsels, though entailing the renunciation of certain values which are to be undoubtedly esteemed, does not detract from a genuine development of the human persons, but rather by its very nature is most beneficial to that development. Indeed the counsels, voluntarily undertaken according to each one's personal vocation, contribute a great deal to the purification of heart and spiritual liberty. They continually stir up the fervor of charity. But especially they are able to more fully mold the Christian man to that type of chaste and detached life, which Christ the Lord chose for himself and which his Mother also embraced. This is clearly proven by the example of so many holy founders. Let no one think that religious have become strangers to their fellowmen or useless citizens of this earthly city by their consecration.

50. Fully conscious of this communion of the whole Mystical Body of Jesus Christ, the

pilgrim Church from the very first ages of the Christian religion has cultivated with great piety the memory of the dead, and "because it is a holy and wholesome thought to pray for the dead that they may be loosed from their sins", also offers suffrages for them. The Church has always believed that the apostles and Christ's martyrs who had given the supreme witness of faith and charity by the shedding of their blood, are closely joined with us in Christ, and she has always venerated them with special devotion, together with the Blessed Virgin Mary and the holy angels. The Church has piously implored the aid of their intercession. To these were soon added also those who had more closely imitated Christ's virginity and poverty, and finally others whom the outstanding practice of the Christian virtues and the divine charisms recommended to the pious devotion and imitation of the faithful. . . .

Our union with the Church in heaven is put into effect in its noblest manner especially in the sacred Liturgy, wherein the power of the Holy Spirit acts upon us through sacramental signs. Then, with combined rejoicing we celebrate together the praise of the divine majesty; then all those from every tribe and tongue and people and nation who have been redeemed by the blood of Christ and gathered together into one Church, with one song of praise magnify the one and triune God. Celebrating the Eucharistic sacrifice therefore, we are most closely united to the Church in heaven in communion with and venerating the memory first of all of the glorious ever-Virgin Mary, of Blessed Joseph and the blessed apostles and martyrs and of all the saints.

Chapter 8 is devoted entirely to the Blessed Virgin Mary, Mother of God in the Mystery of Christ and the Church, 52–69 *(see Appendix B)*.

Orientalium Ecclesiarum (Decree on the Catholic Churches of the Eastern Rite), 1964.

30. The Sacred Council feels great joy in the fruitful zealous collaboration of the Eastern and the Western Catholic Churches and at the same time declares: All these directives of law are laid down in view of the present situation till such time as the Catholic Church and the separated Eastern Churches come together into complete unity. Meanwhile, however, all Christians, Eastern as well as Western, are earnestly asked to pray to God fervently and assiduously, nay, indeed daily, that, with the aid of the most holy Mother of God, all may become one.

Unitatis Redintegratio (Decree on Ecumenism), 1964.

14. Similarly it must not be forgotten that from the beginning the Churches of the East have had a treasury from which the Western Church has drawn extensively-in liturgical practice, spiritual tradition, and law. Nor must we undervalue the fact that it was the ecumenical councils held in the East that defined the basic dogmas of the Christian faith, on the Trinity, on the Word of God who took flesh of the Virgin Mary. To preserve this faith these Churches have suffered and still suffer much.

15. In this liturgical worship, the Christians of the East pay high tribute, in beautiful hymns of praise, to Mary ever Virgin, whom the ecumenical Council of Ephesus solemnly proclaimed to be the holy Mother

of God, so that Christ might be acknowledged as being truly Son of God and Son of Man, according to the Scriptures. Many also are the saints whose praise they sing, among them the Fathers of the universal Church.

20. Our thoughts turn first to those Christians who make open confession of Jesus Christ as God and Lord and as the sole Mediator between God and men, to the glory of the one God, Father, Son and Holy Spirit. We are aware indeed that there exist considerable divergences from the doctrine of the Catholic Church concerning Christ himself, the Word of God made flesh, the work of redemption, and consequently, concerning the mystery and ministry of the Church, and the role of Mary in the plan of salvation. But we rejoice to see that our separated brethren look to Christ as the source and center of Church unity. Their longing for union with Christ inspires them to seek an ever closer unity, and also to bear witness to their faith among the peoples of the earth.

Christus Dominus (Decree Concerning the Pastoral Office of Bishops in the Church), 1965.

No references to Mary.

Perfectae Caritatis (Decree on Renewal of Religious Life), 1965.

25. Religious institutes, for whom these norms of adaptation and renewal have been laid down, should respond generously to the specific vocation God gave them as well as their work in the Church today. The sacred synod highly esteems their way of life in poverty, chastity and obedience, of which Christ the Lord is himself the exemplar.

Moreover, their apostolate, most effective, whether obscure or well known, offers this synod great hope for the future. Let all religious, therefore, rooted in faith and filled with love for God and neighbor, love of the cross and the hope of future glory, spread the good news of Christ throughout the whole world so that their witness may be seen by all and our Father in heaven may be glorified (Matt. 5:16). Therefore, let them beseech the Virgin Mary, the gentle Mother of God, "whose life is a model for all," that their number may daily increase and their salutary work be more effective.

Optatam Totius (Decree on Priestly Training), 1965.

8. The spiritual training should be closely connected with the doctrinal and pastoral, and, with the special help of the spiritual director, should be imparted in such a way that the students might learn to live in an intimate and unceasing union with the Father through his Son Jesus Christ in the Holy Spirit. Conformed to Christ the Priest through their sacred ordination they should be accustomed to adhere to him as friends, in an intimate companionship, their whole life through. They should so live his paschal mystery themselves that they can initiate into it the flock committed to them. They should be taught to seek Christ in the faithful meditation on God's word, in the active participation in the sacred mysteries of the Church, especially in the Eucharist and in the divine office, in the bishop who sends them and in the people to whom they are sent, especially the poor, the children, the sick, the sinners and the unbelievers. They should love and venerate with a filial trust the most blessed Virgin Mary, who was

given as mother to the disciple by Christ Jesus as he was dying on the cross. Those practices of piety that are commended by the long usage of the Church should be zealously cultivated; but care should be taken lest the spiritual formation consist in them alone or lest it develop only a religious affectation. The students should learn to live according to the Gospel ideal, to be strengthened in faith, hope and charity, so that, in the exercise of these practices, they may acquire the spirit of prayer, learn to defend and strengthen their vocation, obtain an increase of other virtues and grow in the zeal to gain all men for Christ.

Gravissimum Educationis (Declaration on Christian Education), 1965.

No references to Mary.

Nostra Aetate (Declaration on the Relation of the Church to Non-Christian Religions), 1965.

3. The Church regards with esteem also the Moslems. They adore the one God, living and subsisting in himself; merciful and all-powerful, the Creator of heaven and earth, who has spoken to men; they take pains to submit wholeheartedly to even his inscrutable decrees, just as Abraham, with whom the faith of Islam takes pleasure in linking itself, submitted to God. Though they do not acknowledge Jesus as God, they revere him as a prophet. They also honor Mary, his virgin Mother; at times they even call on her with devotion.

4. As the sacred synod searches into the mystery of the Church, it remembers the bond that spiritually ties the people of the New Covenant to Abraham's stock. . . . The Church keeps ever in mind the words of the Apostle about his kinsmen: "theirs is the sonship and the glory and the covenants and the law and the worship and the promises; theirs are the fathers and from them is the Christ according to the flesh" (Rom. 9:4–5), the Son of the Virgin Mary. She also recalls that the Apostles, the Church's mainstay and pillars, as well as most of the early disciples who proclaimed Christ's Gospel to the world, sprang from the Jewish people.

Dei Verbum (Dogmatic Constitution on Divine Revelation), 1965.

No references to Mary.

Apostolicam Actuositatem (Decree on the Apostolate of the Laity), 1965.

4. The perfect example of this type of spiritual and apostolic life is the most Blessed Virgin Mary, Queen of Apostles, who while leading the life common to all here on earth, one filled with family concerns and labors, was always intimately united with her Son and in an entirely unique way cooperated in the work of the Savior. Having now been assumed into heaven, with her maternal charity she cares for these brothers of her Son who are still on their earthly pilgrimage and remain involved in dangers and difficulties until they are led into the happy fatherland. All should devoutly venerate her and commend their life and apostolate to her maternal care.

Dignitatis Humanae (Declaration on Religious Freedom), 1965.

No references to Mary.

Ad Gentes (Decree on the Mission Activity of the Church), 1965.

4. To accomplish this, Christ sent from the Father his Holy Spirit, who was to carry on

REGINA APOSTOLORUM.

ant perfeverantes cum Maria Matre Iefu. Act. 1

Queen of Apostles

inwardly his saving work and prompt the Church to spread out. Doubtless, the Holy Spirit was already at work in the world before Christ was glorified. Yet on the day of Pentecost, he came down upon the disciples to remain with them forever (cf. John 14:16). The Church was publicly displayed to the multitude, the Gospel began to spread among the nations by means of preaching, and there was presaged that union of all peoples in the catholicity of the faith by means of the Church of the New Covenant, a Church which speaks all tongues, understands and accepts all tongues in her love, and so supersedes the divisiveness of Babel. For it was from Pentecost that the "Acts of the Apostles" took again, just as Christ was – conceived when

the Holy Spirit came upon the Virgin Mary, and just as Christ was impelled to the work of his ministry by the same Holy Spirit descending upon him while he prayed.

Presbyterorum Ordinis (*Decree on the Ministry and Life of Priests*), 1965.

18. In order that, in all conditions of life, they may be able to grow in union with Christ, priests, besides the exercise of their conscious ministry, enjoy the common and particular means, old and new, which the Spirit never ceases to arouse in the People of God and which the Church commends, and sometimes commands, for the sanctification of her members. . . . Nourished by spiritual reading, under the light of faith, they can more diligently seek signs of God's will and impulses of his grace in the various events of life, and so from day to day become more docile to the mission they have assumed in the Holy Spirit. They will always find a wonderful example of such docility in the Blessed Virgin Mary, who was led by the Holy Spirit to dedicate herself totally to the mystery of man's redemption. Let priests love and venerate with filial devotion and veneration this mother of the Eternal Highpriest, Queen of Apostles and Protector of their own ministry.

Gaudium et Spes (*Pastoral Constitution on the Church In the Modern World*), 1965.

22. He who is "the image of the invisible God" (Col. 1:15), is himself the perfect man. To the sons of Adam he restores the divine likeness which had been disfigured from the first sin onward. Since human nature as he assumed it was not annulled, by that very fact it has been raised up to a divine dignity in our respect too. For by his incarnation the Son of God has united him-

self in some fashion with every man. He worked with human hands, he thought with a human mind, acted by human choice and loved with a human heart. Born of the Virgin Mary, he has truly been made one of us, like us in all things except sin.

See also Appendix B, Excerpt from **Lumen Gentium.**

VELIKA GOSPA

Croatian celebration marked on August 15.

Tradition holds *Velika Gospa* dates back to Sinj, in the province of Dalmatia, Croatia. In 1716, the army of the Turkish Empire was advancing on its way toward Vienna and, it seemed, was certain to wipe out the small town on its way. The people turned to Mary, and throughout the night of August 14, prayed before an image of *Our Lady of Grace.* The next morning, an apparition of a beautiful lady, whom everyone recognized as Mary, appeared in the sky. The Turkish soldiers became violently ill and were unable to cross the river into Sinj, and so they retreated. They never returned.

In gratitude for this great victory against such a superior force, the Croatians increased their love and devotion to Mary. They built a larger church in her honor, and it became the central Marian shrine for all of Dalmatia. Annually, thousands of pilgrims, especially from Dalmatia and Bosnia, make a pilgrimage to the church.

VENERATION OF MARY

The proper honor given to Mary. In technical and traditional terms, devotion to Mary is a form *dulia,* or the homage and honor owed the saints, both angelic and human in heaven. It is not *latria,* or adoration and worship, which can be given only to God. Because of her unique relationship to Christ in salvation history, the special degree of devotion due to Mary has traditionally been called *hyperdulia.*

See Devotions, Marian.

VESSEL OF HONOR

Marian title used in the Litany of the Blessed Virgin Mary (also known as the Litany of Loreto), which was originally approved in 1587 by Pope Sixtus V. The image refers to Mary as the Mother of God.

See also Litany of the Blessed Virgin Mary.

VIA MATRIS

Latin for "the way of the mother."

This devotion, known as The Way of the Sorrowful Mother, is based on private revelations reported by the founders of the Servants of Mary in the thirteenth century. It is one of many devotions that grew out of the fervent preaching of the Servites. One historical study indicates that the devotion existed as early as the fourteenth century in Flanders.

Patterned on the Stations of the Cross, the *Via Matris* is a set of seven stations commemorating the seven sorrows of Our Lady. The stations are canonically erected in churches; although the blessing and erection of these stations used to be reserved to the Servite Order, since Vatican II, any priest may perform the ritual.

One version of the devotion reads:

An Act of Contrition

Virgin most afflicted, how ungrateful have I been in the past to my God, in return for all His benefits. Now, I repent in bitterness of heart, humbly asking pardon for the offence done to His infinite goodness, and resolved by the help of heavenly grace to offend Him no more. Ah, by all the pains which you did suffer in the cruel Passion of your dear Jesus, I pray you, with fervent sighs, to obtain for me pardon and mercy for all my grievous sins. Receive this holy exercise wherein I am going to engage in memory of your Sorrows. Obtain that the same sword which pierced your soul may pierce mine also, that I may live and die in the love of my Lord, and share eternally in that glory, which He has purchased for me with His most precious blood. Amen.

First Station: The Prophecy of Simeon

Leader: *How great was the shock to Mary's heart at hearing the sorrowful words, in which holy Simeon told the bitter Passion and death of her sweet Jesus, since in that same moment she realized in her mind all the insults, blows, and torments which the impious men were to offer to the Redeemer of the world. But a still sharper sword pierced her soul. It was the thought of men's ingratitude to her beloved Son. Now consider that because of your sins you art unhappily among the ungrateful, and casting yourself at the feet of the Mother of Dolors, say with sorrow:*

People: *Virgin beloved, who did feel so bitter pangs of soul at seeing the abuse which I, wretch that I am, would make of the Blood of your dear Son, obtain for me, I pray you, by your riven heart, that in time to come I may better correspond to God's mercies, profit by His heavenly grace, receive not in vain His lights and inspirations, and so be among the blessed number of those who are saved by the bitter Passion of Jesus. Amen*

Hail Mary . . .

Virgin, most sorrowful: Pray for us.

Second Station: The Flight into Egypt

Leader: *Consider the sharp sorrow which Mary felt when, St. Joseph being warned by an angel, she had to flee by night in order to preserve her beloved Child from the slaughter decreed by Herod. What anguish was hers, in leaving Judea, lest she should be overtaken by the soldiers of the cruel king! How great her privations in that long journey! What sufferings she bore in that land of exile, what sorrow amid that people given to idolatry! But consider how often you have renewed that bitter grief of Mary, when your sins have caused her Son to flee from your heart. Wherefore repent, and turn to her, humbly saying:*

People: *Sweetest Mother, once and once only Herod obliged you to fly with your Jesus, to escape the slaughter which he had commanded; but I, how often have I forced my Redeemer and you with Him, to fly from my heart, when I have admitted into it accursed sin, hateful to you and to my loving Lord. With tears and contrition I humbly sue for pardon. Mercy, dear Lady mine, mercy!, and I promise you that, for the future, with the help of God, I will ever maintain my Savior and you in complete possession of my soul. Amen.*

Hail Mary . . .

Virgin, most sorrowful: Pray for us.

287

Third Station: The Loss of Jesus in the Temple

Leader: How dread was the grief of Mary, when she saw that she had lost her beloved Son! And as if to increase her sorrow, when she sought him diligently among her kinsfolk and acquaintance, she could hear no tidings of Him. No hindrances stayed her, nor weariness, nor danger; but she forthwith returned to Jerusalem, and for three long days sought Him sorrowing. Great be your confusion, O my soul, who has so often lost your Jesus by your sins, and has given no heed to seek Him at once, a sign that you do make of very little or of no account the precious treasure of divine love. Weep then for your blindness, and turning you to that Lady of sighs, your Mother, say with compunction:

People: Virgin most afflicted, obtain that I may learn from you to seek Jesus, when I have lost Him by giving ear to my passions and to the evil suggestions of the devil; obtain that I may find Him again, and when I possess Him once more, that I may ever repeat the words of the Spouse, "I found Him whom my soul loveth; I held Him, and I will not let Him go." Amen.

Hail Mary . . .

Virgin, most sorrowful: Pray for us.

Fourth Station: Mary Meets Jesus on the Way to Calvary

Leader: Come, O you sinners, come and see if you can endure so sad a sight. This Mother, so tender and loving, meets her beloved Son, meets Him amid an impious rabble, who drag Him to a cruel death, wounded, torn by stripes, crowned with thorns, streaming with blood, bearing His heavy cross. Ah, consider, my soul, the grief of the blessed Virgin thus beholding her Son! Who would not weep at seeing this Mother's grief? But who has been the cause of such woe? I, it is I, who with my sins have so cruelly wounded the heart of my sorrowing Mother! And yet I am not moved; I am as a stone, when my heart should break because of my ingratitude.

People: Virgin most holy, I crave pardon for the sorrows I have caused you. I know and confess that I deserve it not, for it is I through whom your Jesus was so treated; yet call to mind that you are the Mother of mercy. Show mercy, then, to me, and I promise to be more faithful to my Redeemer in the time to come, and thus to console you for the many sorrows I have offered to your afflicted heart. Amen.

Hail Mary . . .

Virgin, most sorrowful: Pray for us.

Fifth Station: Jesus Dies on the Cross

Leader: Look, devout soul, look to Calvary, whereon are raised two altars of sacrifice, one on the body of Jesus, the other on the heart of Mary. Sad is the sight of that dear Mother drowned in a sea of woe, seeing her beloved Son, part of her very self, cruelly nailed to the shameful tree the cross. Ah me!, how every blow of the hammer, how every stripe which fell on the Savior's form, fell also on the disconsolate spirit of the Virgin. As she stood at the foot of the cross, pierced by the sword of sorrow, she turned her eyes on Him, until she knew that He lived no longer and had resigned His spirit to His Eternal Father. Then her own soul was like to have left the body and joined itself to that of Jesus.

People: *Mother of Sorrows, who would not leave Calvary until you had drunk the last drop of the chalice of your woe, how great is my confusion of face, that I so often refuse to take up my cross, and in all ways endeavor to avoid those slight sufferings which the Lord, for my good, is pleased to send upon me. Obtain for me, I pray you, that I may see clearly the value of suffering, and may be enabled, if not to cry with St. Francis Xavier, "More to suffer, my God, ah, more!" at least to bear meekly all my crosses and trials. Amen.*

Hail Mary . . .

Virgin, most sorrowful: Pray for us.

Sixth Station: Mary Receives the Dead Body of Jesus in Her Arms

Leader: *Consider the most bitter sorrow which rent the soul of Mary, when she saw the dead body of her dear Jesus on her knees, covered with blood, all torn with deep wounds. O mournful Mother, a bundle of myrrh, indeed, is your Beloved to you. Who would not pity you? Whose heart would not be softened, seeing affliction which would move a stone? Behold John not to be comforted, Magdalen and the other Mary in deep affliction, and Nicodemus, who can scarcely bear his sorrow.*

People: *And I, shall I alone be tearless amid such grief? Ingrate and hard am I! Grant, dear Mother, that my heart may be pierced with the same sword that pierced your sorrowful soul, that it may be softened, and may indeed lament those my heavy sins which were the cause of your cruel suffering. Amen.*

Hail Mary . . .

Virgin, most sorrowful: Pray for us.

Seventh Station: Jesus Is Placed in the Tomb

Leader: *Consider the sighs which burst from Mary's sad heart when she saw her beloved Jesus laid within the tomb. What grief was hers when she saw the stone lifted to cover that sacred tomb! She gazed a last time on the lifeless body of her Son, and could scarce detach her eyes from those gaping wounds. And when the great stone was rolled to the door of the sepulcher, oh, then indeed her heart seemed torn from her body!*

People: *O Mother most desolate, who did indeed in body depart from the sepulcher, but did leave your heart where was your only treasure, obtain that all our desires, all our love may rest there with you. Surely our hearts must melt with love to our Savior, who has shed His Blood for our salvation. Surely we must love you, who has suffered so much for us. Oh, by all your sorrows, grant that the memory of them may be ever imprinted on our mind, that our hearts may burn with love to God, and to you, sweet Mother, who did pour out all your soul in sorrow for the Passion of Jesus: to Him be honor, glory, and thanksgiving for ever and ever. Amen.*

Hail Mary . . . .

Virgin, most sorrowful: Pray for us.

To Mary in Her Desolation:

I pity you, most Holy Mother, with all the tenderness of which my heart is capable, in your extreme desolation. Deep indeed was your grief, when you did witness the passion and death of your beloved Son. But then His presence could in a measure sustain you and comfort you in the stormy waves of sorrow. Now are you wholly desolate. Oh, grief unequalled! Oh, lonely bitterness! Oh, by that grievous loss, have pity on me, who so often have, by my sins, lost my beloved Lord. Obtain, O tender Mother, that I may never again cause my Jesus to remove from me through my wickedness and want of fervor, but may serve Him faithfully in this earthly life, to see and enjoy Him hereafter in heaven. Amen.

See Three Hail Marys.

VICTORY, OUR LADY OF

Ancient Marian title of undetermined origin. Our Lady of Victory has been venerated independently in Constantinople, Paris, Sicily, Prague, and elsewhere. The title may have resulted from prayers to Our Lady during times a region was being threatened, attacked or invaded. A famous victory over the Turks in the naval battle of Lepanto (1571) was attributed entirely to Our Lady's intercession, and Pope Pius V established the day of the battle, October 7, as a feast of Our Lady of Victory. Two years later, the name of the feast was changed to Our Lady of the Rosary.

VIRGINITY OF MARY, PERPETUAL

Doctrine that Mary remained a virgin throughout her life on earth.

The teaching traditionally includes three major components: her virginal conception of Christ (*virginitas ante partum*); her virginity in parturition, or giving birth to Christ (*virginitas in* [or *durante*] *partu*); and her perpetual virginity (*virginitas post partum*).

This triple formula became the standard with St. Augustine (353–430), St. Peter Chrysologus (c. 400–c. 450), and Pope St. Leo the Great (r. 440–461).

The Marian title "ever virgin" became extremely popular from the latter part of the fourth century.

Mary's virginity in conceiving Christ at the moment of her *fiat* (her completely free consent to God's calling that she become the Mother of his own Son incarnate at the Annunciation) is also called "pneumatological" conception. That is, it took place through the power of the Holy Spirit.

St. Augustine

This teaching is included not only in Scripture (in the infancy narratives of Matthew [1:18–25] and Luke [1:26–38]) but also in the very early witness of an Apostolic Father: St. Ignatius of Antioch (died c. 110). The testimony of the virginal conception is constant in patristic testimony. From the Church's earliest creeds, Christians have professed "by the power of the Holy Spirit he was born of the Virgin Mary and became man."

Among the great theologians who have written on the fittingness of the Christ's birth by a virgin are St. Augustine and St. Thomas Aquinas (1225–1274), who note that if God had not predestined that his Son be conceived and born of a virgin and, thus, St. Joseph had been his natural father, Christ's divine origins would have been obscured because God the Father would not have been Jesus' only Father.

With regard to Mary's virginity in parturition, Matthew reveals in his infancy narrative (1:25) that Mary remained a virgin giving birth to Jesus. The evangelist sees in her bringing forth of Christ the fulfillment of the Old Testament prophecy in Is. 7:14 that a virgin would conceive and *bear* a child. In the testimony of the Fathers of the West, this came to be understood as meaning her bodily integrity remained intact, and she did not experience the ordinary pains of childbirth. The Fathers of the East stressed the aspect of her joy and freedom in giving birth to Jesus. General agreement regarding Mary's remaining a virgin while giving birth to Christ was formalized by both the East and West in the period between 375 and 425.

In writing of Mary's perpetual virginity, the Second Vatican Council (1962–1965) confirmed the dogma that Mary remained a virgin throughout her life:

Joined to Christ the Head and in communion with all his saints, the faithful must in the first place reverence the memory "of the glorious ever virgin Mary, Mother of God and of our Lord Jesus Christ." (*Dogmatic Constitution on the Church, Lumen Gentium*, 52)

The council also took note of the dogmatic status of the first two major components of Mary's perpetual virginity:

This union of the Mother with her Son in the work of salvation is made manifest from the time of Christ's conception up to his death . . .

and:

. . . then also at the birth of Our Lord, who did not diminish his mother's virginal integrity but sanctified it, the Mother of God joyfully showed her firstborn Son to the shepherds and the Magi. (*Lumen Gentium*, 57)

For centuries, and even today, New Testament references to the "brothers" and "sisters" of the Lord (Mk. 6:3; Jn. 2:12) have been presented as an objection against Mary's perpetual virginity. St. Jerome (c. 347–420), the outstanding Scripture scholar among the Fathers and Doctors of the Church, countered that the terms really referred to Jesus' cousins. Later, he repudiated this view, since the Greek of the New Testament did have a definite word for "cousins." But, as Pope John Paul II noted, there is no word for "cousin" in Hebrew and Aramaic, and the "terms 'brother' and 'sister' therefore had a far broader meaning which included several degrees of relationship" (*Marian Catechesis*, August 28, 1996).

Another interpretation was offered by Epiphanius (Patriarch of Constantinople, d. 535) who was of the opinion that these were the sons and daughters of Joseph from a previous marriage. Although this would be in accord with faith in Mary's perpetual virginity, it was contrary to the beliefs of St. Jerome and St. Augustine, who both considered St. Joseph also to be a virgin.

The *Catechism of the Catholic Church* explains that "they [the "brothers" and "sisters"] are close relations of Jesus, according to an Old Testament expression" (500).

See also Doctrines of the Church, Marian.

VIRGIN MOST PRUDENT, MOST VENERABLE, MOST RENOWNED, MOST POWERFUL, MOST MERCIFUL, MOST FAITHFUL — *See Litany of the Blessed Virgin Mary.*

VIRGIN MOTHER OF EMMANUEL

Reference to Mary as Christ's mother.
The term *Emmanuel* is Hebrew for "God [is] with us" or "[may] God [be] with us" (Is. 7:14, 8:8). In Matthew's Gospel, the name is given to Christ and is traditionally seen as a prediction of the virgin birth of Jesus (Mt. 1:23).

See Virginity of Mary, Perpetual.

VIRGIN OF MIRACLES — *See Caacupe, Our Lady of the Miracles of.*

VIRGIN OF POZZENTA — *See Caravaggio, Our Lady of.*

VIRGIN OF THE FOUNTAIN — *See Caravaggio, Our Lady of.*

VIRGIN OF THE GATE — *See Iviron, Our Lady of.*

VIRGIN OF THE POOR — *See Banneux, Our Lady of.*

VIRGIN OF THE SEA — *See Boulogne, Our Lady of.*

VIRGIN OF VIRGINS

Marian title used in the Litany of the Blessed Virgin Mary (also known as the Litany of Loreto), which was originally approved in 1587 by Pope Sixtus V.

See Litany of the Blessed Virgin Mary.

VIRGIN WITH THE GOLDEN HEART — *See Beauraing, Our Lady of.*

VIRTUES OF THE BLESSED VIRGIN MARY, CHAPLET OF THE TEN EVANGELICAL VIRTUES

Prayer promoted by the Marian Order, featuring a string of ten beads with a medal on one end and a crucifix at the other.

After the Sign of the Cross, there is one Our Father followed by ten Hail Marys. During each Hail Mary, after saying "Holy Mary, Mother of God," one virtue is offered in prayer, proceeding from Most Pure to Most Sorrowful. The prayer then concludes with "pray for us sinners, now and at the hour of our death. Amen."

The virtues are:

most pure
most prudent
most humble
most faithful
most devout
most obedient
most poor
most patient
most merciful
most sorrowful.

The chaplet concludes with:

Glory to the Father and to the Son and to the Holy Spirit. As it was in the beginning, is now and will be forever. Amen.

In Your Conception, O Virgin Mary, You were Immaculate.

Pray for us to the Father whose son, Jesus, you brought forth into the world.

Let us pray. Father, you prepared the Virgin Mary to be the worthy mother of your Son. You let her share beforehand in the salvation Christ would bring by his death, and kept her sinless from the first moment of her conception. Help us by her prayers to live in your presence without sin. We ask this in the name of Jesus the Lord. Amen.

The Virgin Mary's Immaculate Conception: Be our Health and our Protection.

VISIONS OF MARY — *See Apparitions of Mary.*

VISITATION OF MARY — *See Rosary; Scripture, Mary in.*

VLADIMIR, OUR LADY OF

Image and devotion.

The origin of this ancient Marian icon can be traced back to 1125. Its style is that of an *Eleousa*, the Greek for *Mother of Tenderness*. The Christ Child snuggles in Mary's arms and his right hand gently touches her left cheek. The original large painting is of the type known as the St. Luke icons.

For many, "The Lady Who Saves Russia" is the most beloved image of the Eastern Church.

The oldest known representation of *Our Lady of Vladimir* is located at the Tretjakow Gallery in Moscow. According to research, it was commissioned in Constantinople by a Russian, who then had the painting taken from city to city during the period of united Ukrainian-Russian history. In 1169, Duke Andrej Bogoljubskij had the icon brought from Kiev to the new cathedral of Vladimir. Due to the honor and reverence of the people, who attributed gracious assistance to Our Lady's help throughout the Ukraine, a large cathedral was built for her in Vladimir.

In 1395, when the Mongol invasion threatened Moscow, the image was brought to that city where Mary was honored as the unconquerable shield of the Russian people. Important state transactions took place before her image, and her blessing was invoked before battle. Over time, the image became the principal symbol of the Russian Orthodox Church. Her image is in countless Orthodox

Our Lady of Vladimir

In 1995, on the 600th anniversary of the transference of the icon from Vladimir to Moscow, an academic conference was held in the Tretjakow Fine Arts Gallery.

See also **Eleousa** *and* **Oumilenie.**

churches and homes. The intimate relationship of *Our Lady of Tenderness* with her divine Son is seen as an ideal representation the Christian's relationship to Christ.

W–Z

WALSINGHAM, OUR LADY OF

Marian image and devotion based on apparitions reported by Lady Richeldis de Faverches in Walsingham, England, in 1061.

This widow of a Norman landowner said Mary instructed her to build a replica of the Holy Family's home, and that pilgrims who visited this shrine would receive the same graces as if they had made the long and dangerous journey to Palestine. "The Holy House" — referred to as "England's Nazareth" — became the fourth great shrine of medieval Christendom, joining those of Jerusalem, Rome, and St. James Compostela in Spain.

Over the years, many miracles were attributed to the intercession of Our Lady of Walsingham, including King Edward I being saved from harm when a piece of masonry fell.

Devotion was interrupted for some three-and-a-half centuries when the shrine was destroyed during the English Reformation. In 1538, King Henry VIII confiscated and razed the building and sold its lands into private ownership.

In the nineteenth century, Charlotte Pearson Boyd, a devout Anglican, developed a personal devotion to Our Lady of Walsingham. Around 1863, she noticed a small stone building (then being used as a barn) that seemed to be a late medieval chapel. Located about a mile from the site of the shrine, it had been "The Slipper Chapel" in which pilgrims had left their shoes before walking the last distance barefoot as a form of penance. Boyd purchased the building in the 1890s and restored it. During this time, she was also received into the Roman Catholic Church.

Eventually, the chapel was donated to the local Catholic bishop and, in 1934, it was declared the Roman Catholic National Shrine of Our Lady of Walsingham. Marist Fathers and Sisters administer and care for the shrine today.

In the 1920s, the Anglican vicar of Walsingham, Alfred Hope Patton, built a shrine to Our Lady of Walsingham in his parish church. Later, he moved it to its own nearby site. Eastern Orthodox Christians maintain yet a third shrine in the village. Modern pilgrims often visit all of them.

Today, Our Lady of Walsingham is venerated as the patroness of England. The Feast of Our Lady of Walsingham is celebrated on the Feast of the Annunciation, March 25.

WASHING OF THE SILVER — *See* Immaculate Conception of El Viejo, Our Lady of the.

WAY OF THE CROSS; STATIONS OF THE CROSS

A form of devotion commemorating the Passion and death of Christ, consisting of a series of meditations (stations).

The traditional fourteen are:

1. Jesus is condemned to death.
2. Jesus takes up his cross.
3. Jesus falls for the first time on the way to Calvary.
4. Jesus meets Mary, his Mother.
5. Simon of Cyrene helps Jesus carry his cross.
6. Veronica wipes Jesus' face with a veil.
7. Jesus falls the second time.
8. Jesus meets the women of Jerusalem.
9. Jesus falls the third time.
10. Jesus is stripped of his clothes.
11. Jesus is nailed to the cross.
12. Jesus dies on the cross.
13. Jesus' body is removed from the cross.
14. Jesus is buried.

Images of these scenes are mounted in most churches and chapels, and, in some outdoor-places, on posts. A person making the Way of the Cross passes before these stations, or stopping points, pausing at each for meditation. If the stations are made by a group of people indoors, only the leader walks from station to station.

The stations originated from the practice of Holy Land pilgrims who visited the actual scenes of incidents in the Passion of Christ (Jerusalem's *Via Dolorosa*). Representations elsewhere of at least some of these scenes were known as early as the fifth century. Later, the stations evolved in connection with, and as a consequence of, strong devotion to the Passion in the twelfth and thirteenth centuries. Franciscans, who were given custody of the Holy Places in 1342, promoted the devotion widely; one of them, St. Leonard of Port Maurice, became known as the greatest preacher of the Way of the Cross in the eighteenth century. The general features of the devotion were fixed by Clement XII in 1731.

See also Via Matris.

WEDDING (OR LASSO) ROSARY

Large rosary used during a Mexican wedding ceremony. The lasso is draped around the bride and groom as they kneel at the altar.

WEDNESDAYS OF MOUNT CARMEL
— *See* **Brown Virgin.**

WEEPING MADONNAS

Statues or images of Mary that reportedly shed tears. One example is *Our Lady of Akita*, Japan.

See **Akita, Our Lady of;** *Miracle.*

WHITE — *See Liturgical Colors for Marian feasts.*

WHITE SCAPULAR — *See Scapular of Our Lady of Good Counsel; Scapular of Our Lady of Ransom.*

WOMAN CLOTHED WITH THE SUN

Description from Rev. 12:1 sometimes used to describe Mary. Scripture scholars note that the woman adorned with the sun, the moon, and the stars (images taken from Gen. 37:9–10) symbolizes God's people in the Old and the New Testament.

See Scripture, Mary in.

WORLD MISSION ROSARY

Sacramental and method of praying the Rosary.

Introduced by Archbishop Fulton J. Sheen in the mid-twentieth century to encourage prayers for the missions and missionaries, the Rosary is made with each decade a different color to symbolize the continents: green for Africa, red for the Americas, white for Europe, blue for Oceania, and yellow for Asia. As the beads are prayed, the supplicant is encouraged to offer those prayers for the missionary efforts of the Church in each continent.

ZAPOPAN, OUR LADY OF

Image and devotion.

Tzapopa (later Zapopan), Mexico, a town about two miles from Guadalajara, was founded in 1541 by Francisco de Bobadilla, a conquistador who defeated the Tochos Indians after they had gone to war against the Spaniards.

Among the Franciscans who came to evangelize the people in the area was Fr. Antonio of Segovia, who brought a statue of Mary Immaculate with him. Pious legend says the priest volunteered to act as a mediator between the Indians and Spaniards, so that there would be no more fighting. He stood before the Tochos holding a crucifix in one hand and a small statue of Mary in the other. The Indians noticed a light shimmering around the Marian image and chose to lay down their weapons.

An adobe shrine was constructed to hold the Marian statue, and in 1641, it was placed under the care of the diocesan clergy. (The present shrine was dedicated by the bishop of Guadalajara on September 8, 1730.)

In the years that followed, there was an official inquiry into miracles attributed to the intercession of Our Lady of Zapopan, and the local bishop transferred her feast to December 18. He also gave the devotion the name *Nuestra Señora de la O* or *de la Expectación*, but people have continued to use the original title.

Whenever nearby Guadalajara — now one of largest cities in Mexico — was in danger (as in 1721, when a plague threatened the residents), the statue was moved there. In 1734, Our Lady of Zapopan was proclaimed patroness against storms and lightning. After Mexico became independent in 1821, Our Lady of Zapopan was proclaimed Patroness of the State of Jalisco and its army, and was canonically crowned in 1921. Today, the statue is in Guadalajara from June 13 to October 5.

The statue itself, made of light wood, is about thirteen inches tall. Our Lady wears a red tunic and blue mantle. There are traces of an earlier golden color. She stands on a crescent moon and her hands, in a prayerful position, hold a scepter. Most often, the statue is

Our Lady of Zapopan

placed in a silver vase that goes up to her hips and the vase is set on a pedestal.

The statue is clothed in rich garments and wears a lavish wig with an imperial crown on it. Mary also wears a blue scarf, emblematic of a general, and there is a golden staff hanging from her right arm, which could be a commander's baton. Below her hands there is a golden circular frame that features an image of the Christ Child in its center. It is speculated that this disc is what is being referred to in the title *de la O.*

ZARAGOZA — *See* Pilar, Our Lady of.

ZION, DAUGHTER OF — *See Daughter of Zion.*

ZO-SE, OUR LADY OF

Shrine near Shanghai that developed from a small church built in the latter half of the nineteenth century by Fr. Della Corte, S.J.

The priest had placed a small picture of Our Lady, Help of Christians in the building. After members were spared from floods and bandit attacks, the congregation erected a larger church. It features a statue of Mary holding the Christ Child aloft.

Reports of Mary appearing to a religious in Zo-se in the mid-twentieth century received a negative assessmenl of any supernatural character related to the event.

Appendix A

Excerpt from the *Directory on Popular Piety and the Liturgy*

In its 2001 document, *Directory on Popular Piety and the Liturgy*, the Congregation for Divine Worship and the Discipline of the Sacraments noted that "some of the earliest forms of veneration of the Blessed Virgin Mary also reflect popular piety, among them the *Sub tuum praesidium* and the Marian iconography of the catacombs of St. Priscilla in Rome."

In Chapter Five, titled "Veneration of the Holy Mother of God," the authors wrote:

183. Popular devotion to the Blessed Virgin Mary is an important and universal ecclesial phenomenon. Its expressions are multifarious and its motivation very profound, deriving as it does from the People of God's faith in, and love for, Christ, the Redeemer of mankind, and from an awareness of the salvific mission that God entrusted to Mary of Nazareth, because of which she is mother not only of Our Lord and Savior Jesus Christ, but also of mankind in the order of grace.

Indeed, "the faithful easily understand the vital link uniting Son and Mother. They realize that the Son is God and that she, the Mother, is also their mother. They intuit the immaculate holiness of the Blessed Virgin Mary, and in venerating her as the glorious queen of Heaven, they are absolutely certain that she who is full of mercy intercedes for them. Hence, they confidently have recourse to her patronage. The poorest of the poor feel especially close to her. They know that she, like them, was poor, and greatly suffered in meekness and patience. They can identify with her suffering at the crucifixion and death of her Son, as well as rejoice with her in his resurrection. The faithful joyfully celebrate her feasts, make pilgrimage to her sanctuary, sing hymns in her honor, and make votive offerings to her. They instinctively distrust whoever does not honor her and will not tolerate those who dishonor her." (208)

The Church exhorts all the faithful — sacred minister, religious and laity — to develop a personal and community devotion to the Blessed Virgin Mary through the use of approved and recommended pious exercises.(209) Liturgical worship, notwithstanding its objective and irreplaceable importance, its exemplary efficacy and normative character, does not in fact exhaust all the expressive possibilities of the People of God for devotion to the Holy Mother of God. (210)

184. The relationship between the Liturgy and popular Marian piety should be regu-

lated by the principles and norms already mentioned in this document. (211) In relation to Marian devotion, the Liturgy must be the "exemplary form,"(212) source of inspiration, constant reference point and ultimate goal of Marian devotion.

185. Here, it will be useful to recall some pronouncements of the Church's Magisterium on Marian devotions. These should always be adhered to when elaborating new pious exercises or in revising those already in use, or simply in activating them in worship. (213) The care and attention of the Pastors of the Church for Marian devotions are due to their importance, since they are both a fruit and an expression of Marian piety among the people and the ecclesial community, and a significant means of promoting the "Marian formation" of the faithful, as well as in determining the manner in which the piety of the faithful for the Blessed Virgin Mary is molded.

186. The fundamental principle of the Magisterium with regard to such pious exercises is that they should be derivative from the "one worship which is rightly called Christian, because it efficaciously originates in Christ, finds full expression in Christ, and through Him, in the Holy Spirit leads to the Father." (214) Hence, Marian devotions, in varying degrees and modes, should:

give expression to the Trinitarian note which characterizes worship of the God revealed in the New Testament, the Father, Son and Holy Spirit; the pneumatological aspect, since every true form of piety comes from the Spirit and is exercised in the Spirit; the ecclesial character, in virtue of which the faithful are constituted as the holy people of God, gathered in prayer in the Lord's

name (cf. Mt. 18:20) in the vital Communion of Saints; (215)

have constant recourse to Sacred Scripture, as understood in Sacred Tradition; not overlook the demands of the ecumenical movement in the Church's profession of faith; consider the anthropological aspects of cultic expressions so as to reflect a true concept of man and a valid response to his needs; highlight the eschatological tension which is essential to the Gospel message; make clear missionary responsibility and the duty of bearing witness, which are incumbent on the Lord's disciples. (216)

Times of Pious Marian Exercises
Celebration of feasts

187. Practically all Marian devotions and pious exercises are in some way related to the liturgical feasts of the General Calendar of the Roman Rite or of the particular calendars of dioceses and religious families. Sometimes, a particular devotion antedates the institution of the feast (as is the case with the feast of the Holy Rosary), in other instances, the feast is much more ancient than the devotion (as with the *Angelus Domini*). This clearly illustrates the relationship between the Liturgy and pious exercises, and the manner in which pious exercises find their culmination in the celebration of the feast. In so far as liturgical, the feast refers to the history of salvation and celebrates a particular aspect of the relationship of the Virgin Mary to the mystery of Christ. The feast, however, must be celebrated in accordance with liturgical norm, and bear in mind the hierarchical difference between "liturgical acts" and associated "pious exercises." (217)

It should not be forgotten that a feast of the Blessed Virgin, in so far as it is popular manifestation, also has important anthropological implications that cannot be overlooked.

Saturdays

188. Saturdays stand out among those days dedicated to the Virgin Mary. These are designated as *memorials of the Blessed Virgin Mary.* (218) This memorial derives from carolingian time (ninth century), but the reasons for having chosen Saturday for its observance are unknown.(219) While many explanations have been advanced to explain this choice, none is completely satisfactory from the point of view of the history of popular piety. (220)

Prescinding from its historical origins, today the memorial rightly emphasizes certain values to which contemporary spirituality is more sensitive: it is a remembrance of the maternal example and discipleship of the Blessed Virgin Mary who, strengthened by faith and hope, on that great Saturday on which Our Lord lay in the tomb, was the only one of the disciples to hold vigil in expectation of the Lord's resurrection; it is a prelude and introduction to the celebration of Sunday, the weekly memorial of the Resurrection of Christ; it is a sign that the "Virgin Mary is continuously present and operative in the life of the Church." (221)

Popular piety is also sensitive to the Saturday memorial of the Blessed Virgin Mary. The statutes of many religious communities and associations of the faithful prescribe that special devotion be paid to the Holy Mother of God on Saturdays, sometimes through specified pious exercises composed precisely for Saturdays (222).

Tridua, Sepinaria, Marian Novenas

189. Since it is a significant moment, a feast day is frequently preceded by a preparatory triduum, septinaria or novena. The "times and modes of popular piety," however, should always correspond to the "times and modes of the Liturgy."

Tridua, septinaria, and novenas can be useful not only for honoring the Blessed Virgin Mary through pious exercises, but also to afford the faithful an adequate vision of the positions she occupies in the mystery of Christ and of the Church, as well as the role she plays in it.

Pious exercises cannot remain indifferent to the results of biblical and theological research on the Mother of Our Savior. These should become a catechetical means diffusing such information, without however altering their essential nature.

Tridua, septinaria, and novenas are truly preparations for the celebration of the various feast days of Our Lady, especially when they encourage the faithful to approach the Sacraments of Penance and Holy Eucharist, and to renew their Christian commitment following the example of Mary, the first and most perfect disciple of Christ.

In some countries, the faithful gather for prayer on the 13th of each month, in honor of the apparitions of Our Lady at Fatima.

Marian Months

190. With regard to the observance of "Marian months," which is widespread in the Latin and Oriental Churches (223), a number of essential points can be mentioned. (224)

In the West, the practice of observing months dedicated to the Blessed Virgin emerged from a context in which the Liturgy was not always regarded as the normative form of Christian worship. This caused, and continues to cause, some difficulties at a liturgico-pastoral level that should be carefully examined.

191. In relation to the western custom of observing a "Marian month" during the month of May (or in November in some parts of the Southern hemisphere), it would seem opportune to take into account the demands of the Liturgy, the expectations of the faithful, their maturity in the faith, in an eventual study of the problems deriving from the "Marian months" in the overall pastoral activity of the local Church, as might happen, for example, with any suggestion of abolishing the Marian observances during the month of May.

In many cases, the solution for such problems would seem to lay in harmonizing the content of the "Marian months" with the concomitant season of the Liturgical Year. For example, since the month of May largely corresponds with the fifty days of Easter, the pious exercises practiced at this time could emphasize Our Lady's participation in the Paschal mystery (cf. John 19, 25-27), and the Pentecost event (cf. Acts 1:14) with which the Church begins: Our Lady journeys with the Church having shared in the novum of the Resurrection, under the guidance of the Holy Spirit. The fifty days are also a time for the celebration of the sacraments of Christian initiation and of the mystagogy. The pious exercises connected with the month of May could easily highlight the earthly role played by the glorified Queen of Heaven, here and now, in the celebration of the Sacraments of Baptism, Confirmation and Holy Eucharist. (225)

The directives of *Sacrosanctum Concilium* on the need to orient the "minds of the faithful . . . firstly to the feasts of the Lord, in which, the mysteries of salvation are celebrated during the year," (226) and with which the Blessed Virgin Mary is certainly associated, should be closely followed.

Opportune catechesis should remind the faithful that the weekly Sunday memorial of the Paschal Mystery is "the primordial feast day." Bearing in mind that the four weeks of Advent are an example of a Marian time that has been incorporated harmoniously into the Liturgical Year, the faithful should be assisted in coming to a full appreciation of the numerous references to the Mother of our Savior during this particular period.

Pious Exercises Recommended by the Magisterium

192. This is not the place to reproduce the list of Marian exercises approved by the Magisterium. Some, however, should be mentioned, especially the more important ones, so as to make a few suggestions about their practice and emendation.

Prayerfully Hearing the Word of God

193. The Council's call for the "sacred celebration of the word of God" at significant moments throughout the Liturgical Year, (227) can easily find useful application in devotional exercises made in honor of the Mother of the Word Incarnate. This corresponds perfectly with the orientation of Christian piety (228) and reflects the conviction that it is already a worthy way to honor the Blessed Virgin Mary, since it involves acting as she did in relation to the Word of God. She lovingly accepted the Word and treasured it in her heart, meditated on it in her mind and spread it with

her lips. She faithfully put it into practice and modeled her life on it . (229)

194. "Celebrations of the Word, because of their thematic and structural content, offer many elements of worship which are at the same time genuine expressions of devotion and opportunities for a systematic catechesis on the Blessed Virgin Mary. Experience, however, proves that celebrations of the Word should not assume a predominantly intellectual or didactic character. Through hymns, prayers, and participation of the faithful they should allow for simple and familiar expressions of popular piety which speak directly to the hearts of the faithful." (230)

Angelus Domini

195. The *Angelus Domini* is the traditional form used by the faithful to commemorate the holy annunciation of the angel Gabriel to Mary. It is used three times daily: at dawn, mid-day and at dusk. It is a recollection of the salvific event in which the Word became flesh in the womb of the Virgin Mary, through the power of the Holy Spirit in accordance with the salvific plan of the Father.

The recitation of the *Angelus* is deeply rooted in the piety of the Christian faithful, and strengthened by the example of the Roman Pontiffs. In some places changed social conditions hinder its recitation, but in many other parts every effort should be made to maintain and promote this pious custom and at least the recitation of three *Aves*. The *Angelus* "over the centuries has conserved its value and freshness with its simple structure, biblical character [. . .] quasi liturgical rhythm by which the various

times of the day are sanctified, and by its openness to the Paschal Mystery." (231)

It is therefore "desirable that on some occasions, especially in religious communities, in shrines dedicated to the Blessed Virgin, and at meetings or conventions, the *Angelus* be solemnly recited by singing the Ave Maria, proclaiming the Gospel of the Annunciation" (232) and by the ringing of bells.

Regina Coeli

196. By disposition of Benedict XIV (2 April 1742), the *Angelus* is replaced with the antiphon *Regina Coeli* during paschaltide. This antiphon, probably dating from the tenth or eleventh century, (233) happily conjoins the mystery of the Incarnation of the Word (*quem meruisti portare*) with the Paschal event (*resurrexit sicut dixit*). The ecclesial community addresses this antiphon to Mary for the Resurrection of her Son. It adverts to, and depends on, the invitation to joy addressed by Gabriel to the Lord's humble servant who was called to become the Mother of the saving Messiah (*Ave, gratia plena*).

As with the *Angelus,* the recitation of the *Regina Coeli* could sometimes take a solemn form by singing the antiphon and proclaiming the Gospel of the resurrection.

The Rosary

197. The Rosary, or Psalter of the Blessed Virgin Mary, is one of the most excellent prayers to the Mother of God. (234) Thus, "the Roman Pontiffs have repeatedly exhorted the faithful to the frequent recitation of this biblically inspired prayer which is centered on contemplation of the salvific events of Christ's life, and their close association with the his Virgin Mother. The value

and efficacy of this prayer have often been attested by saintly Bishops and those advanced in holiness of life." (235)

The Rosary is essentially a contemplative prayer, which requires "tranquillity of rhythm or even a mental lingering which encourages the faithful to meditate on the mysteries of the Lord's life." (236) *Its use is expressly recommended in the formation and spiritual life of clerics and religious.* (237)

198. *The Blessing for Rosary Beads* (238) indicates the Church's esteem for the Rosary. This rite emphasizes the community nature of the Rosary. In the rite, the blessing of Rosary beads is followed by the blessing of those who meditate on the mysteries of the life, death and resurrection of Our Lord so as to "establish a perfect harmony between prayer and life." (239)

As indicated in the *Benedictionale*, Rosary beads can be blessed publicly, on occasions such as a pilgrimage to a Marian shrine, a feast of Our Lady, especially that of the Holy Rosary, and at the end of the month of October. (240)

199. With due regard for the nature of the Rosary, some suggestions can now be made which could make it more proficuous.

On certain occasions, the recitation of the Rosary could be made more solemn in tone "by introducing those Scriptural passages corresponding with the various mysteries, some parts could be sung, roles could be distributed, and by solemnly opening and closing of prayer." (241)

200. Those who recite a third of the Rosary sometimes assign the various mysteries to particular days: joyful (Monday and Thursday), sorrowful (Tuesday and Friday), glorious (Wednesday, Saturday and Sunday).

Where this system is rigidly adhere to, conflict can arise between the content of the mysteries and that of the Liturgy of the day: the recitation of the sorrowful mysteries on Christmas day, should it fall on a Friday. In cases such as this it can be reckoned that "the liturgical character of a given day takes precedence over the usual assignment of a mystery of the Rosary to a given day; the Rosary is such that, on particular days, it can appropriately substitute meditation on a mystery so as to harmonize this pious practice with the liturgical season." (242) Hence, the faithful act correctly when, for example, they contemplate the arrival of the three Kings on the Solemnity of the Epiphany, rather than the finding of Jesus in the Temple. Clearly, such substitutions can only take place after much careful thought, adherence to Sacred Scripture and liturgical propriety.

201. The custom of making an insertion in the recitation of the Hail Mary, which is an ancient one that has not completely disappeared, has often been recommended by the Pastors of the Church since it encourages meditation and the concurrence of mind and lips. (243)

Insertions of this nature would appear particularly suitable for the repetitive and meditative character of the Rosary. It takes the form of a relative clause following the name of Jesus and refers to the mystery being contemplated. The meditation of the Rosary can be helped by the choice of a short clause of a Scriptural and Liturgical nature, fixed for every decade.

202. "In recommending the value and beauty of the Rosary to the faithful, care should be taken to avoid discrediting other forms of prayer, or of overlooking the exis-

tence of a diversity of other Marian chaplets which have also been approved by the Church." (244) It is also important to avoid inculcating a sense of guilt in those who do not habitually recite the Rosary: "The Rosary is an excellent prayer, in regard to which, however, the faithful should feel free to recite it, in virtue of its inherent beauty." (245)

Litanies of the Blessed Virgin Mary

203. Litanies are to be found among the prayers to the Blessed Virgin recommended by the Magisterium. These consist in a long series of invocations of Our Lady, which follow in a uniform rhythm, thereby creating a stream of prayer characterized by insistent praise and supplication. The invocations, generally very short, have two parts: the first of praise (*Virgo clemens*), the other of supplication (*Ora pro nobis*).

The liturgical books contain two Marian litanies (246): The *Litany of Loreto,* repeatedly recommended by the Roman Pontiffs; and the *Litany for the Coronation of Images of the Blessed Virgin Mary* (247), which can be an appropriate substitute for the other litany on certain occasions .(248)

From a pastoral perspective, a proliferation of litanies would not seem desirable, (249) just as an excessive restriction on them would not take sufficient account of the spiritual riches of some local Churches and religious communities. Hence, the Congregation for Divine Worship and the Discipline of the Sacraments recommends "taking account of some older and newer formulas used in the local Churches or in religious communities which are notable for their structural rigor and the beauty of their invocations." (250) This exhortation, natu-rally, applies to the specific authorities in the local Churches or religious communities.

Following the prescription of Leo XIII that the recitation of the Rosary should be concluded by the Litany of Loreto during the month of October, the false impression has arisen among some of the faithful that the Litany is in some way an appendix to the Rosary. The Litanies are independent acts of worship. They are important acts of homage to the Blessed Virgin Mary, or as processional elements, or form part of a celebration of the Word of God or of other acts of worship.

Consecration and Entrustment to Mary

204. The history of Marian devotion contains many examples of personal or collective acts of "consecration or entrustment to the Blessed Virgin Mary" (*oblatio, servitus, commendatio, dedicatio*). They are reflected in the prayer manuals and statutes of many associations where the formulas and prayers of consecration, or its remembrance, are used.

The Roman Pontiffs have frequently expressed appreciation for the pious practice of "consecration to the Blessed Virgin Mary" and the formulas publicly used by them are well known. (251)

Louis Grignon the Montfort is one of the great masters of the spirituality underlying the act of "consecration to Mary". He " proposed to the faithful consecration to Jesus through Mary, as an effective way of living out their baptismal commitment." (252)

Seen in the light of Christ's words (cf. John 19, 25–27), the act of consecration is a conscious recognition of the singular role of Mary in the Mystery of Christ and of the

Church, of the universal and exemplary importance of her witness to the Gospel, of trust in her intercession, and of the efficacy of her patronage, of the many maternal functions she has, since she is a true mother in the order of grace to each and every one of her children. (253)

It should be recalled, however, that the term "consecration" is used here in a broad and non-technical sense: "the expression is use of 'consecrating children to Our Lady'," by which is intended placing children under her protection and asking her maternal blessing (254) for them." Some suggest the use of the alternative terms "entrustment" or "gift." Liturgical theology and the consequent rigorous use of terminology would suggest reserving the term *consecration* for those self-offerings which have God as their object, and which are characterized by totality and perpetuity, which are guaranteed by the Church's intervention and have as their basis the Sacraments of Baptism and Confirmation.

The faithful should be carefully instructed about the practice of consecration to the Blessed Virgin Mary. While such can give the impression of being a solemn and perpetual act, it is, in reality, only analogously a "consecration to God." It springs from a free, personal, mature, decision taken in relation to the operation of grace and not from a fleeting emotion. It should be expressed in a correct liturgical manner: to the Father, through Christ in the Holy Spirit, imploring the intercession of the Blessed Virgin Mary, to whom we entrust ourselves completely, so as to keep our baptismal commitments and live as her children. The act of consecration should take place outside of the celebration of the Eucharistic Sacrifice, since it is a devotional act which cannot be assimilated to the Liturgy. It should also be borne in mind that the act of consecration to Mary differs substantially from other forms of liturgical consecration.

The Brown Scapular and other Scapulars

205. The history of Marian piety also includes "devotion" to various scapulars, the most common of which is devotion to the Scapular of Our Lady of Mount Carmel. Its use is truly universal and, undoubtedly, its is one of those pious practices which the Council described as "recommended by the Magisterium throughout the centuries." (255)

The Scapular of Mount Carmel is a reduced form of the religious habit of the Order of the Friars of the Blessed Virgin of Mount Carmel. Its use is very diffuse and often independent of the life and spirituality of the Carmelite family.

The Scapular is an external sign of the filial relationship established between the Blessed Virgin Mary, Mother and Queen of Mount Carmel, and the faithful who entrust themselves totally to her protection, who have recourse to her maternal intercession, who are mindful of the primacy of the spiritual life and the need for prayer.

The Scapular is imposed by a special rite of the Church which describes it as "a reminder that in Baptism we have been clothed in Christ, with the assistance of the Blessed Virgin Mary, solicitous for our conformation to the Word Incarnate, to the praise of the Trinity, we may come to our heavenly home wearing our nuptial garb" (256).

The imposition of the Scapular should be celebrated with "the seriousness of its origins. It should not be improvised. The

Scapular should be imposed following a period of preparation during which the faithful are made aware of the nature and ends of the association they are about to join and of the obligations they assume." (257)

Medals

206. The faithful like to wear medals bearing effigies of the Blessed Virgin Mary. These are a witness of faith and a sign of veneration of the Holy Mother of God, as well as of trust in her maternal protection.

The Church blesses such objects of Marian devotion in the belief that "they help to remind the faithful of the love of God, and to increase trust in the Blessed Virgin Mary." (258) The Church also points out that devotion to the Mother of Christ also requires "a coherent witness of life." (259)

Among the various medals of the Blessed Virgin Mary, the most diffuse must be the "Miraculous Medal". Its origins go back to the apparitions in 1830 of Our Lady to St. Catherine Labouré, a humble novice of the Daughters of Charity in Paris. The medal was struck in accordance with the instructions given by Our Lady and has been described as a "Marian microcosm" because of its extraordinary symbolism. It recalls the mystery of Redemption, the love of the Sacred Heart of Jesus and of the Sorrowful Heart of Mary. It signifies the mediatory role of the Blessed Virgin Mary, the mystery of the Church, the relationship between Heaven and earth, this life and eternal life.

St. Maximilian Kolbe (+1941) and the various movements associated with him, have been especially active in further popularizing the miraculous medal. In 1917 he

adopted the miraculous medal as the badge of the "Pious Union of the Militia of the Immaculate Conception" which he founded in Rome while still a young religious of the Conventual Friars Minor.

Like all medals and objects of cult, the Miraculous Medal is never to be regarded as a talisman or lead to any form of blind credulity. (260) The promise of Our Lady that "those who wore the medal will receive great graces" requires a humble and tenacious commitment to the Christian message, faithful and persevering prayer, and a good Christian life.

The "Akathistos" Hymn

207. In the Byzantine tradition, one of the oldest and most revered expressions of Marian devotion is the hymn "Akathistos" — meaning the hymn sung while standing. It is a literary and theological masterpiece, encapsulating in the form of a prayer, the universally held Marian belief of the primitive Church. The hymn is inspired by the Scriptures, the doctrine defined by the Councils of Nicaea (325), Ephesus (431), and Chalcedon (451), and reflects the Greek fathers of the fourth and fifth centuries. It is solemnly celebrated in the Eastern Liturgy on the Fifth Saturday of Lent. The hymn is also sung on many other liturgical occasions and is recommended for the use of the clergy and faithful.

In recent times the Akathistos has been introduced to some communities in the Latin Rite. (261) Some solemn liturgical celebrations of particular ecclesial significance, in the presence of the Pope, have also helped to popularize the use of the hymn in Rome. (262) This very ancient hymn, (263) the mature fruit of the undivided Church's earliest devotion to the Blessed Virgin Mary, constitutes an appeal and invocation for the unity of Christians under the guidance of the Mother of God: "Such richness of praise, accumulated from the various forms of the great tradition of the Church, could help to ensure that she may once again breathe with 'both lungs': the East and the West." (264)

NOTES

(208) CONGREGATION FOR DIVINE WORSHIP, Circular Letter *Guidelines and proposals for the celebration of the Marian Year* (3.4.1987), 67.

(209) Cf. LG 67; Decree *Presbyterorum Ordinis*, 18; Decree *Optatam totius,* 8; Decree *Apostolicam actuositatem*, 4; CIC, canons 76, ' 2, 5; 663, ''2–4; 246 ' 3.

(210) Cf. CCC 971. 2673–2679.

(211) Cf. supra nn. 47–59, 70–75.

(212) Cf. PAUL VI, Apostolic Exhortation *Marialis Cultus,* 1; CONGREGATION FOR DIVINE WORSHIP, Circular Letter *Guidelines and proposals for the celebration of the Marian Year* 7; *Collectio missarum de beata Maria Virgine, Praetanda,* 9–18.

(213) Cf. PAUL VI, Apostolic Exhortation *Marialis Cultus,* 24.

(214) *Ibid,* Intro..

(215) Cf. *Ibid.,* 25–39; CONGREGATION FOR DIVINE WORSHIP, Circular Letter *Guidelines and proposals for the celebration of the Marian Year,* 8.

(216) Cf. *Ibid.,* 8.

(217) Cf. n. 232.

(218) The *Missale Romanum* contains diverse formularies for the celebration of Mass in honor of the Blessed Virgin Mary on Saturday mornings during "ordinary time", the use of which is optional. See also the *Collectio missarum de beata Maria Virgine, Praenotanda* 34–36; and the *Liturgia Horarum* for Saturdays of "ordinary time" which permits the Office of the Blessed Virgin Mary on Saturdays.

(219) Cf. ALCUIN, *Le sacramentaire grégorien,* II, ed. J. DESHUSSES, Editions Universitaires, Fribourg 1988, pp. 25–27 and 45; PL 101, 455–456.

(220) Cf. UMBERTO DE ROMANIS, *De vita regulari,* II, Cap. XXIV, *Quare sabbatum attribuitur Beatae Virgini,* Typis A. BEFANI, Romae 1889, pp. 72–75.

(221) CONGREGATION FOR DIVINE WORSHIP, Circular Letter *Guidelines and proposals for the celebration of the Marian Year,* 5.

(222) An example of which is to be found in *Felicitacion sabatina a Maria Inmaculada* composed by Fr. Manuel Garcia Navarro, who subsequently entered the Carthusians (+1903).

(223) In the Byzantine rite, the liturgy for the month of August is centered on the solemnity of the Dormition of Our Lady (15 August). Until the twelfth century, it was observed as a "Marian month"; in the Coptic rite the "Marian month" is that of kiahk, corresponding approximately to January-February, and is structured in relation to Christmas. In the West the first indications of a Marian month date from the sixteenth century. By the eighteenth century, the Marian month — in its modern sense — is well attested, but during this period the pastors of souls concentrate their apostolic efforts — including Penance and the Eucharist — not so much on the Liturgy but on pious exercises, which were much favored by the faithful.

(224) Cf. CONGREGATION FOR DIVINE WORSHIP, Circular Letter *Guidelines and proposals for the celebration of the Marian Year,* 64–65.

(225) For comments on the Blessed Virgin Mary and the Sacraments of Christian initiation cf. *Ibid.,* 25–31.

(226) SC 108.

(227) Cf. SC 35, 4.

(228) Cf. PAUL VI, Apostolic Exhortation *Marialis Cultus,* 30.

(229) Cf. *Ibid.,* 17; *Collectio missarum de beata Virginis Mariae, Praenotanda ad lectionarium,* 10.

(230) CONGREGATION FOR DIVINE WORSHIP, Circular Letter *Guidelines and proposals for the celebration of the Marian Year,* 10.

(231) Cf. PAUL VI, Apostolic Exhortation *Marialis Cultus,* 41.

(232) CONGREGATION FOR DIVINE WORSHIP, Circular Letter, *Guidelines and proposals for the celebration of the Marian Year,* 61.

(233) The antiphon is found in the twelfth century Antiphonary of the Abbey of San Lupo in Benevento. Cf. R. J. HESBERT (ed.) *Corpus Antiphonalium Officii,* vol. II, Herder, Roma 1965, pp. XX–XXIV; vol. III, Herder, Roma 1968, p. 440.

(234) Regarding indulgences cf. EI, *Aliae concessiones,* 17, p. 62. For a commentary on the Ave Maria cf. CCC 2676–2677.

(235) CONGREGATION FOR DIVINE WORSHIP, Circular Letter *Guidelines and proposals for the celebration of the Marian Year,* 62.

(236) PAUL VI, Apostolic Exhortation *Marialis Cultus,* 62.

(237) Cf. CIC, canons 246, ' 3; 276, ' 2,5; 663, ' 4; CONGREGATION FOR THE CLERGY, *Directory for the Ministry and Life of Priests,* Libreria Editrice Vaticana, Città del Vaticano 1994, 39.

(238) Cf. RITUALE ROMANUM, *de Benedictionibus, Ordo benedictionis coronarum Roasrii,* cit., 1183–1207.

(239) *Ibid.*

(240) Cf. *ibid.,*1183–1184.

(241) CONGREGATION FOR DIVINE WORSHIP, Circular Letter *Guidelines and proposals for the celebration of the Marian Year,* 62, a.

(242) *Ibid.,* 62, b.

(243) Cf. SC 90.

(244) CONGREGATION FOR DIVINE WORSHIP, Circular Letter *Guidelines and proposals for the celebration of the Marian Year,* 62, c.

(245) PAUL VI, Apostolic Exhortation *Marialis Cultus,* 55.

(246) The Litany of Loreto was first included in the *Rituale Romanum* in 1874, as an appendix. Regarding indulgences connected with it cf. EI, Aliae concessiones, 22, p. 68.

(247) Cf. *Ordo coronandi imaginem beatae Mariae Virginis,* Editio Typica, Typis Polyglotis Vaticanis 1981, n. 41, pp. 27–29.

(248) Cf. CONGREGATION FOR DIVINE WORSHIP, Circular Letter *Guidelines and proposals for the celebration of the Marian Year,* 63, c.

(249) Litanies multiplied in the sixteenth century. Often, they were in poor taste and the results of an uninformed piety. In 1601, Clement VIII had the Holy Office issue *Quoniam Multi,* which was intended to curb the excessive and uncontrolled production of litanies. According to the terms of this decree, only the more ancient litanies contained in the Breviary, Missal, Pontifical, and Ritual, as well as the Litany of Loreto, were approved for the use of the faithful (cf. *Magnum Bullarium Romanum,* III, Lugduni 1656, p. 1609).

(250) CONGREGATION FOR DIVINE WORSHIP, Circular Letter *Guidelines and proposals for the celebration of the Marian Year,* 63, d.

(251) See the *Atto di affidamento alla Beata Vergine Maria* pronounced by John Paul II on Sunday, 8 October 2000, together with the Bishops gathered in Rome for the celebration of the Great Jubilee.

(252) JOHN PAUL II, Encyclical Letter, *Redemptoris Mater,* 48.

(253) Cf. LG 61; JOHN PAUL II, Encyclical Letter, *Redemptoris Mater,* 40–44.

(254) CONGREGATION FOR DIVINE WORSHIP, Circular Letter *Guidelines and proposals for the celebration of the Marian Year,* 86.

(255) LG 67; cf. PAUL VI, Letter to Cardinal Silva Henriquez, Papal Legate to the Marian Congress in Santo Domingo, in AAS 57 (1965) 376–379.

(256) CONGREGATION FOR DIVINE WORSHIP, Circular Letter *Guidelines and proposals for the celebration of the Marian Year,* 88.

(257) RITUALE ROMANUM, *De Benedictionibus, Ordo benedictionis et impositionis scapularis,* cit., 1213.

(258) RITUALE ROMANUM, *De benedicionibus, Ordo benedictionis rerum quae ad pietatem et devotionem exercendam destinatur,* cit., 1168.

(259) *Ibid.*

(260) Cf. LG 67; PAUL VI, Apostolic Exhortation *Marialis Cultus,* 38; CCC 2111.

(261) In addition to the *Akathistos* other prayers deriving from the Oriental traditions have received grants of indulgences: cf. EI *Aliae concessiones,* 23, pp. 68–69.

(262) The singing of the *Akathistos* at Santa Maria Maggiore on 7 June 1981 marked the anniversaries of the Councils of Constantinople (381) and Ephesus (431); the hymn was also sung to commemorate the 450th anniversary of the apparitions of Guadalupe in Mexico, 10–12 December 1981. On 25 March 1988, John Paul II presided at Matins in Santa Maria Supra Minerva during which the hymn was sung in the Slavonic Rite. It is again explicitly mentioned among the indulgenced devotions for the Jubilee Year in the Bull *Incarnationis Mysterium.* It was sung at Santa Maria Maggiore on 8 December 2000 in Greek, Old Slavonic, Hungarian, Romanian and Arabic at a solemn celebration with the representatives of the Byzantine Catholic Churches at which John Paul II presided.

(263) While its author is unknown, modern scholarship tends to place its composition some time after the Council of Chalcedon. A Latin version was written down around 800 by Christopher, Bishop of Venice, which had enormous influence on the piety of the Western middle ages. It is associated with Germanus of Constantinople, who died in 733.

(264) JOHN PAUL II, Circular Letter *Redemptoris Mater,* 34.

Appendix B

Excerpt from *Lumen Gentium*

CHAPTER VIII

The Blessed Virgin Mary, Mother of God in the Mystery of Christ and the Church

I. Introduction

52. Wishing in His supreme goodness and wisdom to effect the redemption of the world, "when the fullness of time came, God sent His Son, born of a woman, . . . that we might receive the adoption of sons."(283) "He for us men, and for our salvation, came down from heaven, and was incarnate by the Holy Spirit from the Virgin Mary." [1] This divine mystery of salvation is revealed to us and continued in the Church, which the Lord established as His body. Joined to Christ the Head and in the unity of fellowship with all His saints, the faithful must in the first place reverence the memory "of the glorious ever Virgin Mary, Mother of our God and Lord Jesus Christ." [2]

53. The Virgin Mary, who at the message of the angel received the Word of God in her heart and in her body and gave Life to the world, is acknowledged and honored as being truly the Mother of God and Mother of the Redeemer. Redeemed by reason of the merits of her Son and united to Him by a close and indissoluble tie, she is endowed with the high office and dignity of being the Mother of the Son of God, by which account she is also the beloved daughter of the Father and the temple of the Holy Spirit.

Because of this gift of sublime grace she far surpasses all creatures, both in heaven and on earth. At the same time, however, because she belongs to the offspring of Adam she is one with all those who are to be saved. She is "the mother of the members of Christ . . . having cooperated by charity that faithful might be born in the Church, who are members of that Head." [3] Wherefore she is hailed as a pre-eminent and singular member of the Church, and as its type and excellent exemplar in faith and charity. The Catholic Church, taught by the Holy Spirit, honors her with filial affection and piety as a most beloved mother.

54. Wherefore this Holy Synod, in expounding the doctrine on the Church, in which the divine Redeemer works salvation, intends to describe with diligence both the role of the Blessed Virgin in the mystery of the Incarnate Word and the Mystical Body, and the duties of redeemed mankind toward the Mother of God, who is mother of Christ and mother of men, particularly of the faithful. It does not, however, have it in mind to give a complete doctrine on Mary, nor does it wish to decide those questions which the work of theologians has not yet fully clarified. Those opinions therefore may be lawfully retained which are propounded in Catholic schools concerning her, who occupies a place in the

Church which is the highest after Christ and yet very close to us.[4]

II. *The Role of the Blessed Mother in the Economy of Salvation*

55. The Sacred Scriptures of both the Old and the New Testament, as well as ancient Tradition show the role of the Mother of the Savior in the economy of salvation in an ever clearer light and draw attention to it. The books of the Old Testament describe the history of salvation, by which the coming of Christ into the world was slowly prepared. These earliest documents, as they are read in the Church and are understood in the light of a further and full revelation, bring the figure of the woman, Mother of the Redeemer, into a gradually clearer light. When it is looked at in this way, she is already prophetically foreshadowed in the promise of victory over the serpent which was given to our first parents after their fall into sin. (284) Likewise she is the Virgin who shall conceive and bear a son, whose name will be called Emmanuel. (285) She stands out among the poor and humble of the Lord, who confidently hope for and receive salvation from Him. With her the exalted Daughter of Sion, and after a long expectation of the promise, the times are fulfilled and the new Economy established, when the Son of God took a human nature from her, that He might in the mysteries of His flesh free man from sin.

56. The Father of mercies willed that the incarnation should be preceded by the acceptance of her who was predestined to be the mother of His Son, so that just as a woman contributed to death, so also a woman should contribute to life. That is true in outstanding fashion of the mother of Jesus, who gave to the world Him who is Life itself and who renews all things, and who was enriched by God with the gifts which befit such a role. It is no wonder therefore that the usage prevailed among the Fathers whereby they called the mother of God entirely holy and free from all stain of sin, as though fashioned by the Holy Spirit and formed as a new creature.[5] Adorned from the first instant of her conception with the radiance of an entirely unique holiness, the Virgin of Nazareth is greeted, on God's command, by an angel messenger as "full of grace,"(286) and to the heavenly messenger she replies: "Behold the handmaid of the Lord, be it done unto me according to thy word." (287) Thus Mary, a daughter of Adam, consenting to the divine Word, became the mother of Jesus, the one and only Mediator. Embracing God's salvific will with a full heart and impeded by no sin, she devoted herself totally as a handmaid of the Lord to the person and work of her Son, under Him and with Him, by the grace of almighty God, serving the mystery of redemption. Rightly therefore the holy Fathers see her as used by God not merely in a passive way, but as freely cooperating in the work of human salvation through faith and obedience. For, as St. Irenaeus says, she "being obedient, became the cause of salvation for herself and for the whole human race."[6] Hence not a few of the early Fathers gladly assert in their preaching, "The knot of Eve's disobedience was untied by Mary's obedience; what the virgin Eve bound through her unbelief, the Virgin Mary loosened by her faith."[7] Comparing Mary with Eve, they call her "the Mother of the living,"[8] and still more often they say: "death through Eve, life through Mary."[9]

57. This union of the Mother with the Son in the work of salvation is made manifest from the time of Christ's virginal conception up to His death it is shown first of all when Mary, arising in haste to go to visit Elizabeth, is greeted by her as blessed because of her belief in the promise of salvation and the precursor leaped with joy in the womb of his mother. (288) This union is manifest also at the birth of Our Lord, who did not diminish His mother's virginal integrity but sanctified it,[10] when the Mother of God joyfully showed her firstborn Son to the shepherds and Magi. When she presented Him to the Lord in the temple, making the offering of the poor, she heard Simeon foretelling at the same time that her Son would be a sign of contradiction and that a sword would pierce the mother's soul, that out of many hearts thoughts might be revealed. (289) When the Child Jesus was lost and they had sought Him sorrowing, His parents found Him in the temple, taken up with the things that were His Father's business; and they did not understand the word of their Son. His Mother indeed kept these things to be pondered over in her heart. (290)

58. In the public life of Jesus, Mary makes significant appearances. This is so even at the very beginning, when at the marriage feast of Cana, moved with pity, she brought about by her intercession the beginning of miracles of Jesus the Messiah. (291) In the course of her Son's preaching she received the words whereby in extolling a kingdom beyond the calculations and bonds of flesh and blood, He declared blessed (292) those who heard and kept the word of God, as she was faithfully doing. (293) After this manner the Blessed Virgin advanced in her pilgrimage of faith, and faithfully persevered in her union with her Son unto the cross, where she stood, in keeping with the divine plan, (294) grieving exceedingly with her only begotten Son, uniting herself with a maternal heart with His sacrifice, and lovingly consenting to the immolation of this Victim which she herself had brought forth. Finally, she was given by the same Christ Jesus dying on the cross as a mother to His disciple with these words: "Woman, behold thy son." (295)[11]

59. But since it has pleased God not to manifest solemnly the mystery of the salvation of the human race before He would pour forth the Spirit promised by Christ, we see the apostles before the day of Pentecost "persevering with one mind in prayer with the women and Mary the Mother of Jesus, and with His brethren,"(296) and Mary by her prayers imploring the gift of the Spirit, who had already overshadowed her in the Annunciation. Finally, the Immaculate Virgin, preserved free from all guilt of original sin,[12] on the completion of her earthly sojourn, was taken up body and soul into heavenly glory,[13] and exalted by the Lord as Queen of the universe, that she might be the more fully conformed to her Son, the Lord of lords (297) and the conqueror of sin and death.[14]

III. On the Blessed Virgin and the Church

60. There is but one Mediator as we know from the words of the apostle, "for there is one God and one mediator of God and men, the man Christ Jesus, who gave himself a redemption for all." (298) The maternal duty of Mary toward men in no wise obscures or diminishes this unique mediation of Christ, but rather shows His power. For all the salvific influence of the Blessed Virgin on men originates, not from some inner necessity,

but from the divine pleasure. It flows forth from the superabundance of the merits of Christ, rests on His mediation, depends entirely on it and draws all its power from it. In no way does it impede, but rather does it foster the immediate union of the faithful with Christ.

61. Predestined from eternity by that decree of divine providence which determined the incarnation of the Word to be the Mother of God, the Blessed Virgin was in this earth the virgin Mother of the Redeemer, and above all others and in a singular way the generous associate and humble handmaid of the Lord. She conceived, brought forth and nourished Christ. she presented Him to the Father in the temple, and was united with Him by compassion as He died on the Cross. In this singular way she cooperated by her obedience, faith, hope and burning charity in the work of the Savior in giving back supernatural life to souls. Wherefore she is our mother in the order of grace.

62. This maternity of Mary in the order of grace began with the consent which she gave in faith at the Annunciation and which she sustained without wavering beneath the cross, and lasts until the eternal fulfillment of all the elect. Taken up to heaven she did not lay aside this salvific duty, but by her constant intercession continued to bring us the gifts of eternal salvation.[15] By her maternal charity, she cares for the brethren of her Son, who still journey on earth surrounded by dangers and cultics, until they are led into the happiness of their true home. Therefore the Blessed Virgin is invoked by the Church under the titles of Advocate, Auxiliatrix, Adjutrix, and Mediatrix.[16] This, however, is to be so understood that it neither takes away from nor adds anything to the dignity and efficaciousness of Christ the one Mediator.[17]

For no creature could ever be counted as equal with the Incarnate Word and Redeemer. Just as the priesthood of Christ is shared in various ways both by the ministers and by the faithful, and as the one goodness of God is really communicated in different ways to His creatures, so also the unique mediation of the Redeemer does not exclude but rather gives rise to a manifold cooperation which is but a sharing in this one source.

The Church does not hesitate to profess this subordinate role of Mary. It knows it through unfailing experience of it and commends it to the hearts of the faithful, so that encouraged by this maternal help they may the more intimately adhere to the Mediator and Redeemer.

63. By reason of the gift and role of divine maternity, by which she is united with her Son, the Redeemer, and with His singular graces and functions, the Blessed Virgin is also intimately united with the Church. As St. Ambrose taught, the Mother of God is a type of the Church in the order of faith, charity and perfect union with Christ.[18] For in the mystery of the Church, which is itself rightly called mother and virgin, the Blessed Virgin stands out in eminent and singular fashion as exemplar both of virgin and mother.[19] By her belief and obedience, not knowing man but overshadowed by the Holy Spirit, as the new Eve she brought forth on earth the very Son of the Father, showing an undefiled faith, not in the word of the ancient serpent, but in that of God's messenger. The Son whom she brought forth is He whom God placed as the first-born among many brethren, (299) namely

the faithful, in whose birth and education she cooperates with a maternal love.

64. The Church indeed, contemplating her hidden sanctity, imitating her charity and faithfully fulfilling the Father's will, by receiving the word of God in faith becomes herself a mother. By her preaching she brings forth to a new and immortal life the sons who are born to her in baptism, conceived of the Holy Spirit and born of God. She herself is a virgin, who keeps the faith given to her by her Spouse whole and entire. Imitating the mother of her Lord, and by the power of the Holy Spirit, she keeps with virginal purity an entire faith, a firm hope and a sincere charity.[20]

65. But while in the most holy Virgin the Church has already reached that perfection whereby she is without spot or wrinkle, the followers of Christ still strive to increase in holiness by conquering sin. (300) And so they turn their eyes to Mary who shines forth to the whole community of the elect as the model of virtues. Piously meditating on her and contemplating her in the light of the Word made man, the Church with reverence enters more intimately into the great mystery of the Incarnation and becomes more and more like her Spouse. For Mary, who since her entry into salvation history unites in herself and re-echoes the greatest teachings of the faith as she is proclaimed and venerated, calls the faithful to her Son and His sacrifice and to the love of the Father. Seeking after the glory of Christ, the Church becomes more like her exalted Type, and continually progresses in faith, hope and charity, seeking and doing the will of God in all things. Hence the Church, in her apostolic work also, justly looks to her, who, conceived of the Holy Spirit, brought forth

Christ, who was born of the Virgin that through the Church He may be born and may increase in the hearts of the faithful also. The Virgin in her own life lived an example of that maternal love, by which it behooves that all should be animated who cooperate in the apostolic mission of the Church for the regeneration of men.

IV. The Cult of the Blessed Virgin in the Church

66. Placed by the grace of God, as God's Mother, next to her Son, and exalted above all angels and men, Mary intervened in the mysteries of Christ and is justly honored by a special cult in the Church. Clearly from earliest times the Blessed Virgin is honored under the title of Mother of God, under whose protection the faithful took refuge in all their dangers and necessities.[21] Hence after the Synod of Ephesus the cult of the people of God toward Mary wonderfully increased in veneration and love, in invocation and imitation, according to her own prophetic words: "All generations shall call me blessed, because He that is mighty hath done great things to me." (301) This cult, as it always existed, although it is altogether singular, differs essentially from the cult of adoration which is offered to the Incarnate Word, as well to the Father and the Holy Spirit, and it is most favorable to it. The various forms of piety toward the Mother of God, which the Church within the limits of sound and orthodox doctrine, according to the conditions of time and place, and the nature and ingenuity of the faithful has approved, bring it about that while the Mother is honored, the Son, through whom all things have their being (302) and in whom it has pleased the Father that all fullness should dwell, (303) is rightly known,

loved and glorified and that all His commands are observed.

67. This most Holy Synod deliberately teaches this Catholic doctrine and at the same time admonishes all the sons of the Church that the cult, especially the liturgical cult, of the Blessed Virgin, be generously fostered, and the practices and exercises of piety, recommended by the magisterium of the Church toward her in the course of centuries be made of great moment, and those decrees, which have been given in the early days regarding the cult of images of Christ, the Blessed Virgin and the saints, be religiously observed.[22] But it exhorts theologians and preachers of the divine word to abstain zealously both from all gross exaggerations as well as from petty narrow-mindedness in considering the singular dignity of the Mother of God.[23] Following the study of Sacred Scripture, the Holy Fathers, the doctors and liturgy of the Church, and under the guidance of the Church's magisterium, let them rightly illustrate the duties and privileges of the Blessed Virgin which always look to Christ, the source of all truth, sanctity and piety. Let them assiduously keep away from whatever, either by word or deed, could lead separated brethren or any other into error regarding the true doctrine of the Church. Let the faithful remember moreover that true devotion consists neither in sterile or transitory affection, nor in a certain vain credulity, but proceeds from true faith, by which we are led to know the excellence of the Mother of God, and we are moved to a filial love toward our mother and to the imitation of her virtues.

V. Mary the sign of created hope and solace to the wandering people of God

68. In the interim just as the Mother of Jesus, glorified in body and soul in heaven, is the image and beginning of the Church as it is to be perfected is the world to come, so too does she shine forth on earth, until the day of the Lord shall come, (304) as a sign of sure hope and solace to the people of God during its sojourn on earth.

69. It gives great joy and comfort to this holy and general Synod that even among the separated brethren there are some who give due honor to the Mother of our Lord and Savior, especially among the Orientals, who with devout mind and fervent impulse give honor to the Mother of God, ever virgin.[24] The entire body of the faithful pours forth instant supplications to the Mother of God and Mother of men that she, who aided the beginnings of the Church by her prayers, may now, exalted as she is above all the angels and saints, intercede before her Son in the fellowship of all the saints, until all families of people, whether they are honored with the title of Christian or whether they still do not know the Savior, may be happily gathered together in peace and harmony into one people of God, for the glory of the Most Holy and Undivided Trinity.

NOTES

(1) Credo in Missa Romana: Symbolum Constantinopolitanum: Mansi 3, 566. Cfr. Conc. Ephesinum, ib. 4, 1130 (necnon ib. 2, 665 et 4, 1071); Conc. Chalcedonense, ib. 7, 111–116; Cow. Constantinopolitanum II, ib. 9, 375–396.

(2) Canon Missae Romanae.

(3) S. Augustine, De S. Virginitate. 6: PL 40, 399.

(4) Cfr. Paulus Pp. VI, allocutio in Concilio, die 4 Dec. 1963: AAS 56 (1964) p. 37.

(5) Cfr. S. Germanus Const., Nom. in annunt. Deiparae: PG 98, 328 A; In Dorm. 2: col. 357. Anastasius Antioch., Serm. 2 de Annunt., 2: PG 89, 1377 AB; Serm. 3, 2: col. 1388 C. S. Andrcas Cret. Can. in B. V. Nat. 4: PG 97, 1321 B. In B. V. Nat., 1: col. 812 A. Hom. in dorm. 1: col. 1068 C. — S. Sophronius, Or. 2 in Annunt., 18: PG 87 (3), 3237 BD.

(6) S. Irenaeus, Adv. Hacr. III, 22, 4: PG 7, 9S9 A; Harvey, 2, 123.

(7) S. Irenaeus, ib.; Harvey, 2, 124.

(8) S. Epiphanius, Nacr. 78, 18: PG 42, 728 CD; 729 AB.

(9) S. Hieronymus, Epist. 22, 21: PL 22, 408. Cfr. S. Augwtinus, Serm. Sl, 2, 3: PL 38, 33S; Serm. 232, 2: col. 1108. — S. Cyrillus Hieros., Catech. 12, 15: PG 33, 741 AB. — S. Io. Chrysostomus, In Ps. 44, 7: PG SS, 193. — S. Io. Damascenus, Nom. 2 in dorm. B.M.V., 3: PG 96, 728.

(10) Cfr. Conc. Lateranense anni 649, Can. 3: Mansi 10, 1151. S. Leo M., Epist. ad Flav.: PL S4, 7S9. — Conc. Chalcedonense: Mansi 7, 462. — S. Ambrosius, De inst. virg.: PL 16, 320.

(11) Cfr. Pius XII, Litt. Encycl. Mystici Corporis, 29 iun. 1943: AAS 35 (1943) pp. 247–248.

(12) Cfr. Pius IX, Bulla Ineffabilis 8 Dec. 1854: acta Pii IX, I, I, p. 616; Denz. 1641 (2803).

(13) Cfr. Pius XII, Const. Apost. Munificensissimus, 1 no. 1950: AAS 42 (1950) ú Denz. 2333 (3903). Cfr. S. Io. Damascenus, Enc. in dorm. Dei genitricis, Hom. 2 et 3: PG 96, 721–761, speciatim col. 728 B. — S. Germanus Constantinop., in S. Dei gen. dorm. Serm. 1: PG 98 (6), 340–348; Serm. 3:

col. 361. — S. Modestus Hier., In dorm. SS. Deiparae: PG 86 (2), 3277–3312.

(14) Cfr. Pius XII Litt. Encycl. Ad caeli Reginam, 11 Oct. 1954: AAS 46 (1954), pp. 633–636; Denz. 3913 ss. Cfr. S. Andreas Cret., Hom. 3 in dorm. SS. Deiparae: PG 97, 1089–1109. — S. Io. Damascenus, De fide orth., IV, 14: PG 94, 1153–1161.

(15) Cfr. Kleutgen, textus reformstus De mysterio Verbi incarnati, cap. IV: Mansi 53, 290. cfr. S. Andreas Cret., In nat. Mariac, sermo 4: PG 97, 865 A. — S. Germanus Constantinop., In annunt. Deiparae: PG 98, 321 BC. In dorm. Deiparae, III: col. 361 D. S. Io. Damascenus, In dorm. B. V. Mariae, Hom. 1, 8: PG 96, 712 BC–713 A.

(16) Cfr. Leo XIII, Litt. Encycl. Adiutricem populi, 5 sept. 1895: ASS 15 (1895–96), p. 303. — S. Pius X, Litt. Encycl. Ad diem illum, 2 Febr. 1904: Acta, I, p. 154 Denz. 1978 a (3370) . Pius XI, Litt. Encycl. Miserentissimus, 8 Maii 1928: AAS 20 (1928) p. 178. Pius XII, Nuntius Radioph., 13 Maii 1946: AAS 38 (1946) p. 266.

(17) S. Ambrosius, Epist. 63: PL 16, 1218.

(18) S. Ambrosius, Expos. Lc. II, 7: PL 15, 1555.

(19) Cfr. Ps.–Petrus Dam. Serm. 63: PL 144, 861 AB. Godefridus a S. Victore. In nat. B. M., Ms. Paris, Mazarine, 1002, fol. 109 r. Gerhohus Reich., De gloria et honore Filii hominis, 10: PL 194, 1105AB.

(20) S. Ambrosius, l. c. et Expos. Lc. X, 24–25: PL 15, 1810. S. Augustinus, In lo. Tr. 13, 12: PL 35 1499. Cfr. Serm. 191, 2, 3: PL 38 1010; etc. Cfr. etiam Ven. Beda, In Lc. Expos. I, cap. 2: PL 92, 330. Isaac de Stella, Serm. 51. PL 194, 1863 A.

(21) Sub tuum praesidium.

(22) Conc. Nicaenum II, anno 787: Mansi 13. 378–379; Denz. 302 (600–601) . Conc. Trident., sess. 2S: Mansi 33, 171–172.

(23) Cfr. Pius XII, Nunius radioph., 24 Oct. 1954: AAS 46 (1954) p. 679. Litt. Encycl. Ad caeli Reginam, 11 Oct. 1954: AAS 46 (1954) p. 637.

(24) Cfr. Pius XI, Litt. Encycl. Ecclesiam Dei, 12 nov. 1923: AAS 15 (1923) p. 581. Pius XII, Litt. Encycl. Fulgens corona, 8 Sept. 1953: AAS 45 (1953) pp. 590–591.

Scripture References

283 Gal. 4:4–5.
284 Cf. Gen. 3:15.
285 Cf Is 7:14; cf. Mich. 5:2–3; Mt. 1:22–23.
286 Cf. Lk. 1:28.
287 Lk. 1:38.
288 Cf. Lk. 1:41–45.
289 Cf. Lk. 2:34–35.
290 Cf. Lk. 2:41–51.
291 Cf. Jn. 2:1-11.

292 Cf. Mk. 3:35; 27–28.
293 Cf. Lk. 2:19, 51.
294 Cf. Jn. 19:25.
295 Cf. Jn. 19:26–27.
296 Acts 1:14.
297 Cf. Apoc.19:16
298 1 Tim. 2:5-6.
299 Rom. 8:29.
300 Cf. Eph. 5:27.
301 Lk. 1:48.

Index

A

Academia Mariana:
    Pontifical International Marian
        Academy – 225-226
Ad Caeli Reginam – **9**
    Coronation of the Blessed
        Virgin Mary – 73 -74
    Queenship of Mary – 234
Ad Diem Illum Laetissimum – **10**
Ad Gentes: Decree On the Mission
    Activity of the Church:
    Vatican II – 284
Ad Jesum Per Mariam – **11**
Admirable Heart of Mary, The – **11**
Admirable Secret of the Most Holy
    Rosary – **12**
Adoration – **12**
Advocate of Grace – **12-14**
Africa:
    Africa, Our Lady of – 14
    Help of Christians, Our Lady, –
      122-123
Africa, Our Lady of – **14**
Agreda, Venerable Mary of –**14**
    Alexander VII –18
    Most Blessed Sacrament, Our
      Lady of the – 191
Ain-Karin – **15**
Akathistos – **16**
    Eastern Church, Mary in the –
      99
Akita, Our Lady of – **17**
Albania:
    Good Counsel, Our Lady of –
      114
Alexandarian Rite:
    Eastern Church, Mary in the –
      99
Alexander VII – **18**
All Souls' Rosary – **18**
Alma Redemptoris Mater – **18-19**
Almudena, Our Lady of – **19**
Altagracia, Our Lady of – **19**
Altötting, Our Lady of – **20**
Ancestors of Mary – **20**
Ancrene Riwle:
    Alma Redemptoris Mater – 18

Angelic Salutation – **20**
Angels, Our Lady of the – **20-21**
Angelus – **21**
Anglican Church, Mary in the –
    22
    Walsingham, Our Lady of – 295
Anglican-Roman Catholic Interna-
    tional Commission
      Anglican Church,
        Mary in the – 22;
      Book of Common Prayer,
        Mary in the – 48
Anna – **23**
    Scripture, Mary in – 256-260
Annociade – **23**
Annunciata, The – **23**
Annunciation – **23-24**
    Annociade – 23
    Fiat in the Name of Humanity
      –107
    Marymas –183
Annunciation Bread – **24**
Antigua, Our Lady of – **24**
Antiochan Rite:
    Eastern Church, Mary in the –
      99
Antiphons of Our Lady – **25**
    Alma Redemptoris Mater – 18
    Hymns, Marian – 129
Antipolo, Our Lady of – **25-26**
    Brown Virgin – 50
Aparecida, Our Lady – **26**
Apocryphal Writing, Mary in – **26-
28**
Apostles – **28**
Apostleship of Prayer:
    Morning Offering – 190
Apostolate of Mary:
    Blue Army – 48
Apostolic Rosary – **28**
Apostolicam Actuositatem (Decree
    On the Apostolate of the Laity):
      Vatican II – 285
Apparitions of Mary – **28**
Arantzazu, Our Lady of – **29**
Arcachon, Our Lady of – **29**
Archaeology and Mary – **30**
Argentina:

Knots, The Virgin Who Unties
    – 151
    Lujan, Our Lady of – 171
Ark of the Covenant – **30**
Armenian Rite:
    Eastern Church, Mary in the –
      99
Art, Mary in – **31**
    Eastern Church, Mary in the –
      99
    Eleousa and Oumilenie – 100
    Icons – 131
    Panagia – 213
Associate of the Redeemer – **33**
Assumption – **33-34**
    Glorified Body – 112-113
    La Conquistadora – 153
Assumption, Feast of the –**35-36**
Athanasian Creed – **36**
Atocha, Our Lady of –**36-37**
Atonement, Our Lady of – **37-38**
Augustinians:
    Consolation, Our Lady of – 70-
      71
    Perpetual Help, Our Lady of –
      218-219
Australia:
    Help of Christians,
      Our Lady, – 122-123
Austria:
    Mariazell, Our Lady of – 179-
      180
Ave Maria – **38**
Ave Maria Salutation – **38**
Ave Maris Stella – **39**
    Star of the Sea – 272
Ave Regina Caelorum – **39-40**
    Antiphons of Our Lady – 25
Avioth, Our Lady of – **40**

B

Baconthorpe, John:
    Carmel, Our Lady of Mount –
      54-56
Bai Dau, Our Lady of – **41**
Banneux, Our Lady of – **41**
Barnabite Fathers:

Our Lady, Mother of Divine
Providence – 93
Basilica of the National Shrine of
the Immaculate Conception:
See index listing at *Immaculate
Conception, Basilica of the
National Shrine of the*
Battle of Lepanto:
Help of Christians, Our Lady –
122-123
Battle of Vienna:
Help of Christians, Our Lady –
122-123
Beads – **41**
Beauraing, Our Lady of – **42**
Beco, Mariette:
Banneux, Our Lady of – 41
Belgium:
Banneux, Our Lady of – 41
Beauraing, Our Lady of – 42
Hal, Our Lady of – 121
Benedict XV – **42**
Benedict XVI – **43**
Benedictus:
Canticle – 52
Birth of Mary – **44**
Bistrica, Our Lady of – **45**
Black Madonna, The:
Czestochowa, Our Lady of – 79
Black Madonnas – **46**
Art, Mary in – 33
Einsiedeln, Our Lady of – 99
Hal, Our Lady of – 121
Le Puy, Our Lady of – 159
Montserrat – 190
Black Virgin, The:
Chartes, Our Lady of – 62
Blackbirds, Our Lady of the – **46**
Blagovescenije Marii:
Annunciation – 23-24
Blessed Roses – **47**
Blessed Sacrament:
Most Blessed Sacrament, Our
Lady of the – 191
Blessed (Title of Mary) – **47**
Blue:
Liturgical Colors for Marian
Feasts – 168
Blue Army – **48**
Pilgrim Virgin Statue – 221
Bolivia:
Copacabana, Our Lady of – 71
Book of Common Prayer, Mary in
the – **48**
Bosnia-Herzegovina:

Medjugorje, Our Lady of –186;
Velika Gospa – 286
Boulogne, Our Lady of – **48-49**
Bowed Head, Our Lady of the;
Grace, Our Lady of – 118
Brazil:
Aparecida, Our Lady – 26
Lujan, Our Lady of – 171
Brentano, Clemens:
Emmerich, Blessed Anne
Catherine –100
Brigettine Office – **49**
Brigettine Rosary – 49
Brothers and Sisters of Jesus:
Virginity of Mary, Perpetual –
290-292
Brown One, The Little:
Guadalupe, Our Lady of – 118
Brown Scapular:
Carmel, Our Lady of Mount –
54-56
Brown Scapular Confraternity of
Carmel: Confraternity,
Archconfraternity – 68
Brown Virgin – **50**
Byzantine Rite:
Akathistos – 16
Angelic Salutation – 21
Assumption, Feast of the – 35-
36
Eastern Church, Mary in the –
99;
Entreaty (or Supplication) of
the Mother of God
–102;
Feasts of Mary – 107
Girdle of Our Lady, Feast of
the – 112
Help of Christians, Our Lady
– 122-123
Hypapante –129

C

Caacupé, Our Lady of the Miracles
of – 51
Calvin, John:
Reformation and Mary –
237
Trent, Council of – 277
Camairago ("Shrine of the Virgin
of the Fountain"):
Caravaggio, Our Lady of – 53
Canada:
Cape, Our Lady of the – 52-53
Candelaria – **51-52**

Candlemas – **52**
Canterbury Tales, The:
Alma Redemptoris Mater –18
Boulogne, Our Lady of – 48-49
Canticle – **52**
Hannah's Hymn of Praise – 121
Hymns, Marian –129
Magnificat –174
Nunc Dimittis – 207
Cap-de-la-Madeleine, Shrine of:
Cape, Our Lady of the – 52-53
Cape, Our Lady of the – **52-53**
Caravaggio, Our Lady of – **53**
Caregiver, Our Lady's – **53**
Ephesus – 102
Carmel of the Maipú, Our Lady of
– **54**
Carmel, Mount – **54**
Carmel, Our Lady of Mount – **54-
56**
Novena to Our Lady of Mount
Carmel – 202
Carmelites:
Carmel, Our Lady of Mount –
54-56
Casa Santa Maria – **56**
Casimir's Hymn, St. – **57**
Catacomb:
Art, Mary in – 31
Catacombs – **57**
La Leche, Our Lady of – 153
Catechism of the Catholic Church,
Mary in the – **58-59**
Catholic Foreign Mission Society
of America:
Maryknoll – 182
Cause of Our Joy – **59**
Liesse, Our Lady of – 159
Cenacle, Our Lady of the – **59**
Most Blessed Sacrament, Our
Lady of the – 191
Cerlango ("Church of the Virgin
of Pozzenta"):
Caravaggio, Our Lady of – 53
Cerro San Cristóbal,
La Virgen del – **60**
Chaldean Rite:
Eastern Church, Mary in the –
99
Chaminade, Blessed William
Joseph:
Daughters of Mary Immaculate
– 85
Marian Library/

International Marian
Research Center – 176
Chapi, Our Lady of – **60**
Candelaria – 51
Chaplet – **60**
Brigettine Rosary – 49
Charity of El Cobre,
Our Lady of – **61**
Chartes, Our Lady of – **61-62**
Chaucer:
Alma Redemptoris Mater – 18
Chevalier, Jules:
Sacred Heart,
Our Lady of the – 247
Child of Mary – **62**
Children of Mary – **62**
Virginity of Mary, Perpetual –
292
Chile:
Carmel of the Maipú,
Our Lady of – 54
*Cerro San Cristóbal,
La Virgen del* – 60
China:
China, Our Lady of – 62-63
Zo-se, Our Lady of – 298
China, Our Lady of – **62-63**
Chiquinquira, Our Lady of – **63-
64**
Chosen Daughter of the Father –
64
Christi Matri – **64**
Paul VI – 214
Christian Life Community – **64-
65**
Christokos:
Mother of God –194
Circumcision, Feast of – **65**
Solemnity of Mary,
Mother of God – 266
Claretians – **65**
Cocharcas, Our Lady of – **65**
Candelaria – 51
Coins – **66**
*Collections of Masses of the Blessed
Virgin Mary* – 66
Colors, Marian:
Art, Mary in – 31
Colombia:
Chiquinquira, Our Lady of –
63-64
Column, St. Mary's – **66**
Comforter of the Afflicted – **66**
Kevelaer, Our Lady of – 149
Communion of Saints – **67**

Company of Mary – **67**
Composers of Marian music:
Hymns, Marian – 129
Conference, Marian – **67**
Confidence, Our Lady of – **67**
Confraternity, Archconfraternity –
68
Confraternity:
of the Holy Rosary:
Cape, Our Lady of the –
52-53
of the Immaculate Conception
of the Most Blessed Virgin
Mary: Confraternity,
Archconfraternity – 68
of the Immaculate Conception
of Our Lady of Lourdes:
Confraternity,
Archconfraternity – 68
of the Lady of All Nations:
Confraternity,
Archconfraternity – 68
of Mary, Help of Christians:
Confraternity
Archconfraternity – 68
of Mary, Queen of All Hearts:
Confraternity,
Archconfraternity – 68
of Our Lady of Sorrows:
Confraternity,
Archconfraternity – 68
of Our Mother of Perpetual
Help: Confraternity,
Archconfraternity – 68
Congregation of the
Blessed Sacrament:
Most Blessed Sacrament,
Our Lady of the –191
Congregations of Christian
Brothers: Liesse, Our Lady of
– 159
Congress, Marian – **68-69**
Consecration of World:
Immaculate Heart of Mary –
136
Consecration to Jesus Through
Mary – **69-70**
Consolation, Our Lady of – **70**
Consolation,
Chaplet of Our Lady of – **70**
Consueverunt Romani Pontifices:
Rosary – 241-243
Copacabana, Our Lady of – **71-72**
Candelaria – 51
Cocharcas, Our Lady of – **65**

Cord – **72**
Co-Redemptrix, Co-Redemptorist
– **72**
Benedict XVI – 43
Coromoto, Our Lady of – **73**
Corona of Our Mother of
Consolation – **73**
Coronation of the Blessed Virgin
Mary – **73-74**
May – 183-184
Costa Rica:
Angels, Our Lady of the – 21
Croatia:
Bistrica, Our Lady of – 46
Velika Gospa – 286
Crosier Fathers:
Crosier Rosary –74-75
Crosier Rosary – **74-75**
Crown of the Blessed Virgin Mary,
Little – **75**
Crown of the Seven Decades – **77**
Crowning of Mary – **78**
Cuba:
Charity of El Cobre, Our Lady
of – 61
Cuapa, Nicaragua – **78-79**
Cult – **79**
Czech:
Hostyn, Our Lady of – 127
Czestochowa, Our Lady of –
79-81
Marians of the Immaculate
Conception – 179
Czestochowa, Chaplet of
Our Lady of – **79**

D

Daily, Daily Sing to Mary – **83**
Dalmatia:
Loreto, Holy House of – 169
Velika Gospa – 286
Dark Virgin of the Lake:
Copacabana, Our Lady of – 71
Daughter of Zion – **83**
Daughters
of Mary, Help of Christians –
85
of Mary Immaculate – **85**
of Our Lady of
Compassion – **86**
of Our Lady of Mercy – **86**
of Our Lady of the Holy
Rosary – **86**
of Our Lady of the Sacred
Heart – **87**

Dayton, University of:
    Marian Library/International
        Marian Research Center –
        176
de Chemino, Jean:
    Carmel, Our Lady of Mount –
        54-56
Death of Mary – **87**
Decade – **87**
Dedication of Basilica of St. Mary
    Major – **87**
Deipara – **87**
De la Roche (de Rupe), O.P.,
    Blessed Alan – **87-88**
    Dominicans – 96
Descendimiento:
    Desolata –88
    Soledad, Virgen de – 266
Desolata – **88**
Deus Caritas Est:
    Benedict XVI – 43
Devotions, Marian – **88-91**
*Directory on Popular Piety and
    Liturgy* – **299-310**
    Popular Piety – 227
Divina Infantita – **91**
*Divine Life of the Most Holy Virgin,
    The:* Agreda, Venerable Mary
    of –15
Divine Mercy
    Marian Helpers, Association of
        – 176
Divine Praises – **92**
    Spouses of the Blessed Virgin
        Mary – 269
Divine Privilege – **92**
Divine Providence, Our Lady,
    Mother of – **92-94**
Doctors of the Church, Marian –
    94-95
Doctrine, Development of – **95**
Doctrines of the Church, Marian –
    95
Dominican Republic
    Altagracia, Our Lady of – 19
Dominicans – **96**
    De la Roche (de Rupe), O.P.,
        Blessed Alan – 87-88
    Queen of Preachers – 234
    Rosary, Dominican – 243
    Rosary, Our Lady of the – 245
    Rosary Sunday– 246
    Rose – 246
Dormition of Mary – **97**

Assumption, Feast of the – 35-
    36
dos Santos, Lucia
    Fatima, Our Lady of – 105-106
Dowry, Our Lady's – **97**
Dragon in Apocalypse:
    Scripture, Mary in – 256-260
Duff, Frank:
    Legion of Mary – 157
Dulia, hyperdulia, latria:
    Devotions, Marian – 91

E

Eastern Church, Mary in the – **99**
Ecuador:
    Quinche, Our Lady of – 235
Egypt, Flight into:
    Scripture, Mary in – 256-260
    Via Matris – 288
    *Sub Tuum Praesidium – 272-
    273*
Einsiedeln, Our Lady of – **99**
El Salvador:
    Peace, Our Lady of – 216
Eleousa and *Oumilenie* – **100**
    Art, Mary in – 32
    Grace, Our Lady of – 118
    Vladimir, Our Lady of – 293
Elizabeth and Zechariah:
    Scripture, Mary in – 256-260
Emblems of Mary – **100**
Emmanuel:
    Virgin Mother of Emmanuel –
        290
Emmerich, Blessed Anne
        Catherine – **100**
    Ephesus – 102
    Panagia – 213
    Tomb of Mary – 276
Encyclicals, Marian – 101
    Leo XIII –101
    St. Pius X – 101
    Pius XI – 102
    Pius XII –102
    John XXIII –102
    John Paul II – 102
England:
    Atonement, Our Lady of – 27
    Boulogne, Our Lady of – 48-49
    Carmel, Our Lady of Mount –
        54-56
    Dowry, Our Lady's – 97
    Walsingham, Our Lady of –
        295

Entreaty (or Supplication) of the
    Mother of God –**102**
Ephesus – **102**
    Panagia – 213
    Tomb of Mary – 276
Ephesus, Council of – **103**
    Lux Veritatis – 171
    Mother of God – 192
    Solemnity of Mary, Mother of
        God – 266
Ephesus, Our Lady of – **103**
Eschatological Icon of the Church
    – **103**
Evangelical and Fundamentalist
    Churches, Mary in – **103**
Evangelismos:
    Annunciation – 23-24
Eve:
    Knots, The Virgin Who Unties
        – 151
    New Eve – 198
    Original Sin – 210

F

Family Rosary Crusade – **105**
Fatima, Our Lady of – **105-106**
    Blue Army– 48
    First Saturday Devotion – 108
Feast of Swallows:
    Annunciation – 23-24
Feasts of Mary – **107**
Fiat in the Name of Humanity –
    107
Fifteen Saturdays – **107**
Finding in the Temple:
    Rosary – 241-243
    Scripture, Mary in – 256-260
First Saturday Devotion – **108**
Florence, Italy:
    Annunciata, The – 23
Flores de Mayo – **108**
Florida:
    La Leche, Our Lady of – 153
Flos Carmeli – **108**
Flower of Carmel:
    Flos Carmeli –108
Flowers, Plants:
    Mary Garden – 181
Fountain
    of Beauty:
        Litany of Mary, Queen –
            163
    of Elijah:
        Carmel, Our Lady of Mount
            – 54-56

Fountain, Our Lady of the:
 Caravaggio, Our Lady of – 53
France:
 Arcachon, Our Lady of – 29
 Avioth, Our Lady of – 40
 Boulogne, Our Lady of – 48-49
 Chartes, Our Lady of – 61-62
 Hope, Our Lady of – 127
 Le Puy, Our Lady of – 159
 Lourdes, Our Lady of – 169
 Pellevoisin, Our Lady of – 216-217
 Pontmain, Our Lady of – 226
Franciscan Crown Rosary:
 Rosary of the Seven Joys of Our Lady – 245
Franciscans – 109
 Pontifical International Marian Academy – 226
 Portiuncula – 227
 Zapopan, Our Lady of –297
Friar Servants of Mary:
 Annunciata, The – 23
Fullness of Grace, Mary's – 109

G

Gabriel
 Angelic Salutation – 20
 Annunciation – 23-24
 Apocryphal Writing, Mary in – 26
 Fiat in the Name of Humanity – 107
Gabriel Bell – 111
Garabandal – 111
Gate, Virgin of the:
 Iviron, Our Lady of – 142
Gate of Heaven – 111
Gaudium et Spes (Pastoral Constitution On the Church In the Modern World)
 Vatican II –286
Genealogy of Mary:
 Ancestors of Mary – 20
Germany:
 Altötting, Our Lady of – 20
 Column, St. Mary's – 66
 Golden Saturdays, The – 113
 Good Counsel, Our Lady of – 114-115
 Kevelaer, Our Lady of –149
 Knots, The Virgin Who Unties – 151
Gietrzwald, Poland – 111

Girdle of Our Lady, Feast of the – 112
Glories of Mary, The – 112
Glorified Body – 112-113
Glorious Mother of God:
 Litany of Mary, Queen – 163
Glorious Mysteries:
 Rosary – 241-243
Glory of the Holy Spirit:
 Litany of Mary, Queen –163
Glory of the Human Race – 113
Golden Saturdays, The – 113
Good Counsel, Our Lady of – 114
Good Friday:
 Desolata – 88
Good Health, Our Lady of – 116
Good Hope, Our Lady of:
 Confidence, Our Lady of – 67
Good Remedy, Our Lady of – 117
 Novena to Our Lady of Good Remedy – 201
Gospel of Pseudo-Matthew
 Apocryphal Writing, Mary in – 26
Grace – 118
Grace, Our Lady of – 118
 Velika Gospa – 286
Graymoor:
 Atonement, Our Lady of – 37-38
Great Return, Our Lady of the:
 Boulogne, Our Lady of – 48-49
Green Scapular:
 Scapular of the Immaculate Heart –253
Gregory XIII:
 Christian Life Community – 64-65
Griteria:
 Immaculate Conception of El Viejo, Our Lady of the – 135-136
Grotto, The:
 Sorrowful Mother, National Sanctuary of Our – 267
Guadalupe, Our Lady of – 118-120
 Brown Virgin – 50
Guard of Honor of the Immaculate Heart of Mary – 120
Guatemala:
 Rosary, Our Lady of the – 245

H

Hail, Holy Queen:

Salve Regina – 252
Hail Mary:
 Ave Maria – 38
Hail Queen of the Heavens:
 Ave Regina Caelorum – 39-40
Hal, Our Lady of – 121
Handmaid of the Lord – 121
 Annunciation – 23-24
Hannah's Hymn of Praise – 121-122
Health of the Sick:
 Litany of the Blessed Virgin Mary – 160
Help of Christians, Our Lady – 122-123
 China, Our Lady of – 62-63
Help of the Sick, Our Lady:
 Scapular of St. Camillus – 255
Heresy – 123
Herologian:
 Athanasian Creed – 36
Herman the Cripple:
 Alma Redemptoris Mater –18
Hermits, Abbey of Our Lady of the:
 Einsiedeln, Our Lady of – 99
Herod – 124
Heroine of the Quran – 124
Hodegitria – 124
 Art, Mary in – 31
Holy Family – 124
Holy Innocents –125
Holy Mary –125
Holy Mother of God – 126
Holy Name of Mary – 126
Holy Rosary, Feast of the:
 Blessed Roses – 47
Holy Spirit and Mary – 126-127
 Incarnation – 137
 Spouses of the Blessed Virgin Mary – 268
Holy Virgin of Virgins – 127
Honduras:
 Suyapa, Our Lady of – 273
Honestis, Blessed Peter de:
 Children of Mary – 63
Hope, Our Lady of – 127
 Pontmain, Our Lady of – 226
Hostyn, Our Lady of – 127-128
Hours of Our Lady – 128
House, Mary's:
 Loreto, Holy House of – 169
House of Gold – 128
 Litany of the Blessed Virgin Mary – 160

Hymns, Marian – **128**
Akathistos – 16
Hypapante – **129**
Hyperdulia – **129**

I

Icons – **131**
Iconstasis –**131**
Id Albishara:
　Annunciation – 23-24
Idolatry – **131**
Illyricus of Osimo, Blessed
　Thomas: Arcachon,
　　Our Lady of – 29
Imitation of Christ:
　Imitation of Our Lady – 131
Imitation of Our Lady – 131
Immaculate Conception – **131-
　133**
　Ad Caeli Reginam – 9
　Ad Diem Illum Laetissimum – 10
　Redemptoris Mater – 13
　Advocate of Grace – 12-14
　Alexander VII – 18
　Apocryphal Writing, Mary in –
　　26
　*Cerro San Cristóbal, La Virgen
　　del* – 60
　Grace – 118
　Lourdes, Our Lady of – 170
　Novena in Honor of the Immac-
　　ulate Conception – 200
　Novena to the Immaculate Con-
　　ception – 201
　Original Sin – 210
Immaculate Conception, Archcon-
　fraternity of the – **133**
Immaculate Conception, Basilica
　of the National Shrine of the –
　　133-134
　Catacombs – 57
　China, Our Lady of – 62-63
　Our Lady, Mother of Divine
　　Providence – 93-94
　Ephesus, Our Lady of – 103
　Good Health, Our Lady of –
　　117
　Hostyn, Our Lady of – 128
　Mary Garden –181
Immaculate Conception, Chaplet
　of the – **133**
Immaculate Conception of El
　Viejo, Our Lady of the –
　　135-136

Immaculate Conception, Feast of
　the – **135**
Immaculate Heart of Mary – **136**
　Admirable Heart of Mary, The –
　　11
　Claretians – 65
Immaculate Heart of Mary, Chap-
　let of the – **137**
Incarnation – **137**
Incomparable Virgin Mary, The –
　137-138
India:
　Good Health, Our Lady of –
　　116
Ineffabilis Deus –**138**
　Fullness of Grace, Mary's – 109
Infancy Narratives – **138**
　Scripture, Mary in – 256-260
Ingrascentibus malis:
　Pius XI – 223
Inkpot, Our Lady of the:
　Star of the Sea – 272
Institute of the Blessed Virgin
　Mary – **138**
Institution of the First Monks,
　The: Carmel, Our Lady of
　　Mount – 54-56
Intercession of Mary –**138-140**
International Marian Research
　Center:
　Marian Library/International
　　Marian Research Center –
　　176
International Union of Prayer:
　Banneux, Our Lady of – 41
Ireland:
　Knock, Our Lady of – 150
Irish Penal Rosary – 140
Islam, Mary in – **140-141**
Italy:
　Caravaggio, Our Lady of – 53
Iviron, Our Lady of – **141-142**

J

Janssoone, O.F.M, Frederic:
　Cape, Our Lady of the – 52-53
Japan:
　Akita, Our Lady of – 17
Jasna Gora, Our Lady of:
　Czestochowa, Our Lady of – 79-
　　81
Jesse Tree:
　Ancestors of Mary – 20
Jesuits – 143

Christian Life Community – 64-
　65
Good Counsel, Our Lady of –
　114
John XXII:
　Angelus – 21
John XXIII – **143-145**
　Encyclicals, Marian – 102
John Paul II – **145-147**
　Advocate of Grace – 13-14
　Associate of the Redeemer – 33
　Czestochowa, Our Lady of –
　　79-81
　Daughter of Zion – 83
　Encyclicals, Marian –101-102
　Eschatological Icon of the
　　Church – 103
　Fatima, Our Lady of – 105-106
　Totus Tuus – 277
Jordan of Saxony:
　Antiphons of Our Lady – 25
Joyful Mysteries:
　Rosary – 241-243
Joy of Israel – **147**
Joy, Our Lady of – **147**
Joys of Mary – **147-148**

K

Kateri Indian Rosary – **149**
Kempis, Thomas à:
　Imitation of Our Lady – 131
Keng-Hsin, S.V.D., Thomas Tien:
　China, Our Lady of – 62-63
Kevelaer, Our Lady of – **149**
Kibeho (Rwanda), Our Lady of –
　149
Knights of Columbus:
　Bai Dau, Our Lady of – 41
　Pilgrim Virgin Statue – 221
Knock, Our Lady of – **150**
Knots, The Virgin Who Unties –
　151
Krolowa Polski (Queen of Poland):
　Czestochowa, Our Lady of – 79-
　　81

L

La Chapelle, Our Lady of – **153**
La Conquistadora – **153**
La Coyeta:
　Copacabana, Our Lady of – 71-
　　72
La Leche, Our Lady of – **153-154**
La Morenita:

Guadalupe, Our Lady of – 118-120

La Naval – **154**

La Negrita:
Angels, Our Lady of the – 20-21

La Salette, Our Lady of – **154**

La Vang, Our Lady of – **155**

La Virgen Hallade:
Antigua, Our Lady of – 24

Ladder Rosary – **156**

Lady Altar – **157**

Lady Chapel – **157**

Lady Day:
Annunciation – 23-24

Lakes, Our Lady of St. John of the:
San Juan, Our Lady of – 252

Lala Meriem:
Africa, Our Lady of – 14

Lanteri, Bruno:
Oblates of the Virgin Mary – 209

Last Supper:
Cenacle, Our Lady of the – 59

Laudesi – **157**

Legends of Mary – **157**

Legion of Mary – **157-158**
Column, St. Mary's – 66
Slavery of Mary, Slave of Mary – 264

Leo XIII – **158-159**
Encyclicals, Marian –101-102
Good Counsel, Our Lady of – 114

Le Puy, Our Lady of – **159**
Einsiedeln, Our Lady of – 99

Liesse, Our Lady of – **159**

Life of the Blessed Virgin Mary, The:
Emmerich, Blessed Anne Catherine – 100

Lily:
Symbols of Mary – 273

Litany – **159**

Litany of the Blessed Virgin Mary – **160**
Ark of the Covenant – 31
Cause of Our Joy – 59
Devotions, Marian – 90
Gate of Heaven –111
Mirror of Justice – 189
Morning Star – 191
Mother Thrice Admirable – 194
Mystical Rose – 195
Singular Vessel of Devotion – 263
Spiritual Vessel – 268

Tower of David, Tower of Ivory – 277

Vessel of Honor – 287

Litany of Loreto:
Litany of the Blessed Virgin Mary –160

Litany of Mary, Eleventh Century Irish – **163**

Litany of Mary, Queen – **163**
Chosen Daughter of the Father – 64
Glorious Mother of God – 113
Joy of Israel – 147

Litany of Our Lady of Hope (Our Lady of Pontmain) – **164-165**

Litany of Our Lady of Pontmain:
Litany of Our Lady of Hope –164-165

Litany of Our Lady of Lourdes – **165-166**

Litany of Our Lady of the Seven Sorrows – **166-167**

Litany of the Immaculate Heart of Mary – **161-163**

Lithuania:
Siluva, Our Lady of – 263

Little Company of Mary, Sisters of the – **167**

Little Crown of the Blessed Virgin Mary:
Crown of the Blessed Virgin Mary – 75

Little Flower Rosary – **168**

"Little Lourdes":
Chapi, Our Lady of – 60

Little Office of the Blessed Virgin Mary – **168**
Saturday Devotion to Mary – 252

Little Office of the Immaculate Conception – **168**

Little Rosary of St. Anne – **168-169**

Liturgical Colors for Marian Feasts – **169**

Liturgy of the Hours:
Ave Regina Caelorum – *41*
Canticle – 52
Nunc Dimittis – 207
Regina Caeli – 238
Salve Regina – 252
Sub Tuum Praesidium – *272-273*

Living Rosary – **169**

Living Rosary, Association of the – **169**

Locutions:
Apparitions of Mary – 28-29

Longo, Blessed Bartolo:
Pompeii, Our Lady of the Rosary of – 225

Loreto, Holy House of; Loreto, Our Lady of – **169**

Loreto Sisters – **170**

Lourdes, Our Lady of – **170**"Lourdes of Germany":
Altötting, Our Lady of – 20

"Lourdes of Italy":
Caravaggio, Our Lady of – 53

Lourdes Water – **171**
Lourdes, Our Lady of –170

Loving Mother of the Redeemer:
Alma Redemptor Mater – 18

Lujan, Our Lady of **171**

Lumen Gentium (Dogmatic Constitution on the Church):
Adoration – 12
Assumption – 33-34
Devotions, Marian – 88-91
Excerpt, Chapter VIII – 311-318
Intercessions of Mary – 138-140
Vatican II – 281

Luther, Martin:
Reformation and Mary – 237
Trent, Council of – 277

Lux Veritatis – **172**

Luxembourg
Consolation, Our Lady of – 70

M

Madonna and Child of Soweto:
Black Madonnas – 46

Madonna del Parto:
Smooth Delivery, Our Lady of – 265

Madonna della Fiducia:
Confidence, Our Lady of – 67

Madonna of the Crucifix:
Hope, Our Lady of – 127
Pontmain, Our Lady of – 226

"Madonna of Mercy":
Casa Santa Maria –56

Madrid:
Almudena, Our Lady of – 19

Magi:
Scripture, Mary in – 256-260

Magnificat – **174**

Canticle – 52
Hannah's Hymn of Praise – 121-122
Scripture, Mary in – 256-260
Maria Bambina – 174
Maria Hilif (Mary, Help):
Help of Christians, Our Lady – 122-123
Maria Niña:
Divina Infantita – 91
Maria Stein – 174-175
Marialis Cultus – 175-176
Associate of the Redeemer – 33
Perfect Follower of Christ – 218
Rosary – 241-243
Mariam:
Name of Mary –197
Marian Congress,
Marian Conference:
Congress, Marian – 68-69
Marian Devotions:
Devotions, Marian – 88-91
Marian Helpers, Association of – 176
Marian Library/
International Marian Research Center – 176
Marian Library Studies:
Marian Library/International Marian Research Center – 176-177
Marian Medal – 177
Marian Movement of Priests – 177-178
Cenacle, Our Lady of the – 59
Marian Year –178
Ad Caeli Reginam –9
Marianists:
Society of Mary – 265
Marianist Sisters:
Daughters of Mary Immaculate – 85
Marianites of the Holy Cross – 178
Mariannhill Missionaries – 179
Marians of the Immaculate Conception – 179
Marian Helpers, Association of – 176
Mariapolis – 179
Mariazell, Our Lady of – 179-180
Mariolatry – 180
Mariological Society of America:

Marian Library/International Marian Research Center – 176
Mariology – 181
Marists:
Society of Mary – 265
Walsingham, Our Lady of – 295
Marto, Francisco and Jacinta
Fatima, Our Lady of – 105-106
Martyrs, Our Lady of – 181
Mary Altar:
Lady Altar –157
Mary Garden – 181
Mary: Grace and Hope in Christ:
Anglican Church, Mary in the – 22
Mary, Help of Christians:
Help of Christians, Our Lady, – 122-123
Mary Immaculate:
Immaculate Conception – 131-133
Mary Major:
Basilica of St. – 268
Mary Reparatrix (Restorer) – 182
Mary's Dowry:
Atonement, Our Lady of – 37-38
Dowry, Our Lady's – 97
Maryknoll – 182
Marymas – 183
Mater Dolorosa – 183
May – 183-184
May Crowning:
Coronation of the
Blessed Virgin Mary – 73
Mediator Dei – 184-185
Mediatrix – 185
Medjugorje, Our Lady of – 186
Memorare – 186
Mense Maio:
Paul VI – 214-215
Mercedarians:
Crown of the Twelve Stars – 77
Mercy, Our Lady of – 186
Mercy, Our Lady of – 186-187
China, Our Lady of – 62-63
Mercy, Our Lady of – 186
Altagracia, Our Lady of – 19
Antigua, Our Lady of – 24
Meritxell, Our Lady of – 187
Messages and Communications
from Mary: Revelation, Divine
and Private – 240
Mexico:

Antipolo, Our Lady of – 25-26
Guadalupe, Our Lady of – 118
La Conquistadora – 153
Ocotlan, Our Lady of – 210
San Juan, Our Lady of – 252
Zapopan, Our Lady of – 297
Milan, Italy:
Maria Bambina – 174
Militia of the Immaculate
Conception – 187
Miracle – 188
Miraculous Medal – 188
Children of Mary – 62
Smile, Our Lady of the – 264-265
Miraculous Medal,
Association of the – 188-189
Miriam:
Name of Mary – 197
Mirror of Justice – 189
Litany of the Blessed Virgin Mary – 160
Mirror of Our Lady:
Brigettine Office – 49
Missionaries of Our Lady of La Salette: La Salette, Our Lady of – 154-155
Missionary Oblates of Mary Immaculate:
Cape, Our Lady of the – 52-53
Oblates of Mary Immaculate – 209
Missionary Rosary – 189-190
Missionaries of Our Lady of Africa:
Africa, Our Lady of –14
Missionary of the Sacred Heart of Jesus: Sacred Heart, Our Lady of the – 247
Model of Faith and Charity – 190
Montfort Missionaries:
Company of Mary – 67
Month of May:
May – 183-184
Month of the Rosary:
October –210
Monthly Devotions – 190
Montserrat – 190
Moreau, Basil:
Marianites of the Holy Cross – 178-179
Morgan, Henry:
Antigua, Our Lady of – 24
Morning Offering – 190-191
Morning Star – 191

Litany of the Blessed Virgin
Mary – 160
Most Blessed Sacrament,
Our Lady of the – **191**
Most Excellent Fruit of
Redemption – **192**
Mother of Consolation:
Consolation, Our Lady of – 70
Mother of Emmanuel – **192**
Mother of God – **192-194**
Fullness of Grace, Mary's – 109
Mother of Good Health:
Good Health, Our Lady of –
116
Mother of Refugees:
Bai Dau, Our Lady of – 41
Mother of the Church – **194**
Mother Thrice Admirable – **194-
195**
Schoenstatt, Our Lady of – 256
Munificentissimus Deus:
Assumption – 33-34
Pius XII – 223
"My Mother, my confidence":
Confidence, Our Lady of – 67
Mysteries of the Rosary:
Rosary – 241-243
Mystery Plays and Mary – **195**
Mystical City of God, The:
Agreda, Venerable Mary of – 14
Mystical Rose – **195**
Litany of the Blessed Virgin
Mary – 160

N

Name of Mary – **197**
Name of Mary, Most Holy – **197**
Naples, Italy:
Brown Virgin – 50
Nativity:
Scripture, Mary in – 256-260
Nativity of Mary:
Apocryphal Writing, Mary in –
26
Birth of Mary – 44
Nativity of Mary, The:
Apocryphal Writing, Mary in –
26
Nazareth:
Archaeology and Mary – 30
Scripture, Mary in – 256-260
Need, Our Lady in – **197**
Netherlands:
Star of the Sea – 272
New Eve – **198**

New Millennium, Our Lady of the
– **198**
Newman, Venerable John Henry:
Litany of the Immaculate Heart
of Mary –161-163
Nicaragua:
Cuapa, Nicaragua – 78
Immaculate Conception of El
Viejo, Our Lady of the –
135-136
Nicene Creed – **199**
*Nostra Aetate , Declaration On the
Relation Of the Church to Non-
Christian Religions:*
Vatican II – 284
Notre Dame du Cap:
Cape, Our Lady of the – 52-53
Novena – **199**
in honor of the Immaculate
Conception – **200-201**
to Our Lady of Good Remedy
– **201**
to Our Lady of Mount Carmel
– **201-203**
to Our Lady of Perpetual Help
– **203-204**
to Our Lady of the Rosary –
204
to Our Sorrowful Mother –
204-206
to the Immaculate Conception
– **206-207**
Nunc Dimittis – **207**
Canticle – 52
"Nursing Madonna":
Art, Mary in – 31

O

Oblates of Mary Immaculate –
209-210
Pontmain, Our Lady of – 227
St. Mary Major, Basilica of –
268
Oblates of the Virgin Mary –
209-210
Ocotlan, Our Lady of – 210
October – **210**
Odigitria:
Art, Mary in – 31
Salus Populi Romani – 251
Office of Our Lady:
Little Office of the Blessed
Virgin Mary – 168-169
*Optatam Totius (Decree On Priestly
Training):* Vatican II – 283

Order of Crowning:
Coronation of the Blessed Vir-
gin Mary – 73
Order of the Most Holy Trinity:
Good Remedy, Our Lady of –
117
Order of Preachers:
Dominicans – 96
*Orientalium Ecclesiarum (Decree
On the Catholic Churches of the
Eastern Rite):* Vatican II – 282
Original Sin – **210**
Orthodox Church, Mary in the –
211
Panagia – 213
Walsingham, Our Lady of – 295
Our Lady:
Titles of Mary – 276
Our Lady of the . . .
See *(Name), Our Lady of the*
Our Lady's Altar:
Lady Altar – 157
Our Lady's Chapel:
Lady Chapel – 157
Our Lady's Day:
Lady Day – 157
Our Lady's Psalter – **211**
Rosary – 241-243
Our Lady's Rosary Makers – 211
Our Lady's Tank:
Good Health, Our Lady of –
116
Our Nursing Mother of Happy
Delivery:
La Leche, Our Lady of – 153-
154
Ozanam, Frederick:
Stabat Mater Speciosa – 271

P

Palestine – **213**
Paloma, Virgin de la:
Atocha, Our Lady of – 37
Panaghia Kapoli – **213**
Panagia – **213**
Panama:
Antigua, Our Lady of – 24
Paraguay:
Caacupé, Our Lady of the
Miracles of – 51
Lujan, Our Lady of –171
Passing of Mary:
Apocryphal Writing, Mary in –
26
Patroness, Mary as – **214**

Paul VI – 214-215
  Associate of the Redeemer – 33
  Marialis Cultus – 175-176
  Mother of the Church –194
Pauline Fathers:
  Czestochowa, Our Lady of – 79-81
Peace and Good Voyage, Our Lady of:
  Antipolo, Our Lady of – 25-26
Peace, Our Lady of – **216**
Peking (Beijing), Our Lady of:
  China, Our Lady of – 62-63
Pellevoisin, Our Lady of – **216-217**
Pentecost – **217-218**
  Cenacle, Our Lady of the – 59
  Novena – 199-200
  Scripture, Mary in – 256-260
Perfect Follower of Christ – **218**
Perfectae Caritatis, Decree On Renewal of Religious Life:
  Vatican II – 283
Perpetual Help, Our Lady of – **218-219**
  Icons –131
  Novena to Our Lady of Perpetual Help – 204
Perpetual Rosary for the Dead – **219-220**
Peru:
  Chapi, Our Lady of – 60
  Cocharcas, Our Lady of – 65
  Mercy, Our Lady of –186
Peyton, C.S.C., Father Patrick:
  Family Rosary Crusade –105
Philippines:
  Antipolo, Our Lady of – 25-26
  Flores de Mayo –108
  La Naval – 154
Piekary, Our Lady of – **220**
Pietà – **220**
  Art, Mary in – 33
  Sorrowful Mother, National Sanctuary of Our – 267
Pilar, Our Lady of – **221**
Pilgrim Virgin – **221**
  Blue Army – 48
Pilgrimage – **221-222**
  Walsingham, Our Lady of – 295
Pillar, Our Lady of the:
  Pilar, Our Lady of – 221
Pity, Our Lady of:
  Pietà – 220
Pius IX – **222**

Alexander VII – 118
  Immaculate Conception – 131-133
  Ineffabilis Deus –138
(St.) Pius X – **222-223**
  Ad Diem Illum Laetissimum – 10
  Encyclicals, Marian – 101-102
Pius XI – **223-224**
  Encyclicals, Marian – 102
Pius XII – **223**
  Ad Caeli Reginam – 9
  Assumption –33-34
  Encyclicals, Marian –102
  Immaculate Heart of Mary – 136
  Mediator Dei – 184
Poland:
  Czestochowa, Our Lady of – 79-81
  Gietrzwald, Poland – 111
  Piekary, Our Lady of – 220
Pompeii, Our Lady of the Rosary of – **224-225**
Pontifical International Marian Academy – 225-**226**
Pontifical North American College: Casa Santa Maria – 56
Pontmain, Our Lady of – **226**
  Hope, Our Lady of – 127
Popular Piety – **227**
Portiuncula – **227**
Praisers of Our Lady:
  Laudesi – 157
"Praying Madonna":
  Art, Mary in – 31
Predestination of Mary – **227-228**
Prefaces of Our Lady – **229**
Presbyterorum Ordinis, Decree On the Ministry and Life of Priests:
  Vatican II – 285
Presentation of Jesus in the Temple, Feast of the – **228-229**
  Hypapante – 129
  Scripture, Mary in – 256-260
Presentation of Mary – **229-230**
  Apocryphal Writing, Mary in – 26
Privileges of Mary – **230**
Pro Maria Committee:
  Beauraing, Our Lady of – 42
Prompt Succor, Our Lady of – **230-231**

Prophecies in the Old Testament, Mary in – **231-232**
  Scripture, Mary in – 256-260
Protestant Churches, Mary in
  Mainline: Reformation and Mary – 237
  Trent, Council of – 277
Protoevangelium of James:
  Apocryphal Writing, Mary in – 26
Psalter, Marian:
  Our Lady's Psalter – 211
Puerto Rico:
  Our Lady, Mother of Divine Providence – 93
Purification of the Blessed Virgin Mary, Feast of the – **232**
  Candlemas – 52
  Presentation of Jesus in the Temple, Feast of the – 228-229
Purisima:
  Candelaria –51
  Immaculate Conception of El Viejo, Our Lady of the – 135-136

Q

Queen of: angels, of patriarchs, of prophets, of apostles, of martyrs, of confessors, of virgins, of all saints, conceived without original sin, assumed into heaven, of the most holy Rosary, of peace:
  Litany of the Blessed Virgin Mary – 160
Queen of: love, of mercy, of peace, of angels, of patriarchs and prophets, of apostles and martyrs, of confessors and virgins, of all saints, conceived without original sin, assumed into heaven, of all the earth, of heaven, of the universe
  Litany of Mary, Queen – 163-164
Queen of All Hearts, Confraternity of Mary – **233**
Queen of the Americas – **233**
Queen of the Americas Guild – **233**
Queen of Angels, Our Lady:
  Angels, Our Lady of the – 20-21
Queen of Peace, Our Lady – **234**

China, Our Lady of – 62-63
Medjugorje, Our Lady of – 186
Queen of Preachers – **234**
Queenship of Mary – **234**
   Ad Caeli Reginam – 9
Quinche, Our Lady of – **235**

R

Ransom, Order of Our Lady of:
   Crown of the Twelve Stars – 77
   Mercy, Our Lady of – 186
   Seven Saturdays in Honor of
     Our Lady of Ransom – 262
Recurrens Mensis October:
   Paul VI – 214-215
Redemptoris Mater:
   Mother of Emmanuel – 192
   John Paul II – 145-147
Redemptorists – **237**
   Perpetual Help, Our Lady of –
     218-219
Reformation and Mary – **237**
Refuge of Sinners – **237-238**
   Schoenstatt, Our Lady of – 256
Regina Caeli – **238**
   Angelus – 21
   Antiphons of Our Lady – 25
Reims, Tapestry of Our Lady of –
   239
Relics of Mary – **239**
   Chartes, Our Lady of – 61-62
   Cord – 72
Resurrection:
   Rosary – 241-243
Revelation, Book of:
   Scripture, Mary in – 256-260
Revelation, Divine and Private –
   240-241
Rites:
   Eastern Church, Mary in the –
     99
Rivers, Our Lady of the – **241**
Rockies, Our Lady of the – **241**
Rosa Mystica:
   Mystical Rose – 195
Rosary – 241-243
   De la Roche (de Rupe), O.P.,
     Blessed Alan – 87-88
   Dominicans – 96
   Help of Christians, Our Lady, –
     122-123
Rosary Bridge:
   Cape, Our Lady of the – 52
     Rosary Confraternity – 243
Rosary, Dominican – **243**

Rosary in Honor of St. Joseph –
   243
Rosary of the Dead – **244**
Rosary of Our Lady of Sorrows
   (Servite) – **244**
Rosary of Our Lady of Tears – **244**
Rosary, Our Lady of the – **245**
   Chiquinquira, Our Lady of, 63
   Fifteen Saturdays – 107
   La Naval – 154
   Novena to Our Lady of the
     Rosary – 204
   Victory, Our Lady of – 290
Rosary of the Seven Joys of Our
   Lady – **245-246**
"Rosary Priest":
   Family Rosary Crusade – 105
Rosary Sunday – **246**
Rose – **246**
   Banneux, Our Lady of – 41
   Blessed Roses – 47
   Guadalupe, Our Lady of –
     118-120
   Knock, Our Lady of – 150-
     151
   La Salette, Our Lady of – 154
   Litany of the Blessed Virgin
     Mary – 160
   Little Flower Rosary – 168
   Lourdes, Our Lady of – 170
   Mary Garden – 181
   Meritxell, Our Lady of – 187
   Mystical Rose – 195
   Rosary – 241-243
   Rosary, the Secret of the – 260
   St. Mary Major, Basilica of –
     268
Rosemary – **246**
Rue Du Bac Paris, Our Lady of:
   Miraculous Medal –188
Russia:
   Fatima, Our Lady of – 105-106
   Iviron, Our Lady of – 141-142
   Vladimir, Our Lady of – 293
Rwanda:
   Kibeho (Rwanda), Our Lady of
     – 149-150

S

Sabbatine Privilege – **247**
Sacramentals, Marian – **247**
Sacred Congregation for the
   Doctrine of Faith:
     Apparitions of Mary – 28

Sacred Heart, Our Lady of the –
   247
Sacred Hearts of Jesus and Mary,
   Congregation of the:
   Queen of Peace, Our Lady –
     234
Sacrosanctum concilium (*Constitu-
   tion on the Sacred Liturgy*):
   Vatican II – 281
Saint – **248**
St. Albert the Great – **248**
   Assumption – 33-34
   Dominicans – 96
   Immaculate Conception –
     131-133
St. Aloysius Gonzaga:
   Annunciata, The – 23
St. Alphonsus Liguori:
   Ad Caeli Reginam – 10
   Assumption – 33-34
   Child of Mary – 62
   Glories of Mary, The – 112
   Redemptorists – 237
   Three Hail Marys – 276
   *True Devotion to the Blessed
     Virgin Mary, A Treatise on* –
     278
St. Alphonsus Rodriguez:
   Little Office of the Immaculate
     Conception – 168
St. Ambrose:
   Gate of Heaven – 111
St. Andrew:
   Chiquinquira, Our Lady of –
     63-64
St. Anne (and St. Joachim) –**143**
   Apocryphal Writing, Mary in –
     26
   Birth of Mary – 44
   Little Rosary of St. Anne –
     168-169
   Scripture, Mary in – 256-260
St. Anselm of Canterbury:
   Child of Mary – 62
   Daily, Daily Sing to Mary – 83
St. Anthony Mary Claret:
   Claretians – 65
St. Anthony of Padua:
   Chiquinquira, Our Lady of –
     63-64
St. Augustine:
   Admirable Heart of Mary, The –
     11
   Consolation, Our Lady of – 70

Virginity of Mary, Perpetual –
290-292
St. Bernadette:
Apparitions of Mary – 28
Immaculate Conception –133
Lourdes, Our Lady of – 169
St. Bernadine of Siena:
Assumption – 33-34
Glory of the Human Race –113
Rosary of the Seven Joys of Our
Lady – 246
St. Bernard of Clairvaux:
Immaculate Conception –132
Memorare – 186
St. Bonaventure:
Assumption – 33-34
Hail Mary of Our Sorrowful
Mother – 121
Immaculate Conception – 131-
133
St. Bridget of Sweden:
Brigettine Office – 49
Brigettine Rosary– 49
St. Camillus of Lellis:
Scapular of St. Camillus – 254
St. Casimir:
Daily, Daily Sing to Mary – 83
St. Catherine Labouré:
Miraculous Medal – 188
St. Catherine of Siena:
Pompeii, Our Lady of the
Rosary of – 225
St. Conrad of Parzham:
Altötting, Our Lady of – 20
St. Dominic:
De la Roche (de Rupe), O.P.,
Blessed Alan – 87-88
Dominicans – 96
Ladder Rosary – 156
Pompeii, Our Lady of the
Rosary of – 224-225
Scapular of St. Dominic – 255
St. Elizabeth:
Ain-Karin – 15
Ave Maria – 38
Devotions, Marian – 88-91
Magnificat – 174
Scripture, Mary in – 256-260
St. Elizabeth of Hungary:
Hal, Our Lady of – 121
St. Eugene De Mazenod:
Oblates of Mary Immaculate –
209
St. Faustina Kowalska:

Marian Helpers, Association of
– 176
St. Francis of Assisi:
Angels, Our Lady of the – 20-21
Portiuncula – 227
St. Francis de Sales:
Assumption – 33-34
Imitation of Our Lady – 131
Ladder Rosary – 156
St. Gabriel of the Sorrowful Virgin:
Benedict XV – 42
St. Gregory Nazianzen:
Ad Caeli Reginam – 9
St. Helena:
Czestochowa, Our Lady of – 79-
81
Flores de Mayo – 108
St. Ignatius of Antioch:
Consolation, Our Lady of – 70
Virginity of Mary, Perpetual –
290-292
St. Ignatius Loyola:
Arantzazu, Our Lady of – 29
Christian Life Community – 65
Jesuits – 143
Oblates of the Virgin Mary –
209-210
St. Irenaeus:
Knots, Virgin Who Unties –
151
New Eve – 198
St. Isidore:
Almudena, Our Lady of – 19
St. James:
Pilar, Our Lady of – 221
Pilgrimage – 221
Walsingham, Our Lady of – 295
St. Jerome:
Ad Caeli Reginam – 9
Virginity of Mary, Perpetual –
296
St. Joachim (and St. Anne) – **143**
Apocryphal Writing, Mary in –
26
Birth of Mary – 44
Scripture, Mary in – 256-260
St. Joan Valois:
Annociade – 23
St. John:
Caregiver, Our Lady's – 53
Czestochowa, Our Lady of – 79-
81
Knock, Our Lady of – 150
Need, Our Lady in – 197
Scripture, Mary in – 256-260

Tomb of Mary – 276
St. John of Avila:
Imitation of Our Lady – 131
St. John Baptist de la Salle:
Liesse, Our Lady of – 159
St. John the Baptist:
Birth of Mary – 45
Herod – 124
Scripture, Mary in – 256-260
St. John Berchmans:
Crown of the Blessed Virgin
Mary, Little – 75-76
Immaculate Conception,
Chaplet of the – 134-135
St. John Bosco:
Daughters of Mary, Help of
Christians – 84
Help of Christians, Our
Lady – 122-123
St. John Damascene:
Ad Caeli Reginam – 9
St. John Eudes:
Admirable Heart of Mary, The –
11
Ave Maria Salutation – 39
Divine Providence, Our Lady of,
First Saturday Devotion –
108
Immaculate Heart of Mary –
136
St. John of Matha:
Good Remedy, Our Lady of –
117
St. John Neumann:
Hostyn, Our Lady of – 127-128
St. Joseph:
Apocryphal Writing, Mary in –
26
Holy Family – 124
Knock, Our Lady of – 150
Rosary in Honor of St. Joseph –
243
Scripture, Mary in – 256-260
Spouses of the Blessed Virgin
Mary – 268
St. Juan Diego:
Apparitions of Mary – 28
Guadalupe, Our Lady of – 118-
120
St. Leo the Great:
Virginity of Mary, Perpetual –
290-292
St. Leonard of Port Maurice:
Three Hail Marys – 276
St. Louis Marie de Montfort:

Company of Mary – 67

Consecration to Jesus Through Mary – 69-70

Crown of the Blessed Virgin Mary, Little – 75-76

Legion of Mary – 157

Queen of All Hearts, Confraternity of Mary – 233

Salus Populi Romani – 251

Secret of the Rosary, The – 260

Slavery of Mary, Slave of Mary – 264

Totus Tuus – 277

St. Luke:
Art, Mary in – 31
Atocha, Our Lady of – 36-37
Czestochowa, Our Lady of – 79-81
Grace, Our Lady of – 118
Infancy Narratives, 138
St. Mary Major, Basilica of – 268
Scripture, Mary in – 256-260
Vladimir, Our Lady of – 293-294

St. Margaret Mary Alacoque:
Benedict XIV – 42
Pellevoisin, Our Lady of – 216-217

St. Maria Mazzarello:
Daughters of Mary, Help of Christians – 85

St. Martin I:
Ad Caeli Reginam – 10

St. Mary Josepha Rosello:
Daughters of Our Lady of Mercy – 86

St. Mary Magdalene:
Scripture, Mary in – 256-260

St. Matthew:
Infancy Narratives – 138
Scripture, Mary in – 256-260

St. Maximilian Kolbe:
Militia of the Immaculate Conception – 187

St. Mechtilde of Helfta:
Three Hail Marys – 276
Trinity, Our Lady of the – 277-278

St. Meinrad:
Einsiedeln, Our Lady of – 99

St. Michael:
Golden Saturdays, The – 113

St. Monica:

Consolation, Our Lady of – 70-71

St. Peter Canisius:
Assumption – 33-34
Incomparable Virgin Mary, The – 137-138
Litany of the Blessed Virgin Mary – 160

St. Peter Chrysologus:
Virginity of Mary, Perpetual – 290-292

St. Peter Damian:
Little Office of the Blessed Virgin Mary – 168-169

St. Peter Julian Eymard:
Most Blessed Sacrament, Our Lady of the – 191

St. Peter Nolasco:
Crown of the Twelve Stars – 77
Mercy, Our Lady of – 186
Seven Saturdays in Honor of Our Lady of Ransom – 261

St. Philip Benizi:
Divine Providence, Our Lady, Mother of – 92-94

St. Philip Neri:
May – 183-184

St. Pio of Petrelcina:
Perfect Sanctity – 218

Pius X, St.
See *Pius X*

St. Raymond of Peñafort:
Crown of the Twelve Stars – 77
Mercy, Our Lady of –186

St. Robert Bellarmine:
Assumption – 33-34

St. Rose:
Pompeii, Our Lady of the Rosary of – 224-225

St. Simon Stock:
Carmel, Our Lady of Mount – 54-56
Flos Carmeli – 108

St. Teresa of Ávila:
Immaculate Conception of El Viejo, Our Lady of the – 135-136

St. Thérèse of Lisieux:
Little Flower Rosary –168
Smile, Our Lady of the – 264-265

St. Thomas Aquinas:
Assumption – 33-34
Dominicans – 96

Immaculate Conception – 131-133
Virginity of Mary, Perpetual – 296

St. Zechariah:
Ain-Karin – 15
Scripture, Mary in – 256-260

Salesian Sisters:
Daughters of Mary, Help of Christians – 85

Salesians:
Help of Christians, Our Lady – 122-123

Salus Populi Romani – 251
St. Mary Major, Basilica of – 268

Salve Regina:
Antiphons of Our Lady – 25
Glories of Mary, The – 112

San Juan, Our Lady of – 252

Sasagawa, Sister Agnes:
Akita, Our Lady of – 17

Saturday Devotion to Mary – 252-253

Scapular; Scapular Medal – 253

Scapular of Our Lady of Good Counsel – 253

Scapular of Our Lady of Mount Carmel – 253

Scapular of Our Lady of Ransom – 254

Scapular of St. Camillus – 254

Scapular of St. Dominic – 254

Scapular of the Immaculate Conception – 254

Scapular of the Immaculate Heart – 255

Scapular of the Immaculate Heart of Mary – 255

Scapular of the Most Sacred Heart of Jesus – 255

Scapular of the Sacred Hearts of Jesus and Mary – 255

Scapular of the Seven Sorrows – 255-256

Schubert, Franz:
Hymns, Marian – 128

Schoenstatt, Our Lady of – 256

Schoenstatt Movement:
Mother Thrice Admirable – 194-195

Schrocken Rosary – 256

Scotus, John Duns:
Immaculate Conception – 131-133

Scriptural Rosary – 256
Scripture, Mary in – 256-260
Secret of the Rosary, The – 260
Sedes Sapientiae – 260
Servants of Mary:
Laudesi – 157
Servites – 261
Rosary of Our Lady of Sorrows
(Servite) – 244
Sorrowful Mother, National
Sanctuary of Our – 267
Sorrows, Our Lady of – 267
Sorrows of Mary, Seven Sorrows
of Mary – 268
Seven Saturdays in Honor of Our
Lady of Ransom – 262
Seven Sorrows, Chaplet of the –
262
Seven Words – 262
Sheen, Archbishop Fulton J.:
World Mission Rosary – 297
Shepherds:
Scripture, Mary in – 256-260
Shkodra, Our Lady of:
Good Counsel, Our Lady of –
114
Sicily:
Syracuse, Our Lady of –
273-274
Signum Magnum:
Paul VI – 214
Silence, Our Lady of:
Knock, Our Lady of –151
Silence, Virgin of:
Litany of Our Lady of Hope –
164
Siluva, Our Lady of – 263
Simeon:
Nunc Dimittis – 207
Scripture, Mary in – 256-260
Sin – 263
Singular Vessel of Devotion – 263
Litany of the Blessed Virgin
Mary – 160
Sinj, Our Lady of:
Velika Gospa – 286
Sixtus V:
Litany of the Blessed Virgin
Mary – 160
Slavery of Mary, Slave of Mary –
264
Smile, Our Lady of the – 264-265
Smooth Delivery, Our Lady of –
265
Snows, Our Lady of:

St. Mary Major, Basilica of –
269
Oblates of Mary Immaculate –
209
Society of the Admirable Heart of
Mary:
Admirable Heart of Mary, The –
11
Society of the Divine Word:
Missionary Rosary – 189
Society of Mary – 265
Daughters of Mary Immaculate
– 86
Marian Library/International
Marian Research Center –
176
Society of Our Lady of the Most
Holy Trinity – 265
Society of St. Vincent de Paul:
Stabat Mater Speciosa – 271
Sodalities of Our Lady:
Christian Life Community – 65
Soledad, Virgen de (Our Lady of
Solitude) – 266
Solemnity of Mary, Mother of God
– 266
Solitude, Our Lady of:
Soledad, Virgen de (Our Lady of
Solitude) – 266
Sollicitudo omnium eccelarium:
Alexander VII – 18
Sopetrán, Our Lady of:
Antigua, Our Lady of – 25
Sorrowful and Immaculate Heart
of Mary – 267
Sorrowful Mother: Novena to Our
Sorrowful Mother – 205
Sorrowful Mother, National
Sanctuary of Our – 267
Sorrows, Our Lady of – 267
*Stabat Mater, Stabat Mater
Dolorosa* – 270
Sorrows of Mary, Seven Sorrows of
Mary – 267
Soul – 268
Source of Life:
Art, Mary in – 31
Spain:
Almudena, Our Lady of – 19
Arantzazu, Our Lady of – 29
Atocha, Our Lady of – 36-37
Claretians – 65
Garabandal – 111
La Leche, Our Lady of – 153
La Salette, Our Lady of – 154

Pilar, Our Lady of – 221
"Spinning" of the Sun:
Fatima, Our Lady of – 105-106
Spiritual Vessel – 268
Litany of the Blessed Virgin
Mary – 160
Splendor of the Church – 268
Litany of Mary, Queen –163
Spouses of the Blessed Virgin Mary
– 268
St. Mary Major, Basilica of – 268
*Stabat Mater, Stabat Mater
Dolorosa* – 270-271
Stabat Mater Speciosa –271
Stamps – 271
Star of the Sea – 272
Star of the Sea, Chaplet of Our
Lady – 272
Stations of the Cross:
Via Matris – 286-290
Way of the Cross – 295-296
Stations of the Seven Sorrows:
Via Matris – 286-290
Story of a Soul:
Smile, Our Lady of the –
264-265
Strata, Blessed Victoria:
Annociade – 23
Sub Tuum Praesidium – 272- 273
Mother of God – 192-194
Suyapa, Our Lady of – 273
Switzerland:
Einsiedeln, Our Lady of – 99
Maria Stein – 174-175
Symbols of Mary – 273
Syracuse, Our Lady of – 273 -274

T

Taper, Our Lady of the – 275
Tank, Our Lady's:
Good Health, Our Lady of –
116
Tarivá, Our Lady of:
Antigua, Our Lady of – 24
Tekakwitha, Blessed Kateri:
Kateri Indian Rosary – 149
Temple, Finding in the:
Scripture, Mary in – 256-260
Tenderness, Our Lady of:
Vladimir, Our Lady of – 294
Theotokos:
Devotions, Marian – 88-91
Eastern Church, Mary in the –
99

Ephesus, Council of – 103
    Mother of God – 192
"Third Secret of Fatima":
    Fatima, Our Lady of – 105-106
Thirty-Three, Our Lady of the –
    275-276
Three Hail Marys – **276**
Three Privileges:
    Trinity, Our Lady of the –
        277-278
Titles of Mary – **276**
Tomb of Mary – **276**
Tonglu, Holy Mother of:
    China, Our Lady of – 62-63
Totus Tuus – **277**
Tower of David, Tower of Ivory –
    277
    Litany of the Blessed Virgin
        Mary – 160
Trent, Council of – **277**
    Devotions, Marian – 88-91
    Relics of Mary – 239
Trezzo sull'Adda ("Shrines of the
    Madonna of the Milk"):
    Caravaggio, Our Lady of – 53
Trinity and Mary – **277**
Trinity, Our Lady of the –
    277-278
True Devotion to Mary – **278**
    Legion of Mary – 157
Trust, Our Lady of:
    Confidence, Our Lady of – 67
Turkey:
    Ephesus – 102
    Girdle of Our Lady, Feast of the
        – 112
    Vladimir, Our Lady of –
        293-294

U

Underground, Our Lady:
    Chartes, Our Lady of – 61-62
Unitatis Redintegratio (*Decree on
    Ecumenism*): Vatican II – 282
Upper Room:
    Cenacle, Our Lady of the – 59
Uruguay:
    Lujan, Our Lady of – 171
Ursulines:
    Prompt Succor, Our Lady of –
        230
    Thirty-Three, Our Lady of the –
        275-276

V

Vacchi, Giovanna:
    Caravaggio, Our Lady of – 53
Vailankanni, Our Lady of:
    Good Health, Our Lady of –
        116
Vatican II – **281-286**
Veil of the Blessed Virgin
    Chartes, Our Lady of – 62
Velika Gospa – **286**
Veneration of Mary – **286**
Venezuela:
    Coromoto, Our Lady of – 73
Vessel of Honor – **286**
    Litany of the Blessed Virgin
        Mary – 160
Via Matris – **286-290**
Victory, Our Lady of – **290**
    Help of Christians, Our Lady,
        –123
Vietnam:
    Bai Dau, Our Lady of – 41
    La Vang, Our Lady of – 155
Virginity of Mary, Perpetual –
    290-291
Virgin: most prudent, most
    venerable, most renowned,
    most powerful, most merciful,
    most faithful: Litany of the
    Blessed Virgin Mary –160
Virgin Mother of Emmanuel –
    292
Virgin of Charity:
    of El Cobre, Our Lady of – 61
Virgin of the Fountain:
    Caravaggio, Our Lady of – 53
Virgin of the Gate:
    Iviron, Our Lady of – 141-142
Virgin of High Grace:
    Altagracia, Our Lady of – 19
Virgin of Miracles:
    Caacupé, Our Lady of the Mira-
        cles of – 51
Virgin of the Poor:
    Banneux, Our Lady of – 41
Virgin of Pozzenta:
    Caravaggio, Our Lady of – 53
Virgin of the Sea:
    Boulogne, Our Lady of – 48-49
Virgin of Tenderness:
    Art, Mary in – 31
    Eleousa and Oumilenie – 100
Virgin of Virgins – **292**

Litany of the Blessed Virgin
    Mary – 160
Virgin with the Golden Heart:
    Beauraing, Our Lady of – 42
Virgo Paritura:
    Chartes, Our Lady of – 62
Virtues of the Blessed Virgin Mary,
    Chaplet of the Ten Evangelical
    292-293
Visitation Rosary – 241
Visions:
    Apparitions of Mary – 28
Vladimir, Our Lady of – **293-294**

W-Z

Wales:
    Taper, Our Lady of the – 275
Walsingham, Our Lady of – 295
Washing of the Silver:
    Immaculate Conception of El
        Viejo, Our Lady of the –
        135-136
Way of the Cross, Stations of the
    Cross – **295-296**
    *Stabat Mater, Stabat Mater
        Dolorosa* – 270
Wedding (or Lasso) Rosary – **296**
Wednesdays of Mount Carmel:
    Brown Virgin – 50
Weeping Madonna:
    Akita, Our Lady of – 17
    Syracuse, Our Lady of –
        273-274
White:
    Liturgical Colors for Marian
        Feasts – 169
White Fathers; White Sisters
    (Missionaries of Our Lady of
    Africa) – 14
        Africa, Our Lady of –14
Woman Clothed in the Sun – **296**
    Scripture, Mary in – 256-260
World Mission Rosary – **297**
Zapopan, Our Lady of – **297**
Zion, Daughter of:
    Daughter of Zion – 83
Zona:
    Girdle of Our Lady, Feast of the
        – 112
Zo-se, Our Lady of – **298**
Zwingli, Huldrych:
    Trent, Council of – 277

Images and Art

Pope St. Pius X – 10
Adoration of the Magi – 15
Our Lady of Akita – 17
St. John Eudes – 11
Annunciation – 24
Madonna of the Streets by Ferruzi – 31
Eleousa, the "Virgin of Tenderness" – 32
The Sistine Madonna by Raphael – 33
Assumption – 33-34
St. Francis de Sales – 35
Our Lady of Atonement – 37
Pope Benedict XVI – 43
Our Lady of Bistrica – 45
Our Lady of Einsiedeln – 46
Madonna and Child of Soweto – 47
Blue Army logo – 48
Candelaria – 51
Our Lady's Caregiver – 53
Our Lady of Mount Carmel – 55
La Virgen Del Cerro San Cristobal – 60
Our Lady of Charity of El Cobre – 61
Our Lady of China – 63
St. Ignatius Loyola – 64
St. Anthony Claret – 65
Our Lady of Czestochowa – 80
St. Maria Mazzarello – 85
Blessed William Joseph Chaminade – 85
Bishop Dominic Mary Hồ Ngọc Cẩn – 87
Our Lady of La Salette – 91
Our Lady, Mother of Divine Providence – 93
St. Bernard – 95
St. Thomas Aquinas – 95
St. Dominic – 96
Blessed Anne Catherine Emmerich – 100

Jacinta and Francisco Marto, Lucia dos Santos – 106
St. Francis of Assisi – 109
St. Alphonsus Liguori – 112
Our Lady of Shkodra – 114
Our Lady of Good Counsel – 115
Our Lady of Good Counsel by Sarullo – 115
Our Lady of Good Health, Vailankanni – 116
Our Lady of Good Remedy – 117
Our Lady of Guadalupe – 119
Our Lady, Help of Christians – 122
Mary, Help of Christians – 123
Rest on the Flight into Egypt – 124
Holy Family by Batoni – 124
Flight into Egypt – 125
Our Lady of Hostyn – 128
Immaculate Conception – 133
Basilica of the National Shrine of the Immaculate Conception – 134
Immaculate Heart of Mary – 136
St. Peter Canisius – 138
St. Anne – 143
Pope John XXIII – 144
Pope John Paul II – 146
La Conquistadora – 153
Our Lady of La Vang – 155
St. Louis de Montfort – 157
St. John Baptist de la Salle – 159
Venerable John Henry Newman – 162
St. Bernadette and Our Lady of Lourdes – 170
Our Lady of Lourdes – 171
Pope Paul VI – 175
Marian Library Medal – 176
Our Lady of Mariazell – 180
St. Philip Neri – 183
St. Maximilian Kolbe – 187

St. Catherine Labouré – 188
Our Lady of the Miraculous Medal – 189
Theotokos – 193
Mystical Rose – 195
John and Mary – 197
Sorrowful Mother by Kaulbach – 205
Our Lady of Ocotlan – 210
Platytera Mary and the Child Jesus – 213
St. Margaret Mary Alacoque – 217
Pentecost – 217
St. Pio of Pietrelcina – 218
Our Lady of Perpetual Help – 219
Pietà by Michelangelo – 220
Pope Pius IX – 222
Pope St. Pius X – 223
Our Lady of the Rosary of Pompeii – 225
Presentation of Jesus in the Temple – 229
Refuge of Sinners by Crosio – 237
Refuge of Sinners – 238
Tapestry of Our Lady of Reims – 239
St. Joseph – 243
Our Lady of the Sacred Heart – 247
Salus Populi Romani – 251
Sedes Sapientiae – 261
Our Lady of Siluva – 263
St. Thérèse of Lisieux – 264
Belize stamp, 1980 – 271
Weeping Madonna of Syracuse – 274
Mary and the Trinity – 278
Queen of Apostles – 285
St. Augustine – 290
Our Lady of Vladimir – 294
Our Lady of Zapopan – 297

A
Marian
BIBLE STUDY

Bringing Scripture
to Life for Moms

Laura Marie Wells

OurSundayVisitor

Bringing Your Catholic Faith to Life

www.osv.com